AIDS

SOURCEBOOK

Sixth Edition

Health Reference Series

Sixth Edition

AIDS
SOURCEBOOK

Basic Consumer Health Information about the Human Immunodeficiency Virus (HIV) and Acquired Immunodeficiency Syndrome (AIDS), Including Facts about Its Origins, Symptoms, Stages, Types, Transmission, Risk Factors, and Prevention, and Featuring Details about Diagnostic Testing, Treatments, Side Effects, and Co-Occurring Infections, such as Mycobacterium Avium Complex, Tuberculosis, Cryptococcal Meningitis, Toxoplasmosis, and Human Papillomavirus.

Along with Tips for Living with HIV/AIDS, Information on Clinical Trials and Current Research, a Glossary of Related Terms, and a List of Resources for Additional Help and Information

OMNIGRAPHICS

155 W. Congress, Suite 200 Detroit, MI 48226

Bibliographic Note

Because this page cannot legibly accommodate all the copyright notices, the Bibliographic Note portion of the Preface constitutes an extension of the copyright notice.

* * *

Omnigraphics, Inc.
Editorial Services provided by Omnigraphics, Inc.,
a division of Relevant Information, Inc.

Keith Jones, *Managing Editor*

* * *

Copyright © 2016 Relevant Information, Inc.
ISBN 978-0-7808-1381-6
E-ISBN 978-0-7808-1405-9

Library of Congress Cataloging-in-Publication Data

AIDS sourcebook : basic consumer health information about the human immunodeficiency virus (HIV) and acquired immunodeficiency syndrome (aids), including facts about its origins, stages, types, transmission, risk factors, and prevention, and featuring details about diagnostic testing, antiretroviral treatments, and co-occurring infections, such as cytomegalovirus, mycobacterium avium complex, pneumocystis carinii pneumonia, and toxoplasmosis; along with tips for living with hiv/aids, updated statistics, reports on current research initiatives, a glossary of related terms, and a list of resources for additional help and information / Keith Jones, managing editor. – Sixth edition
    pages cm. – (Health reference series)
Summary: "Provides basic consumer health information about transmission, testing, stages, and treatment of human immunodeficiency virus (HIV), with facts about prevention, related complications, and tips for living with HIV/AIDS. Includes index, glossary of related terms and directory of resources" – Provided by publisher.
    ISBN 978-0-7808-1381-6 (hardcover : alk. paper) – ISBN 978-0-7808-1405-9 (ebook)
    1. AIDS (Disease)–Popular works. I. Jones, Keith.
    RC606.64.A337 2016
    616.97'92--dc23
                                                          2015035127

Printed in the United States

Table of Contents

Part III: HIV/AIDS Diagnosis

Part IV: Treatments and Therapies for HIV/AIDS

Part V: Common Co-Occurring Infections and Complications of HIV/AIDS

Part VII: Clinical Trials and Ongoing Research

Part VIII: Additional Help and Information

Preface

About This Book

According to the Centers for Disease Control and Prevention, more than 1.2 million Americans are living with human immunodeficiency virus (HIV) infection. An estimated 50,000 people in the United States are newly infected with HIV each year. This devastating disease attacks the immune system and affects all parts of the body, eventually leading to acquired immunodeficiency syndrome (AIDS), it's most deadly and advanced stage, for which there is currently no cure. Yet there is hope for the many Americans living with HIV infection or AIDS. Researchers are developing new and more effective drug combinations, and scientists are growing ever closer to a vaccine. Improvements in medication and earlier diagnosis mean that those infected with HIV are living longer, healthier, and more productive lives. Still, many Americans are unaware of even the basic facts about HIV—how it is transmitted, how HIV progresses to AIDS, and how HIV and AIDS are treated.

AIDS Sourcebook, Sixth Edition, provides basic consumer information about the human immunodeficiency virus (HIV) and acquired immunodeficiency syndrome (AIDS), including information about the stages of the disease and about how it is transmitted. It includes guidelines for preventing disease transmission and details about how it is diagnosed and the various drug regimens used in its treatment. Information on co-occurring infections, complications, and tips for living with HIV infection are also included. The book concludes with a glossary of related terms and a list of resources for additional help and information.

How to Use This Book

This book is divided into parts and chapters. Parts focus on broad areas of interest. Chapters are devoted to single topics within a part.

Part I: Basic Information about Human Immunodeficiency Virus (HIV) / Acquired Immunodeficiency Syndrome (AIDS) defines HIV and AIDS and explains what is known about the origin of the virus. It describes the life cycle, and stages of HIV infection. It also includes a brief discussion of the prevalence and incidence of HIV and AIDS in the United States and around the world.

Part II: HIV/AIDS Transmission, Risk Factors, and Prevention presents the facts about the transmission of the human immunodeficiency virus and debunks some of the rumors about how this infection is transmitted. It explains the factors that put people at risk for HIV infection, such as risky sexual behavior, smoking, alcohol, and substance abuse, and provides tips for avoiding these risks.

Part III: HIV/AIDS Diagnosis describes the different types of HIV testing and explains consumer rights regarding confidentiality. It provides a detailed explanation of what the test results mean and how to determine if you have AIDS. Finally, it provides tips for choosing a provider and navigating the healthcare system.

Part IV: Treatment and Therapies for HIV/AIDS details the antiretroviral treatment process, describes the common side effects and complications of this treatment, and explains how the effectiveness of treatment is monitored. It also discusses complementary and alternative HIV/AIDS treatments, other treatments currently being developed, the use of Marijuana in HIV treatment, and how treatment varies in the special cases of children and pregnant women.

Part V: Common Co-Occurring Infections and Complications of HIV/AIDS describes the bacterial, fungal, parasitic, and viral infections that often accompany HIV and AIDS. It also offers tips on how to avoid these infections and explains how they are treated when they do occur. In addition, AIDS-related cancer, wasting syndrome, neurological complications, and other AIDS-related health concerns are discussed.

Part VI: Living with HIV Infection offers advice on coping with an HIV/AIDS diagnosis and explains how diet and exercise can help maintain positive physical, mental, and sexual health. It discusses legal responsibility regarding disclosure of HIV status, as well as provides information about your rights in the workplace. The part concludes with a discussion about laws that apply to people with HIV and a description of the public benefits, insurance, and housing options available for persons with HIV.

Part VII: Clinical Trials and Ongoing Research provides basic information about clinical trials, and ongoing research on health-risk behaviors that contribute to the leading causes of HIV infection among youth and adults.

Part VIII: Additional Help and Information includes a glossary of terms related to AIDS and HIV and a directory of resources for additional help and support.

Bibliographic Note

This volume contains documents and excerpts from publications issued by the following U.S. government agencies: AIDS.gov and AIDS*info*, services of the U.S. Department of Health and Human Services (HHS); Centers for Disease Control and Prevention (CDC); Eunice Kennedy Shriver National Institute of Child Health and Human Development (NICHD); National Cancer Institute (NCI); National Institute of Dental and Craniofacial Research (NIDCR); National Institute of Neurological Disorders and Stroke (NINDS); National Institute on Drug Abuse (NIDA); U.S. Department of Veterans Affairs (VA); U.S. Food and Drug Administration (FDA); and National Cancer Institute (NCI).

About the Health Reference Series

The *Health Reference Series* is designed to provide basic medical information for patients, families, caregivers, and the general public. Each volume takes a particular topic and provides comprehensive coverage. This is especially important for people who may be dealing with a newly diagnosed disease or a chronic disorder in themselves or in a family member. People looking for preventive guidance, information about disease warning signs, medical statistics, and risk factors for health problems will also find answers to their questions in the *Health Reference Series*. The *Series*, however, is not intended to serve as a tool for diagnosing illness, in prescribing treatments, or as a substitute for the physician/patient relationship. All people concerned about medical symptoms or the possibility of disease are encouraged to seek professional care from an appropriate health care provider.

A Note about Spelling and Style

Health Reference Series editors use *Stedman's Medical Dictionary* as an authority for questions related to the spelling of medical terms and the *Chicago Manual of Style* for questions related to grammatical structures, punctuation, and other editorial concerns. Consistent adherence is not always possible, however, because the individual volumes within the *Series* include many documents from a wide variety of different producers, and the editor's primary goal is to present material from each source as accurately as is possible. This sometimes means that information in different chapters or sections may follow other guidelines and alternate spelling authorities.

Our Advisory Board

We would like to thank the following board members for providing guidance to the development of this Series:

- Dr. Lynda Baker, Associate Professor of Library and Information Science, Wayne State University, Detroit, MI

- Nancy Bulgarelli, William Beaumont Hospital Library, Royal Oak, MI

- Karen Imarisio, Bloomfield Township Public Library, Bloomfield Township, MI

- Karen Morgan, Mardigian Library, University of Michigan-Dearborn, Dearborn, MI

- Rosemary Orlando, St. Clair Shores Public Library, St. Clair Shores, MI

Health Reference Series Update Policy

The inaugural book in the *Health Reference Series* was the first edition of Cancer Sourcebook published in 1989. Since then, the Series has been enthusiastically received by librarians and in the medical community. In order to maintain the standard of providing high-quality health information for the layperson the editorial staff at

Omnigraphics felt it was necessary to implement a policy of updating volumes when warranted.

Medical researchers have been making tremendous strides, and it is the purpose of the *Health Reference Series* to stay current with the most recent advances. Each decision to update a volume is made on an individual basis. Some of the considerations include how much new information is available and the feedback we receive from people who use the books. If there is a topic you would like to see added to the update list, or an area of medical concern you feel has not been adequately addressed, please write to:

Managing Editor
Health Reference Series
Omnigraphics, Inc.
155 W. Congress, Suite 200
Detroit, MI 48226

Part One

Basic Information about Human Immunodeficiency Virus (HIV) / Acquired Immunodeficiency Syndrome (AIDS)

Chapter 1

Definition and Origin of HIV and AIDS

What is HIV?

HIV stands for the human immunodeficiency virus.

> **H** – Human. This virus infects human beings.
>
> **I** – Immunodeficiency. This virus attacks a person's immune system. The immune system is the body's defense against infections, such as bacteria and viruses. Once attacked by HIV, the immune system becomes deficient and doesn't work properly.
>
> **V** – Virus. A virus is a type of germ too small to be seen even with a microscope.

HIV is a virus. Some viruses, such as the ones that cause colds or flu, stay in the body for only a few days. HIV, however, never goes away. A person who is infected with HIV is said to be "HIV

This chapter includes excerpts from "What Is HIV/AIDS?" AIDS.gov, August 27, 2015; and text from "HIV/AIDS Basics," U.S. Department of Veterans Affairs (VA), September 17, 2015.

Figure 1.1. *Basic Information about HIV*

positive." Once a person is HIV positive, that person will always be HIV positive.

What does the virus do?

All viruses must infect living cells to reproduce. HIV takes over certain immune system cells that are supposed to defend the body. These cells are called CD4 cells, or T cells.

When HIV takes over a CD4 cell, it turns the cell into a virus factory. It forces the cell to produce thousands of copies of the virus. These copies infect other CD4 cells. Infected cells don't work well and die early. Over time, the loss of CD4 cells weakens the immune system, making it harder for the body to stay healthy.

> CD4 cells are the cells in the body that fight HIV. They are part of the body's immune system.

What is AIDS?

AIDS stands for acquired immunodeficiency syndrome.

AIDS was first reported in the United States in 1981 and has since become a major worldwide epidemic. AIDS is the most

> **A** – Acquired. This condition is acquired, meaning that a person becomes infected with it.

I – Immuno. HIV affects a person's immune system, the part of the body that fights off germs such as bacteria or viruses.

D – Deficiency. The immune system becomes deficient and does not work properly.

S – Syndrome. A person with AIDS may experience other diseases and infections because of a weakened immune system.

advanced stage of infection caused by HIV. The names HIV and AIDS can be confusing because both terms describe the same disease. Most people who are HIV positive do not have AIDS. An HIV-positive person is said to have AIDS when his or her immune system becomes so weak it can't fight off certain kinds of infections and cancers, such as PCP (a type of pneumonia) or KS (Kaposi sarcoma, a type of cancer that affects the skin and internal organs in HIV), wasting syndrome (involuntary weight loss), memory impairment, or tuberculosis.

Even without one of these infections, an HIV-positive person is diagnosed with AIDS if his or her immune system becomes severely weakened. This is measured by a lab test that determines the number of CD4 cells a person has. A CD4 cell count less than 200 in an HIV-infected person counts as a diagnosis of AIDS. It can take between 2 to 10 years, or longer, for an HIV-positive person to develop AIDS, even without treatment.

HIV means you have the Human Immunodeficiency Virus. AIDS means your immune system is so weak it cannot fight certain infections or cancers because you have HIV.

Once a person has been diagnosed with AIDS, she or he is always considered to have AIDS, even if that person's CD4 count goes up again and/or they recover from the disease that defined their AIDS diagnosis.

Where did HIV come from?

Scientists identified a type of chimpanzee in West Africa as the source of HIV infection in humans. They believe that the chimpanzee version of the immunodeficiency virus (called simian immunodeficiency virus, or SIV) most likely was transmitted to humans and mutated into HIV when humans hunted these chimpanzees for meat and came into contact with their infected blood. Studies show that HIV may have jumped from apes to humans as far back as the late 1800s. Over decades, the virus slowly spread across Africa and later into other parts of the world. We know that the virus has existed in the United States since at least the mid- to late 1970s.

How is HIV spread?

HIV is spread through four body fluids:

- semen
- vaginal fluid
- blood
- breast milk

HIV is NOT spread through:

- tears
- sweat
- feces
- urine

How is HIV spread through sex?

You can get infected from sexual contact with someone who is infected with HIV. Sexual contact that can transmit HIV includes:

- vaginal sex (penis in the vagina)
- anal sex (penis in the anus of either a man or a woman)
- oral sex (penis in the mouth)

If you have sex, the best thing to do is to practice "safer sex" all the time. To do so, always use a condom, dental dam, or other latex barrier and avoid "rough sex" or other activities that might cause bleeding. If you use lube with a condom, make sure it is water based, not oil-based. Oil-based lube causes latex condoms to break.

If you have unprotected sex with someone who is infected, it doesn't mean that you will be infected, too. But there is always a chance, especially if your partner is not on effective HIV medicines. Using a condom reduces your risk.

HIV is NOT spread by:

- hugging or massage
- masturbation
- fantasizing
- dry kissing
- phone sex
- cyber sex
- sex toys you don't share
- daily living with someone who has HIV

How is HIV spread through blood?

You can become infected if you have contact with the blood of some-one who is infected with HIV. Blood-borne infection with HIV can occur through:

- sharing needles when shooting drugs
- tattoos or body piercings with unsterilized needles
- accidental needle sticks
- blood transfusions
- splashing blood in your eyes

HIV is NOT spread by blood passed through insect bites.

Can mothers give HIV to their babies?

Infection can occur from HIV positive pregnant women to their babies in the womb and during birth. Taking anti-HIV drugs during pregnancy and childbirth can dramatically lower the risk.

After birth, transmission can occur through breast milk of infected women. The highest risk may be in the early months after birth. New mothers should try to bottle-feed their babies rather than breast-feed.

If you are an HIV-positive woman and intend to become pregnant, or you find out that you are HIV positive during your pregnancy, talk to your doctor about ways to reduce the chances that your baby will become infected, too.

What are the symptoms?

You can't tell if a person is HIV positive by looking at them. Most people with HIV infection don't look sick. Even so, when a person first becomes infected, he or she may get certain symptoms. This period of early infection is called **acute HIV infection**.

Symptoms can be different for each person. Sometimes there are no symptoms at all. Other times symptoms are strong. You may feel as if you have a cold or the flu. You may experience:

- fever

- headache

- sore throat

- swollen lymph nodes, usually on the neck

- fatigue

- rash

- sores in the mouth

If symptoms appear, they usually do so within days or weeks after infection, and end after 1 to 2 weeks.

The only way to tell if your symptoms are from a cold, the flu, or HIV is to have an HIV test.

What is an HIV test?

The HIV test is designed to determine whether you have been infected with HIV–the virus that causes AIDS.

When you get infected with HIV, the HIV virus replicates itself and spreads through the body, and your body produces cells and particles (antibodies) to fight the virus.

There are different types of HIV tests, some that can detect HIV itself (HIV antigen), and some that can detect antibodies to HIV in your body. If you have either HIV antigens or HIV antibodies, then you have been infected with HIV. The HIV test does not tell you if you have AIDS, how long you have been infected, or how sick you might be—for this you need other kinds of tests.

Using newer HIV testing methods, it is possible to identify most cases of HIV 2–3 weeks after infection.

Should you get tested?

The U.S. Centers for Disease Control and Prevention (CDC) currently recommends that all adults in the United States get tested for HIV infection at least once, regardless of risk factors for HIV infection, and that they be tested repeatedly if there is an ongoing risk of HIV infection.

The U.S. Department of Veterans Affairs recommends that voluntary HIV testing be provided to all patients who receive medical care—even for those Veterans who do not think that they have risk factors. That way, people who are infected will be diagnosed early and can get the most benefits from treatment. They also can take steps to avoid spreading the disease to others. For example, a woman who tests positive for HIV during a pregnancy can take medication to help prevent her baby from becoming infected. Or, a man who thought he was HIV negative but finds out he is infected can take steps to avoid infecting his sex partner.

How is HIV treated?

There are many treatments now that can help people with HIV. As a result, many people with HIV are living much longer and healthier lives than before.

Currently, medicines can slow the growth of the virus or stop it from making copies of itself. Although these drugs don't eliminate the virus from the body, they keep the amount of virus in the blood low. The amount of virus in the blood is called the **viral load**, and it can be measured by a test.

There are several types of anti-HIV drugs. Each type attacks the virus in its own way. It's similar to the way the military plans an attack using the different strengths of the Army, Navy, Air Force, and Marines.

> **HIV drugs cannot eliminate HIV virus from the body, but they can reduce it to very, very low levels. The main goal of HIV drugs is to reduce viral load as much as possible for as long as possible.**

How are the drugs taken?

Most people who are getting treated for HIV take 3 or more drugs. This is called combination therapy or "the cocktail." (It also has a longer name: Anti-Retroviral Therapy (ART) or Highly Active Anti-Retroviral Therapy (HAART.) Combination therapy is the most effective treatment for HIV.

People who are HIV positive need to work closely with their doctors to decide when to start treatment and which drugs to take.

Is it hard to take these drugs?

HIV medicines have become much easier to take in recent years. Some newer drug combinations package 3 separate medicines into only 1 pill, taken once a day, with minimal side effects. For the great majority of people, HIV medicines are tolerable and effective, and let people infected with HIV live longer and healthier lives. Still, for some people taking medicine for HIV can be complicated. Some of the drugs are difficult to take, can cause serious side effects, and don't work for everyone. Even when a drug does help a particular person, it may become less effective over time or stop working altogether.

Once on medications, patients must work with their health care providers to monitor how well the drugs are working, deal with side effects, and decide what to do if the drugs stop working.

The good news is that experts are learning more about the virus and creating new treatments for HIV, making it easier to take these medicines.

Do you have to be treated for the rest of your life?

Right now, there is no cure for HIV infection or AIDS. So, once you start treatment, you have to continue to be sure the virus doesn't multiply out of control.

> **The most effective treatment for HIV is combination therapy. Different anti-HIV drugs attack the virus in different ways, so combining three or more drugs is the best way to fight the virus.**

Are there long-term effects?

Over time, HIV-positive people may experience symptoms from the infection and side effects from their anti-HIV drugs. Sometimes it is not clear whether the virus or the medications are causing the problems.

One long-term effect that some people experience is a change in the way their bodies handle fats and sugars. In some cases, these changes can raise the person's risk for heart disease and diabetes. Some people have experienced visible changes in body shape and appearance, including increased fat in the belly, neck, shoulders, breasts, or face — or loss of fat in the face, legs, or arms.

Experts aren't sure whether these changes in body fat are due to HIV itself, or to the anti-HIV drugs. There are no proven cures at this time, but there are steps people can take to reduce the effects. These include changes in diet, exercise, medication, even plastic surgery.

Over time, HIV infects and kills off immune cells. This leaves the body unable to fight certain kinds of serious, sometimes deadly, infections. These are called **opportunistic infections** because they take the opportunity to attack when a person's immune system is weak. Having HIV can also increase the risk of getting certain cancers. They may reach the advanced stage of infection called AIDS.

Is HIV always fatal?

Most people who do not receive treatment for HIV will eventually (over years) become ill and die of complications of HIV infection. With treatment (called antiretroviral therapy), though, most people with HIV infection can lead long and healthy lives; this is especially true if they start HIV treatment when their immune system is still relatively strong.

Chapter 2

HIV Life Cycle – How HIV Causes AIDS

HIV Life Cycle

- HIV gradually destroys the immune system by attacking and killing CD4 cells. CD4 cells are a type of white blood cell that play a major role in protecting the body from infection.

- HIV uses the machinery of the CD4 cells to multiply (make copies of itself) and spread throughout the body. This process, which includes seven steps or stages, is called the HIV life cycle. HIV medicines protect the immune system by blocking HIV at different stages of the HIV life cycle.

- Antiretroviral therapy or ART is the use of HIV medicines to treat HIV infection. People on ART take a combination of HIV medicines from at least two different HIV drug classes every day. Because HIV medicines in different drug classes block HIV at different stages of the HIV life cycle, ART is very effective at preventing HIV from multiplying. ART also reduces the risk of HIV drug resistance.

- ART can't cure HIV, but HIV medicines help people with HIV live longer, healthier lives. ART also reduces the risk of sexual transmission of HIV.

Text in this chapter is excerpted from "HIV Overview – The HIV Life Cycle," AIDS*info*, September 22, 2015.

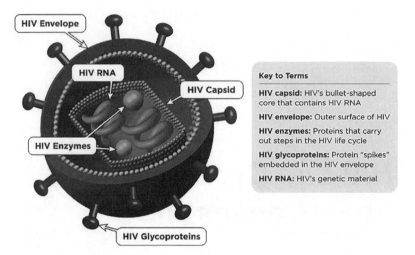

Figure 2.1. *Human Immunodeficiency Virus*

Once a person is infected with HIV, the virus begins to attack and destroy the CD4 cells of the immune system. CD4 cells are a type of white blood cell that play a major role in protecting the body from infection. HIV uses the machinery of the CD4 cells to multiply (make copies of itself) and spread throughout the body. This process, which includes seven steps or stages, is called the HIV life cycle.

What is the connection between HIV medicines and the HIV life cycle?

Antiretroviral therapy (ART) is the use of HIV medicines to treat HIV infection. HIV medicines protect the immune system by blocking HIV at different stages of the HIV life cycle.

HIV medicines are grouped into different drug classes according to how they fight HIV. Each class of drugs attacks HIV at a different stage of the HIV life cycle.

People on ART take a combination of HIV medicines from at least two different HIV drug classes every day. Because HIV medicines in different drug classes block HIV at different stages of the HIV life cycle, ART is very effective at preventing HIV from multiplying. Having less HIV in the body protects the immune system and prevents HIV from advancing to AIDS. ART also reduces the risk of HIV drug resistance.

ART can't cure HIV, but HIV medicines help people with HIV live longer, healthier lives. HIV medicines also reduce the risk of sexual transmission of HIV.

What are the seven stages of the HIV life cycle?

The seven stages of the HIV life cycle are: 1) binding, 2) fusion, 3) reverse transcription, 4) integration, 5) replication, 6) assembly, and 7) budding. To understand each stage in the HIV life cycle, it helps to first imagine what HIV looks like.

Now follow each stage in the HIV life cycle, as HIV attacks a CD4 cell and uses the machinery of the cell to multiply.

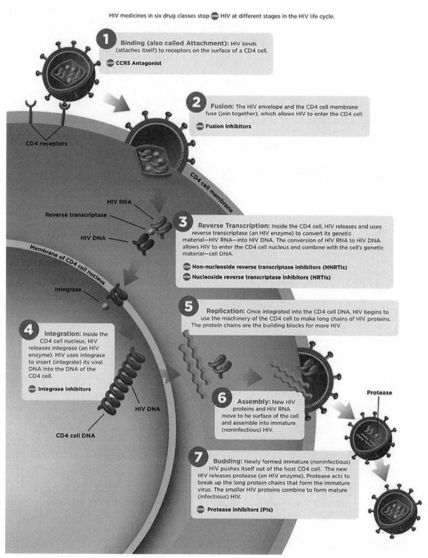

Figure 2.2. *HIV Life Cycle*

Chapter 3

Stages of HIV Infection

Overview

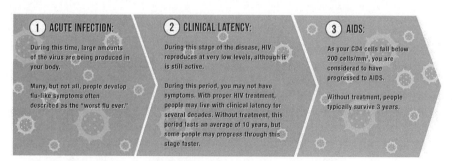

1 ACUTE INFECTION:

During this time, large amounts of the virus are being produced in your body.

Many, but not all, people develop flu-like symptoms often described as the "worst flu ever."

2 CLINICAL LATENCY:

During this stage of the disease, HIV reproduces at very low levels, although it is still active.

During this period, you may not have symptoms. With proper HIV treatment, people may live with clinical latency for several decades. Without treatment, this period lasts an average of 10 years, but some people may progress through this stage faster.

3 AIDS:

As your CD4 cells fall below 200 cells/mm³, you are considered to have progressed to AIDS.

Without treatment, people typically survive 3 years.

Figure 3.1. *Stages of HIV Infection*

How Does HIV Progress in Your Body?

Without treatment, HIV advances in stages, overwhelming your immune system and getting worse over time. The three stages of HIV infection are: (1) acute HIV infection, (2) clinical latency, and (3) AIDS (acquired immunodeficiency syndrome).

However, there's good news: by using HIV medicines (called antiretroviral therapy or ART) consistently, you can prevent HIV from progressing to AIDS. ART helps control the virus so that you can live a longer, healthier life and reduce the risk of transmitting HIV to others.

These are the three stages of HIV infection:

Text in this chapter is excerpted from "Stages of HIV Infection," AIDS.gov, August 27, 2015.

Acute HIV Infection Stage

Within 2–4 weeks after HIV infection, many, but not all, people develop flu-like symptoms, often described as "the worst flu ever." Symptoms can include fever, swollen glands, sore throat, rash, muscle and joint aches and pains, fatigue, and headache. This is called "acute retroviral syndrome" (ARS) or "primary HIV infection," and it's the body's natural response to the HIV infection.

During this early period of infection, large amounts of virus are being produced in your body. The virus uses *CD4 cells* to replicate and destroys them in the process. Because of this, your *CD4 count* can fall rapidly. Eventually your immune response will begin to bring the level of virus in your body back down to a level called a *viral set point*, which is a relatively stable level of virus in your body. At this point, your CD4 count begins to increase, but it may not return to pre-infection levels. It may be particularly beneficial to your health to begin ART during this stage.

During the acute HIV infection stage, you are at high risk of transmitting HIV to your sexual or drug using partners because the levels of HIV in your blood stream are very high. For this reason, it is very important to take steps to reduce your risk of transmission.

Clinical Latency Stage

After the acute stage of HIV infection, the disease moves into a stage called the "clinical latency" stage. "Latency" means a period where a virus is living or developing in a person without producing symptoms. During the clinical latency stage, people who are infected with HIV experience no HIV-related symptoms, or only mild ones. (This stage is sometimes called "asymptomatic HIV infection" or "chronic HIV infection.")

During the clinical latency stage, the HIV virus continues to reproduce at very low levels, although it is still active. If you take ART, you may live with clinical latency for several decades because treatment helps keep the virus in check. For people who are not on ART, the clinical latency stage lasts an average of 10 years, but some people may progress through this stage faster.

People in this symptom-free stage are still able to transmit HIV to others, even if they are on ART, although ART greatly reduces the risk of transmission.

If you have HIV and you are not on ART, then eventually your viral load will begin to rise and your CD4 count will begin to decline. As this happens, you may begin to have *constitutional symptoms* of HIV as the virus levels increase in your body.

AIDS

This is the stage of HIV infection that occurs when your immune system is badly damaged and you become vulnerable to *opportunistic infections*. When the number of your CD4 cells falls below 200 cells per cubic millimeter of blood (200 cells/mm^3), you are considered to have progressed to AIDS. (In someone with a healthy immune system, CD4 counts are between 500 and 1,600 cells/mm^3.) You are also considered to have progressed to AIDS if you develop one or more opportunistic illnesses, regardless of your CD4 count.

Without treatment, people who progress to AIDS typically survive about 3 years. Once you have a dangerous opportunistic illness, life-expectancy without treatment falls to about 1 year. However, if you are taking ART and maintain a low viral load, then you may enjoy a near normal life span. You will most likely never progress to AIDS.

Factors Affecting Disease Progression

People living with HIV may progress through these stages at different rates, depending on a variety of factors, including their genetic makeup, how healthy they were before they were infected, how soon after infection they are diagnosed and linked to care and treatment, whether they see their healthcare provider regularly and take their HIV medications as directed, and different health-related choices they make, such as decisions to eat a healthful diet, exercise, and not smoke.

Not everyone is diagnosed early. Some people are diagnosed with HIV and AIDS concurrently, meaning that they have been living with HIV for a long time and the virus has already done damage to their body by the time they find out they are infected. These individuals need to seek a healthcare provider immediately and be linked to care so that they can stay as healthy as possible, as long as possible.

Time between HIV Infection and AIDS

Factors that may shorten the time between HIV and AIDS:

- Older age
- HIV subtype
- Co-infection with other viruses (like tuberculosis or hepatitis C)
- Poor nutrition

- Severe stress
- Your genetic background

Factors that may delay the time between HIV and AIDS:

- Taking antiretroviral therapy consistently
- Staying in regular HIV care
- Closely adhering to your doctor's recommendations
- Eating healthful foods
- Taking care of yourself
- Your genetic background

By making healthy choices, you have some control over the progression of HIV infection.

Chapter 4

A Statistical Overview

Chapter Contents

21

Section 4.1

HIV/AIDS Prevalence and Incidence in the United States and Worldwide

This section includes excerpts from "Statistics Overview," Centers for Disease Control and Prevention (CDC), June 30, 2015; text from "U.S. Statistics," AIDS.gov, December 2, 2014; and text from "Global Statistics," AIDS.gov, November 13, 2014.

Statistics Overview

Definitions

- *Diagnosis of HIV infection:* The term refers to persons diagnosed with HIV infection, regardless of the stage of disease at diagnosis (i.e., HIV infection Stage 1, 2, 3 [AIDS], or unknown), from 50 states, the District of Columbia, and 6 U.S. dependent areas.

- *HIV infection, stage 3 (AIDS):* The term refers specifically to persons with diagnosed HIV whose infection was ever classified as stage 3 (AIDS), based on CDC's 2008 revised surveillance case definitions for adults, adolescents, and children.

- *6 U.S. dependent areas included in the data:* American Samoa, Guam, the Northern Mariana Islands, Puerto Rico, the Republic of Palau, and the U.S. Virgin Islands.

- *Transmission category:* The term for summarizing the multiple risk factors that a person may have had by selecting the one most likely to have resulted in HIV transmission. For surveillance purposes, persons with more than one reported risk factor for HIV infection are classified in the transmission category listed first in a hierarchy of transmission categories, and therefore counted only once. The exception is men who had sexual contact with other men and injected drugs; this group makes up a separate transmission category.

- *HIV incidence:* The estimated number of persons newly infected with HIV during a specified time period (e.g., a year).

- *HIV prevalence:* The number of persons living with HIV at a given time regardless of the time of infection, whether the person has received a diagnosis (aware of infection), or the stage of HIV disease.

HIV Prevalence Estimate

Prevalence is the number of people living with HIV infection at a given time, such as at the end of a given year.

At the end of 2012, an estimated 1.2 million persons aged 13 and older were living with HIV infection in the United States, including 156,300 (12.8%) persons whose infections had not been diagnosed.

HIV Incidence Estimate

Incidence is the number of new HIV infections that occur during a given year. CDC estimates that approximately 50,000 people in the United States are newly infected with HIV each year. In 2010 (the most recent year that data are available), there were an estimated 47,500 new HIV infections. Nearly two thirds of these new infections occurred in gay and bisexual men. Black/African American men and women were also highly affected and were estimated to have an HIV incidence rate that was almost 8 times as high as the incidence rate among whites.

Diagnoses of HIV Infection

In 2013, the estimated number of diagnoses of HIV infection in the United States was 47,352. There were 37,887 diagnoses in adult and adolescent males and 9,278 in adult and adolescent females. There were an estimated 187 diagnoses of HIV infection among children aged less than 13 years at diagnosis.

Diagnoses of HIV Infection, by Age

In 2013, the estimated number of diagnoses of HIV infection in the United States, by age at diagnosis, was as follows:

Table 4.1. HIV Infection Diagnoses by Age

Age (Years)	Estimated Number of Diagnoses of HIV Infection, 2013
Under 13	187
Ages 13–14	45
Ages 15–19	1,863

Table 4.1. Continued

Age (Years)	Estimated Number of Diagnoses of HIV Infection, 2013
Ages 20–24	8,053
Ages 25–29	7,825
Ages 30–34	6,165
Ages 35–39	4,858
Ages 40–44	4,820
Ages 45–49	4,961
Ages 50–54	3,747
Ages 55–59	2,467
Ages 60–64	1,316
Ages 65 or older	1,045

Diagnoses of HIV Infection, by Race / Ethnicity

CDC tracks diagnoses of HIV infection information on seven racial and ethnic groups: American Indian/Alaska Native, Asian, black/African American, Hispanic/Latino, Native Hawaiian/other Pacific Islander, white, and multiple races.

In 2013, the estimated number of diagnoses of HIV infection in the United States was as follows:

Table 4.2. HIV Infection Diagnoses by Race/Ethnicity

Race or Ethnicity	Estimated Number of Diagnoses of HIV Infection, 2013
American Indian/Alaska Native	218
Asian	973
Black/African American	21,836
Hispanic/Latino[a]	10,117
Native Hawaiian/Other Pacific Islander	67
White	13,101
Multiple Races	1,039

[a]*Hispanics/Latinos can be of any race.*

Diagnoses of HIV Infection, by Transmission Category

Six common transmission categories are male-to-male sexual contact, injection drug use, male-to-male sexual contact and injection drug use, heterosexual contact, mother-to-child (perinatal) transmission, and other (includes blood transfusions and unknown cause).

The distribution of the estimated number of diagnoses of HIV infection among adults and adolescents in the United States by transmission category follows. A breakdown by sex is provided where appropriate.

Table 4.3. HIV Infection Diagnoses by Transmission Category

Transmission Category	Estimated Number of Diagnoses of HIV Infection, 2013		
	Adult and Adolescent Males	Adult and Adolescent Females	Total
Male-to-male sexual contact	30,689	NA	30,689
Injection drug use	1,942	1,154	3,096
Male-to-male sexual contact and injection drug use	1,270	NA	1,270
Heterosexual contact[a]	3,887	8,031	11,918
Other[b]	99	93	192

[a]Heterosexual contact with a person known to have, or to be at high risk for, HIV infection.
[b]Includes hemophilia, blood transfusion, perinatal exposure, and risk factor not reported or not identified.

The distribution of the estimated number of diagnoses of HIV infection among children aged less than 13 years at the time of diagnosis in the United States, by transmission category, follows:

Table 4.4. HIV Infection Diagnoses by Transmission Category for Children Aged under 13

Transmission Category	Estimated Number of Diagnoses of HIV Infection, 2013
Perinatal	107
Other[a]	80

[a]Includes hemophilia, blood transfusion, and risk factor not reported or not identified.

HIV Diagnoses, by Top 10 States / Dependent Areas

These are the 10 states or dependent areas reporting the highest number of HIV diagnoses in 2013:

Table 4.5. Top 10 States/Dependent Areas with Highest HIV Diagnoses

State/Dependent Area	Number of Diagnoses of HIV Infection, 2013
Florida	5,377
California	5,334
Texas	4,854
New York	3,803
Georgia	3,020
New Jersey	2,177
Maryland	2,174
Illinois	2,091
North Carolina	1,578
Pennsylvania	1,425

Persons Living with Diagnosed HIV Infection

At the end of 2012, there were an estimated 914,826 persons living with diagnosed HIV infection in the United States.

Data include persons with a diagnosis of HIV infection regardless of the stage of disease at diagnosis. Estimated numbers resulted from statistical adjustment that accounted for delays in reporting to the health department (but not for incomplete reporting) and missing transmission category, where appropriate.

Because of delays in reporting of deaths, death and prevalence data are only available through the end of 2012. The exclusion of data from the most recent year allows at least 18 months for deaths to be reported and for these persons to be removed from calculations of persons living with diagnosed HIV infection.

Totals include persons of unknown race/ethnicity. Because totals for the estimated numbers were calculated independently of the values for the subpopulations, the subpopulation values may not equal these totals.

Stage 3 (AIDS)

In 2013, the estimated number of persons with diagnosed HIV infection classified as stage 3 (AIDS) in the United States was 26,688.

Of these, 20,256 stage 3 (AIDS) classifications were among adult and adolescent males, 6,424 were among adult and adolescent females, and 8 were among children aged less than 13 years.

The cumulative estimated number of persons with diagnosed HIV infection ever classified as stage 3 (AIDS) through 2012 in the United States was 1,194,039.

Estimated numbers resulted from statistical adjustment that accounted for delays in reporting to the health department (but not for incomplete reporting) and missing transmission category, where appropriate.

Cumulative totals include persons of unknown race/ethnicity. Because totals for the estimated numbers were calculated independently of the values for the subpopulations, the subpopulation values may not equal these totals.

Stage 3 (AIDS), by Age

In 2013, the estimated number of stage 3 (AIDS) classifications in the 50 states and the District of Columbia, by distribution of ages at time of classification, was as follows:

Table 4.6. Age Based Classification of Stage 3 AIDS

Age (Years)	Estimated Number of Persons with Diagnosed HIV infection Ever Classified as Stage 3 (AIDS), 2013
Under 13	8
Ages 13–14	30
Ages 15–19	435
Ages 20–24	2,239
Ages 25–29	3,123
Ages 30–34	3,268
Ages 35–39	3,200
Ages 40–44	3,496
Ages 45–49	3,781
Ages 50–54	3,135
Ages 55–59	1,998
Ages 60–64	1,144
Ages 65 or older	831

Stage 3 (AIDS), by Race / Ethnicity

CDC tracks AIDS information on seven racial and ethnic groups: American Indian/Alaska Native, Asian, black/African American, Hispanic/Latino, Native Hawaiian/other Pacific Islander, white, and multiple races.

In 2013, the estimated number of persons with diagnosed HIV infection ever classified as stage 3 (AIDS) in the United States, by race or ethnicity was as follows:

Table 4.7. Stage 3 (AIDS) Diagnosed in the United States by Race or Ethnicity

Race or Ethnicity	Estimated Number of Persons with Diagnosed HIV Infection Ever Classified as Stage 3 (AIDS), 2013	Cumulative Estimated Number of Persons with Diagnosed HIV Infection Ever Classified as Stage 3 (AIDS), Through 2013[a]
American Indian/Alaska Native	104	3,514
Asian[b]	415	9,712
Black/African American	13,172	497,267
Hispanic/Latino[c]	5,336	215,685
Native Hawaiian/Other Pacific Islander	37	855
White	6,759	436,557
Multiple Races	867	30,448

[a]*From the beginning of the epidemic through 2013.*
[b]*Includes Asian/Pacific Islander legacy cases.*
[c]*Hispanics/Latinos can be of any race.*

Stage 3 (AIDS), by Transmission Category

CDC collects HIV and stage 3 (AIDS) data using six common transmission categories: male-to-male sexual contact, injection drug use, male-to-male sexual contact and injection drug use, heterosexual contact, mother-to-child (perinatal) transmission, and other (includes blood transfusions and unknown cause).

The distribution of the estimated number of persons with HIV infection ever classified as stage 3 (AIDS) among adults and adolescents in the United States, by transmission category, follows. A breakdown by sex is provided where appropriate.

Table 4.8. Stage 3 (AIDS) in the United States Among Adults and Adolescents by Transmission Category

| Transmission Category | Estimated Number of Persons with Diagnosed HIV infection Ever Classified as stage 3 (AIDS), 2013 | | |
	Adult and Adolescent Males	Adult and Adolescent Females	Total
Male-to-male sexual contact	14,611	NA	14,611
Injection drug use	1,610	1,143	2,753
Male-to-male sexual contact and injection drug use	1,026	NA	1,026
Heterosexual contact[a]	2,865	5,109	7,974
Other[b]	144	172	316

[a]*Heterosexual contact with a person known to have, or to be at high risk for, HIV infection.*
[b]*Includes hemophilia, blood transfusion, perinatal exposure, and risk factor not reported or not identified.*

Table 4.9. Cumulative Report

| Transmission Category | Cumulative Estimated Number of Persons with Diagnosed HIV Infection Ever Classified as Stage 3 (AIDS), Through 2013[a] | | |
	Adult and Adolescent Males	Adult and Adolescent Females	Total
Male-to-male sexual contact	577,403	NA	577,403
Injection drug use	187,218	89,790	277,008
Male-to-male sexual contact and injection drug use	83,828	NA	83,828

Table 4.9. Continued

Transmission Category	Cumulative Estimated Number of Persons with Diagnosed HIV Infection Ever Classified as Stage 3 (AIDS), Through 2013[a]		
	Adult and Adolescent Males	Adult and Adolescent Females	Total
Heterosexual contact[b]	82,447	146,521	228,968
Other[c]	11,545	5,868	17,413

[a]*From the beginning of the epidemic through 2013.*
[b]*Heterosexual contact with a person known to have, or to be at high risk for, HIV infection.*
[c]*Includes hemophilia, blood transfusion, perinatal exposure, and risk factor not reported or not identified.*

Persons Living with Diagnosed HIV Infection Ever Classified as Stage 3 (AIDS)

At the end of 2012, an estimated 508,845 persons in the United States were living with diagnosed HIV infection ever classified as Stage 3 (AIDS). Estimated numbers resulted from statistical adjustment that accounted for delays in reporting to the health department (but not for incomplete reporting) and missing transmission category, where appropriate.

Because of delays in reporting of deaths to the National HIV Surveillance System (NHSS), four years of prevalence data are displayed. The data reflect the persons living with an infection ever classified as stage 3 (AIDS) at the end of a given year during 2009-2012. The exclusion of data from the most recent year allows at least 18 months for deaths to be reported and for these persons to be removed from calculations of persons living with an AIDS diagnosis.

Totals include persons of unknown race/ethnicity. Because totals for the estimated numbers were calculated independently of the values for the subpopulations, the subpopulation values may not equal these totals.

Deaths of Persons with Diagnosed HIV Infection Ever Classified as Stage 3 (AIDS)

In 2012, the estimated number of deaths of persons with diagnosed HIV infection ever classified as stage 3 (AIDS) in the United States was 13,712.

The cumulative estimated number of deaths of persons with diagnosed HIV infection ever classified as stage 3 (AIDS) in the United States, through 2012, was 658,507.

Deaths of persons with diagnosed HIV infection ever classified as stage 3 (AIDS) may be due to any cause.

Estimated numbers resulted from statistical adjustment that accounted for delays in reporting to the health department (but not for incomplete reporting) and missing transmission category, where appropriate. Because of delays in reporting of deaths, data are only available through the end of 2012. The exclusion of data from the most recent year allows at least 18 months for deaths of persons with an AIDS diagnosis to be reported.

Totals include persons of unknown race/ethnicity. Because totals for the estimated numbers were calculated independently of the values for the subpopulations, the subpopulation values may not equal these totals.

HIV in the United States

Fast Facts

- More than 1.2 million people in the United States are living with HIV infection, and almost 1 in 8 (12.8%) are unaware of their infection.
- Gay, bisexual, and other men who have sex with men (MSM[a]), particularly young black/African American MSM, are most seriously affected by HIV.
- By race, blacks/African Americans face the most severe burden of HIV.

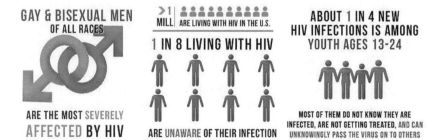

GAY & BISEXUAL MEN OF ALL RACES ARE THE MOST SEVERELY AFFECTED BY HIV

>1 MILL ARE LIVING WITH HIV IN THE U.S.

1 IN 8 LIVING WITH HIV ARE UNAWARE OF THEIR INFECTION

ABOUT 1 IN 4 NEW HIV INFECTIONS IS AMONG YOUTH AGES 13-24

MOST OF THEM DO NOT KNOW THEY ARE INFECTED, ARE NOT GETTING TREATED, AND CAN UNKNOWINGLY PASS THE VIRUS ON TO OTHERS

Figure 4.1. HIV in the United States

CDC estimates that 1,218,400 persons aged 13 years and older are living with HIV infection, including 156,300 (12.8%) who are unaware of their infection. Over the past decade, the number of people living with HIV has increased, while the annual number of new HIV infections has remained relatively stable. Still, the pace of new infections continues at far too high a level—particularly among certain groups.

HIV Incidence (new infections): The estimated incidence of HIV has remained stable overall in recent years, at about 50,000 new HIV infections per year. Within the overall estimates, however, some groups are affected more than others. MSM continue to bear the greatest burden of HIV infection, and among races/ethnicities, African Americans continue to be disproportionately affected.

HIV Diagnoses (new diagnoses, regardless of when infection occurred or stage of disease at diagnosis): In 2013, an estimated 47,352 people were diagnosed with HIV infection in the United States. In that same year, an estimated 26,688 people were diagnosed with AIDS. Overall, an estimated 1,194,039 people in the United States have been diagnosed with AIDS.

Deaths: An estimated 13,712 people with an AIDS diagnosis died in 2012, and approximately 658,507 people in the United States with an AIDS diagnosis have died overall. The deaths of persons with an AIDS diagnosis can be due to any cause—that is, the death may or may not be related to AIDS.

By Risk Group

Gay, bisexual, and other men who have sex with men (MSM) of all races and ethnicities remain the population most profoundly affected by HIV.

In 2010, the estimated number of new HIV infections among MSM was 29,800, a significant 12% increase from the 26,700 new infections among MSM in 2008.

Although MSM represent about 4% of the male population in the United States, in 2010, MSM accounted for 78% of new HIV infections among males and 63% of all new infections. MSM accounted for 54% of all people living with HIV infection in 2011, the most recent year these data are available.

In 2010, white MSM continued to account for the largest number of new HIV infections (11,200), by transmission category, followed closely by black MSM (10,600).

The estimated number of new HIV infections was greatest among MSM in the youngest age group. In 2010, the greatest number of new

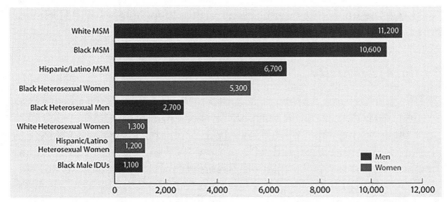

Figure 4.2. Estimated New HIV Infections in the United States, 2010, for the Most Affected Subpopulations

Source: CDC. Estimated HIV incidence among adults and adolescents in the United States, 2007–2010. HIV Surveillance Supplemental Report 2012;17(4). Subpopulations representing 2% or less are not reflected in this figure. Abbreviations: MSM, men who have sex with men; IDU, injection drug user.

HIV infections (4,800) among MSM occurred in young black/African American MSM aged 13–24. Young black MSM accounted for 45% of new HIV infections among black MSM and 55% of new HIV infections among young MSM overall.

Since the epidemic began, an estimated 311,087 MSM with an AIDS diagnosis have died, including an estimated 5,380 in 2012.

Heterosexuals and injection drug users also continue to be affected by HIV.

Since the epidemic began, almost 92,613 persons with AIDS that were infected through heterosexual sex, have died, including an estimated 4,550 in 2012.

New HIV infections among women are primarily attributed to heterosexual contact (84% in 2010) or injection drug use (16% in 2010). Women accounted for 20% of estimated new HIV infections in 2010 and 23% of those living with HIV infection in 2011. The 9,500 new infections among women in 2010 reflect a significant 21% decrease from the 12,000 new infections that occurred among this group in 2008.

Injection drug users represented 8% of new HIV infections in 2010 and 15% of those living with HIV in 2011.

Since the epidemic began, nearly 186,728 people with (AIDS) who inject drugs have died, including an estimated 3,514 in 2012.

By Race / Ethnicity

Blacks/African Americans continue to experience the most severe burden of HIV, compared with other races and ethnicities.

Blacks represent approximately 12% of the U.S. population, but accounted for an estimated 44% of new HIV infections in 2010. They also accounted for 41% of people living with HIV infection in 2011.

Since the epidemic began, an estimated 270,726 blacks with AIDS have died, including an estimated 6,540 in 2012.

Hispanics/Latinos are also disproportionately affected by HIV.

Hispanics/Latinos represented 16% of the population but accounted for 21% of new HIV infections in 2010. Hispanics/Latinos accounted for 20% of people living with HIV infection in 2011.

Disparities persist in the estimated rate of new HIV infections in Hispanics/Latinos. In 2010, the rate of new HIV infections for Latino males was 2.9 times that for white males, and the rate of new infections for Latinas was 4.2 times that for white females.

Since the epidemic began, more than 100,888 Hispanics/Latinos with an AIDS diagnosis have died, including 2,155 in 2012.

[a]*For assessing disease risk, the term MSM is often used instead of gay, homosexual, or bisexual because it refers to a risk behavior, rather than an identity that may or may not be tied to a behavior.*

Global Statistics

35 MILLION PEOPLE WORLDWIDE ARE CURRENTLY LIVING WITH HIV/AIDS.

THE VAST MAJORITY OF PEOPLE LIVING WITH HIV ARE IN LOW- AND MIDDLE-INCOME COUNTRIES, PARTICULARLY IN SUB-SAHARAN AFRICA.

3.2 MILLION CHILDREN WORLDWIDE ARE LIVING WITH HIV. MOST OF THESE CHILDREN WERE INFECTED BY THEIR HIV-POSTIVE MOTHERS DURING PREGNANCY, CHILDBIRTH OR BREASTFEEDING.

Figure 4.3. Prevalence of HIV/AIDS

The Global HIV/AIDS Epidemic

HIV, the virus that causes AIDS, is one of the world's most serious health and development challenges:

- According to the World Health Organization (WHO), there were approximately 35 million people worldwide living with HIV/AIDS in 2013. Of these, 3.2 million were children (<15 years old).

- According to WHO, an estimated 2.1 million individuals world-wide became newly infected with HIV in 2013. This includes over 240,000 children (<15 years). Most of these children live in sub-Saharan Africa and were infected by their HIV-positive mothers during pregnancy, childbirth or breastfeeding.

- A UNAIDS report shows that 19 million of the 35 million people living with HIV today do not know that they have the virus.

- The vast majority of people living with HIV are in low- and middle-income countries. According to WHO, sub-Saharan Africa is the most affected region, with 24.7 million people living with HIV in 2013. Seventy-one percent of all people who are living with HIV in the world live in this region.

- HIV is the world's leading infectious killer. According to WHO, an estimated 39 million people have died since the first cases were reported in 1981 and 1.5 million people died of AIDS-related causes in 2013.

- Even today, despite advances in our scientific understanding of HIV and its prevention and treatment as well as years of significant effort by the global health community and leading government and civil society organizations, most people living with HIV or at risk for HIV do not have access to prevention, care, and treatment, and there is still no cure. However, effective treatment with antiretroviral drugs can control the virus so that people with HIV can enjoy healthy lives and reduce the risk of transmitting the virus to others.

- The HIV epidemic not only affects the health of individuals, it impacts households, communities, and the development and economic growth of nations. Many of the countries hardest hit by HIV also suffer from other infectious diseases, food insecurity, and other serious problems.

- Despite these challenges, there have been successes and promising signs. New global efforts have been mounted to address the epidemic, particularly in the last decade. Prevention has helped to reduce HIV prevalence rates in a small but growing number of countries and new HIV infections are believed to be on the decline. In addition, the number of people with HIV receiving treatment in resource-poor countries has dramatically increased in the past decade. According to WHO, at the end of 2013, 12.9 million people living with HIV were receiving antiretroviral therapy (ART) globally, of which 11.7 million were receiving ART in low- and middle-income countries. About 740,000 of those were children. This is a 5.6 million increase in the number of people receiving ART since 2010. However, almost 22 million other people living with HIV, or 3 of 5 people living with HIV, are still not accessing ART.

- Progress has been made in preventing mother-to-child transmission of HIV and keeping mothers alive. According to WHO, in 2013, 67% of pregnant women living with HIV in low- and middle-income countries (970,000 women) received ART to avoid transmission of HIV to their children. This is up from 47% in 2010.

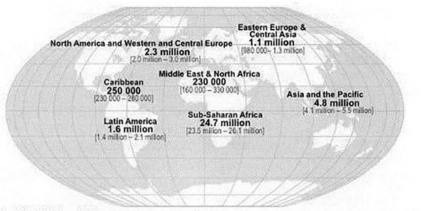

Total: 35.0 million [33.2 million – 37.2 million]

Source: UNAIDS

&UNAIDS

Figure 4.4. *Adults and Children Estimated to be Living with HIV – 2013*

Section 4.2

HIV/AIDS and Minority Populations

Text in this section is excerpted from "HIV/AIDS Fact Sheets,"
Centers for Disease Control and Prevention (CDC), August 4, 2015.

HIV among African Americans

Fast Facts

- African Americans are the racial/ethnic group most affected by HIV.
- The rate of new HIV infection in African Americans is 8 times that of whites based on population size.
- Gay and bisexual men account for most new infections among African Americans; young gay and bisexual men aged 13 to 24 are the most affected of this group.

Blacks/African Americans have the most severe burden of HIV of all racial/ethnic groups in the United States. Compared with other races and ethnicities, African Americans account for a higher proportion of new HIV infections, those living with HIV, and those ever diagnosed with AIDS.

The Numbers

New HIV Infections[a]

- African Americans accounted for an estimated 44% of all new HIV infections among adults and adolescents (aged 13 years or older) in 2010, despite representing only 12% of the US population; considering the smaller size of the African American population in the United States, this represents a population rate that is 8 times that of whites overall.

- In 2010, men accounted for 70% (14,700) of the estimated 20,900 new HIV infections among all adult and adolescent African Americans. The estimated rate of new HIV infections for African American men (103.6/100,000 population) was 7 times that of white men, twice that of Latino men, and nearly 3 times that of African American women.

- In 2010, African American gay, bisexual, and other men who have sex with men[b] represented an estimated 72% (10,600) of new infections among all African American men and 36% of an estimated 29,800 new HIV infections among all gay and bisexual men. More new HIV infections (4,800) occurred among young African American gay and bisexual men (aged 13-24) than any other subgroup of gay and bisexual men.

- In 2010, African American women accounted for 6,100 (29%) of the estimated new HIV infections among all adult and adolescent African Americans. This number represents a decrease of 21% since 2008. Most new HIV infections among African American women (87%; 5,300) are attributed to heterosexual contact.[c] The estimated rate of new HIV infections for African American women (38.1/100,000 population) was 20 times that of white women and almost 5 times that of Hispanic/Latino women.[d]

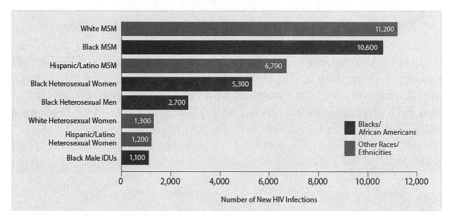

Figure 4.5. *Estimates of New HIV Infections in the United States for the Most-Affected Subpopulations, 2010*

Source: CDC. Estimated HIV incidence among adults and adolescents in the United States, 2007–2010. HIV Surveillance Supplemental Report 2012;17(4). Subpopulations representing 2% or less are not reflected in this figure.
Abbreviations: MSM, men who have sex with men; IDU, injection drug user.

HIV and AIDS Diagnoses[e] and Deaths

- At some point in their lifetimes, an estimated 1 in 16 African American men and 1 in 32 African American women will be diagnosed with HIV infection.

- In 2012, African Americans had the largest percentage (47%) of the estimated 47,989 diagnoses of HIV infection in the United States.

- In 2012, an estimated 14,102 African Americans were diagnosed with HIV infection ever classified as stage 3 (AIDS) in the United States.

- By the end of 2011, an estimated 265,812 African Americans diagnosed with HIV infection ever classified as stage 3 (AIDS) had died in the United States.

Prevention Challenges

African Americans face a number of challenges that contribute to the higher rates of HIV infection. The **greater number of people living with HIV (prevalence)** in African American communities and the fact that African Americans tend to **have sex with partners of the same race/ethnicity** means that they face a greater risk of HIV infection with each new sexual encounter.

African American communities continue to experience higher rates of **other sexually transmitted infections (STIs)** compared with other racial/ethnic communities in the United States. Having an STI can significantly increase the chance of getting or transmitting HIV.

Lack of awareness of HIV status can affect HIV rates in communities. Almost 73,600 HIV-infected people in the African American community in 2011 were unaware of their HIV status. Diagnosis late in the course of HIV infection is common, which results in missed opportunities to get early medical care and prevent transmission to others.

The poverty rate is higher among African Americans than other racial/ethnic groups. The **socioeconomic issues** associated with poverty—including limited access to high-quality health care, housing, and HIV prevention education—directly and indirectly increase the risk for HIV infection, and affect the health of people living with and at risk for HIV. These factors may explain why African Americans have worse outcomes on the HIV continuum of care, including lower rates of linkage to care, retention in care, being prescribed HIV treatment, and viral suppression. New data from 2010 indicate that 75%

of HIV-infected African Americans aged 13 or older are linked to care, 48% are retained in care, 46% are prescribed antiretroviral therapy, and only 35% are virally suppressed.

Stigma, fear, discrimination, homophobia, and negative perceptions about HIV testing can also place too many African Americans at higher risk. Many at risk for HIV fear discrimination and rejection more than infection and may choose not to seek testing.

[a]*New HIV infections refer to HIV incidence, or the number of people who are newly infected with HIV within a given period of time, whether they are aware of their infection or not.*

[b]*The term men who have sex with men (MSM) is used in CDC surveillance systems. It indicates a behavior that transmits HIV infection, not how individuals self-identify in terms of their sexuality.*

[c]*Heterosexual contact with a person known to have, or to be at high risk for, HIV infection.*

[d]*Hispanics/Latinos can be of any race.*

[e]*HIV and AIDS diagnoses indicate when a person is diagnosed with HIV infection or AIDS, but do not indicate when the person was infected.*

HIV/AIDS among American Indians and Alaska Natives

Fast Facts

- HIV affects American Indians and Alaska Natives (AI/AN) in ways that are not always obvious because of their small population sizes.
- Of all races/ethnicities, AI/AN had the highest percentages of diagnosed HIV infections due to injection drug use.
- AI/AN face HIV prevention challenges, including poverty, high rates of STIs, and stigma.

HIV is a public health issue among the approximately 5.2 million American Indians and Alaska Natives (AI/AN), who represent about 1.7%[a] of the US population. Compared with other racial/ethnic groups, AI/AN ranked fifth in estimated rates of HIV infection diagnoses in 2013, with lower rates than in blacks/African Americans, Hispanics/

Latinos[b], Native Hawaiians/Other Pacific Islanders, and people reporting multiple races, but higher rates than in Asians and whites.

The Numbers

Overall, the effect of HIV infection on AI/AN is proportional to their US population size. However, within the overall statistics of new HIV infections and diagnoses, certain measures are disproportionate in this population group relative to other races/ethnicities.

New HIV Infections[c]

- In 2010, fewer than 1% (210) of the estimated 47,500 new HIV infections in the United States were among AI/AN.

HIV and AIDS Diagnoses[d] and Deaths

- AI/AN men accounted for 78% (169) and AI/AN women accounted for 22% (49) of the estimated 218 AI/AN diagnosed with HIV infection in the United States in 2013.

- Of the estimated 169 HIV diagnoses among AI/AN men in 2013, most (71%; 120) were attributed to male-to-male sexual contact.

- Of the estimated 49 HIV diagnoses among AI/AN women in 2013, the majority (69%, 34) were attributed to heterosexual contact.

- In the United States in 2013, both male and female AI/AN had the highest percent of estimated diagnoses of HIV infection attributed to injection drug use, compared with all races/ethnicities. Among men, 13% (22) of new HIV diagnoses were attributed to injection drug use and 6% (10) were attributed to both male-to-male sex and injection drug use. Among women 29% (14) of new HIV diagnoses were attributed to injection drug use.

- In 2013, an estimated 104 AI/AN were diagnosed with AIDS, a number that has remained relatively stable since 2009.

- By the end of 2012, an estimated 1,867 AI/AN with AIDS had died in the United States.

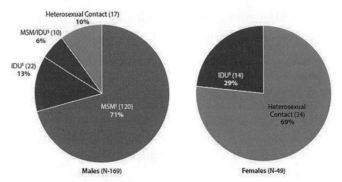

Figure 4.6. *Estimated Diagnoses of HIV Infection among Adult and Adolescent American Indians/Alaska Natives by Transmission Category and Sex, 2011 – United States*

†Male-to-male sexual contact ‡Injection drug use §Male-to-male sexual contact and injection drug use
The terms male-to-male sexual contact (MSM) and male-to-male sexual contact and injection drug use (MSM/IDU) are used in CDC surveillance systems. They indicate the behaviors that transmit HIV infection, not how individuals self-identify in terms of their sexuality

Why Are American Indians and Alaska Natives Affected by HIV?

Race and ethnicity alone are not risk factors for HIV infection. However, AI/AN may face challenges associated with risk for HIV.

- **Lack of awareness of HIV status.** Overall, approximately one in 7 (14%) adults and adolescents living with HIV infection in the United States at the end of 2011 were unaware of their HIV infection. Of the 3,700 American Indians and Alaska Natives estimated to be living with HIV in 2011, 18.9% (700) are estimated to be undiagnosed.

- **Sexually transmitted diseases (STDs).** AI/AN have the second highest rates of chlamydia and gonorrhea and the fourth highest rate of syphilis among all racial/ethnic groups. STDs increase the susceptibility to HIV infection.

- AI/AN gay and bisexual men may face **culturally based stigma and confidentiality concerns** that could limit opportunities for education and HIV testing, especially among those who live in rural communities or on reservations.

- **Cultural diversity.** There are over 560 federally recognized AI/AN tribes, whose members speak over 170 languages. Because each tribe has its own culture, beliefs, and practices and can be subdivided into language groups, it can be challenging to create culturally appropriate prevention programs for each group.

- **Socioeconomic issues.** Poverty, including lack of housing and HIV prevention education, directly and indirectly increases the risk for HIV infection and affects the health of people living with and at risk for HIV infection. Compared with other racial/ethnic groups, AI/AN have higher poverty rates, have completed fewer years of education, are younger, are less likely to be employed, and have lower rates of health insurance coverage.

- **Mistrust of government and its health care facilities.** The federally funded Indian Health Service (IHS) provides health care for approximately 2 million AI/AN and consists of direct services delivered by the IHS, tribally operated health care programs, and urban Indian health care services and resource centers. However, because of confidentiality and quality-of-care concerns and a general distrust of the US government, some AI/AN may avoid IHS.

- **Alcohol and illicit drug use.** Although alcohol and substance use do not cause HIV infection, they can reduce inhibitions and impair judgment and lead to behaviors that increase the risk of HIV. Injection drug use directly increases the risk of HIV through contaminated syringes and works. Compared with other racial/ethnic groups, AI/AN tend to use alcohol and drugs at a younger age, use them more often and in higher quantities, and experience more negative consequences from them.

- **Data limitations.** Racial misidentification of AI/AN may lead to the undercounting of this population in HIV surveillance systems and may contribute to the underfunding of AI/AN-targeted services.

[a]*Census population estimates for AI/AN include those reporting Hispanic ethnicity or one or more races.*

[b]*Hispanics/Latinos can be of any race.*

[c]*New HIV infections refer to HIV incidence, or the number of people who are newly infected with HIV, whether or not they are aware of their infection.*

[d]*HIV and AIDS diagnoses refer to the number of people diagnosed with HIV infection (regardless of stage of disease) and the number of people diagnosed with AIDS, respectively, during a given time period. The terms do not indicate when they were infected.*

HIV Infection among Asians in the United States

Fast Facts

- The number of HIV diagnoses among Asians has increased in recent years, along with the growth of the Asian population in the United States.
- Among Asians, gay and bisexual men are most affected by HIV.
- More than 1 in 5 Asians living with HIV do not know they have it.

According to the most recent U.S. census data, the Asian population in the United States grew 43%, or more than four times as fast as the total US population between 2000 and 2010. Corresponding with this significant growth, the number of Asians receiving a diagnosis of HIV has increased in recent years. Overall, Asians continue to account for only 2% of new HIV infections in the United States and dependent areas.[a]

The Numbers

New HIV Infections[b]

- Asians accounted for 2% (950) of the estimated 47,500 new HIV infections in the United States in 2010.

- The rate of estimated new HIV infections among Asians decreased from 10.4 per 100,000 in 2007 to 8.4 in 2010.

HIV and AIDS Diagnoses[c] and Deaths
In the United States and dependent areas:

- Of the estimated 973 adult and adolescent Asians diagnosed with HIV infection in 2013, 82% (799) were men and 16% (159) were women.

- Eighty-eight percent (703) of the estimated 799 HIV diagnoses among Asian men in 2013 were attributed to male-to-male sexual contact. Ninety-four percent (150) of the estimated 159 HIV diagnoses among Asian women were attributed to heterosexual contact.[d]

- At the end of 2012, Asians accounted for 1% (11,075) of the esti-mated 933,996 people living with diagnosed HIV infection.

- In 2013, an estimated 415 Asians were diagnosed with AIDS, representing 2% of the estimated 27,135 AIDS diagnoses.

- By the end of 2012, an estimated 3,477 Asians ever diagnosed with AIDS had died.

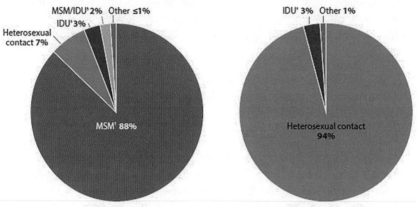

Figure 4.7. *Estimated Diagnoses of HIV Infection among Adult and Adolescent Asians, by Transmission Category and Gender, United States and 6 US Dependent Areas, 2011*

*Due to rounding, percentages might not total 100%.

†Male-to-male sexual contact ‡Injection drug use §Male-to-male sexual contact and injection drug use

The terms male-to-male sexual contact (MSM) and male-to-male sexual contact and injection drug use (MSM/IDU) are used in CDC surveillance systems. They indicate the behaviors that transmit HIV infection, not how individuals self-identify in terms of their sexuality.

Why Are Asians Affected by HIV?

There are some behaviors that put everyone at risk for HIV, including Asians. These include having vaginal or anal sex without a condom or without being on medicines that prevent HIV, or sharing injection drug equipment with someone who has HIV. Other factors that particularly affect Asians include:

- **Undiagnosed HIV.** CDC research shows that more than 1 in 5 (22%) Asians living with HIV do not know they have it. People living with undiagnosed HIV cannot obtain the care they need to stay healthy and may transmit HIV to others.

- **Cultural factors** may affect the risk of HIV infection. Some Asians may avoid seeking testing, counseling, or treatment because of language barriers or fear of discrimination, the stigma of homosexuality, immigration issues, or fear of bringing shame to their families. Traditional Asian cultures may emphasize male-dominated gender roles that empower men and deprive women of sexual negotiating power. This factor may affect the rate of heterosexual HIV transmission to Asian women.

- **Limited research** about Asian health and HIV infection has resulted in few targeted prevention programs and behavioral interventions in this population.

- **The low number of HIV cases** among Asians may not reflect the true burden of HIV in this population because of **race/ethnicity misidentification** that could lead to the **underestimation of HIV infection in this population.**

  [a]*Dependent areas: American Samoa, Guam, the Northern Mariana Islands, Puerto Rico, the Republic of Palau, and the US Virgin Islands.*

  [b]*New HIV infections refer to HIV incidence, or the number of people who are newly infected with HIV, whether they know it or not.*

  [c]*HIV and AIDS diagnoses refer to the estimated number of people diagnosed with HIV infection regardless of stage of disease at diagnosis and the estimated number of people diagnosed with AIDS, respectively, during a given time period. The terms do not indicate when they were infected.*

  [d]*Heterosexual contact with a person known to have, or to be at high risk for, HIV infection.*

HIV among Latinos

HIV infection is a serious threat to the health of the Hispanic/Latino community. In 2010, Hispanics/Latinos accounted for over one-fifth (21% or 9,800) of all new HIV infections in the United States and 6 dependent areas[b] despite representing about 16% of the total U.S. population.

Fast Facts

- Hispanics / Latinos[a] are disproportionately affected by HIV, relative to other races/ethnicities.
- The estimated new HIV infection rate among Hispanics or Latinos in 2010 in the United States was more than 3 times as high as that of whites.
- Socioeconomic factors such as poverty and language barriers may contribute to Hispanic / Latino HIV infection rates.

The Numbers

New HIV Infections[c]

- In 2010, Hispanic/Latino men accounted for 87% (8,500) of all estimated new HIV infections among Hispanics/Latinos in the United States. Most (79% or 6,700) of the estimated new HIV infections among Hispanic/Latino men were attributed to male-to-male sexual contact.

- Among Hispanic/Latino men who have sex with men (MSM[d]), 67% of estimated new HIV infections occurred in those under age 35.

- Hispanic women/Latinas accounted for 14% (1,400) of the estimated new infections among all Hispanics/Latinos in the United States in 2010.

- The estimated rate of new HIV infection among Hispanics/Latinos in the United States in 2010 was more than 3 times as high as that of whites (27.5 vs. 8.7 per 100,000 population).

HIV and AIDS Diagnoses[e] and Deaths

- At some point in their lives, an estimated 1 in 36 Hispanic/Latino men and 1 in 106 Hispanic/Latino women will be diagnosed with HIV.

- In 2012, Hispanics/Latinos accounted for 22% (10,705) of the estimated 48,893 new diagnoses of HIV infection in the United States and 6 dependent areas. Of the 10,694 adult and adolescent Hispanics/Latinos diagnosed with HIV infection in 2012, 86% (9,168) were in men and 14% (1,526) were in women.

47

- Eighty-one percent (7,405) of the estimated 9,168 HIV diagnoses among Hispanic/Latino men in the United States and dependent areas in 2012 were attributed to male-to-male sexual contact. Eighty-six percent (1,315) of the estimated 1,526 HIV diagnoses among Hispanic/Latino women were attributed to heterosexual contact.[f]

- In 2011, Hispanics/Latinos accounted for 20% (242,000) of the estimated 1.2 million people living with HIV infection in the United States.

- In 2012, an estimated 5,796 Hispanics/Latinos were diagnosed with HIV infection ever classified as stage 3 (AIDS) in the United States and 6 dependent areas.

- By the end of 2011, an estimated 122,848 Hispanics/Latinos who had ever been diagnosed with HIV infection ever classified as stage 3 (AIDS) had died in the United States and 6 dependent areas. In 2012, HIV was the seventh leading cause of death among Hispanics/Latinos aged 25-34 in the United States and the ninth leading cause of death among Hispanics/Latinos aged 35-54.

- In 2011, data from the National HIV Surveillance System (NHSS) and the Medical Monitoring Project showed that 80.8% of Hispanics/Latinos with diagnosed HIV infection were linked to care, 53.6% were retained in care, 49.8% were prescribed antiretroviral therapy (ART), and 41.3% had achieved viral suppression.

Prevention Challenges

A number of factors contribute to the HIV epidemic in Latino communities.

- **There is a greater number of people living with HIV (prevalence)** in Hispanic/Latino communities and Hispanics/ Latinos tend to have sex with partners of the same race/ethnicity. This means that Hispanics/Latinos face a greater risk of HIV infection.

- While data suggest that most Hispanic/Latino men with HIV were infected through sexual contact with other men, the **behavioral risk factors for HIV infection differ by country of birth.** For example, men born in Puerto Rico have a higher percentage of diagnosed HIV infections attributed to injection drug use (IDU).

- The majority of HIV infections diagnosed among Hispanic/Latino men and women are attributed to sexual contact with men. Being unaware of a partners' risk factors (for example, IDU, multiple sexual partners, and male-to-male sexual contact) may place Hispanic/Latino men and women at increased risk for HIV.

- Research shows that the presence of a **sexually transmitted disease (STD)** makes it easier to become infected with HIV. Hispanics/Latinos have the third highest rates for STDs including chlamydia, gonorrhea, and syphilis.

- **Cultural factors** may affect the risk of HIV infection. Some Hispanics/Latinos may avoid seeking testing, counseling, or treatment if infected because of immigration status, stigma, or fear of discrimination. Traditional gender roles, cultural norms *("machismo,"* which stresses virility for Hispanics/Latino men, and *"marianismo,"* which demands purity from Latina women), and the stigma around homosexuality may add to prevention challenges.

- **Socioeconomic factors** such as poverty, migration patterns, lower educational accomplishment, inadequate or no health insurance, limited access to health care, and language barriers may contribute to HIV infection among Hispanics/Latinos. Those factors may limit awareness about HIV infection risks and opportunities for counseling, testing, and treatment.

- Because of **fear of disclosing immigration status and possible deportation,** undocumented Hispanic/Latino immigrants may be less likely to access HIV prevention services, get an HIV test, or receive adequate treatment and care if they are living with HIV.

[a]*Hispanics / Latinos can be of any race.*
[b]*Dependent areas: American Samoa, Guam, the Northern Mariana Islands, Puerto Rico, the Republic of Palau, and the US Virgin Islands.*
[c]*New HIV infections refer to HIV incidence or the number of people who are newly infected with HIV, whether they are aware of their infection or not.*
[d]*The term men who have sex with men (MSM) is used in CDC surveillance systems. It indicates the behaviors that transmit HIV infection, rather than how individuals.*
[e]*HIV and AIDS diagnoses refer to the estimated number of people diagnosed with HIV infection regardless of stage of disease at diagnosis,*

and the estimated number of people diagnosed with AIDS, respectively, during a given time period.

[Heterosexual contact with a person known to have, or be at high risk for, HIV infection.

HIV among Native Hawaiians and Other Pacific Islanders in the United States

Fast Facts

- HIV affects Native Hawaiians and Other Pacific Islanders (NHOPI) in ways that are not always apparent because of their small population size.
- One in four NHOPI living with HIV are unaware of their infection.
- NHOPI cultural taboos on talking about sex may interfere with HIV prevention.

National estimates show that Native Hawaiians and Other Pacific Islanders (NHOPI) in the United States and dependent areas[a,b] represent a very small proportion of HIV infections, compared with other races/ethnicities.

The Numbers

New HIV Infections[c]

- In 2010, NHOPI accounted for less than 1% (70) of the estimated 47,500 new HIV infections in the United States.

- The estimated number of new HIV infections among NHOPI remained stable from 2008 to 2010.

HIV and AIDS Diagnoses[d] and Deaths

In the United States:

- In 2013, NHOPI had the fourth highest estimated rates of HIV diagnoses (12.7 per 100,000 people) in the United States by race/ethnicity, behind blacks/African Americans, Hispanics/Latinos,[e] and those of multiple races.

- In 2013, the rate of HIV diagnoses in NHOPI was almost twice as high as rates among whites.

- In 2011, an estimated 1,200 NHOPI were living with HIV. Of those, 75% had been diagnosed.

In the United States and six dependant areas:

- In 2013, less than 1% (67) of 48,145 estimated HIV diagnoses were among NHOPI; 52 diagnoses were in men, and 15 were in women.

- In 2013, 47 of the 52 estimated HIV diagnoses among NHOPI men were attributed to male-to-male sexual contact, and 13 of the estimated 15 HIV diagnoses among NHOPI women were attributed to heterosexual contact.[f]

- In 2013, an estimated 37 NHOPI were diagnosed with AIDS.

- By the end of 2012, an estimated 361 NHOPI ever diagnosed with AIDS had died.

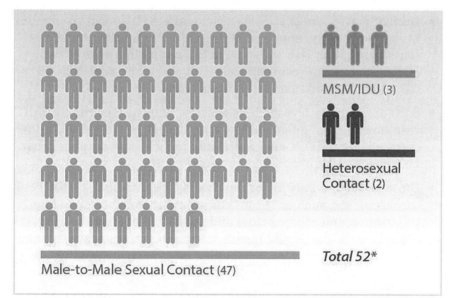

Figure 4.8. NHOPI transmission category –men

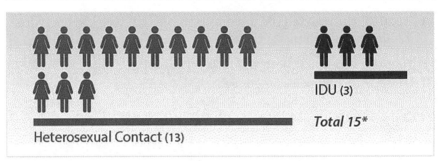

Figure 4.9. NHOPI transmission category – women

* Because totals were calculated independently of the values of the subpopulation, the subpopulation values do not sum to the total. Numbers less than 12 should be interpreted with caution because they have underlying relative standard errors greater than 30% and are considered unreliable.

Prevention Challenges

There are some behaviors that put everyone at risk for HIV, including NHOPI. These include having vaginal or anal sex without a condom or without being on medicines that prevent HIV, or sharing injection drug equipment with someone who has HIV. Other factors that particularly affect NHOPI include:

- Lack of awareness of HIV status can affect HIV rates in communities. Nationally, approximately 14% of US adults and adolescents living with HIV infection in 2011 were unaware of their HIV infection. However, 25% of adult and adolescent NHOPI with HIV were unaware of their infection.

- Socioeconomic factors such as poverty, inadequate or no health care coverage, language barriers, and lower educational attainment among NHOPI may contribute to lack of awareness about HIV risk and higher-risk behaviors.

- Cultural factors may affect the risk of HIV infection. NHOPI cultural customs, such as those that prioritize obligations to family (reputation and ethnic pride) and taboos on intergenerational sexual topics and sexual health discussion, may stigmatize sexuality in general, and homosexuality specifically, as well as interfere with HIV risk-reduction strategies, such as condom use.

- Limited research about NHOPI health and HIV infection has resulted in few targeted prevention programs and behavioral interventions in this population.

- The low reported number of HIV cases among NHOPI may not reflect the true burden of HIV in this population because of race/ethnicity misidentification that could lead to the underestimation of HIV infection in this population.

[a]Dependent areas: American Samoa, Guam, the Northern Mariana Islands, Puerto Rico, the Republic of Palau, and the US Virgin Islands.

[b]Certain data are presented for the United States only. Incidence estimates are available for the 50 states and the District of Columbia only. Estimated subpopulation rates of HIV and AIDS diagnoses by race/ethnicity for the 6 US dependent areas are not available because the US Census Bureau does not collect information from all dependent areas.

[c]New HIV infections refer to HIV incidence or the number of people who are newly infected with HIV in a given time period, whether they are aware of their infection or not.

[d]HIV and AIDS diagnoses refer to the estimated number of people diagnosed with HIV infection, regardless of stage of disease at diagnosis, and the estimated number of people diagnosed with AIDS, respectively, during a given time period. The terms do not indicate when they were infected.

[e]Hispanics/Latinos can be of any race. [f]Heterosexual contact with a person known to have, or to be at high risk for, HIV infection.

Part Two

HIV/AIDS Transmission, Risk Factors, and Prevention

Chapter 5

HIV and Its Transmission: An Overview

HIV Transmission

HIV CAN BE TRANSMITTED THROUGH...

| Sexual Contact | Injection Drug Use | Pregnancy, Childbirth & Breast Feeding | Occupational Exposure | and rarely, Blood Transfusion/Organ Transplant |

Figure 5.1. *HIV Transmission Modes*

How Is HIV Spread?

HIV is spread from an infected person to another person through direct contact with some of the body's fluids. It is not spread easily. Only certain body fluids from an HIV-infected person can transmit HIV:

- Blood

Text in this chapter is excerpted from "How Do You Get HIV or AIDS?" AIDS .gov, August 27, 2015.

- Semen (cum)

- Pre-seminal fluid (pre-cum)

- Rectal fluids

- Vaginal fluids

- Breast milk

These body fluids must come into contact with a mucous membrane or damaged tissue or be directly injected into your bloodstream (by a needle or syringe) for transmission to possibly occur. Mucous membranes are the soft, moist areas just inside the openings to your body. They can be found inside the rectum, the vagina or the opening of the penis, and the mouth.

If you think you may have been exposed to HIV, get tested. You can get tested at your healthcare provider's office, a clinic, and other locations. You can also get a HIV home test kit from your local pharmacy.

Ways HIV Is Transmitted

In the United States, HIV is spread mainly by:

1. Having sex with someone who has HIV.

   In general:

   Anal sex is the highest-risk sexual behavior. Receptive anal sex ("bottoming") is riskier than insertive anal sex ("topping").

   Vaginal sex is the second highest-risk sexual behavior.

   Having multiple sex partners or having sexually transmitted infections can increase the risk of HIV infection through sex.

2. Sharing needles, syringes, rinse water, or other equipment ("works") used to prepare injection drugs with someone who has HIV.

Less commonly, HIV may be spread by:

- Being born to an infected mother. HIV can be passed from mother to child during pregnancy, birth, or breastfeeding.

- Being stuck with an HIV-contaminated needle or other sharp object. This is a risk mainly for health care workers.

- Receiving blood transfusions, blood products, or organ/tissue transplants that are contaminated with HIV. This risk is extremely small because of rigorous testing of the US blood supply and donated organs and tissues.

- Eating food that has been pre-chewed by an HIV-infected person. The contamination occurs when infected blood from a caregiver's mouth mixes with food while chewing, and is very rare.

- Being bitten by a person with HIV. Each of the very small number of documented cases has involved severe trauma with extensive tissue damage and the presence of blood. There is no risk of transmission if the skin is not broken.

- Oral sex—using the mouth to stimulate the penis, vagina, or anus (fellatio, cunnilingus, and rimming). Giving fellatio (mouth to penis oral sex) and having the person ejaculate (cum) in your mouth is riskier than other types of oral sex.

- Contact between broken skin, wounds, or mucous membranes and HIV-infected blood or blood-contaminated body fluids. These reports have also been extremely rare.

- Deep, open-mouth kissing if the person with HIV has sores or bleeding gums and blood is exchanged. HIV is not spread through saliva. Transmission through kissing alone is extremely rare.

HIV is NOT spread by:

- Air or water

- Insects, including mosquitoes or ticks

- Saliva, tears, or sweat

- Casual contact, like shaking hands, hugging or sharing dishes/ drinking glasses

- Drinking fountains

- Toilet seats

HIV is not spread through the air and it does not live long outside the human body.

People with HIV who are using antiretroviral therapy (ART) consistently and who have achieved viral suppression (having the virus reduced to an undetectable level in the body) are very unlikely to transmit the virus to their uninfected partners. However, there is still some risk of transmission, so even with an undetectable viral load, people with HIV should continue to take steps to reduce HIV transmission.

If I Have HIV, Does That Mean I Have AIDS?

No. The terms "HIV" and "AIDS" can be confusing because both terms refer to the same disease. However, "HIV" refers to the virus itself, and "AIDS" refers to the late stage of HIV infection, when an HIV-infected person's immune system is severely damaged and has difficulty fighting diseases and certain cancers. Before the development of certain medications, people with HIV could progress to AIDS in just a few years. But today, most people who are HIV-positive do not progress to AIDS. That's because if you have HIV and you take ART consistently, you can keep the level of HIV in your body low. This will help keep your body strong and healthy and reduce the likelihood that you will ever progress to AIDS. It will also help lower your risk of transmitting HIV to others.

Chapter 6

Risky Behaviors and HIV

Chapter Contents

Section 6.1

Alcohol and Substance Use – HIV Risk

This section includes excerpts from "Substance Abuse/Use,"
AIDS.gov, January 14, 2014; and text from "Substance Abuse Issues,"
AIDS.gov, May 9, 2014.

Substance Abuse/Use

HIV CAN BE TRANSMITTED BY SHARING DRUG
PREPARATION OR INJECTING EQUIPMENT
("WORKS") WITH A PERSON WHO HAS HIV.

ALCOHOL AND DRUGS CAN IMPAIR YOUR JUDGMENT
AND AFFECT YOUR ABILITY TO MAKE SAFE CHOICES,
PUTTING YOU AT GREATER RISK FOR HIV.

THE CDC RECOMMENDS THAT PEOPLE WHO INJECT
DRUGS OR ENGAGE IN OTHER RISKY BEHAVIORS
GET TESTED FOR HIV AT LEAST ONCE EVERY YEAR.

Figure 6.1. *Alcohol and Substance Abuse*

How Are Drug Use and HIV Related?

Acohol and other drug use can play a significant role in the spread
of HIV. For example:

- Injection drug use is one of the causes of HIV in the United
  States and is responsible for approximately 10% of HIV cases
  annually.

- If you inject drugs, you can get HIV from sharing drug preparation or injecting equipment ("works") with a person who has
  HIV. You can also then pass HIV to your sex and drug-using
  partners.

- Drinking alcohol or taking other drugs can increase your risk
  for HIV and other sexually transmitted diseases (STDs). Being
  drunk or high affects your ability to make safe choices and lowers your inhibitions, leading you to take risks you are less likely

to take when sober, such as having sex without a condom or sex with multiple partners.

- Transactional sex (trading sex for drugs or money) can also increase your risk for getting HIV.

- If you use drugs, you at are a higher risk for HIV infection and therefore should seek HIV testing.

- If you already have HIV, drinking alcohol or taking other drugs can affect your immune system and may speed up the progression of the disease. Drinking or taking drugs also can affect your HIV treatment adherence.

What Are The HIV Risks Of Using Different Types of Drugs?

It's important to know how different types of drugs can increase your risk of getting HIV or passing it to others.

Injected Drugs

Injected drugs are drugs that are introduced into the bloodstream using a needle and syringe. Sharing drug preparation or injecting equipment ("works") can expose you to HIV-infected blood. If you share works with someone who is HIV-positive, that person's blood can stay on needles or spread to the drug solution. In that case, you can inject HIV directly into your body.

HIV-infected blood can also get into drug solutions by:

- Using blood-contaminated syringes to prepare drugs

- Reusing water

- Reusing bottle caps, spoons, or other containers ("cookers") to dissolve drugs into water and to heat drugs solutions

- Reusing small pieces of cotton or cigarette filters ("cottons") to filter out particles that could block the needle

"Street sellers" of syringes may repackage used syringes and sell them as sterile syringes. For this reason, people who inject drugs should get syringes from reliable sources of sterile syringes, such as pharmacies or needle-exchange programs.

It is important to know that sharing a needle or syringe for any use, including skin popping and injecting steroids, hormones, or silicone, can put you at risk for HIV and other blood-borne infections.

Methamphetamine

Methamphetamine ("meth") is a very addictive stimulant that can be snorted, smoked, or injected. It has many street names, including crystal, tina, black beauties, and more.

Meth can reduce your inhibitions and interfere with you sound judgment regarding your behavior, which may make you less likely to protect yourself or others. This increases your risk of getting or transmitting HIV infection, both through sex and injection drug use.

Even though using meth is an HIV risk factor for anyone who does it, **there is a strong link between meth use and HIV transmission for men who have sex with men (MSM).** Studies show that MSM who use meth may increase their sexual AND drug-use risk factors. They may:

- Use condoms less often

- Have more sex partners

- Engage in unprotected anal sex (especially as the receptive partner, which is the highest risk behavior)

- Inject meth instead of smoking or snorting it

Meth use can also make the effects of HIV worse for people who already have HIV.

Alcohol

Drinking alcohol, particularly binge drinking, can increase your risk for HIV. Being drunk affects your ability to make safe choices and lowers your inhibitions, which may lead you to take risks you are less likely to take when sober, such as having sex without a condom.

Alcohol use and abuse can also make the effects of HIV worse if you already have HIV. For example, alcohol use and abuse may make it difficult for you to follow your HIV treatment plan. In addition, alcohol abuse can contribute to health conditions such as liver disease that have an impact on the progression of HIV infection.

Crack Cocaine

Cocaine is a powerfully addictive stimulant drug. The powdered form of cocaine is either inhaled through the nose (snorted), or dissolved in water and injected into the bloodstream. Crack is a form of cocaine that has been processed to make a rock crystal that users smoke.

If you use crack cocaine, you put yourself at risk for contracting HIV because crack impairs your judgment, which can lead to risky sexual behavior.

In addition, crack's short-lived high and addictiveness can create a compulsive cycle in which you quickly exhaust your resources and may turn to other ways to get the drug, including trading sex for drugs or money, which increases your HIV infection risk.

Compared to nonusers, crack cocaine users report:

- A greater number of recent and lifetime sexual partners

- Infrequent condom use

- Using more than one substance

- Being less responsive to HIV prevention programs

Other Drugs

Other drugs are also associated with increased risk for HIV infection. For example:

- Using "club drugs" like Ecstasy, ketamine, gamma-Hydroxy-butyric acid (GHB), and poppers can alter your judgment and impair your decisions about sex or other drug use. You may be more likely to have unplanned and unprotected sex or use other drugs, including injection drugs or meth. Those behaviors can increase your risk of exposure to HIV. If you have HIV, this can also increase your risk of spreading HIV to others.

- The use of amyl nitrite (an inhalant known as "poppers") has also been associated with HIV risk. Poppers, which are sometimes used in anal sex because they relax the sphincter, have long been linked to risky sexual behaviors, illegal drug use, and sexually transmitted infections among gay and bisexual men. They also have recently been linked to increased use among adolescents.

Injection Drug Use and Hepatitis Risk

Hepatitis is broad term referring to inflammation of the liver. This condition is most often caused by a virus. In the United States, the most common causes of viral hepatitis are hepatitis A virus (HAV), hepatitis B virus (HBV), and hepatitis C virus (HCV). HBV and HCV are common among people who are at risk for, or living with, HIV.

You can get some forms of viral hepatitis the same way you get HIV—through unprotected sexual contact and injection drug use. In fact, **about 80% of HIV-infected injection drug users in the U.S. are also infected with HCV.**

HCV infection sometimes results in an acute illness, but most often becomes a chronic condition that can lead to *cirrhosis* of the liver and liver cancer. HCV infection is more serious in people living with HIV because it leads to liver damage more quickly.

Co-infection with HCV may also affect the treatment of HIV infection. Therefore, it's important for people who inject drugs to know whether they are also infected with HCV and, if they aren't, to take steps to prevent infection. To find out if you are infected with HCV, ask your doctor or other healthcare provider to test your blood. HCV can be treated successfully, even in people who have HIV.

If I Use Drugs, How Can I Reduce My Risk of HIV Infection?

If you are using drugs—including injection drugs, meth, alcohol, or other drugs—the best way to reduce your risk of HIV is to stop using drugs. Substance abuse treatment programs can help you do this.

Many substance abuse treatment programs include HIV counseling to help people stop or reduce their risk behaviors, including risky injection practices and unsafe sex, so that they can stay healthy and reduce their risk of contracting HIV or transmitting it to others.

If you are injecting drugs and believe you cannot stop using yet, here are some other things that will reduce your risk of getting HIV or transmitting it to others:

- Never use or "share" syringes (needles), water, "works," or drug preparation equipment that has already been used by someone else.

- Use a new, sterile syringe each time you prepare and inject drugs. You can get clean needles from pharmacies or syringe services programs (often also called needle-exchange programs).

- Only use syringes that come from a reliable source (e.g., pharmacies or syringe exchange programs).

- Use sterile water to prepare drugs, such as water that has been boiled for 5 minutes or clean water from a reliable source (such as fresh tap water).

- Use a new or disinfected container ("cooker") and a new filter ("cotton") each time you prepare drugs.

- Before you inject, clean the injection site with a new alcohol swab.

- Safely dispose of syringes after one use.

Also, if you engage in sexual activity, reduce your sexual risk factors for HIV infection.

The Importance Of HIV Testing For People Who Use Drugs

The CDC and the U.S. Preventive Services Task Force recommend that people who inject drugs or engage in other behaviors that put them at increased risk get tested for HIV at least once every year. (CDC also recommends that sexual partners of those who inject drugs also get tested at least once per year.)

Thanks to the *Affordable Care Act*, HIV tests for people aged 15-65 as well as younger and older individuals at high risk (such as those who inject drugs) are covered by most private health insurance plans without co-pays or deductibles.

Talk to your healthcare provider about getting tested for HIV. You can use the HIV Testing and Care Services Locator (locator.aids.gov) or call 1-800-458-5231 to find a confidential HIV testing site near you and learn about what kinds of HIV tests are offered at each site.

HIV home test kits are also available and can be obtained from a drugstore. Currently, there are two home test kits approved by the FDA: the Home Access HIV-1 Test System and the OraQuick In-Home HIV Test. If you buy your home test online, make sure it is FDA-approved.

What If I Already Have HIV?

If you are already living with HIV, you need to take care of yourself so that you stay healthy. Substance use and abuse can negatively affect your health and well-being in a variety of ways.

Frequently Asked Questions

Can I get HIV from sharing needles or drug equipment?

Yes. Used needles and equipment (or "works") can have HIV-infected blood on or inside them. If they do, you put that blood—and possibly HIV—directly into your body when you use them to inject or prepare your drugs. Only sterile equipment carries no risk of HIV contamination. If you inject drugs (including steroids, insulin, etc.), don't share used needles or equipment with anyone.

Where can I go to find drug treatment or rehab?

You can use the HIV/AIDS Prevention and Services Locator to find a substance abuse treatment facility, as well as HIV testing sites and other services. For other resources, see SAMHSA's Substance Abuse and Mental Health Treatment Resources page (www.samhsa. gov/treatment/index.aspx).

If I'm not ready to quit, how can I protect myself from HIV?

Quitting or getting into rehab is the best way to reduce your drug-related risk of getting HIV. But if you're not ready to quit, you can at least protect yourself and others from HIV and other diseases by using clean equipment if you inject drugs. Syringe services programs let you turn in your used needles and equipment for clean ones. They can also give you information on where you can get help to quit drugs.

To find a needle exchange or syringe services program near you, use the Harm Reduction Coalition's Interactive Harm Reduction Resources Locator (harmreduction.org/connect-locally). Even though some service organizations provide syringe services, it may not be legal in a particular jurisdiction so be sure to check before participating in the program.

Do syringe services programs increase drug use?

No. National and international studies show that syringe services programs do not increase drug use. The research also shows that syringe services programs are very effective in decreasing blood-borne illnesses (like HIV and hepatitis) among injection drug users when they are included as part of medical and substance abuse treatment and prevention services. Syringe services programs protect injection drug users' sexual partners or children, who could otherwise be at risk for HIV infection. These programs also serve as important doorways to health information, treatment, and rehab. Because of the overwhelming evidence that they do not increase drug use and because of their clear effectiveness in decreasing HIV and other diseases, Congress voted to lift a previously imposed ban on federal funding for syringe services programs in December 2009. Subsequently, however, on December 17, 2011, Congress passed HR 2055, the Consolidated Appropriations Act of 2012, which the President signed into law on December 23, 2011. This act reinstated the ban that was in place prior to December 2009. As a result, using federal funds for the distribution of needles or syringes for the hypodermic injection of any illegal drug is prohibited.

The Importance of Treatment for Drug and Alcohol Use

Treatment for substance use disorders is effective and readily available. The main goal for substance use treatment is for individuals to stop using and start their journey toward recovery. People can recover and can lead full and active lives in their communities and workplaces, and with their families and friends. One continual challenge, however, is helping people to stay in treatment long enough for them to achieve this goal.

If you are living with HIV, getting treatment for a substance use disorder can help you improve your adherence to ART, stick to other parts of your care plan, and support you in making healthy choices that will reduce your risk of transmitting HIV to others.

In order to be successful, drug and alcohol treatment must be tailored to your individual needs. Outcomes will depend on the severity of your drug or alcohol problem, if you have previous experience with treatment and what that experience was, the type of treatment you receive, and other factors.

If the treatment you receive for a substance use disorder includes medication, and you are also taking medication to treat your HIV, it's very important to tell your health care providers and treatment providers. This is because there may be a risk of drug interactions that can decrease the effectiveness of either or both treatments. You will need to work very closely with your providers to find a plan that works for you. There are many professionals in both fields who have experience working with people receiving treatment for both conditions.

The main thing to remember is that treatment for substance use disorders is available and you can begin recovery to lead an active life in your family, community, and workplace.

Section 6.2

Smoking and HIV

This section includes excerpts from "Smoking & Tobacco Use," AIDS. gov, August 12, 2014.

Figure 6.2. *Smoking and HIV*

Tobacco use is the leading cause of preventable illness and death in the United States, causing nearly one out of five deaths in the United States each year.

Smoking increases your risk of developing lung cancer and other cancers, heart disease, chronic obstructive pulmonary disease (COPD), asthma, and other diseases, and of dying early.

For these reasons, smoking is a significant health issue for all individuals, but it is even more of a concern for people living with HIV, who tend to smoke more than the general population. According to the U.S. Centers for Disease Control and Prevention (CDC), approximately 19% of adults in the United States are smokers. However, **the smoking rate is two to three times higher among adults who are HIV-positive.**

If you smoke and you HIV, you're more likely to get HIV-related infections, including:

- Thrush (a mouth infection, also called oral candidiasis)

- Hairy leukoplakia (white mouth sores)

- Bacterial pneumonia

- Pneumocystis pneumonia (a dangerous lung infection)

Smoking when you have HIV also makes you more likely to get other serious illnesses than nonsmokers with HIV. These illnesses can make you too sick to work (disabled) or even lead to early death. They include:

- COPD (chronic obstructive pulmonary disease, a serious lung disease that causes severe breathing problems and includes emphysema and chronic bronchitis)
- Heart disease and stroke
- Lung cancer, head and neck cancer, cervical cancer, and anal cancer

People with HIV who smoke are also less likely to keep to their HIV treatment plan.

The Benefits of Quitting Smoking

Quitting smoking has major and immediate health benefits for all tobacco users, including those living with HIV/AIDS. Quitting reduces your chances of developing disease, helps you feel better, and improves your quality of life.

Also, stay away from secondhand smoke, which is smoke in the air from other people smoking. Secondhand smoke has immediate harmful effects on your blood and blood vessels, which can raise your risk for a heart attack. People who already have heart disease are at especially high risk for a heart attack. Secondhand smoke can also cause a stroke or lead to lung cancer.

Talk with your health care provider about programs and products that can help you quit.

The Role of Healthcare Providers

Surveys have found that two-thirds of smokers living with HIV/AIDS want to quit smoking. Healthcare providers can play an important role in encouraging and supporting them.

Healthcare providers who talk to their patients about quitting smoking—even for just 3 minutes or less—can have a positive impact on those smokers' decision to quit.

In fact, in a large-scale study of thousands of people with HIV, researchers concluded that smoking represented such a significant risk factor for developing serious clinical diseases and death that healthcare providers should routinely make "*stop smoking*" programs part of the HIV care they provide.

Help to Quit Smoking

The Affordable Care Act offers several resources to help people quit smoking. Under the Affordable Care Act (ACA), private health insurance policies created after March 23, 2010 are required to cover recommended preventive health services at no extra cost to the consumer. This includes tobacco use screenings for all adults and cessation interventions for tobacco users.

The Act also provides for Medicaid coverage of tobacco cessation services for pregnant women, at no extra cost, along with expanded Medicare coverage of tobacco cessation counseling, making it available to approximately 5 million Medicare tobacco users—not just those with tobacco-related diseases.

In addition, the Affordable Care Act expands employment-based wellness programs, such as those that focus on helping employees stop smoking.

The CDC's National Center for HIV/AIDS, Viral Hepatitis, STD, and TB Services (NCHHSTP) offers a helpful table of recommended preventive services for people at risk for HIV and shows which health insurance plans cover these services without cost sharing under the ACA.

The Federal Government also has several other resources to assist individuals in quitting smoking:

- **Smartphone Apps**—The National Institutes of Health (NIH) has launched *QuitPal*, a free smartphone app to help smokers change their behavior. Also, the VA has developed the *StayQuit Coach* app to help individuals stay quit after they have stopped smoking.

- **Tips from Former Smokers**—The CDC offers *"Tips from Former Smokers,"* featuring people discussing the health effects they are living with as a result of their tobacco use, as well as resources and tools to help individuals quit smoking.

- **Information and Resources**—The website, *BeTobaccoFree. hhs.gov*, provides information on avoiding or ending tobacco use.

- **Chat/Phone Support**—The National Cancer Institute's (NCI) Smokefree.gov provides free resources to help people quit smoking, including real-time live instant messaging help from a counselor. You can also call 1-800-QUIT-NOW for free quit coaching and referrals to local resources.

- **Help for the Military**—The U.S. Department of Defense (DOD) website, *Quit Tobacco. Make Everyone Proud* (www. ucanquit2.org), offers resources for members of the U.S. military and their families.

I'm thinking about quitting, but even just thinking about it is making me anxious. What should I do?

Quitting works best when you're prepared. Before you quit START by taking these five important steps:

S – Set a quit date.

T – Tell family, friends, and coworkers that you plan to quit.

A – Anticipate and plan for the challenges you'll face while quitting.

R – Remove cigarettes and other tobacco products from your home, car, and work.

T – Talk to your doctor about getting help to quit.

Section 6.3

Sexual Risk Factors and HIV Transmission

Text in this section is excerpted from "Lower Your Sexual Risk of HIV," AIDS.gov, August 13, 2015.

Lower Your Sexual Risk of HIV

Figure 6.3. *Sexual Risk and HIV*

How Can I Reduce My Risk of Getting HIV through Sexual Contact?

In the United States, HIV is mainly spread by having sex with someone who has HIV. There are several steps you can take to reduce your risk of getting HIV through sexual contact, and the more of these actions you take, the safer you can be. These actions include:

- **Choose less risky sexual behaviors.** Oral sex is much less risky than anal or vaginal sex. Anal sex is the highest-risk sexual activity for HIV transmission. If you are HIV-negative, insertive anal sex ("topping") is less risky for getting HIV than receptive anal sex ("bottoming"). Remember: HIV can be sexually transmitted via blood, semen (cum), pre-seminal fluid (pre-cum), rectal fluid, and vaginal fluid. Sexual activities that do not involve the potential exchange of these bodily fluids (e.g. touching) carry no risk for getting HIV.

- **Use condoms consistently and correctly.** When used consistently and correctly, condoms are highly effective in preventing HIV.

- **Reduce the number of people you have sex with.** The number of sex partners you have affects your HIV risk. The more partners you have, the more likely you are to have a partner with HIV whose viral load is not suppressed or to have a sex partner with a sexually transmitted disease. Both of these factors can increase the risk of HIV transmission. Remember: one in eight people living with HIV in the U.S. are unaware of their infection.

- **Talk to your doctor about pre-exposure prophylaxis (PrEP).** PrEP is taking HIV medicine daily to prevent HIV infection. PrEP should be considered if you are HIV-negative and in an ongoing sexual relationship with an HIV-positive partner. PrEP also should be considered if you are HIV-negative and have had a sexually transmitted disease (STD) or any anal sex (receptive or insertive) with a male partner without condoms in the past six months and are not in an exclusive relationship with a recently tested, HIV-negative partner.

- **Talk to your doctor right away (within 3 days) about post-exposure prophylaxis (PEP) if you have a possible exposure to HIV.** An example of a possible exposure is if you have anal or vaginal sex without a condom with someone who is or may be HIV-positive, and you are HIV-negative and not taking PrEP. Your chance of exposure to HIV is lower if your HIV-positive partner is taking antiretroviral therapy (ART) consistently and correctly, especially if his/her viral load is undetectable. Starting PEP immediately and taking it daily for 4 weeks reduces your chance of getting HIV.

- **Get tested and treated for other sexually transmitted diseases (STDs) and encourage your partners to do the same.** If you are sexually active, get tested at least once a year. STDs can have long-term health consequences. They can also increase your chance of getting HIV or transmitting it to others. Find an STD testing site.

- **If your partner is HIV-positive, encourage your partner to get and stay on treatment.** ART reduces the amount of HIV virus (viral load) in blood and body fluids. If taken consistently and correctly, ART can keep people with HIV healthy for many years, and greatly reduce their chance of transmitting HIV to sex partners.

Of course, you can also reduce your risk of getting HIV by not having sex. If you aren't having sexual contact, you are 100% protected from getting HIV in that way. Alternatively, if you are having sex, you can reduce your risk if you and your partner have both been tested and know that you are both HIV-negative and you practice monogamy. Being monogamous means: 1) You are in a sexual relationship with only one person and 2) Both of you are having sex only with each other. However, monogamy won't protect you completely unless you know for sure that both you and your partner are not infected with HIV.

Sexual Practices and HIV Risk

The risk of getting HIV through sexual contact varies widely depending on the type of sexual activity. Some activities carry a much higher risk of HIV transmission than others.

Your risk depends on several other factors as well, including whether you and your partner are using a condom and—if one of you is HIV-positive—whether the partner who is HIV-positive is using ART consistently and correctly and has achieved a suppressed viral load, and whether the partner who is HIV-negative is using PrEP consistently and correctly. Condoms and HIV medicines can greatly lower the risk of transmitting HIV.

Here is a list of some sexual practices, the risks they pose for transmitting HIV, and steps you can take to lower your risk of getting HIV:

Receptive Anal Sex (Bottoming)

- The risk of getting HIV from receiving anal sex (penis in the anus or "bottoming") without a condom is higher than any other sexual activity.

- The partner receiving anal sex (bottom) is at greater risk of getting HIV than the partner performing anal sex (top) because the lining of the rectum is thin and may allow HIV to enter the body.

- HIV can found in the blood, semen (cum), pre-seminal fluid (pre-cum), or rectal fluid of a person infected with the virus, so having your partner pull out before he ejaculates (cums) may not decrease your risk.

- Do not douche before anal sex. Douching irritates the lining of your rectum and this can increase your risk for getting HIV. If you are concerned about cleanliness, clean the rectum gently, with a soapy finger and water.

- If you are bottoming, always use a new condom with a water-based lubricant. This will help minimize damage to your rectum during sex and lower your risk of getting HIV and other STDs.

Insertive Anal Sex (Topping)

- Insertive anal sex (penis in the anus of either a man or a woman or "topping") without a condom is considered a high-risk behavior for HIV transmission, but the risk is not as high as receptive anal sex (bottoming).

- The partner receiving anal sex (bottom) is at greater risk of getting HIV than the partner performing anal sex (top), however the top is also at risk because HIV can enter through the opening of the penis or through small cuts, abrasions, or open sores on the penis.

- If you are topping, always use a new condom with a water-based lubricant. This will help lower your risk of getting HIV and other STDs.

Receptive Vaginal Sex (Risks for Women)

- Receptive vaginal sex (penis in the vagina) without a condom is considered a high-risk behavior for HIV transmission.

- In women, HIV can be directly absorbed through the mucous membranes that line the vagina and cervix. The lining of the vagina can also sometimes tear and possibly allow HIV to enter the body.

- Your risk of HIV infection increases if you or your partner also has an STD.

- You can lower your risk of getting HIV and other STDs by always using a new condom.

- Oral or hormonal contraceptives (e.g., birth control pills) do not protect women against HIV or other STDs.

- Many barrier methods used to prevent pregnancy (e.g., diaphragm, cervical cap) do not protect against HIV or other STDs because they still allow infected semen (cum) to come in contact with the lining of the vagina. If you use one of these methods, be sure to also use a male condom correctly every time you have vaginal sex.

- When worn in the vagina, female condoms are just as effective as male condoms at preventing STDs, HIV, and pregnancy. Don't use a male condom and a female condom at the same time; they do not work together and could break.

- Don't use nonoxynol-9 (N-9). Some contraceptives, like condoms, suppositories, foams, and gels contain the spermicide N-9. Don't use these gels, foams, or suppositories to prevent against HIV— these methods only lower your chances of pregnancy, not of getting HIV and other STDs. N-9 actually makes your risk of HIV infection higher, because it can irritate the vagina, which might make it easier for HIV to get into your body.

- Don't douche before sex. Douching removes some of the normal bacteria in the vagina that protects you from infection. This can increase your risk of getting HIV.

Insertive Vaginal Sex (Risks for Men)

- Insertive vaginal sex (penis in the vagina) without a condom is considered a high-risk behavior for HIV transmission, but it is less risky for the male partner than the female partner.

- In men, HIV can enter the body through the urethra (the opening at the tip of the penis) or through small cuts or open sores on the penis. Men who are not circumcised are at greater risk of HIV infection through vaginal sex than are circumcised men.

- Your risk of HIV infection increases if you or your partner also has an STD.

- Use a new condom with a water-based lubricant every time you have insertive vaginal sex to prevent STDs, including HIV.

Performing Oral Sex on a Man

- The risk of getting HIV by performing oral sex (your mouth on someone's penis or "fellatio") is low, but it is not zero risk. It is difficult to measure the exact risk because people who practice oral sex may also practice other forms of sex during the same encounter.

- Performing oral sex on an HIV-infected man, with ejaculation in the mouth, is the riskiest type of oral sex activity.

- If the man you are performing oral sex on has HIV, his blood, semen, or pre-seminal fluid may contain the virus.

- Performing oral sex also puts you at risk for getting other STDs, including herpes.

- Your risk of getting HIV or other STDs is reduced if you do not have open sores or cuts in your mouth.

- You can reduce your risk of getting HIV and other STDs through oral sex if you avoid having your partner ejaculate (cum) in your mouth, and if you use a condom.

Receiving Oral Sex If You Are a Man

- The risk of getting HIV by receiving oral sex (someone's mouth on your penis or "fellatio") if you are a man is low, but it is not zero risk. It is difficult to measure the exact risk because people who practice oral sex may also practice other forms of sex during the same encounter.

- If the person giving you oral sex has HIV, blood from their mouth may enter your body through the lining of your urethra (the opening at the tip of your penis) or your anus, or through cuts and sores.

- Receiving oral sex also puts you at risk of contracting other STDs, including herpes.

- Your risk of getting HIV is reduced if you do not have open sores or cuts on your penis.

Performing Oral Sex on a Woman

- The risk of getting HIV by performing oral sex on a woman (your mouth on a woman's genitals or "cunnilingus") is low, but it is not zero risk. It is difficult to measure the exact risk because people who practice oral sex may also practice other forms of sex during the same encounter.

- If the woman you are performing oral sex on has HIV, her vaginal fluid may contain the virus.

- Performing oral sex also puts you at risk of contracting other STDs.

- There are effective barriers you can use to protect you from contact with your partner's vaginal fluids. These include natural rubber latex sheets, dental dams, or using cut-open nonlubricated condoms between your mouth and your partner's genitals or rectum.

Receiving Oral Sex If You Are a Woman

- The risk of getting HIV by receiving oral sex (someone's mouth on your genitals or "cunnilingus") if you are a woman is low, but it is not zero risk. It is difficult to measure the exact risk because people who practice oral sex may also practice other forms of sex during the same encounter.

- If the person giving you oral sex has HIV, blood from their mouth may enter your body through your vagina, cervix, or anus, or through cuts and sores.

- Your risk of HIV is increased if you have genital sores or other STDs.

- Receiving oral sex also puts you at risk of getting other STDs, such as herpes, syphilis, gonorrhea, genital warts (human papillomavirus or HPV), intestinal parasites (amebiasis), or hepatitis A or B infection.

- There are effective barriers you can use to protect you from contact with your partner's mouth. These include natural rubber latex sheets, dental dams, or using cut-open nonlubricated condoms between your partner's mouth and your genitals or rectum.

Oral-Anal Contact (Rimming)

- The risk of getting HIV by giving or receiving oral stimulation to the anus (your mouth on someone's anus, also called "anilingus" or "rimming") is low, but it is not zero risk.

- This kind of sexual contact comes with a high risk of transmitting hepatitis A and B, parasites, and other bacteria to the partner who is doing the rimming. There are effective vaccines that protect against hepatitis A and B and human papillomavirus infections. Talk to your health care provider to see if these are right for you, if you have not already been vaccinated.

- You can reduce your risk of getting HIV or other STDs if you use a cut-open unlubricated condom, dental dam, or non-microwaveable plastic wrap over the anus to protect against infection.

Digital Stimulation (Fingering)

- There is a very small risk of getting HIV from fingering your partner if you have cuts or sores on your fingers and your partner has cuts or sores in the rectum or vagina. HIV transmission this way is technically possible but unlikely and not well documented.

- Use medical-grade gloves and lots of water-based lubricant to eliminate this risk.

Sex Toys

- There is a very small risk of getting HIV from sharing sex toys. HIV transmission this way is technically possible, but unlikely and not well documented.

- Using sex toys can be a safe practice, as long as you do not share your toys with your partner.

- If you share your toy with your partner, use a condom on the toy, if possible, and change the condom before your partner uses it.

- Clean your toys with soap and water, or a stronger disinfectant if indicated on the cleaning instructions. It is important to do this after each use!

No-Risk Sexual Activities

These activities carry no risk of HIV transmission:

- Non-sexual massage

- Casual or dry kissing

- Phone sex, cyber sex, sexy talk

- Masturbation (without your partner's body fluids)

- Frottage—also known as "dry humping" or body-to-body rubbing

You can still contract other STDs, like herpes, HPV, or pubic lice ("crabs") if you have bare skin-to-skin contact with your partner.

Using Condoms

When used consistently and correctly, condoms are highly effective in preventing HIV. They are also effective at preventing STDs transmitted through body fluids, like gonorrhea, chlamydia, and HIV. However, they provide less protection against STDs spread through skin-to-skin contact like human papillomavirus (genital warts), genital herpes, and syphilis.

Taking HIV Medicines to Prevent HIV

As noted above, there are ways to prevent getting HIV by taking some of the medicines used to treat HIV. These methods are PrEP (taking HIV medicine daily to prevent HIV infection) and PEP (taking medicine to prevent HIV after a possible exposure).

Circumcision

Male circumcision reduces the risk that a man will get HIV from an infected female partner, and also lowers the risk of other STDs, penile cancer, and infant urinary tract infection. Studies have not consistently shown that it prevents HIV among men who have sex with men. Circumcision is only partly effective and should be used with other prevention measures. Men who are considering circumcision should weigh its risks and costs against its potential benefits.

In December 2014, CDC issued a request for public comment on draft counseling recommendations about elective male circumcision for the prevention of HIV, STDs, and other health outcomes in the United States. The guidance is designed to help health care providers provide accurate information to individual men, as well as to parents, to help them make informed decisions about circumcision.

Section 6.4

Sexually Transmitted Diseases and HIV Risk

This section includes excerpts from "Sexually Transmitted Diseases (STDs): Overview," *Eunice Kennedy Shriver* National Institute of Child Health and Human Development (NICHD), 28 May 2013; text from "STDs and HIV – CDC Fact Sheet," Centers for Disease Control and Prevention (CDC), April 23, 2015; and text from "STDs & Pregnancy – CDC Fact Sheet," Centers for Disease Control and Prevention (CDC), December 16, 2014.

Sexually transmitted diseases (STDs), also known as sexually transmitted infections (STIs), are typically caused by bacteria or viruses and passed from person to person during sexual contact with the penis, vagina, rectum, or mouth. The symptoms of STDs/STIs vary between individuals, depending on the cause, and many people may not experience symptoms at all. Many STDs/STIs have significant health consequences. Together with other scientists' investigations at the NIH, the NICHD's research focuses on understanding sexual risk-taking behaviors that increase the likelihood of individuals contracting STDs/STIs, on developing more effective educational interventions to prevent STDs/STIs, and on defining the consequences and optimal treatments for STIs, especially in pregnant women.

Are some STDs associated with HIV?

Yes. In the United States, people who get syphilis, gonorrhea, and herpes often also have HIV, or are more likely to get HIV in the future.

Why does having an STD put me more at risk for getting HIV?

If you get an STD you are more likely to get HIV than someone who is STD-free. This is because the same behaviors and circumstances that may put you at risk for getting an STD can also put you at greater risk for getting HIV. In addition, having a sore or break in the skin from an STD may allow HIV to more easily enter your body.

What activities can put me at risk for both STDs and HIV?

- Having anal, vaginal, or oral sex without a condom;
- Having multiple sex partners;
- Having anonymous sex partners;
- Having sex while under the influence of drugs or alcohol can lower inhibitions and result in greater sexual risk-taking.

What can I do to prevent getting STDs and HIV?

The only way to avoid STDs is to not have vaginal, anal, or oral sex. If you are sexually active, you can do the following things to lower your chances of getting STDs and HIV:

- Choose less risky sexual behaviors;
- Use condoms consistently and correctly;
- Reduce the number of people with whom you have sex;
- Limit or eliminate drug and alcohol use before and during sex;
- Have an honest and open talk with your healthcare provider and ask whether you should be tested for STDs and HIV;
- Talk to your healthcare provider and find out if pre-exposure prophylaxis, or PrEP, is a good option for you to prevent HIV infection.

If I already have HIV, and then I get an STD, does that put my sex partner(s) at an increased risk for getting HIV?

It can. If you already have HIV, and then get another STD, it can put your HIV-negative partners at greater risk of getting HIV from you.

Your sex partners are less likely to get HIV from you, if you

- Use antiretroviral therapy (ART). ART reduces the amount of virus (viral load) in your blood and body fluids. ART can keep you healthy for many years, and greatly reduce your chance of transmitting HIV to sex partners, if taken consistently.

- Choose less risky sexual behaviors.

- Use condoms consistently and correctly.

The risk of getting HIV may also be reduced if your partner takes pre-exposure prophylaxis, or PrEP, after discussing this option with his or her healthcare provider and determining whether it is appropriate.

Will treating STDs prevent me from getting HIV?

No. It's not enough.

If you get treated for an STD, this will help to prevent its complications, and prevent spreading STDs to your sex partners. Treatment for an STD other than HIV does not prevent the spread of HIV.

If you are diagnosed with an STD, talk to your doctor about ways to protect yourself and your partner(s) from getting reinfected with the same STD, or getting HIV.

Women who are pregnant can become infected with the same sexually transmitted diseases (STDs) as women who are not pregnant. Pregnant women should ask their doctors about getting tested for STDs, since some doctors do not routinely perform these tests.

Can pregnant women become infected with STDs?

Women who are pregnant can become infected with the same sexually-transmitted diseases (STDs) as women who are not pregnant. Pregnancy does not provide women or their babies any additional protection against STDs. Many STDs are 'silent,' or have no symptoms, so women may not know they are infected. A pregnant woman should be tested for STDs, including HIV (the virus that causes AIDS), as a part of her medical care during pregnancy. The results of an STD can be more serious, even life-threatening, for a woman and her baby if the woman becomes infected while pregnant. It is important that women be aware of the harmful effects of STDs and how to protect themselves and their children against infection. Sexual partners of infected women should also be tested and treated.

How do STDs affect a pregnant woman and her baby?

STDs can complicate pregnancy and may have serious effects on both a woman and her developing baby. Some of these problems may be seen at birth; others may not be discovered until months or years later. In addition, it is well known that infection with an STD can make it easier for a person to get infected with HIV. Most of these problems can be prevented if the mother receives regular medical care during pregnancy. This includes tests for STDs starting early in pregnancy and repeated close to delivery, as needed.

Human Immunodeficiency Virus

Human immunodeficiency virus (HIV) is the virus that causes acquired immune deficiency syndrome, or AIDS. HIV destroys specific blood cells that are crucial to helping the body fight diseases. According to CDC's 2011 HIV surveillance data, women make up 25% of all adults and adolescents living with diagnosed HIV infection in the United States. The most common ways that HIV passes from mother to child are during pregnancy, labor and delivery, or through breast-feeding. However, when HIV is diagnosed before or during pregnancy and appropriate steps are taken, the risk of mother-to-child transmission can be lowered to less than 2%. *HIV testing is recommended for all pregnant women.* A mother who knows early in her pregnancy that she is HIV-positive has more time to consult with her healthcare provider and decide on effective ways to protect her health and that of her unborn baby.

Chapter 7

HIV Risk in the Healthcare Setting

Chapter Contents

Section 7.1

Occupational Exposure

This section includes excerpts from "HIV in the Workplace –
Occupational Transmission," Centers for Disease Control and
Prevention (CDC), June 22, 2015; and text from "Division of Oral
Health – Infection Control," Centers for Disease Control and
Prevention (CDC), October 25, 2013.

Occupational HIV Transmission and Prevention among Health Care Workers

- Occupational transmission of HIV to health care workers is extremely rare.
- CDC recommends proper use of safety devices and barriers to prevent exposure to HIV in the health care setting.
- For workers who are exposed, CDC has developed recommendations to minimize the risk of developing HIV.

Only 58 cases of confirmed occupational transmission of HIV to health care workers have occurred in the United States. The proper use of gloves and goggles, along with safety devices to prevent injuries from sharp medical devices, can help minimize the risk of exposure to HIV in the course of caring for patients with HIV. When workers are exposed, the Centers for Disease Control and Prevention (CDC) recommends immediate treatment with a short course of antiretroviral drugs to prevent infection.

The Numbers

As of December 31, 2013, 58 confirmed occupational transmissions of HIV and 150 possible transmissions had been reported in the United States. Of these, only one confirmed case has been reported since 1999. Underreporting of cases to CDC is possible, however, because case reporting is voluntary.

Health care workers who are exposed to a needlestick involving HIV-infected blood at work have a 0.23% risk of becoming infected. In other words, 2.3 of every 1,000 such injuries, if untreated, will result in infection. Risk of exposure due to splashes with body fluids is thought to be near zero even if the fluids are overtly bloody. Fluid splashes to intact skin or mucous membranes are considered to be extremely low risk of HIV transmission, whether or not blood is involved.

Prevention Strategies

To prevent transmission of HIV to health care workers in the workplace, health care workers must assume that blood and other body fluids from all patients are potentially infectious. They should therefore follow these infection control precautions at all times:

- Routinely use barriers (such as gloves and/or goggles) when anticipating contact with blood or body fluids.

- Immediately wash hands and other skin surfaces after contact with blood or body fluids.

- Carefully handle and dispose of sharp instruments during and after use.

Safety devices have been developed to help prevent needlestick injuries. If used properly, these types of devices may reduce the risk of exposure to HIV. Many percutaneous injuries, such as needlesticks and cuts, are related to the disposal of sharp-ended medical devices. All used syringes or other sharp instruments should be routinely placed in "sharps" containers for proper disposal to prevent accidental injuries and risk of HIV transmission.

Although the most important strategy for reducing the risk of occupational HIV transmission is to prevent occupational exposures, plans for postexposure management of health care personnel should be in place. CDC issued updated guidelines in 2013 for the management of health care worker exposures to HIV and recommendations for postexposure prophylaxis (PEP).

Occupational exposure is considered an urgent medical concern and should be managed immediately after possible exposure—the sooner the better; every hour counts. The CDC guidelines outline considerations in determining whether health care workers should receive PEP (antiretroviral medication taken after possible exposure to reduce the chance of infection with HIV) and in choosing the type of PEP regimen. For most

HIV exposures that warrant PEP, a basic 4-week, two-drug regimen is recommended, starting as soon as possible after exposure (within 72 hours). For HIV exposures that pose an increased risk of transmission (based on the infection status of the source and the type of exposure), a three-drug regimen may be recommended. Special circumstances, such as a delayed exposure report, unknown source person, pregnancy in the exposed person, resistance of the source virus to antiretroviral agents, and toxicity of PEP regimens, are also discussed in the guidelines.

Building Better Prevention Programs for Health Care Workers

Continued diligence in the following areas is needed to help reduce the risk of occupational HIV transmission to health care workers.

- **Administrative efforts.** All health care organizations should train health care workers in infection control procedures and the importance of reporting occupational exposures immediately after they occur. Organizations should develop and distribute written policies for the management of occupational exposures.

- **Development and promotion of safety devices.** Effective and competitively priced devices engineered to prevent sharps injuries should continue to be developed for health care workers who frequently come into contact with potentially HIV-infected blood. Proper and consistent use of such safety devices should be continuously evaluated.

- **Monitoring the effects of PEP.** Data on the safety and acceptability of different regimens of PEP, particularly regimens that include new antiretroviral agents, should be monitored and evaluated continuously. Furthermore, health professionals who administer PEP must communicate possible side effects before treatment starts and follow patients closely to make sure they take their medicine correctly.

All cases of suspected occupationally acquired HIV should be reported to state health department HIV surveillance staff and the CDC coordinator for "Cases of Public Health Importance" at 404-639-2050.

Bloodborne Pathogens — Occupational Exposure

What constitutes an occupational exposure in dentistry?

An exposure can be defined as a percutaneous injury (e.g., needlestick or cut with a sharp object) or contact of mucous membrane or nonintact skin (e.g., exposed skin that is chapped, abraded, or with dermatitis) with blood, saliva, tissue, or other body fluids that are potentially infectious. Exposure incidents might place dental health care personnel at risk for hepatitis B virus (HBV), hepatitis C virus (HCV), or human immunodeficiency virus (HIV) infection, and therefore should be evaluated immediately following treatment of the exposure site by a qualified health care professional.

What body fluids are potentially infectious during an occupational exposure?

When evaluating occupational exposures to fluids that might contain hepatitis B virus (HBV), hepatitis C virus (HCV), or human immunodeficiency virus (HIV), health care workers should consider that all blood, body fluids, secretions, and excretions except sweat, may contain transmissible infectious agents. Blood contains the greatest proportion of infectious bloodborne virus particle titers of all body fluids and is the most critical transmission vehicle in the health-care setting. During dental procedures it is predictable that saliva will become contaminated with blood. If blood is not visible, it is still likely that very small quantities of blood are present, but the risk for transmitting HBV, HCV, or HIV is extremely small. Despite this small transmission risk, a qualified health care professional1 should evaluate any occupational exposure to saliva in dental settings, regardless of visible blood.

What is the risk of infection after an occupational exposure?

Hepatitis B Virus (HBV)

Health care workers who have received hepatitis B vaccine and have developed immunity to the virus are at virtually no risk for infection. For an unvaccinated person, the risk from a single needlestick or a cut exposure to HBV-infected blood ranges from 6%–30% and depends on the hepatitis B e antigen (HBeAg) status of the source individual. Individuals who are both hepatitis B surface antigen (HBsAg) positive and HBeAg positive have more virus in their blood and are more likely to transmit HBV.

Hepatitis C Virus (HCV)

Based on limited studies, the estimated risk for infection after a needlestick or cut exposure to HCV-infected blood is approximately

1.8%. The risk following a blood splash is unknown but is believed to be very small; however, HCV infection from such an exposure has been reported.

Human Immunodeficiency Virus (HIV)

- The average risk for HIV infection after a needlestick or cut exposure to HlV-infected blood is 0.3% (about 1 in 300). Stated another way, 99.7% of needlestick/cut exposures to HIV-contaminated blood do not lead to infection.

- The risk after exposure of the eye, nose, or mouth to HIV-infected blood is estimated to be, on average, 0.1% (1 in 1,000).

- The risk after exposure of the skin to HlV-infected blood is estimated to be less than 0.1%. A small amount of blood on intact skin probably poses no risk at all. There have been no documented cases of HIV transmission due to an exposure involving a small amount of blood on intact skin (a few drops of blood on skin for a short period of time). The risk may be higher if the skin is damaged (for example, by a recent cut), if the contact involves a large area of skin, or if the contact is prolonged.

What should be done following an occupational exposure?

Wounds and skin sites that have been in contact with blood or body fluids should be washed with soap and water; mucous membranes should be flushed with water. Immediate evaluation must be performed by a qualified health care professional. Health care providers who evaluate exposed dental health care professionals should be

- Selected before dental health care professionals are placed at risk of exposure.

- Experienced in providing antiretroviral therapy.

- Familiar with the unique nature of dental injuries so they can provide appropriate guidance on the need for antiretroviral prophylaxis.

Employers should follow all federal (including the Occupational Safety and Health Administration (OSHA)) and state requirements for recording and reporting occupational injuries and exposures. The following information should be included in the exposure report, recorded in the exposed person's confidential medical record, and made available to qualified health care professionals:

- Date and time of exposure.

- Details of the procedure being performed, including where and how the exposure occurred, whether the exposure involved a sharp device, the type of device, whether there was visible blood on the device, and how and when during its handling the exposure occurred.

- Details of the exposure, including the type and amount of fluid or material and the severity of the exposure. For a percutaneous injury, details would include the depth of the wound, the gauge of the needle, and whether fluid was injected; for a skin or mucous membrane exposure they would include the estimated volume of material, the duration of contact, and the condition of the skin (e.g., chapped, abraded, or intact).

- Details about the exposure source—whether the patient was infected with hepatitis B virus (HBV) and his or her hepatitis B e antigen (HBeAg) status; hepatitis C virus (HCV); or human immunodeficiency virus (HIV); and, if the source was infected with HIV, the stage of disease, history of antiretroviral therapy, and viral load, if known. If this information is not known from the medical record, then the source patient should be asked to obtain serologic testing for HBV, HCV, and HIV.

- Details about the exposed person (e.g., hepatitis B vaccination and vaccine-response status).

- Details about counseling, post-exposure management, and follow-up.

What factors must qualified health care professionals consider when assessing the need for follow-up of occupational exposures?

The evaluation must include the following factors to determine the need for further follow-up:

Type of exposure

- Percutaneous injury (e.g., depth, extent)
- Mucous membrane exposure

- Nonintact skin exposure

- Bites resulting in blood exposure to either person involved

Type and amount of fluid / tissue

- Blood

- Fluids containing blood

Infectious status of source

- Presence of hepatitis B surface antigen (HBsAg) and hepatitis B e antigen (HBeAg)

- Presence of hepatitis C virus (HCV) antibody

- Presence of human immunodeficiency virus (HIV) antibody

Susceptibility of exposed person

- Hepatitis B vaccine and vaccine response status

- HBV, HCV, or HIV immune status

After conducting this initial evaluation of the occupational exposure, a qualified health care professional must decide whether to conduct further follow-up on an individual basis using all of the information obtained.

What are some measures to reduce the risk of blood contact?

Avoiding occupational exposures to blood is the primary way to prevent transmission of HBV, HCV, and HIV in health care settings. Methods used to reduce such exposures in dental settings include engineering and work practice controls and the use of personal protective equipment (PPE).

Engineering controls isolate or remove the bloodborne pathogens hazard from the workplace. These controls are frequently technology-based and often incorporate safer designs of instruments and devices. Examples include sharps disposal containers, rubber dams, and self-sheathing anesthetic needles. Whenever possible, engineering controls should be used as the primary method to reduce exposures to bloodborne pathogens following skin penetration with sharp instruments or needles.

Work practice controls are behavior-based and are intended to reduce the risk of blood exposure by changing the manner in which a task is performed. Examples include using the "scoop" technique to recap an anesthetic needle, removing burs before placing the hand piece in the dental unit, and restricting the use of fingers during suturing and when administering anesthesia.

Personal protective equipment consists of specialized clothing or equipment worn to protect against hazards. Examples include gloves, masks, protective eyewear with side shields, and gowns to prevent skin and mucous membrane exposures.

Section 7.2

Blood Transfusion and Organ Donation Recipients

This section includes excerpts from "Blood Transfusions & Organ/ Tissue Transplants," AIDS.gov, September 27, 2013; and text from "Keeping Blood Transfusions Safe: FDA's Multi-layered Protections for Donated Blood," U.S.Food and Drug Administration (FDA), June 11, 2015.

OUR NATION'S BLOOD SUPPLY
YOU CANNOT GET HIV FROM DONATING BLOOD. BLOOD COLLECTION PROCEDURES ARE HIGHLY REGULATED AND SAFE.

TESTING DONATED BLOOD
U.S. REGULATIONS REQUIRE THAT EACH UNIT OF DONATED BLOOD IS TESTED FOR INFECTIOUS AGENTS TO ENSURE ITS SAFETY.

ORGAN/TISSUE TRANSPLANTS
THE RISKS OF TRANSPLANT-RELATED HIV INFECTION ARE LOW. ALL DONORS ARE TESTED FOR HIV AND OTHER DISEASES.

Figure 7.1. *Blood Transfusions*

Our Nation's Blood Supply

In the early years of the HIV epidemic, blood transfusions were at increased risk for transmitting HIV infection. In 1985, however, an HIV test became available, and screening of all blood donations rapidly became universal. The U.S. blood supply is now among the safest in the world:

- All blood donors are prescreened for HIV risk factors.

- Blood donations are required to be tested both for presence of antibodies to HIV and for HIV ribonucleic acid (RNA). RNA testing detects HIV at an earlier stage than HIV antibody testing.

- Blood and blood products that test positive for HIV are safely discarded and are not used for transfusions. Donors whose blood tests positive for HIV are notified by the collecting agency and are deferred from further donations.

It is important to know that **you cannot get HIV from donating blood**. Blood collection procedures are highly regulated and safe.

Do Not Donate Blood to Learn Your HIV Status

Some people think that donating blood is a better way to learn their HIV status than asking their doctor for an HIV test or visiting a clinic. This is not true. **You should not donate blood to find out if you are HIV-positive.**

Why? Because the HIV tests used to screen donor blood are highly accurate—but they aren't perfect. If you have been infected with HIV recently, even the most sensitive test may not show it, and you can infect others if your blood is transfused to them.

If you have engaged in high-risk sexual or drug taking behaviors, you should not donate blood. It is important, though, to learn your HIV status. You can get an HIV test at a number of places, including your local health department, public health clinic, or doctor's office or at many local AIDS service organizations, community-based organizations, and even in mobile vans. By getting an HIV test, you can protect your own health, as well as the health of people who need blood. It is also possible to purchase a rapid home-use HIV test kit.

Organ/Tissue Transplants

The risks of transplant-related HIV infection are low. All organ and tissue donors are screened for risk factors, and tested for HIV and other infectious agents that potentially could be transmitted through transplantation. However, although HIV tests are highly accurate, the tests do not always detect the virus in people with very recent infection. Unexpected transmission of HIV, HBV, and HCV from infected donors has been reported in heart, liver, kidney, and pancreas recipients.

Keeping Blood Transfusions Safe: FDA's Multi-layered Protections for Donated Blood

Keeping the United States blood supply the world's safest is the ultimate responsibility of the nation's blood establishments that collect and process the units of whole blood donated by volunteers each year. The Food and Drug Administration, however, has the vital role of ensuring that patients who receive a blood transfusion are protected by multiple overlapping safeguards. This FDA blood-safety system includes measures in the following areas:

- **Donor screening**
- **Blood testing**
- **Donor deferral lists**
- **Quarantine**
- **Problems and Deficiencies**

Donor screening: Donor screening plays an important role in ensuring the safety of the U.S. blood supply. FDA regulations require that a donor be free from any disease transmissible by blood transfusion, in so far as can be determined by health history and examination.

Donors are informed about potential risks and are required to answer questions about factors that may have a bearing on the safety of their blood. For example, donors with a history of intravenous drug abuse are routinely deferred.

In addition to federal regulations, FDA periodically issues guidance documents providing recommendations to decrease the potential for transmission of infectious diseases when new information or testing methodologies becomes available. For example, since November 1999, the FDA has recommended that the blood industry defer potential donors who have lived in the United Kingdom and other European countries to reduce the risk of variant Creutzfeldt-Jakob disease (vCJD), the human form of "mad cow disease."

Blood testing: The FDA reviews and approves all test kits used to detect infectious diseases in donated blood. After donation, each unit of donated blood is required to undergo a series of tests for infectious diseases, including:

Hepatitis B and C viruses

Human Immunodeficiency Virus, Types 1 and 2

Human T-Lymphotropic Virus, Types I and II

Treponema pallidum (Syphilis)

Additionally, FDA recommends testing for the following infectious diseases:

West Nile Virus

Trypanosoma cruzi (Chagas disease)

Donor deferral lists: Blood establishments must keep current a list of deferred donors and use it to make sure that they do not collect blood from anyone on the list.

Quarantine: Donated blood must be quarantined until it is tested and shown to be free of infectious agents.

Problems and deficiencies: Blood centers must investigate manufacturing problems, correct all deficiencies, and notify the FDA when product deviations occur in distributed products.

If any one of these safeguards is breached, the blood component is considered unsuitable for transfusion and is subject to recall.

Chapter 8

HIV Transmission Rumors and Risks

Myths persist about how HIV is transmitted. This chapter provides the facts about HIV risk from different types of sex, injection drug use, and other activities.

How is HIV passed from one person to another?

In the United States, HIV is spread mainly by having sex or sharing injection drug equipment such as needles with someone who has HIV.

Only certain fluids—blood, semen (*cum*), pre-seminal fluid (*pre-cum*), rectal fluids, vaginal fluids, and breast milk—from an HIV-infected person can transmit HIV. These fluids must come in contact with a mucous membrane or damaged tissue or be directly injected into the bloodstream (from a needle or syringe) for transmission to possibly occur. Mucous membranes can be found inside the rectum, the vagina, the opening of the penis, and the mouth.

In the United States, HIV is spread mainly by

- Having sex with someone who has HIV.

- In general:

  - Anal sex is the highest-risk sexual behavior. Receptive anal sex (bottoming) is riskier than insertive anal sex (topping).

Text in this chapter is excerpted from "HIV/AIDS – Transmission," Centers for Disease Control and Prevention (CDC), January 16, 2015.

- Vaginal sex is the second highest-risk sexual behavior.

- Having multiple sex partners or having other sexually transmitted infections can increase the risk of infection through sex.

- Sharing needles, syringes, rinse water, or other equipment (works) used to prepare injection drugs with someone who has HIV.

Less commonly, HIV may be spread by:

- Being born to an infected mother. HIV can be passed from mother to child during pregnancy, birth, or breastfeeding.

- Being stuck with an HIV-contaminated needle or other sharp object. This is a risk mainly for health care workers.

- Receiving blood transfusions, blood products, or organ/tissue transplants that are contaminated with HIV. This risk is extremely small because of rigorous testing of the US blood supply and donated organs and tissues.

- Eating food that has been pre-chewed by an HIV-infected person. The contamination occurs when infected blood from a caregiver's mouth mixes with food while chewing, and is very rare.

- Being bitten by a person with HIV. Each of the very small number of documented cases has involved severe trauma with extensive tissue damage and the presence of blood. There is no risk of transmission if the skin is not broken.

- Oral sex—using the mouth to stimulate the penis, vagina, or anus (fellatio, cunnilingus, and rimming). Giving fellatio (mouth to penis oral sex) and having the person ejaculate (cum) in your mouth is riskier than other types of oral sex.

- Contact between broken skin, wounds, or mucous membranes and HIV-infected blood or blood-contaminated body fluids. These reports have also been extremely rare.

- Deep, open-mouth kissing if the person with HIV has sores or bleeding gums and blood is exchanged. HIV is not spread through saliva. Transmission through kissing alone is extremely rare.

How well does HIV survive outside the body?

HIV does not survive long outside the human body (such as on surfaces), and it cannot reproduce. It **is not** spread by

- Air or water.
- Insects, including mosquitoes or ticks.
- Saliva, tears, or sweat. There is no documented case of HIV being transmitted by spitting.
- Casual contact like shaking hands or sharing dishes.
- Closed-mouth or "social" kissing.
- Toilet seats.

Can I get HIV from anal sex?

Yes. In fact, having anal sex is the riskiest type of sex for getting or spreading HIV.

HIV can be found in the blood, semen (*cum*), preseminal fluid (*precum*), or rectal fluid of a person infected with the virus. The *bottom* is at greater risk of getting HIV because the lining of the rectum is thin and may allow HIV to enter the body during anal sex, but the top is also at risk because HIV can enter through the opening of the penis or through small cuts, abrasions, or open sores on the penis.

Can I get HIV from vaginal sex?

Yes. In general vaginal sex is not as risky anal sex, but is still a high-risk behavior for HIV infection.

Yes. In general, vaginal sex is not as risky anal sex but is still a high-risk behavior for HIV infection. It is possible for either partner to become infected this way. This risk depends on many factors, including whether the partners are using condoms, whether the partner with HIV is using antiretroviral therapy (ART) consistently and correctly and whether the partner who is HIV-negative is using pre-exposure prophylaxis (PrEP) consistently and correctly. Condoms and HIV medicines can greatly lower the risk of transmitting HIV.

In women, HIV can be directly absorbed through the mucous membranes that line the vagina and cervix. The lining of the vagina can also sometimes tear and possibly allow HIV to enter the body.

In men, HIV can enter the body through the urethra (the opening at the tip of the penis) or through small cuts or open sores on the penis.

Men who are not circumcised are at greater risk of HIV infection through vaginal sex than are circumcised men.

Risk for HIV infection increases if you or a partner also has a sexually transmitted disease (STD). See also Is there a connection between HIV and other sexually transmitted infections?

Many barrier methods that women use to prevent pregnancy (e.g., diaphragm, cervical cap) do not protect them against HIV or other STDs because they still allow infected semen (cum) to come in contact with the lining of the vagina.

Oral or hormonal contraceptives (e.g., birth control pills) do not protect women against HIV or other STDs.

Can I get HIV from oral sex?

Yes, but most types of oral sex carry little to no risk of HIV.

Oral sex involves giving or receiving oral stimulation to the penis (fellatio), the vagina (cunnilingus), or the anus (anilingus or rimming). Most types of oral sex carry little to no risk of HIV. The highest oral sex risk is performing oral sex (fellatio) with ejaculation in your mouth. However, the risk is still low, and much lower than anal or vaginal sex. Factors that may increase the risk of transmitting HIV through oral sex are oral ulcers, bleeding gums, genital sores, and the presence of other sexually transmitted diseases (STDs) (which may or may not be visible).

The risk is lower if the partners are using condoms or dental dams, if the partner with HIV is taking antiretroviral therapy (ART) consistently and correctly, and if the partner who is HIV-negative is taking pre-exposure prophylaxis (PrEP) consistently and correctly. Condoms and HIV medicines can greatly lower the risk of transmitting HIV.

Is there a connection between HIV and other sexually transmitted infections?

Yes. Having a sexually transmitted disease (STD) can increase the risk of getting or spreading HIV.

If you are HIV-negative but have an STD, you are at least 2 to 5 times as likely to get HIV if you have unprotected sex with someone who has HIV. There are two ways that having an STD can increase the likelihood of getting HIV. If the STD causes irritation of the skin (e.g., from syphilis, herpes, or human papillomavirus), breaks or sores may make it easier for HIV to enter the body during sexual contact. Even STDs that cause no breaks or open sores (e.g., chlamydia, gonorrhea, trichomoniasis) can increase your risk by causing inflammation that increases the number of cells that can serve as targets for HIV.

If you are HIV-positive and also infected with another STD, you are 3 to 5 times as likely as other HIV-infected people to spread HIV through sexual contact. This appears to happen because there is an increased concentration of HIV in the semen and genital fluids of HIV-positive people who also are infected with another STD.

CDC recommends sexually active gay and bisexual men test for:

- HIV.

- Syphilis.

- Hepatitis B and C.

- Chlamydia and gonorrhea of the rectum if you've had receptive anal sex, or been a "bottom" in the past year.

- Chlamydia and gonorrhea of the penis (urethra) if you have had insertive anal or oral sex in the past year.

- Gonorrhea of the throat if you've performed oral sex (i.e., your mouth on your partner's penis, vagina, or anus) in the past year.

Sometimes your health care provider may suggest a herpes test.

Can I get HIV from someone who is living with HIV but has undetectable viral load?

Yes. Even though having an undetectable viral load greatly lowers the chance that a person with HIV can transmit the virus to a partner, there is still some risk.

Viral load refers to the amount of HIV in the blood. An undetectable viral load is when the amount of HIV in the blood is so low that it can't be measured. Antiretroviral therapy (ART) reduces viral load, ideally to an undetectable level, when taken consistently and correctly. A person with HIV can still potentially transmit HIV to a partner even if they have an undetectable viral load, because.

- HIV may still be found in genital fluids (e.g., semen, vaginal fluids). The viral load test only measures virus in blood.

- A person's viral load may go up between tests. When this happens, they may be more likely to transmit HIV to partners.

- Sexually transmitted diseases (STDs) increase viral load in genital fluids.

Can I get HIV from injecting drugs?

Yes. If you share injection drug equipment with someone who has HIV, your risk is high.

Risk also depends on whether the person who has HIV is using antiretroviral therapy (ART) consistently and correctly, and whether the person who is HIV-negative is using preexposure prophylaxis (PrEP) consistently and correctly.

Sharing drug equipment (*or works*) can also be a risk for spreading HIV. Infected blood can get into drug solutions by

- Using blood-contaminated syringes to prepare drugs.

- Reusing water.

- Reusing bottle caps, spoons, or other containers (*cookers*) to dissolve drugs in water and to heat drug solutions.

- Reusing small pieces of cotton or cigarette filters (*cottons*) to filter out particles that could block the needle.

"Street sellers" of syringes may repackage used syringes and sell them as sterile syringes. For this reason, people who continue to inject drugs should get syringes from reliable sources of sterile syringes, such as pharmacies or needle-exchange programs.

It is important to know that sharing a needle or syringe for any use, including skin popping and injecting steroids, hormones, or silicone, can put you at risk for HIV and other blood-borne infections.

Can I get HIV from using other kinds of drugs?

Not directly, but being drunk or high affects your ability to make safe choices and lowers your inhibitions, which may lead you to take risks such as having sex without a condom.

Methamphetamine (*meth*) is a very addictive stimulant that can be snorted, smoked, or injected. Even though using meth is an HIV risk factor for anyone who does it, there is a strong link between meth use and HIV transmission for men who have sex with men (MSM). MSM who use meth may increase their sexual and drug-use risk factors. They may

- Use condoms less often.

- Have more sex partners and have sex over a longer period of time.

- Engage in unprotected anal sex—especially as the receptive partner.

- Inject meth instead of smoking or snorting it.

Drinking alcohol, particularly binge drinking, and using "club drugs" like Ecstasy, ketamine, GHB, and poppers can alter your judgment and impair your decisions about sex or other drug use. You may be more likely to have unplanned and unprotected sex or use other drugs, including injection drugs or meth. Those behaviors can increase your risk of exposure to HIV. If you have HIV, this can also increase your risk of spreading HIV to others. Treatment programs can help people stop using drugs or alcohol. Find a treatment facility near you or call 1-800-662-HELP (1-800-662-4357).

If I already have HIV, can I get another kind of HIV?

Yes. This is called HIV superinfection. The new strain of HIV can replace the original strain or remain along with the original strain. The effects of superinfection differ from person to person. For some people, superinfection may cause them to get sicker faster because they become infected with a new strain of the virus that is resistant to the medicines they are currently taking to treat their original HIV infection. Research suggests that the kind of superinfection where a person becomes infected with a new strain of HIV that is hard to treat is rare, less than 4%.

Are health care workers at risk of getting HIV on the job?

The risk of health care workers being exposed to HIV on the job (occupational exposure) is very low, especially if they use protective practices and personal protective equipment to prevent HIV and other blood-borne infections. For health care workers on the job, the main risk of HIV transmission is through accidental injuries from needles and other sharp instruments that may be contaminated with the virus; however, even this risk is small. Scientists estimate that the risk of HIV infection from being stuck with a needle used on an HIV-infected person is less than 1%.

Can I get HIV from receiving medical care?

Although HIV transmission is possible in health care settings, it is extremely rare.

Careful practice of infection control, including universal precautions (i.e., using protective practices and personal protective equipment to prevent HIV and other blood-borne infections) protects patients as well as health care providers from possible HIV transmission in medical and dental offices and hospitals.

The risk of getting HIV from receiving blood transfusions, blood products, or organ/tissue transplants that are contaminated with HIV is extremely small because of rigorous testing of the US blood supply and donated organs and tissues.

It is important to know that **you cannot get HIV from donating blood**. Blood collection procedures are highly regulated and safe.

Can I get HIV from casual contact ("social kissing," shaking hands, hugging, using a toilet, drinking from the same glass, or the sneezing and coughing of an infected person)?

No. HIV is not spread by day-to-day contact in the workplace, schools, or social settings. HIV is not spread through shaking hands, hugging, or a casual kiss. You cannot become infected from a toilet seat, a drinking fountain, a door knob, dishes, drinking glasses, food, cigarettes, pets, or insects.

HIV is not spread through the air, and it does not live long outside the body.

Can I get HIV from a tattoo or a body piercing?

Tattooing or body piercing present a potential risk of HIV transmission, but no cases of HIV transmission from these activities have been documented. Be sure that only new needles, ink, and other supplies are used and that the person doing the procedure is properly licensed.

Can I get HIV from being spit on or scratched by an HIV-infected person?

No. HIV cannot be spread through saliva, and there is no documented case of transmission from an HIV-infected person spitting on another person. There is no risk of transmission from scratching because there is no transfer of body fluids between people.

Can I get HIV from mosquitoes?

No. There is no evidence of HIV transmission from mosquitoes or any other insects—even in areas where there are many cases of HIV and large populations of mosquitoes. Unlike organisms that are transmitted by insect bites, HIV does not reproduce (and does not survive) in insects.

Can I get HIV from food?

Except for rare cases in which children consumed food that was pre-chewed by an HIV-infected caregiver, HIV has not been spread through food. The virus does not live long outside the body. You cannot get it from consuming food handled by an HIV-infected person; even if the food contained small amounts of HIV-infected blood or semen, exposure to the air, heat from cooking, and stomach acid would destroy the virus.

Are lesbians or other women who have sex with women at risk for HIV?

Case reports of female-to-female transmission of HIV are rare. The well-documented risk of female-to-male transmission shows that vaginal fluids and menstrual blood may contain the virus and that exposure to these fluids through mucous membranes (in the vagina or mouth) could, potentially, lead to HIV infection.

Is the risk of HIV different for different people?

Although HIV risk factors and routes of transmission apply to everyone equally, some people are at higher risk because of where they live and who their sex partners are.

The percentage of people living with HIV (*prevalence*) is higher in major metropolitan areas, so people who live there are more likely to encounter an HIV-positive person among their possible sex partners. In the same way, because the prevalence of HIV is higher among gay and bisexual men and among black and Latino men and women, members of these groups are more likely to encounter partners who are living with HIV.

Chapter 9

HIV/AIDS Prevention

Chapter Contents

Section 9.1

Safer Sex

This section includes excerpts from "Stop STIs: Six Steps to Safer Sex," AIDS.gov, April 17, 2015; and text from "When one Partner is HIV+," AIDS.gov, March 25, 2015.

Stop Sexually Transmitted Infections: Six Steps to Safer Sex

Whether you call them sexually transmitted infections (STIs) or sexually transmitted diseases (STDs), one thing is true: Women are at risk of infection. Not only does a woman's anatomy make her vulnerable to STIs, women are less likely to have symptoms than men. Untreated STIs can lead to serious health issues, including infertility, cancer, and even death. It's not fun to think about, but protecting yourself from STIs like genital herpes, genital warts, chlamydia, syphilis, gonorrhea, and HIV is an important part of staying healthy.

Here are six ways to protect yourself from STIs:

1. **Get the facts.** About 20 million new STIs occur in the United States every year, affecting people of all ages and backgrounds. Many STIs are spread through intimate sexual contact, but you don't have to have vaginal or anal sex to be at risk—some common STIs are spread easily by oral sex and genital touching. And because many STIs have only mild symptoms or no symptoms at all, you can't tell by looking at someone whether or not they have an infection.

2. **Talk to your partner.** It's important to talk with your partner about STIs and practicing safe sex **before** you have sex. Get tips for talking with your partner, and set the ground rules together. Also, don't assume you're at low risk for STIs if you have sex with only one partner at a time. That person may be having sex with others. If you have been

forced, pressured, or coerced into having sexual contact without protection, there are people who can help you. Everyone deserves to be in control of their own health, including their sexual health.

3. **Get tested.** It's important to know whether or not you have an infection—to make sure it's treated quickly and to avoid spreading it to others. If you are infected, you can take steps to protect yourself and your partner(s). Many Sexually Transmitted Infections (STIs) can be easily diagnosed and treated, and under the Affordable Care Act, STI prevention, screening, and counseling services are fully covered by most insurance plans, at no cost to you. Talk to your health care provider at your annual well-woman visit about which STIs tests you might need. Having an STI can also increase your risk for getting HIV. The same behaviors and situations that put you at risk for STIs also put you at increased risk for getting HIV. Plus, some types of STIs may cause sores or breaks in your skin that make HIV transmission easier. If you test positive for an STI, you should also get tested for HIV.

4. **Practice monogamy.** This means being in a sexual relationship with only one partner who is also faithful to you. Make sure you've both been tested for STIs and know each other's results. Condoms should be used with any partner outside of a long-term, monogamous sexual relationship.

5. **Use condoms.** Use a condom correctly every time you have anal, vaginal, or oral sex to reduce the risk of STI transmission. Get tips for using male and female condoms correctly.

6. **Get vaccinated.** Safe and effective vaccines are available to help prevent the spread of the human papillomavirus (HPV). While it's recommended for kids who are 11 or 12, young women can receive the series of shots through the age of 26. HPV vaccines can help protect you from the types of HPV that cause most cervical cancers. Vaccines for HPV are covered as preventive services under the Affordable Care Act, which means most insurers must cover them at no cost to you. Learn more about HPV, then talk to your doctor about whether the vaccines are right for you.

When One Partner Is HIV+

A "MIXED STATUS" RELATIONSHIP IS A SEXUAL RELATIONSHIP BETWEEN ONE HIV+ PARTNER AND ONE HIV- PARTNER.

IF YOU ARE IN A MIXED-STATUS RELATIONSHIP, YOU CAN

REDUCE THE RISK OF TRANSMITTING HIV

BY USING ART, USING CONDOMS CONSISTENTLY AND CORRECTLY, AND CHOOSING LESS RISKY SEXUAL BEHAVIORS.

IN A RELATIONSHIP WITH SOMEONE WHO IS HIV+?

TALK TO YOUR DOCTOR ABOUT PREP TO REDUCE YOUR RISK OF GETTING HIV.

Figure 9.1. *Mixed Status Relationship*

What Is a "Mixed-Status" Relationship?

A "mixed-status" relationship is a sexual relationship in which one partner is HIV-positive and the other is HIV-negative. This can involve a couple in a long-term relationship or a single encounter between two partners. You may also hear these terms to describe such relationships:

- Serodiscordant
- Discordant
- Serodivergent
- Magnetic
- HIV-positive/negative

Is It Safe for Mixed-Status Couples to Have Sex?

For mixed-status couples, the possibility of HIV infection is a constant reality. There is always a risk of transmitting HIV, but you can minimize it.

Tips for the HIV-Negative Partner

If you are the HIV-negative partner in a mixed-status relationship, here are steps you can take to reduce your chances of getting HIV:

- **Encourage your HIV-positive partner to get and stay on** *antiretroviral therapy* **(ART),** and support your partner in taking all of his/her HIV medications at the right time. This "medication adherence" will lower your partner's viral load, keep your partner healthy, and reduce the risk that HIV can be transmitted.

- **Use condoms consistently and correctly.** When used correctly and consistently, condoms are highly effective in preventing HIV infection, as well as other sexually transmitted diseases (STDs). Both male and female condoms are available.

- **Choose less risky sexual behaviors.** Oral sex is much less risky than anal or vaginal sex. Anal sex is the highest-risk sexual activity for HIV transmission. If you are HIV-negative, insertive anal sex ("topping") is less risky for getting HIV than receptive anal sex ("bottoming"). Remember: HIV can be sexually transmitted via blood, semen (cum), pre-seminal fluid (precum), rectal fluid, and vaginal fluid. Sexual activities that do not involve the potential exchange of these bodily fluids (e.g., touching) carry no risk for getting HIV.

- **Talk to your doctor about pre-exposure prophylaxis (PrEP).** PrEP is a way for people who don't have HIV to prevent HIV infection by taking a pill every day. The pill contains two medicines that are also used to treat HIV. Along with other prevention methods like condoms, PrEP can offer good protection against HIV if taken every day. The CDC recommends PrEP be considered for people who are HIV-negative and at substantial risk for HIV infection. This includes HIV-negative individuals who are in an ongoing relationship with an HIV-positive partner, as well at others at high risk.

- **Talk to your doctor right away (within 3 days) about post-exposure prophylaxis (PEP) if you think you have had a possible exposure to HIV.** An example of a possible exposure is if you had anal or vaginal sex with your HIV-positive partner without a condom, and you are not taking PrEP. Your chance of exposure to HIV is lower if your HIV-positive partner is taking ART consistently and correctly, especially if his/her viral load is undetectable. Starting PEP immediately and taking it daily for 4 weeks reduces your chance of getting HIV.

- **Get tested for HIV.** You should get tested for HIV at least once a year so that you are sure about your HIV status and can take action to keep healthy. Talk to your doctor about whether you may also benefit from more frequent testing (e.g., every 3-6 months). Use the AIDS.gov HIV Testing and Care Services Locator to find a testing site near you, or use a home testing kit.

- **Get tested and treated for other STDs and encourage your partner to do the same.** If either of you are sexually active outside the partnership, you should get tested at least once a year and talk to your provider about whether more frequent testing is of benefit. STDs can have long-term health consequences. They can also increase your chance of getting HIV. Find an STD testing site. Use the AIDS.gov HIV Testing and Care Services Locator to find a testing site near you.

Tips for the HIV-Positive Partner

If you are the HIV-positive partner in a mixed-status relationship, here are steps you can take to reduce your risk of transmitting HIV to your partner:

Get and stay on antiretroviral therapy (ART). ART reduces the amount of virus in your blood and body fluids. ART can keep you healthy for many years, and greatly reduce your chance of transmitting HIV to your sexual partners if you take it consistently and correctly.

If you are taking ART, follow your health care provider's advice. Visit your health care provider regularly and always take your medicine as directed.

Use condoms consistently and correctly. When used correctly and consistently, condoms are highly effective in preventing HIV infection, as well as other sexually transmitted diseases (STDs). Both male and female condoms are available.

Choose less risky sexual behaviors. Oral sex is much less risky than anal or vaginal sex. Anal sex is the highest-risk sexual activity for HIV transmission. During anal sex, it is less risky for you as the HIV-positive partner to be the receptive partner ("bottom") than the insertive partner ("top"). Remember: HIV can be sexually transmitted via blood, semen (cum), pre-seminal fluid (pre-cum), rectal fluid, and vaginal fluid. Sexual activities that do not involve the potential exchange of these bodily fluids (e.g., touching) carry no risk for transmitting HIV.

Talk to your partner about pre-exposure prophylaxis (PrEP), taking HIV medicines daily to prevent HIV infection. The CDC recommends PrEP be considered for people who are HIV-negative and at substantial risk for HIV infection. This includes HIV-negative individuals who are in an ongoing relationship with an HIV-positive partner, as well as others at high risk.

Talk to your partner about post-exposure prophylaxis (PEP) if you think your partner has had a possible exposure to HIV. An example of a possible exposure is if you had anal or vaginal sex without a condom or the condom breaks and your partner is not on PrEP. Your partner's chance of exposure to HIV is lower if you are taking ART consistently and correctly, especially if your viral load is undetectable. Your partner should talk to his/her doctor right away (within 3 days) if they think they have had a possible exposure to HIV. Starting medicine immediately (known as post-exposure prophylaxis, or PEP) and taking it daily for 4 weeks reduces your partner's chance of getting HIV.

Get tested and treated for STDs and encourage your partner to do the same. If either of you are sexually active outside the partnership, you should get tested at least once a year and talk to your provider about whether more frequent testing is of benefit. STDs can have long-term health consequences. They can also increase your risk of transmitting HIV to others. Use the AIDS.gov website's HIV Testing and Care Services Locator to find a testing site near you.

Keep the Lines of Communication Open

If you are part of a mixed-status couple, it is important that you and your partner communicate openly and often about safer sex practices and HIV prevention. Healthcare providers and local HIV/AIDS organizations can be important sources of information and support for you and your partner.

CDC's *Start Talking. Stop HIV.* campaign has information and resources to help you start a conversation about safe sex and HIV.

Section 9.2

Male Circumcision

Text in this section is excerpted from "Male Circumcision," Centers for Disease Control and Prevention (CDC), 2012.

What Is Male Circumcision?

Male circumcision is the surgical removal of some or all of the foreskin (or prepuce) from the penis.

Male Circumcision and Risk for HIV Acquisition by Heterosexual Men

Several types of research have documented that male circumcision significantly reduces the risk of men contracting HIV through penile-vaginal sex.

Biologic Plausibility

Compared with the dry external skin surface of the glans penis and penile shaft, the inner mucosa of the foreskin has less keratinization (deposition of fibrous protein) and a higher density of target cells for HIV infection. Some laboratory studies have shown the foreskin is more susceptible to HIV infection than other penile tissue, although others have failed to show any difference in the ability of HIV to penetrate inner compared with outer foreskin surface. The foreskin may also have greater susceptibility to traumatic epithelial disruptions (tears) during intercourse, providing a portal of entry for pathogens, including HIV. In addition, the microenvironment in the preputial sac between the unretracted foreskin and the glans penis may be conducive to viral survival. Finally, the presence of other sexually transmitted diseases (STDs), which independently may be more common in uncircumcised men, increase the risk for HIV acquisition.

Male Circumcision and Male-to-Female Transmission of HIV

Studies of whether circumcision of males reduces HIV transmission to their female sex partners overall indicate no protective effect.

A RCT of male circumcision in Uganda found no evidence of reduced HIV transmission to female partners. In the study, 922 HIV- infected men with uninfected partners were assigned to either immediate or delayed circumcision. Overall, 18% of women in the intervention group (partners in the immediate circumcision group) acquired HIV during follow-up, compared with 12% of women assigned to the control group (partners in the delayed circumcision group). There was no difference in HIV incidence between the circumcised and control groups when the couples waited to resume sex until the wound had healed, which in 93% of male subjects was within 6 weeks of circumcision. However, women appeared to be at somewhat higher risk for HIV acquisition when the couples resumed sex before the circumcision wounds had healed, although this difference was not statistically significant.

A systematic review and meta-analysis of male circumcision and risk of transmission to women identified 19 studies from 11 populations. The meta-analysis of data from the one RCT and six longitudinal analyses showed little evidence that male circumcision directly affects the risk of transmitting HIV to women (RR, 0.80; 95% CI, 0.53-1.36).

Male Circumcision and Male-to-Male Transmission of HIV

Observational studies have yielded mixed results in attempts to detect a protective effect of male circumcision among men who have sex with men (MSM). While some cross-sectional and prospective studies of MSM have shown statistically significant increases in risk of HIV acquisition by uncircumcised MSM, others have found no evidence that being circumcised was protective against HIV infection among MSM. In a recent meta-analysis of 15 observational studies of male circumcision and HIV acquisition by MSM, a statistically nonsignificant protective association was found (OR, 0.86; 95% CI, 0.65-1.13).

Risks Associated with Male Circumcision

Reported complication rates depend on the type of study (e.g., chart review vs. prospective study), setting (medical vs. nonmedical facility), person operating (traditional vs. medical practitioner), patient age (infant vs. adult), and surgical technique or instrument used.

In large studies of infant circumcision in the United States, reported inpatient complication rates are approximately 0.2%. The most common complications are bleeding and infection, which are usually minor and easily managed.

A recent meta-analysis of 16 prospective studies from diverse settings worldwide that evaluated complications following neonatal, infant, and child male circumcision found that median frequency of severe adverse events was 0% (range, 0%-2%). The median frequency of any complication was 1.5% (range, 0%-16%). Male circumcision by medical providers on children tended to be associated with more complications (median frequency, 6%; range, 2%-14%) than for neonates and infants.

In the three African trials of adult circumcision, complication rates for adult male circumcision ranged from 2% to 8%. The most commonly reported complications were pain, bleeding, infection, and unsatisfactory appearance. There were no reported deaths or long-term sequelae documented.

Minimizing pain is an important consideration for male circumcision. Appropriate use of analgesia is considered standard of care for the procedure at all ages and can substantially control pain. One study found that 93.5% of neonates circumcised in the first week of life using analgesia gave no indication of pain on an objective, standardized neonatal pain rating system.

Effects of Male Circumcision on Penile Sensation and Sexual Function

Well-designed studies of sexual sensation and function in relation to male circumcision are few, and the results present a mixed picture. Taken as a whole, the studies suggest that some decrease in sensitivity of the glans to fine touch can occur following circumcision. However, several studies conducted among men after adult circumcision suggest that few men report their sexual functioning is worse after circumcision; most report either improvement or no change. The three African trials found high levels of satisfaction among the men after circumcision.

HIV Infection and Male Circumcision in the United States

The United States has a much lower population prevalence of HIV infection (0.4%) than sub-Saharan Africa, and an epidemic that is concentrated among men who have sex with men, rather than men who have sex with women. In 2006, it is estimated that approximately 56,300 new HIV infections occurred, of which 73% were in males. Of all new infections, 53% were in MSM, 31% in heterosexuals with reported high risk of exposure, 12% in injection drug users (IDUs), and 4% in MSM-IDUs. Among men, 72% of estimated new infections occurred in the male-to-male sexual contact transmission category, while heterosexual transmission accounted for 13%.

In one prospective study of heterosexual men attending an urban STD clinic, when other risk factors were controlled, uncircumcised men had a 3.5-fold higher risk for HIV infection than men who were circumcised. However, this association was not statistically significant due to small sample size. And in an analysis of clinic records for African American men attending an STD clinic, circumcision was not associated with HIV status overall, but among heterosexual men with known HIV exposure, circumcision was associated with a statistically significant 58% reduction in risk for HIV infection.

Male Circumcision in the United States

In national probability samples of adults surveyed during 1999–2004, the National Health and Nutrition Examination Surveys (NHANES) found that 79% of men reported being circumcised, including 88% of non-Hispanic white men, 73% of non-Hispanic black men, 42% of Mexican American men, and 50% of men of other races/ethnicities. It is important to note that reported circumcision status may be subject to misclassification. In a study of adolescents only 69% of circumcised and 65% of uncircumcised young men correctly identified their circumcision status as verified by physical exam.

According to the National Hospital Discharge Survey (NHDS), 65% of newborns were circumcised in 1999, and the overall proportion of newborns circumcised was stable from 1979 through 1999. In 2007, the NHDS found that 55% of male infants were circumcised. Notably, the proportion of black newborns circumcised increased during this reporting period (58% to 64%); the proportion of white newborns circumcised remained stable (66%). In addition, the proportion of newborns in the Midwest who were circumcised increased during the 20-year period—from 74% in 1979 to 81% in 1999—while the proportion of infants born in the West who were circumcised decreased from 64% in 1979 to 37% in 1999. In another survey, the National Inpatient Sample (NIS), circumcision rates increased from 48% during 1988–1991 to 61% during 1997–2000 but declined to 56% in 2008. Circumcision was more common among newborns who were born to families of higher socioeconomic status, born in the Northeast or Midwest, and who were black.

In 1999, the American Academy of Pediatrics (AAP) changed from a neutral stance on circumcision to a position that the data then available were insufficient to recommend routine neonatal male circumcision.

The Academy also stated, "It is legitimate for the parents to take into account cultural, religious, and ethnic traditions, in addition to medical factors, when making this choice." This position was reaffirmed by the Academy in 2005. AAP is currently reviewing their policy in light of new data. Medicaid does not reimburse the costs of neonatal male circumcision in all states, which poses a barrier to male circumcision for individuals without private insurance. In a recent study conducted in 37 states in which the NIS is conducted, hospitals in states where Medicaid covers routine male circumcision had 24% higher circumcision rates than hospitals in states without such coverage.

Cost-Effectiveness and Ethical Issues for Neonatal Circumcision in the United States

A large, retrospective study of circumcision in nearly 15,000 infants found neonatal circumcision to be highly cost-effective, considering the estimated number of averted cases of infant urinary tract infection and lifetime incidence of HIV infection, penile cancer, balanoposthitis (inflammation of the foreskin and glans), and phimosis (a condition where the male foreskin cannot be fully retracted from the head of the penis). The cost of postneonatal circumcision was 10-fold the cost of neonatal circumcision. There are also studies showing very marginal cost-effectiveness.

A 2010 study estimated that newborn circumcision reduces a U.S. male's lifetime risk of HIV acquisition through heterosexual contact by 15.7% overall, by 20.9% for black males, 12.3% for Hispanic males, and 7.9% for white males. In this model, the number of circumcisions needed to prevent one case of HIV was 298 for all males and ranged from 65 for black males to 1,231 for white males. Based on these estimates, the study concluded that newborn male circumcision was a cost-saving HIV prevention intervention.

Little has been published on the cost-effectiveness of adult circumcision among MSM. A study in Australia found that although a relatively small percentage of HIV infections would be prevented, adult circumcision of MSM could be cost effective or cost saving in some scenarios.

Many parents now make decisions about infant circumcision based on cultural, religious, or parental desires, rather than health concerns. Some have raised ethical objections to parents making decisions about elective surgery on behalf of an infant, particularly when it is done primarily to protect against risks of HIV and STDs that do not occur until young adulthood. But other ethicists have found it an appropriate parental proxy decision.

Considerations for the United States

A number of important differences from sub-Saharan African settings where the three male circumcision trials were conducted must be considered in determining the possible role for male circumcision in HIV prevention in the United States. Notably, the overall risk of HIV infection is considerably lower in the United States, changing risk-benefit and cost-effectiveness considerations. Also, studies to date have demonstrated efficacy only for penile-vaginal sex, the predominant mode of HIV transmission in Africa, whereas the predominant mode of sexual HIV transmission in the United States is by penile-anal sex among MSM. There are as yet no convincing data to help determine whether male circumcision will have any effect on HIV risk for men who engage in anal sex with either a female or male partner, as either the insertive or receptive partner. Receptive anal sex is associated with a substantially greater risk of HIV acquisition than is insertive anal sex. It is more biologically plausible that male circumcision would reduce HIV acquisition risk for the insertive partner rather than for the receptive partner, but relatively few MSM engage solely in insertive anal sex.

In addition, although the prevalence of circumcision may be somewhat lower in U.S. racial and ethnic groups with higher rates of HIV infection, most American men are already circumcised; and it is not known whether men at higher risk for HIV infection would be willing to be circumcised or whether parents would be willing to have their infants circumcised to reduce possible future HIV infection risk.

Section 9.3

Protecting Our Blood Supply

This section includes excerpts from "Blood Safety," Centers for Disease Control and Prevention (CDC), January 31, 2013.

Blood Safety Basics

Overview

The CDC is one of the federal agencies responsible for assuring the safety of the U.S. blood supply by protecting health through investigations and surveillance. The U.S. Food and Drug Administration (FDA) is responsible for regulating how blood donations are collected and blood is transfused. Research on blood transfusion basic science, epidemiology, and clinical practices are carried out by the National Institutes of Health (NIH). Keeping the U.S. blood supply safe is also the responsibility of the blood centers and hospitals that collect and transfuse millions of units of blood each year.

Key Facts

- Each day life-saving blood transfusions are needed in hospitals and emergency treatment facilities across the U.S.

- There are more than 9.5 million blood donors in the United States and an estimated 5 million patients who receive blood annually, resulting in a total of 14.6 million transfusions per year.

- Most patients do not experience any side effects from blood transfusions. On rare occasions, blood transfusions can cause adverse reactions in the patients receiving blood.

- Although the U.S. blood supply is safer than ever before, some bacteria, viruses, prions, and parasites can be transmitted by blood transfusions.

- Each donor is screened for risk of transmissible disease by questionnaire, and each unit of blood donated in the U.S. is routinely screened for various infectious disease pathogens, including five transfusion–transmitted viruses, using nine laboratory tests.

Screening Donated Blood

Blood donors are asked a set of standard questions just before they donate blood to assist in determining if they are in good health and free of any diseases that could be transmitted by blood transfusion. If the donor's answers indicate they are not well or are at risk for having a disease transmissible by blood transfusion, they are not allowed to donate blood.

If the donor is eligible to donate, the donated blood is tested for blood type (ABO group) and Rh type (positive or negative). This is to make sure that patients receive blood that matches their blood type. Before transfusion, the blood is also tested for certain proteins (antibodies) that may cause problems in a person receiving a blood transfusion.

Table 9.1. Tests Used to Screen Donated Blood

Infectious Disease Pathogen	Laboratory Tests Used
Bacterial Contamination	Bacterial culture
Hepatitis B virus (HBV)	Hepatitis B surface antigen (HBsAg) detection Hepatitis B core antibody (anti-HBc) detection
Hepatitis C virus (HCV)	Hepatitis C virus antibody (anti-HCV) detection Nucleic acid amplification testing (NAT) for HCV
Human Immunodeficiency virus Types 1 and 2 (HIV)	HIV-1 and HIV-2 antibody (anti-HIV-1 and anti-HIV-2) detection Nucleic acid amplification testing (NAT) for HIV-1
Human T-Lymphotropic Virus Types I and II (HTLV)	HTLV-I and HTLV-II antibody (anti-HTLV-I and anti-HTLV-II) detection
Treponema pallidum (syphilis)	Anti-treponemal antibody detection
West Nile virus (WNV)	Nucleic acid amplification testing (NAT) for WNV

Table 9.2. Screening Donated Blood for special needs patients

The following tests are not required for all transfusions but are often performed by blood centers or for special needs patients	
Trypanosoma cruzi (Chagas disease)	*T. cruzi antibody detection*
Cytomegalovirus (CMV)	CMV antibody detection

All blood is tested for evidence of certain infectious disease pathogens, such as hepatitis B and C viruses and human immunodeficiency virus (HIV). The tests used to screen donated blood are listed below.

Adverse Reactions Associated with Blood Transfusions

The chance of having a reaction to a blood transfusion is very small. The most common adverse reactions from blood transfusions are allergic and febrile (fever-associated) reactions, which make up over half of all adverse reactions reported. Rare but serious adverse reactions include infection caused by bacterial contamination of blood products and immune reactions due to problems in blood type matching between donor and recipient.

The following is a list of blood transfusion-associated adverse reactions that are tracked through the National Healthcare Safety

Network (NHSN) Hemovigilance Module. These adverse reactions are not common following blood transfusions but are tracked so that CDC can better understand them and develop interventions to prevent them.

- **Allergic reaction**

An allergic reaction results from an interaction of an allergen in the transfused blood with preformed antibodies in the person receiving the blood transfusion. In some instances, infusion of antibodies from the donor may be involved. The reaction may present only with irritation of the skin and/or mucous membranes but can also involve serious symptoms such as difficulty breathing.

- **Acute hemolytic transfusion reaction (AHTR)**

An acute hemolytic transfusion reaction is the rapid destruction of red blood cells that occurs during, immediately after, or within 24 hours of a transfusion when a patient is given an incompatible blood type. The recipient's body immediately begins to destroy the donated red blood cells resulting in fever, pain, and sometimes severe complications such as kidney failure.

- **Delayed hemolytic transfusion reaction (DHTR)**

A delayed hemolytic transfusion reaction occurs when the recipient develops antibodies to red blood cell antigen(s) between 24 hours and 28 days after a transfusion. Symptoms are usually milder than in acute hemolytic transfusion reactions and may even be absent. DHTR is diagnosed with laboratory testing.

- **Delayed serologic transfusion reaction (DSTR)**

A delayed serologic transfusion reaction occurs when a recipient develops new antibodies against red blood cells between 24 hours and 28 days after a transfusion without clinical symptoms or laboratory evidence of hemolysis. Clinical symptoms are rarely associated with DSTR

- **Febrile non-hemolytic transfusion reaction (FNHTR)**

Febrile non-hemolytic transfusion reactions are the most common reaction reported after a transfusion. FNHTR is characterized by fever and/or chills in the absence of hemolysis (breakdown of red blood cells) occurring in the patient during or up to 4 hours after a transfusion. These reactions are generally mild and respond quickly to treatment. Fever can be a symptom of a more severe reaction with more serious causes, and should be fully investigated.

- **Hypotensive transfusion reaction**

A hypotensive transfusion reaction is a drop in systolic blood pressure occurring soon after a transfusion begins that responds quickly to cessation of the transfusion and supportive treatment. Hypotension also can be a symptom of a more severe reaction and should be fully investigated.

- **Post-transfusion purpura (PTP)**

Post-transfusion purpura is a rare but potentially fatal condition that occurs when a transfusion recipient develops antibodies against platelets, resulting in rapid destruction of both transfused and the patient's own platelets and a severe decline in the platelet count. PTP usually occurs 5-12 days after a transfusion and is more common in women than in men.

- **Transfusion-associated circulatory overload (TACO)**

Transfusion-associated circulatory overload occurs when the volume of blood or blood components are transfused cannot be effectively processed by the recipient. TACO can occur due to an excessively high infusion rate and/or volume or due to an underlying heart or kidney condition. Symptoms may include difficulty breathing, cough, and fluid in the lungs.

- **Transfusion-related acute lung injury (TRALI)**

Transfusion-related acute lung injury is a serious but rare reaction that occurs when fluid builds up in the lungs, but is not related to excessive volume of blood or blood products transfused. Symptoms include acute respiratory distress with no other explanation for lung injury such as pneumonia or trauma occurring within 6 hours of transfusion. TRALI is a leading cause of transfusion-related death reported to the FDA. The mechanism of TRALI is not well understood, but is thought to be associated with the presence of antibodies in donor blood.

- **Transfusion-associated dyspnea (TAD)**

Transfusion associated dyspnea is the onset of respiratory distress within 24 hours of transfusion that cannot be defined as TACO, TRALI, or an allergic reaction.

- **Transfusion-associated graft vs. host disease (TAGVHD)**

Transfusion-associated graft vs. host disease is a rare complication of transfusion that occurs when donor T-lymphocytes (the "graft") introduced by the blood transfusion rapidly increase in number in the recipient (the "host") and then attack the recipient's own cells. Symptoms include fever, a characteristic rash, enlargement of the liver, and diarrhea that occur between 2 days and 6 weeks post transfusion. Though very rare, this inflammatory response is difficult to treat and often results in death.

- **Transfusion-transmitted infection (TTI)**

A transfusion-transmitted infection occurs when a bacterium, parasite, virus, or other potential pathogen is transmitted in donated blood to the transfusion recipient.

Section 9.4

Syringe Exchange Programs

Text in this section is excerpted from "Access to Sterile Syringes," Centers for Disease Control and Prevention (CDC), May 4, 2015.

Access to Sterile Syringes

Persons who inject drugs (PWID) can substantially reduce their risk of acquiring and transmitting HIV and other blood borne viral infections by using a sterile needle and syringe for every injection. PWID can access sterile needles and syringes through syringe services programs (SSPs), pharmacies, physician prescription and health care services, though the latter two are rare. SSPs are also sometimes referred to as Syringe Exchange Programs (SEPs).

SSPs are community-based programs that provide access to sterile needles and syringes free of cost and facilitate safe disposal of used needles and syringes. SSPs are an effective component of a comprehensive approach to HIV prevention among PWID and their sex partners, and most SSPs offer other prevention materials (e.g., alcohol swabs, vials of sterile water, condoms) and services, including education on safe injection practices, counseling and testing for HIV and hepatitis C infections, and screening for other sexually transmitted infections. Many SSPs also provide linkage to critical services and programs, thus promoting integration among drug treatment programs, HIV care and treatment services, hepatitis C treatment programs, and other medical, social and mental health services.

In many states pharmacies sell needle and syringes without requiring a prescription and many also have provisions for collecting used syringes, including kiosks and drop boxes.

The Syringe Services Program (SSP) Development and Implementation Guidelines for State and Local Health Departments are guidelines for organizations that wish to support syringe service programs to PWID, including SSPs and pharmacy sales, to prevent transmission of HIV and other blood borne viral infections and to link PWID to vital prevention, medical and social services.

PWID who continue to inject drugs and do not have access to sterile needles and syringes for every injection may consider disinfecting syringes with bleach or other agents to reduce the risk of transmission of HIV and other blood borne viral infections, including hepatitis C. However, disinfection does not sterilize the syringe and the syringe may still carry infectious organisms after disinfection. Therefore, disinfection should be only used if PWID have no other safe options for preventing transmission.

Federal Funding for Syringe Services Programs

Pursuant to 2012 Consolidated Appropriations Act, using federal funds for the distribution of needles or syringes for the hypodermic injection of any illegal drug is prohibited. Specifically, the following activities are no longer permitted with federal funds:

- Human resources used specifically to distribute needles or syringes

- Delivery modes, e.g., vehicles or rent for fixed sites used specifically for distributing needles or syringes

- Purchases of needles or syringes

Chapter 10

Preventing Mother-to-Child Transmission of HIV

Preventing Mother-to-Child Transmission of HIV During Childbirth

- Pregnant women with HIV receive HIV medicines during childbirth (also called labor and delivery) to reduce the risk of mother-to-child transmission of HIV.
- Recommendations on the use of HIV medicines during childbirth consider whether a woman is already taking HIV medicines when she goes into labor and the level of HIV in her blood (HIV viral load).
- Women who are already taking HIV medicines should continue taking their HIV medicines as much as possible during childbirth. Women who have a high or unknown

This chapter includes with excerpts from "Preventing Mother-to-Child Transmission of HIV During Childbirth," *AIDSinfo*, August 17, 2015; and text from "Preventing Mother-to-Child Transmission of HIV After Birth," *AIDSinfo*, August 17, 2015.

HIV viral load near the time of delivery should receive zidovudine (brand name: Retrovir) by intravenous (IV) injection.

- A scheduled cesarean delivery (sometimes called a C-section) at 38 weeks of pregnancy (2 weeks before a woman's expected due date) to reduce the risk of mother-to-child transmission of HIV is recommended for women with a high or unknown HIV viral load near the time of delivery.

Childbirth (also called labor and delivery) is the process of giving birth. A pregnant woman with HIV can pass HIV to her baby at any time during pregnancy, including during childbirth. The risk of mother-to-child transmission of HIV is greatest during delivery when a baby passes through the birth canal and is exposed to any HIV in an HIV-infected mother's blood or other fluids.

How is the risk of mother-to-child transmission of HIV reduced during childbirth?

During childbirth, women with HIV receive HIV medicines to prevent mother-to-child transmission of HIV.

In some situations, a pregnant woman with HIV may have a scheduled cesarean delivery (sometimes called a C-section) at 38 weeks of pregnancy (2 weeks before a woman's expected due date) to reduce the risk of mother-to-child transmission of HIV. A scheduled cesarean delivery is planned ahead of time.

All decisions regarding the use of HIV medicines during childbirth and the choice of a cesarean delivery to prevent mother-to-child transmission of HIV are made jointly by a woman and her health care providers.

Which HIV medicines do women with HIV receive during childbirth?

The choice of HIV medicines to use during childbirth depends on a woman's individual situation. Recommendations on medicines to use consider whether a woman is already taking HIV medicines and the level of HIV in her blood (HIV viral load).

Women who are already taking HIV medicines when they go into labor should continue taking their HIV medicines as much as possible during childbirth. Women who have a high or unknown viral load near the time of delivery should also receive zidovudine (brand name: Retrovir) by intravenous (IV) injection.

Women who did not take HIV medicines during their pregnancies should also receive IV zidovudine during childbirth.

How does zidovudine prevent mother-to-child transmission of HIV during childbirth?

Zidovudine is an HIV medicine that passes easily from a pregnant woman to her unborn baby across the placenta (also called the afterbirth). Once in a baby's system, the HIV medicine protects the baby from infection with any HIV that passed from mother to child during childbirth. For this reason, the use of zidovudine during childbirth prevents mother-to-child transmission of HIV even in women with high viral loads near the time of delivery.

When is a scheduled cesarean delivery recommended to prevent mother-to-child transmission of HIV?

A scheduled cesarean delivery at 38 weeks to prevent mother-to-child transmission of HIV is recommended in the following situations:

- When a woman has a viral load greater than 1,000 copies/mL near the time of delivery
- When a woman's viral load is unknown

In these situations, a woman with HIV should have a scheduled cesarean delivery even if she took HIV medicine during pregnancy. The cesarean delivery should be performed before a woman goes into labor and before her water breaks (also called rupture of membranes).

The risk of mother-to-child transmission of HIV is low for women who take HIV medicines during pregnancy and have a viral load of less than 1,000 copies/mL near the time of delivery. In this situation, a woman with HIV should have a vaginal delivery unless there are other medical reasons for a cesarean delivery.

What happens if an HIV-infected woman goes into labor or her water breaks before her scheduled cesarean delivery?

Once a woman goes into labor or her water breaks, a cesarean delivery may not reduce the risk of mother-to-child transmission of HIV.

In this situation, the decision whether to deliver the baby by cesarean section depends on a woman's individual circumstances.

Preventing Mother-to-Child Transmission of HIV After Birth

- The use of HIV medicines and other strategies have greatly reduced the rate of mother-to-child transmission of HIV. Fewer than 200 babies with HIV are born each year in the United States.
- For 6 weeks after birth, babies born to women with HIV receive an HIV medicine called zidovudine (brand name: Retrovir). The HIV medicine protects the babies from infection with any HIV that passed from mother to child during childbirth.
- HIV testing for babies born to women with HIV is recommended at 14 to 21 days after birth, at 1 to 2 months, and again at 4 to 6 months. The test used (called a virologic HIV test) looks directly for HIV in the blood.
- Results on two virologic tests must be negative to be certain that a baby **is not infected with HIV**. The first negative result must be from a test done when a baby is 1 month or older and the second result from a test done when a baby is 4 months or older. Results on two HIV virologic tests must be positive to know for certain that a baby **is infected with HIV**.
- If testing shows that a baby has HIV, the baby is switched from zidovudine to a combination of HIV medicines. HIV medicines help children infected with HIV live healthier lives.
- Because HIV can spread in breast milk, HIV-infected women in the United States should not breastfeed their babies. In the United States, infant formula is a safe and healthy alternative to breast milk.

How many babies in the United States are born with HIV?

HIV can be passed from an HIV-infected mother to her child during pregnancy, childbirth, or breastfeeding (through breast milk). Fortunately, the use of HIV medicines and other strategies have greatly reduced the rate of mother-to-child transmission of HIV.

Fewer than 200 babies with HIV are born each year in the United States.

The risk of mother-to-child transmission of HIV is low when:

- Women with HIV receive HIV medicine during pregnancy and childbirth and, in certain situations, have a scheduled cesarean delivery (sometimes called a C-section).

- Babies born to women with HIV receive HIV medicines for 6 weeks after birth and are not breastfed.

How soon after birth do babies born to women with HIV receive HIV medicines to prevent mother-to-child transmission of HIV?

Within 6 to 12 hours after birth, babies born to women with HIV receive an HIV medicine called zidovudine (brand name: Retrovir). In general, the babies receive zidovudine for 6 weeks. In certain situations, a baby may receive other HIV medicines in addition to zidovudine. The HIV medicine protects the babies from infection with any HIV that passed from mother to child during childbirth.

Once the 6-week course of zidovudine is finished, babies born to women with HIV receive a medicine called sulfamethoxazole/trimethoprim (brand name: Bactrim). Bactrim helps prevent *Pneumocystis jiroveci* pneumonia (PCP), which is a type of pneumonia that can develop in people with HIV. If HIV testing shows that a baby is not infected with HIV, the Bactrim is stopped.

How soon after birth are babies born to women with HIV tested for HIV?

HIV testing is recommended at 14 to 21 days after birth, at 1 to 2 months, and again at 4 to 6 months. The test used (called a virologic HIV test) looks directly for HIV in the blood.

Results from at least two HIV virologic tests are needed to know whether a baby is HIV negative or HIV positive.

- **HIV-negative (not infected with HIV):**

To know for certain that a baby **is not infected with HIV**, results on two virologic tests must be negative. The first negative result must be from a test done when a baby is 1 month or older, and the second result from a test done when a baby is 4 months or older.

- **HIV-positive (infected with HIV):**

To know for certain that a baby **is infected with HIV**, results on two HIV virologic tests must be positive.

Fortunately, few babies in the United States are born with HIV because most pregnant women with HIV and their newborn babies receive HIV medicines. If testing shows that a baby is HIV positive, the baby is switched from zidovudine to a combination of HIV medicines (called antiretroviral therapy or ART). ART helps people with HIV live longer, healthier lives.

What other steps are used to protect babies from HIV?

Because HIV can spread in breast milk, women with HIV who live in the United States should not breastfeed their babies. In the United States, infant formula is a safe and healthy alternative to breast milk.

There are reports of children becoming infected with HIV by eating food that was previously chewed by a person with HIV. To be safe, babies should not be fed pre-chewed food.

Do women with HIV continue to take HIV medicines after childbirth?

Women work closely with their health care providers to decide whether to continue taking HIV medicines after childbirth. Treatment with HIV medicines is recommended for everyone infected with HIV. HIV medicines prevent HIV from advancing to AIDS and reduce the risk of sexual transmission of HIV.

A woman's decision whether to continue taking HIV medicines after childbirth depends on the following factors:

- Current recommendations for HIV treatment in adults

- The level of HIV in her body (HIV viral load)

- Any issues that may make it hard for her to take HIV medicines exactly as directed

- Whether her partner is infected with HIV

- Her personal preferences and those of her health care provider

Chapter 11

HIV/AIDS Risks and Prevention Strategies in Targeted Populations

Chapter Contents

Section 11.1

Youth

Text in this section is excerpted from "HIV Among Youth," Centers
for Disease Control and Prevention (CDC), June 30, 2015.

> • Youth aged 13 to 24 accounted for an estimated 26% of all
>   new HIV infections in the United States in 2010.
> • Most new HIV infections among youth occur among gay
>   and bisexual males; there was a 22% increase in estimated
>   new infections in this group from 2008 to 2010.
> • Over 50% of youth with HIV in the United States do not
>   know they are infected.

Youth in the United States account for a substantial number of
HIV infections. Gay, bisexual, and other men who have sex with men*
account for most new infections in the age group 13 to 24; black/African
American** or Hispanic/Latino gay and bisexual men are especially
affected. Continual HIV prevention outreach and education efforts,
including programs on abstinence, delaying the initiation of sex, and
negotiating safer sex for the spectrum of sexuality among youth—
homosexual, bisexual, heterosexual, and transgender—are urgently
needed for a new generation at risk.

Referred to as gay and bisexual in this section.

** *Referred to as black in this section.*

The Numbers

New HIV Infections (Aged 13–24)

- In 2010, youth made up 17% of the US population, but
  accounted for an estimated 26% (12,200) of all new HIV infections (47,500) in the United States.

- In 2010, young gay and bisexual men accounted for an estimated
  19% (8,800) of all new HIV infections in the United States and

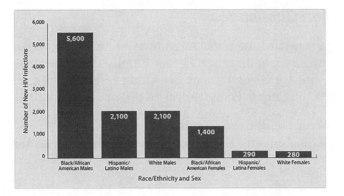

Figure 11.1. *Estimates of New Infections Among Youth Aged 13-24 Years, by Race/Ethnicity and Sex, United States 2010*

72% of new HIV infections among youth. These young men were the only age group that showed a significant increase in estimated new infections—22% from 2008 (7,200) through 2010 (8,800).

- In 2010, black youth accounted for an estimated 57% (7,000) of all new HIV infections among youth in the United States, followed by Hispanic/Latino (20%, 2,390) and white (20%, 2,380) youth.

HIV and AIDS Diagnoses and Deaths among Youth (Aged 13–24)

- An estimated 9,961 youth were diagnosed with HIV infection in the United States in 2013, representing 21% of an estimated 47,352 people diagnosed during that year. Eighty-one percent (8,053) of these diagnoses occurred in those aged 20 to 24, the highest number of HIV diagnoses of any age group.

- At the end of 2012, there were an estimated 62,400 youth living with HIV in the United States. Of these, 32,000 were living with undiagnosed HIV infection.

- In 2013, an estimated 2,704 youth were diagnosed with AIDS, representing 10% of the 26,688 people diagnosed with AIDS that year.

- In 2012, an estimated 156 youth with AIDS died, representing 1% of the 13,712 people with AIDS who died that year.

Prevention Challenges

Low perception of risk. A majority of 15- to 24-year-olds in the United States responding to a Kaiser Family Foundation survey said they were not concerned about becoming infected with HIV, which means they may not take measures to protect their health.

Declining health education. The prevalence of having been taught in school about HIV infection or AIDS decreased from 92% in 1997 to 85% in 2013.

Low rates of testing. It is estimated that in 2010, about 50% of youth aged 13 to 24 with HIV in the United States were unaware of their infection, compared to 12.8% overall. In a 2013 survey, only 13% of high school students (22% of those who had ever had sexual intercourse), and in a 2010 survey, only 35% of adults aged 18 to 24 had been tested for HIV.

Low rates of condom use. In a 2013 survey in the United States, of the 34% of high school students reporting sexual intercourse in the previous 3 months, 41% did not use a condom.

High rates of sexually transmitted diseases (STDs). Some of the highest STD rates in the United States are among youth aged 20 to 24, especially those of minority races and ethnicities. The presence of an STD greatly increases a person's likelihood of acquiring or transmitting HIV.

Older partners. Young gay and bisexual men are more likely to choose older sex partners than those of their own age, and older partners are more likely to be infected with HIV.

Substance use. Nearly half (47%) of youth aged 12 to 20 reported current alcohol use in 2011, and 10% of youth aged 12 to 17 said they were current users of illicit drugs. Among the 34% of currently sexually active students nationwide, 22% had drunk alcohol or used drugs before last sexual intercourse. Substance use has been linked to HIV infection because both casual and chronic substance users are more likely to engage in high-risk behaviors, such as sex without a condom, when they are under the influence of drugs or alcohol.

Homelessness. Runaways, homeless youth, and youth who have become dependent on drugs are at high risk for HIV infection if they exchange sex for drugs, money, or shelter.

Inadequate HIV prevention education. Young people are not always reached by effective HIV interventions or prevention education—especially young gay and bisexual men, because some sex education programs exclude information about sexual orientation.

Feelings of isolation. Gay and bisexual high school students may engage in risky sexual behaviors and substance abuse because they feel isolated and lack support.

Section 11.2

Women

This section includes excerpts from "HIV Among Women," Centers for Disease Control and Prevention (CDC), June 23, 2015; and text from "Women And HIV," AIDS.gov, February 20, 2012.

> - Approximately one in four people living with HIV infection in the United States are women.*
> - Most new HIV infections in women are from heterosexual contact (84%).
> - An estimated 88% of women who are living with HIV are diagnosed, but only 32% have the virus under control.

At the end of 2011, 23% of all people living with HIV in the United States were women. Black/African American** and Hispanic/Latina women continue to be disproportionately affected by HIV, compared with women of other races/ethnicities.

Not all US women who are living with HIV are getting the care they need. Of all women living with HIV in 2011, only 45% were engaged in care, and only 32% had achieved viral suppression.

In this section, women are defined as females aged 13 years and older.

**Referred to as African American in this section.*

The Numbers

New HIV Infections

• Women made up 20% (9,500) of the estimated 47,500 new HIV infections in the United States in 2010. Eighty-four percent of these new infections (8,000) were from heterosexual contact.

• When comparing groups by race/ethnicity, gender, and transmission category, the fourth largest number of all new HIV infections in the United States in 2010 (5,300) occurred among African American women with heterosexual contact (see bar graph). Of the total number of estimated new HIV infections among women, 64% (6,100) were in African Americans, 18% (1,700) were in whites, and 15% (1,400) were in Hispanic/Latina women.

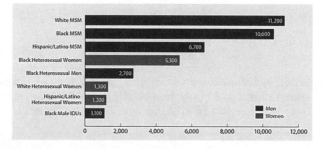

Figure 11.2. *Estimates of New HIV Infections in the United States for the Most-Affected Subpopulations, 2010.*

HIV and AIDS Diagnoses and Deaths

• In 2013, an estimated 9,278 women aged 13 years or older received a diagnosis of HIV infection in the United States (20% of the all estimated diagnoses during 2013), down from the 10,686 new diagnoses among women in 2009.

• Women accounted for 24% (6,424) of the estimated 26,680 AIDS diagnoses among adults and adolescents in 2013 and represent 24% (242,178) of the 1,184,618 cumulative AIDS diagnoses in the United States from the beginning of the epidemic through the end of 2013.

• Among women ever diagnosed with AIDS, an estimated 3,561 died during 2012, and by the end of 2012, an estimated 117,797 had died since the beginning of the epidemic.

Why Are Women Affected by HIV?

- Some women may be **unaware of their male partner's risk factors** for HIV (such as injection drug use or having sex with other men) and may not use condoms.

- The risk of getting HIV during **vaginal sex without a condom or other protection such as** PrEP is much higher for women than it is for men, and **anal sex without a condom** or PrEP is riskier for women than vaginal sex without a condom or PrEP. More than 20% of women aged 20 to 39 who responded to a national survey reported anal sex in the past year.

- Women may be afraid that their partner will leave them or even physically abuse them if they try to talk about condom use.

- Some **sexually transmitted diseases (STDs),** such as gonorrhea and syphilis, greatly increase the likelihood of getting or spreading HIV.

- Women who have been **sexually abused** may be more likely than women with no abuse history to engage in sexual behaviors like exchanging sex for drugs, having multiple partners, or having sex with a partner who is physically abusive when asked to use a condom.

- Some HIV infections among women are due to **injection drug and other substance use**—either directly (sharing drug injection equipment contaminated with HIV) or indirectly (engaging in high-risk behaviors while under the influence of drugs or alcohol).

- The greater number of **people living with HIV (prevalence)** in African American and Hispanic/Latino communities and the fact that people tend to have sex with partners of the same race/ethnicity means that women from these communities face a greater risk of HIV infection with each new sexual encounter.

HIV Care

Both women and men need similar types of HIV care, but there are some important differences:

- Women often have gynecological conditions as a result of HIV infection. These can include persistent and difficult-to-treat vaginal yeast infections, *pelvic inflammatory disease, cervical dysplasia* (abnormal cell changes in the cervix), and an increased likelihood of developing cervical cancer.

- Women may have concerns about pregnancy and childbirth — whether for a current pregnancy or for the future. It is best to talk with your provider about these concerns.

- Women who are diagnosed with HIV should have a Pap smear and a pelvic exam ASAP. They should have a follow-up *Pap smear* **6 months** later.

- Women are less likely to develop *Kaposi's Sarcoma*, a type of cancer that is a common *opportunistic infection* and an AIDS-defining condition.

- Women are often diagnosed later in the stages of HIV infection, so they can be more susceptible to opportunistic infections.

- Women often must be stronger advocates for themselves and their treatment when engaged in HIV care. Many times women face multiple barriers to care.

Section 11.3

Men Who Have Sex with Men

Text in this section is excerpted from "HIV Among Gay and Bisexual Men," Centers for Disease Control and Prevention (CDC), August 12, 2015.

- Gay and bisexual men are more severely affected by HIV than any other group in the United States.

- Among all gay and bisexual men, black/African American gay and bisexual men bear a disproportionate burden of HIV.

- From 2008 to 2010, HIV infections among young black/African American gay and bisexual men increased 20%.

Gay, bisexual, and other men who have sex with men (MSM) represent approximately 2% of the United States population, yet are the population most severely affected by HIV. In 2010, young gay and bisexual men (aged 13-24 years) accounted for 72% of new HIV infections among all persons aged 13 to 24, and 30% of new infections among all gay and bisexual men. At the end of 2011, an estimated 500,022 (57%) persons living with an HIV diagnosis in the United States were gay and bisexual men, or gay and bisexual men who also inject drugs.

The Numbers

New HIV Infections

- In 2010, gay and bisexual men accounted for 63% of estimated new HIV infections in the United States and 78% of infections among all newly infected men. From 2008 to 2010, new HIV infections increased 22% among young (aged 13-24) gay and bisexual men and 12% among gay and bisexual men overall.

- Among all gay and bisexual men, white gay and bisexual men accounted for 11,200 (38%) estimated new HIV infections in 2010. The largest number of new infections among white gay and bisexual men (3,300; 29%) occurred in those aged 25 to 34.

- Among all gay and bisexual men, black/African American gay and bisexual men accounted for 10,600 (36%) estimated new HIV infections in 2010. The largest number of new infections among black/African American gay and bisexual men (4,800; 45%) occurred in those aged 13 to 24. From 2008 to 2010 new infections increased 20% among young black/African American gay and bisexual men aged 13 to 24.

- Among all gay and bisexual men, Hispanic/Latino gay and bisexual men accounted for 6,700 (22%) estimated new HIV infections in 2010. The largest number of new infections among Hispanic/Latino gay and bisexual men (3,300; 39%) occurred in those aged 25 to 34.

HIV and AIDS Diagnoses

- In 2013, in the United States, gay and bisexual men accounted for 81% (30,689) of the 37,887 estimated HIV diagnoses among all males aged 13 years and older and 65% of the 47,352 estimated diagnoses among all persons receiving an HIV diagnosis that year.

143

- In 2013, gay and bisexual men accounted for 55% of the estimated number of persons diagnosed with AIDS among all adults and adolescents in the United States. Of the estimated 14,611 gay and bisexual men diagnosed with AIDS, 40% were blacks/African Americans; 32% were whites; and 23% were Hispanics/Latinos.

- By the end of 2011, an estimated 311,087 gay and bisexual men with AIDS had died in the United States since the beginning of the epidemic, representing 47% of all deaths of persons with AIDS.

- In 2011, CDC data showed that 80.6% of MSM with diagnosed HIV infection were linked to care, 57.5% were retained in care, 52.9% were prescribed antiretroviral therapy (ART), and 44.6% had achieved viral suppression.

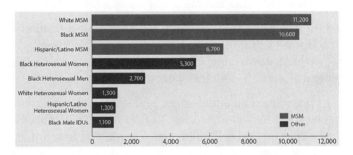

Figure 11.3. *Estimates of New HIV Infections in the United States for the Most-Affected Subpopulations, 2010*

Prevention Challenges

The **large percentage of gay and bisexual men living with HIV** means that, as a group, gay and bisexual men have an increased chance of being exposed to HIV. Results of HIV testing conducted in 20 cities as part of the National HIV Behavioral Surveillance System (NHBS) indicated that 18% of gay and bisexual men tested in 2011 had HIV and that HIV prevalence increased with increasing age.

Many gay and bisexual men with HIV are unaware they have it. Even though the NHBS study showed that the overall percentage of gay and bisexual men with HIV who knew of their HIV infection increased from 56% in 2008 to 66% in 2011, there were still many who did not know they had HIV. Among those infected, only

49% of young gay and bisexual men aged 18 to 24 years knew of their infection, whereas 76% of those aged 40 and older were aware of their HIV infection. Fifty-four percent of black/African American gay and bisexual men knew of their infection, compared with 63% of Hispanic/ Latino gay and bisexual men, and 86% of white gay and bisexual men. People who don't know they have HIV cannot get the medicines they need to stay healthy and may infect others without knowing it. The Centers for Disease Control and Prevention (CDC) recommends that all gay and bisexual men get tested for HIV at least once a year. Sexually active gay and bisexual men may benefit from more frequent testing (e.g., every 3 to 6 months).

Sexual risk behaviors account for most HIV infections in gay and bisexual men. Most gay and bisexual men acquire HIV through anal sex, which is the riskiest type of sex for getting or transmitting HIV. For sexually active gay and bisexual men, the most effective ways to prevent transmitting or becoming infected with HIV are to be on antiretroviral medications (to either treat or prevent infection) and to correctly use a condom every time for anal or vaginal sex. Gay men are at increased risk for sexually transmitted diseases (STDs), like syphilis, gonorrhea, and chlamydia, and CDC recommends that all sexually active gay and bisexual men be tested at least annually for these infections and obtain treatment, if necessary.

Having more sex partners compared to other men means gay and bisexual men have more opportunities to have sex with someone who can transmit HIV or another STD. Similarly, among gay men, those who have more partners are more likely to acquire HIV.

Homophobia, stigma, and discrimination may place gay men at risk for multiple physical and mental health problems and affect whether they seek and are able to obtain high-quality health services.

Section 11.4

Seniors

This section includes excerpts from "HIV Among People Aged 50 and Over," Centers for Disease Control and Prevention (CDC), September 16, 2015; and text from "Newly Diagnosed: Older Adults," AIDS.gov, July 10, 2015.

- Americans aged 50 and older have many of the same HIV risk factors as younger Americans.
- Persons aged 55 and older accounted for 24% (288,700) of the estimated 1.2 million people living with HIV infection in the United States in 2012.
- Older Americans are more likely than younger Americans to be diagnosed with HIV infection later in the course of their disease.

A growing number of people aged 50 and older in the United States are living with HIV infection. People aged 55 and older accounted for about one-quarter (24%, 288,700) of the estimated 1.2 million people living with HIV infection in the United States in 2012.

The Numbers

New HIV Infections (Aged 55 and Older)

- Of an estimated 47,500 new HIV infections in 2010, 5% (2,500) were among Americans aged 55 and older. Of these older Americans:

- 36% (900) of new infections were in white men, and 4% (110) were in white women;

- 24% (590) of new infections were in black men, and 15% (370) were in black women;

- 12% (310) of new infections were in Hispanic/Latino men, and 4% (100) were in Hispanic/Latino women.

- In 2010, 44% (1,100) of the estimated 2,500 new HIV infections among people aged 55 and older were among gay, bisexual, or other men who have sex with men (MSM). Among MSM aged 55 and older, white MSM accounted for an estimated 67% (740) of new HIV infections, Hispanic/Latino MSM 16% (180), and black MSM 15% (160).

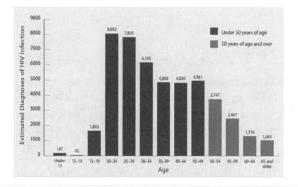

Figure 11.4. *Estimated Diagnoses of HIV Infection by Age, 2013, United States*

HIV and AIDS Diagnoses and Deaths

- In 2013, there were an estimated 8,575 new HIV diagnoses among people aged 50 and over. Most (44%, 3,747) were among those aged 50-54.

- In 2013, the estimated rate (per 100,000) of HIV diagnoses for blacks aged 50-54 was 59.3, compared to 23.3 for Hispanics/Latinos, and 8.7 for whites.

- In 2013, people aged 50 and older accounted for 27% (7,108) of the estimated 26,688 AIDS diagnoses in the United States.

- Of the estimated 13,712 deaths among people with AIDS in 2012, 8,093 (59%) were among people aged 50 and older.

Prevention Challenges

Late HIV Diagnoses and Shorter HIV-to-AIDS Intervals

Older Americans are more likely than younger Americans to be diagnosed with HIV infection late in the course of their disease, meaning a late start to treatment and possibly more damage to their immune system. This can lead to poorer prognoses and shorter survival after an HIV diagnosis. For instance, 98% of people aged 25-29 who were diagnosed with HIV infection during 2004-2009 survived more than 12 months after diagnosis, compared with an estimated 86% of people aged 50 to 59, 82% of people aged 60-64, and 73% of people aged 65 and older. Late diagnoses can occur because health care providers may not always test older people for HIV infection, and older people may mistake HIV symptoms for those of normal aging and don't consider HIV as a cause.

Sexual Risk Factors

Many older Americans are sexually active, including those who are infected with HIV, and have many of the same risk factors for HIV infection as younger Americans, including a lack of knowledge about HIV and how to prevent transmission, and multiple partners. Older people also face unique issues, including:

- Many widowed and divorced people are dating again, and they may be less knowledgeable about HIV than younger people, and less likely to protect themselves.

- Women who no longer worry about getting pregnant may be less likely to use a condom and to practice safer sex. Age-related thinning and dryness of vaginal tissue may raise older women's risk for HIV infection.

- The availability of erectile dysfunction medications may facilitate sex for older men who otherwise would not have been capable of vaginal or anal intercourse.

- Although they visit their doctors more frequently, older Americans are less likely than younger Americans to discuss their sexual habits or drug use with their doctors, who in turn may be less likely to ask their older patients about these issues.

Stigma

Stigma is a particular concern among older Americans because they may already face isolation due to illness or loss of family and friends. Stigma negatively affects people's quality of life, self-image, and behaviors and may prevent them from seeking HIV care and disclosing their HIV status.

First Things First

If you have just been diagnosed with HIV, it's important to **find an HIV care provider, even if you don't feel sick**. Your HIV care provider will be the person who partners with you to manage your HIV. He or she will monitor your health on an ongoing basis and work with you to develop a treatment plan.

It's never too early to start treatment. Current guidelines recommend treatment with ART for all people with HIV, including those over 50 years old or those with early infection. If you don't have a regular doctor, your HIV testing location or your local health department can help you find an HIV care provider.

You should also learn about the steps you can to avoid transmitting HIV to anyone else.

Section 11.5

Prisoners

Text in this section is excerpted from "HIV Among Incarcerated Populations," Centers for Disease Control and Prevention (CDC), July 22, 2015

- HIV is a serious health issue for correctional facilities and their incarcerated populations.
- Most incarcerated people with HIV got the virus before entering a correctional facility.
- HIV testing at a correctional facility may be the first time incarcerated people are tested and diagnosed with HIV.

More than 2 million people in the United States are incarcerated in federal, state, and local correctional facilities on any given day. In 2010, the rate of diagnosed HIV infection among inmates in state and federal prisons was more than five times greater than the rate among people who were not incarcerated. Most inmates with HIV acquire it in their communities, before they are incarcerated.

The Numbers

- In 2012, 1.57 million people were incarcerated in state and federal prisons and at midyear 2013 there were 731,208 people detained in local jails.

- In 2010, there were 20,093 inmates with HIV/AIDS in state and federal prisons with 91% being men.

- Among state and federal jurisdictions reporting in 2010 there were 3,913 inmates living with an AIDS diagnosis.

- Rates of AIDS-related deaths among state and federal prisoners declined an average of 16% per year between 2001 and 2010, from 24 deaths/100,000 in 2001 to 5/100,000 in 2010.

- Among jail populations, African American men are 5 times as likely as white men, and twice as likely as Hispanic/Latino men, to be diagnosed with HIV.

- Among jail populations, African American women are more than twice as likely to be diagnosed with HIV as white or Hispanic/Latino women.

Prevention Challenges

- Lack of awareness about HIV and lack of resources for HIV testing and treatment in inmates' home communities. Most inmates with HIV become infected in their communities, where they may engage in high-risk behaviors or be unaware of available prevention and treatment resources.

- Lack of resources for HIV testing and treatment in correctional facilities. Prison and jail administrators must weigh the costs of HIV testing and treatment against other needs, and some correctional systems may not provide such services. HIV testing can identify inmates with HIV before they are released. Early diagnosis and treatment can potentially reduce the level of HIV in communities to which inmates return.

- Rapid turnover among jail populations. While most HIV programs in correctional facilities are in prisons, most incarcerated people are detained in jails. Nine out of ten jail inmates are released in under 72 hours, which makes it hard to test them for HIV and help them find treatment.

- Inmate concerns about privacy and fear of stigma. Many inmates do not disclose their high-risk behaviors, such as anal sex or injection drug use, because they fear being stigmatized. Health care providers should keep inmate's health care information confidential, know the public health confidentiality and reporting laws, and inform inmates about them.

Chapter 12

HIV Vaccines and Medications

Chapter Contents

Section 12.1

Preventive Vaccines

Text in this section is excerpted from "Vaccines," AIDS.gov, May 12, 2014.

Figure 12.1. *Preventive Vaccines*

What Are Vaccines and What Do They Do?

A vaccine—also called a "shot" or "immunization"—is a substance that teaches your body's immune system to recognize and defend against harmful viruses or bacteria **before** you get infected. These are called "preventive vaccines" or "prophylactic vaccines," and you get them while you are healthy. This allows your body to set up defenses against those dangers ahead of time. That way, you won't get sick if you're exposed to them later. Preventive vaccines are widely used to prevent diseases like polio, chicken pox, measles, mumps, rubella, influenza (flu), and hepatitis A and B.

In addition to preventive vaccines, there are also therapeutic vaccines. These are vaccines that are designed to treat people who already have a disease. Some scientists prefer to refer to therapeutic vaccines as "therapeutic immunogens." Currently, there is only one FDA-approved therapeutic vaccine for advanced prostate cancer in men.

Is There a Vaccine for HIV?

No. There is currently no vaccine that will prevent HIV infection or treat those who have it.

Why Do We Need an HIV Vaccine?

Today, more people living with HIV have access to life-saving *antiretroviral therapy* (ART) than ever before, which is good for their health and reduces the likelihood that they will transmit the virus to others if they adhere to their HIV medication. In addition, others who are at high risk for HIV infection have access to Pre-exposure Prophylaxis (PrEP), or ART being used to prevent HIV. Yet, unfortunately, approximately 50,000 Americans and 2.3 million people worldwide still become newly HIV-infected each year. To control and ultimately end HIV globally, we need a powerful array of HIV prevention tools that are widely accessible to all who would benefit from them.

Vaccines historically have been the most effective means to prevent and even eradicate infectious diseases. They safely and cost-effectively prevent illness, disability and death. Like smallpox and polio vaccines, a preventive HIV vaccine could help save millions of lives. **Developing safe, effective and affordable vaccines that can prevent HIV infection in uninfected people is the best hope for controlling and/or ending the HIV epidemic.**

The long-term goal is to develop a safe and effective vaccine that protects people worldwide from getting infected with HIV. However, even if a vaccine only protects some people, it could still have a major impact on the rates of transmission and help control the epidemic, particularly for populations where there is a high rate of HIV transmission. A partially effective vaccine could decrease the number of people who get infected with HIV, further reducing the number of people who can pass the virus on to others.

A therapeutic immunogen could also be beneficial for people living with HIV by helping slow the progression of the disease and prevent or delay the onset of AIDS.

Why Don't We Have an HIV Vaccine Yet?

HIV is a very complex, highly changeable virus, which makes speedy development of a successful preventive HIV vaccine very difficult, but not impossible. It also takes many years to conduct the research, including the careful clinical testing that will lead to a safe and effective vaccine.

Researchers from around the world have been working for more than two decades to create a vaccine that will protect people against HIV infection. NIAID supports the HIV Vaccine Trials Network (HVTN), an international collaboration of scientists and educators searching for an effective and safe HIV vaccine. The U.S. Military HIV

Research Program (MHRP) is also engaged in HIV vaccine research and led a large collaboration of clinical scientists also funded by NIAID in implementing a vaccine trial that showed for the first time that an HIV vaccine is possible.

How Is HIV Different from Other Viruses?

In part, HIV is different from other viruses because your immune system never fully gets rid of it. Most people who are infected with a virus recover from the infection, and their immune systems "clear" the virus from their bodies. This is true even for viruses that can be deadly, like influenza.

Once your body has cleared a particular virus, you often develop *immunity* to it—meaning it won't make you sick the next time you are exposed to it. We've known since the late 1700s that you can create immunity by exposing people to dead or weakened viruses that will protect them from deadly diseases later.

But the human body can't seem to fully clear HIV and develop immunity to it. The antibodies your immune system makes to fight HIV are not effective—and HIV actually targets, invades, and then destroys some of the most important cells in your immune system itself. This means that, over time, HIV does serious damage to your body's ability to fight disease.

So far, no person with an established HIV infection has managed to clear the virus naturally. This has made it more difficult to develop a preventive HIV vaccine.

What's the Latest on HIV Vaccine Research?

Scientists are continuing to create and test HIV vaccines—in the lab, in animals, and even in human subjects. These vaccine *trials* help researchers to learn whether a vaccine will work and if it can be safely given to people.

In 2009, MHRP and collaborating researchers published findings from a large-scale HIV vaccine trial in Thailand called RV144. That trial involved more than 16,000 adults and showed that a combination vaccine was safe and could prevent about 32 percent of new infections. The scientific community, with leadership from NIAID, is working collaboratively to build on what was learned from RV144 in order to help speed the process of finding an HIV vaccine. Those efforts have provided information that certain antibodies (proteins produced by the body to fight infection) may serve either as a signal or provide a direct role to decreasing the risk of becoming HIV infected. This has led to a better understanding of the type of immune response that may be needed for a preventive HIV vaccine to be effective.

NIAID is also studying other vaccine approaches and several other NIAID-sponsored clinical trials are ongoing.

How can I participate in an HIV vaccine trial?

For more information about HIV vaccines and how you can get involved in HIV vaccine trials, check out Be The Generation. For information about specific HIV vaccine trials, go to the HVTN website at www.HVTN.org or www.AIDSinfo.nih.gov, which has information about all HIV trials.

Can I get HIV from participating in a vaccine clinical trial?

No. You can't get HIV infection from participating in a vaccine trial because the vaccines being tested do not contain the virus itself.

Section 12.2

Microbicides

Text in this section is excerpted from "Microbicides," AIDS.gov, February 27, 2012.

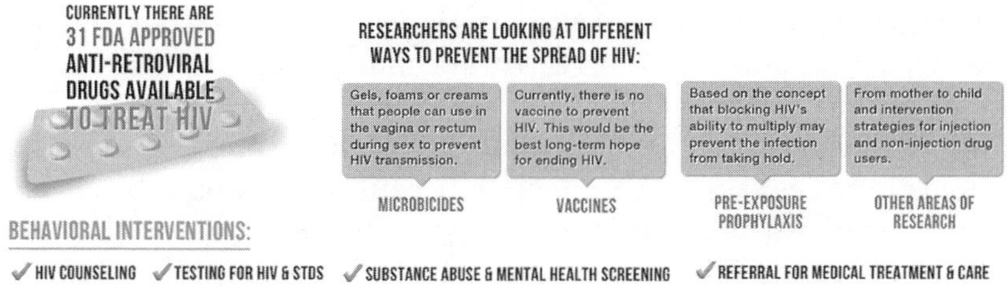

CURRENTLY THERE ARE 31 FDA APPROVED ANTI-RETROVIRAL DRUGS AVAILABLE TO TREAT HIV

RESEARCHERS ARE LOOKING AT DIFFERENT WAYS TO PREVENT THE SPREAD OF HIV:

MICROBICIDES — Gels, foams or creams that people can use in the vagina or rectum during sex to prevent HIV transmission.

VACCINES — Currently, there is no vaccine to prevent HIV. This would be the best long-term hope for ending HIV.

PRE-EXPOSURE PROPHYLAXIS — Based on the concept that blocking HIV's ability to multiply may prevent the infection from taking hold.

OTHER AREAS OF RESEARCH — From mother to child and intervention strategies for injection and non-injection drug users.

BEHAVIORAL INTERVENTIONS:
✓ HIV COUNSELING ✓ TESTING FOR HIV & STDS ✓ SUBSTANCE ABUSE & MENTAL HEALTH SCREENING ✓ REFERRAL FOR MEDICAL TREATMENT & CARE

Figure 12.2. *Treating HIV*

157

What Are Microbicides?

Microbicides are gels, films, or *suppositories* that can kill or neutralize viruses and bacteria. Researchers are studying both *vaginal* and *rectal* microbicides to see if they can prevent sexual transmission of HIV. A safe, effective, and affordable microbicide against HIV could help to prevent many new infections.

Can Microbicides Prevent HIV Infection?

The answer to this question now appears to be "Yes"—though more studies are needed to be sure.

In July, 2010, researchers attending the 2010 International AIDS Conference in Vienna, Austria announced exciting news about the CAPRISA 004 Microbicide Study. In that study, researchers put an *antiretroviral* drug into a vaginal microbicide gel and told the women participating in the trial to use the gel before and after sex to protect against HIV transmission.

The study results found that, overall, the gel was 39% effective in reducing the women's risk of becoming infected with HIV during sex. The more frequently the women used the gel as intended, the more effective it was in protecting them from HIV infection.

The gel was also 51% effective in preventing genital herpes infections. Since having a sexually transmitted infection like herpes increases your risk of contracting HIV, this is another important result.

If other studies of microbicide gels confirm these results and the microbicides are approved for licensure by the appropriate regulatory agency and made available, microbicides could prevent millions of new HIV infections over the next decade.

Why Are Microbicides so Important?

HIV is spread predominantly through sexual transmission. Right now, the best HIV prevention options for sexually active people are being mutually *monogamous* with an HIV-negative partner and using condoms consistently and correctly. For many people, however, these options are not possible.

It is believed that topical microbicides might be more effective than condoms in preventing HIV infection because they would be easier to use and women would not have to negotiate their use, as they often must do with condoms. Worldwide half of the people living with HIV are women. So, public health professionals are particularly interested in developing microbicides for women who aren't able to get their male sex partners to use condoms. Microbicides would make it possible for a woman to protect herself and her partner from HIV without his cooperation or knowledge—a particularly important factor for commercial sex workers (prostitutes) or women in abusive relationships.

Microbicides might also make it possible someday for women to protect themselves from HIV while still allowing them to get pregnant if they wish.

Can I Use a Microbicide to Protect Myself from HIV Infection?

Not yet. The Centre for the Aids Programme of Research in South Africa (CAPRISA) study results are exciting—but even if those results are duplicated in other *clinical trials*, it will probably be several years before microbicides are available to the public. Researchers will have to be sure that the product is both effective in preventing HIV infection and safe for people to use.

For now, the best forms of protection against sexual transmission of HIV continue to be:

- Being mutually monogamous with an HIV-negative partner

- HIV testing—so that you know your own HIV status and your partner's too

- Using condoms consistently and correctly

Chapter 13

HIV Prophylaxis

Chapter Contents

Section 13.1

Pre-Exposure Prophylaxis

Text in this section is excerpted from "HIV Basics—PrEP," Centers for Disease Control and Prevention (CDC), March 24, 2015.

PrEP IS A NEW HIV PREVENTION METHOD IN WHICH PEOPLE WHO DO NOT HAVE HIV INFECTION TAKE A PILL DAILY TO REDUCE THEIR RISK OF BECOMING INFECTED.

ONLY PEOPLE WHO ARE HIV-NEGATIVE SHOULD USE PrEP. AN HIV TEST IS REQUIRED BEFORE STARTING PrEP AND THEN EVERY 3 MONTHS WHILE TAKING PrEP.

PrEP CAN ONLY BE PRESCRIBED BY A HEALTH CARE PROVIDER AND MUST BE TAKEN AS DIRECTED TO WORK.

Figure 13.1. *Pre-exposure prophylaxis (PrEP)*

PrEP

Pre-exposure prophylaxis, or PrEP, is a prevention option for people who are at high risk of getting HIV. It's meant to be used consistently, as a pill taken every day, and to be used with other prevention options such as condoms. Find out if PrEP is right for you.

What Is PrEP?

"PrEP" stands for **Pre-Exposure Prophylaxis**. The word "prophylaxis" means to prevent or control the spread of an infection or disease. The goal of PrEP is to prevent HIV infection from taking hold if you are exposed to the virus. This is done by taking one pill every day. These are some of the same medicines used to keep the virus under control in people who are already living with HIV.

Why Take PrEP?

With 50,000 new HIV infections each year in the United States, and no cure or vaccine available, prevention is key. When taken every day, PrEP can provide a high level of protection against HIV, and is even more effective when it is combined with condoms and other prevention tools.

Is PrEP a Vaccine?

No. PrEP medicine is not injected into the body and does not work the same way as a vaccine. A vaccine teaches your body to fight off infection for several years. For PrEP, you take a pill every day by mouth. The pill that was shown to be safe and to help block HIV infection is called "Truvada". Truvada is a combination of two drugs (tenofovir and emtricitabine). If you take PrEP daily, the presence of the medicine in your bloodstream can often stop HIV from taking hold and spreading in your body. If you do not take PrEP every day, there may not be enough medicine in your bloodstream to block the virus.

Should I Consider Taking PrEP?

CDC recommends that PrEP be considered for people who are HIV-negative and at substantial risk for HIV.

For sexual transmission, this includes anyone who is in an ongoing relationship with an HIV-positive partner. It also includes anyone who 1) is not in a mutually monogamous* relationship with a partner who recently tested HIV-negative, and 2) is a

- gay or bisexual man who has had anal sex without a condom or been diagnosed with an STD in the past 6 months; or

- heterosexual man or woman who does not regularly use condoms during sex with partners of unknown HIV status who are at substantial risk of HIV infection (e.g., people who inject drugs or have bisexual male partners).

For people who inject drugs, this includes those who have injected illicit drugs in the past 6 months and who have shared injection equipment or been in drug treatment for injection drug use in the past 6 months.

For heterosexual couples where one partner has HIV and the other does not, PrEP is one of several options to protect the uninfected partner during conception and pregnancy.

*Mutually monogamous means that you and your partner only have sex with each other and do not have sex outside the relationship.

People who use PrEP must be able to take the drug every day and to return to their health care provider every 3 months for a repeat HIV test, prescription refills, and follow-up.

How Well Does PrEP Work?

In several studies of PrEP, the risk of getting HIV infection was much lower—up to 92% lower—for **those who took the medicines consistently** than for those who didn't take the medicines.

Is PrEP Safe?

Some people in clinical studies of PrEP had early side effects such as an upset stomach or loss of appetite, but these were mild and usually went away in the first month. Some people also had a mild headache. No serious side effects were observed. You should tell your health care provider if these or other symptoms become severe or do not go away.

How Can I Start PrEP?

If you think you may be at substantial risk for HIV (see "Should I consider taking PrEP"), talk to your health care provider about PrEP. If you and your provider agree that PrEP might reduce your risk of getting HIV, he or she will conduct a general physical and test you for HIV and other sexually transmitted diseases. Your blood will also be tested to see if your kidneys and liver are working well. If these tests show that PrEP medicines are likely to be safe for you to take, your provider may give you a prescription. If you do not have health insurance, your provider can talk to you about medication assistance programs that help pay for PrEP for some patients.

If you do take PrEP, you will need to follow up regularly with your health care provider. You will have blood tests for HIV infection and to see if your body is reacting well to Truvada. You will also receive counseling on sexual or injection drug use behaviors.

It is important to take your medicine every day as prescribed. You will receive advice about ways to help you take it regularly so that it has the best chance to help you avoid HIV infection. Tell your provider if you are having trouble remembering to take your medicine or if you want to stop PrEP.

How Can I Get Help to Pay for PrEP?

PrEP is covered by most insurance programs, but if you do not have insurance, your health care provider can talk to you about medication assistance programs that help pay for PrEP medicine.

If I Take PrEP, Can I Stop Using Condoms When I Have Sex?

No, you should not stop using condoms because you are taking PrEP. If PrEP is taken daily, it offers a lot of protection against HIV infection, but not 100%. Condoms also offer a lot of protection against HIV infection if they are used correctly every time you have sex, but not 100%. PrEP medicines don't give you any protection from other infections you can get during sex (like gonorrhea, chlamydia, and hepatitis), but condoms do.

So you will get the most protection from HIV and other sexually transmitted diseases if you consistently take PrEP medicine and consistently use condoms during sex.

How Long Do I Need to Take PrEP?

You should discuss this with your health care provider. There are several reasons that people stop taking PrEP. For example,

- If your risk of getting HIV infections becomes low because of changes in your life, you may want to stop taking PrEP.

- If you find you don't want to take a pill every day or often forget to take your pills, other ways of protecting yourself from HIV infection may work better for you.

- If you have side effects from the medicine that are interfering with your life, or if blood tests show that your body is reacting to PrEP in unsafe ways, your provider may stop prescribing PrEP for you.

How Long Do I Have to Be Taking PrEP before It Is Effective?

Scientists do not yet have an answer on how long it takes PrEP to become fully effective after you start taking it. Some studies suggest that if you take PrEP every day, it reaches its maximum protection in blood at 20 days, in rectal tissue at about 7 days, and in vaginal tissues at about 20 days. Talk to your health care provider about when PrEP might be effective for you.

Can I Stop and Start Taking PrEP?

No. Some people wonder if they can take PrEP for a few days or weeks, stop for awhile, and then start again. This is sometimes called "intermittent" PrEP. All available research shows PrEP's effectiveness declines greatly if it is not taken consistently, so intermittent use is **NOT** recommended. **PrEP must be taken every day to give the best protection against HIV**.

Can You Start PrEP after You Have Been Exposed to HIV?

PrEP is only for people who are at ongoing substantial risk of HIV infection. For people who need to prevent HIV after a single high-risk event of potential HIV exposure—such as sex without a condom, needle-sharing injection drug use, or sexual assault—there is another option called *postexposure* prophylaxis, or PEP. PEP must begin within 72 hours of exposure.

Section 13.2

Post-Exposure Prophylaxis

Text in this section is excerpted from "HIV Basics—PEP," Centers for Disease Control and Prevention (CDC), March 24, 2015.

PEP

PEP is the use of antiretroviral drugs after a single high-risk event to stop HIV from making copies of itself and spreading through your body. PEP must be started as soon as possible to be effective—and always within 3 days of a possible exposure. If you think you may have been exposed to HIV very recently, see a doctor as soon as possible to find out if PEP is right for you.

What Is PEP?

PEP stands for post-exposure prophylaxis. It involves taking antiretroviral medicines as soon as possible, but no more than 72 hours (3 days) after you may have been exposed to HIV, to try to reduce the chance of becoming HIV-positive. These medicines keep HIV from making copies of itself and spreading through your body. Two to three drugs are usually prescribed, and they must be taken for 28 days. PEP is not always effective; it does not guarantee that someone exposed to HIV will not become infected with HIV.

Is PEP Right for Me?

PEP is used for anyone who may have been exposed to HIV very recently during a single event. It is not the right choice for people who may be exposed to HIV frequently.

Your health care provider will consider whether PEP is right for you based on the risk of your exposure.

Health care workers are evaluated for PEP if they are exposed to blood or body fluids of a patient who is infected with HIV. The risk of getting HIV infection this way is less than 1 in 100 exposures.

PEP can also be used to treat people who may have been exposed to HIV during a single event unrelated to work (e.g., unprotected sex, needle-sharing injection drug use, or sexual assault).

Keep in mind that PEP should only be used in situations right after a potential HIV exposure. It is not a substitute for regular use of other proven HIV prevention methods, such as pre-exposure prophylaxis (PrEP), correct and consistent condom use, or use of sterile injection equipment.

If you are prescribed PEP, you will be asked to return for HIV testing at 4 to 6 weeks, 3 months, and 6 months after the potential exposure to HIV. Because PEP is not always effective, you should keep using condoms with sex partners while taking PEP and should not share injection equipment with others.

When Should I Take PEP?

PEP must begin within 72 hours of exposure, before the virus has time to make too many copies of itself in your body.

Starting PEP as soon as possible after a potential HIV exposure is important: research has shown that PEP has little or no effect in preventing HIV infection if it is started more than 72 hours after HIV exposure. HIV makes copies of itself once it enters your body, and it takes about 3 days for it to spread through your body. When HIV is only in a few cells where it entered your body, it can sometimes be stopped by PEP, but when it is in many cells in many places in your body, PEP will not work.

Two to three drugs are usually prescribed, and they must be taken for 28 days.

Does PEP Have Any Side Effects?

PEP is safe but may cause side effects like nausea in some people. These side effects can be treated and are not life-threatening.

Where Can I Get PEP?

Some of the places you can go to seek treatment include your doctor's office, emergency rooms, urgent care clinics, or a local HIV clinic.

How Can I Pay for PEP?

If you are a health care worker who was exposed to HIV on the job, your workplace health insurance or workers' compensation will usually pay for PEP.

If you are prescribed PEP after sexual assault, you may qualify for partial or total reimbursement for medicines and clinical care costs through the Office for Victims of Crime, funded by the US Department of Justice.

If you are prescribed PEP for another reason, and you cannot get insurance coverage (e.g., Medicaid, Medicare, private, or employer-based), your health care provider can apply for free antiretroviral medicines through the medication assistance programs run by the manufacturers. Online applications can be faxed to the company, or some companies have special phone lines. These can be handled urgently in many cases to avoid delay in getting medicine.

Can I Take a Round of PEP Every Time I Have Unprotected Sex?

PEP should only be used right after an uncommon situation with potential HIV exposure. If you are often exposed to HIV, for example, because you often have sex without a condom with a partner who is HIV-positive, repeated uses of PEP are not the right choice. That's because, when drugs are given only after an exposure, more drugs and higher doses are needed to block infection than when they are started before the exposure and continued for a time thereafter. That's an approach called pre-exposure prophylaxis, or PrEP. PrEP means taking a daily pill (brand name, Truvada) for months or years. This keeps medication in your body to keep HIV from making copies of itself and spreading infection through your body anytime you are exposed. If you are at ongoing risk for HIV, speak to your doctor about PrEP.

Part Three

HIV/AIDS Diagnosis

Chapter 14

HIV Testing

Chapter Contents

Section 14.1

HIV Testing Basics

Text in this section is excerpted from "HIV Overview – HIV Testing,"
AIDS *info*, September 24, 2015.

- HIV testing shows whether a person is infected with HIV. HIV stands for human immunodeficiency virus. HIV is the virus that causes AIDS (acquired immunodeficiency syndrome). AIDS is the most advanced stage of HIV infection.
- The Centers for Disease Control and Prevention (CDC) recommends that everyone 13 to 64 years old get tested for HIV at least once and that people at high risk of infection get tested more often.
- Risk factors for HIV infection include having unprotected sex (sex without a condom); having sex with many partners; and injecting drugs and sharing needles, syringes, or other drug equipment with others.
- CDC recommends that all pregnant women get tested for HIV as early as possible during each pregnancy.

What Is HIV Testing?

HIV testing shows whether a person is infected with HIV. HIV stands for human immunodeficiency virus. HIV is the virus that causes AIDS (acquired immunodeficiency syndrome). AIDS is the most advanced stage of HIV infection.

HIV testing can detect HIV infection, but it can't tell how long a person has been HIV infected or if the person has AIDS.

Why Is HIV Testing Important?

Knowing your HIV status can help keep you—and others—safe.

If you are HIV negative:

Testing shows that you don't have HIV. Continue taking steps to avoid getting HIV, such as using condoms during sex.

If you are HIV positive:

Testing shows that you are infected with HIV, but you can still take steps to protect your health. Begin by talking to your health care provider about antiretroviral therapy (ART). ART is the use of HIV medicines to treat HIV infection. People on ART take a combination of HIV medicines every day. ART helps people with HIV live longer, healthier lives. ART also reduces the risk of sexual transmission of HIV. Your health care provider will help you decide when to start ART and what HIV medicines to take.

Who Should Get Tested for HIV?

The Centers for Disease Control and Prevention (CDC) recommends that everyone 13 to 64 years old get tested for HIV at least once and that people at high risk of infection get tested more often.

Factors that increase the risk of HIV infection include:

- Having vaginal or anal sex without using a condom with someone who is HIV positive or whose HIV status you don't know
- Injecting drugs and sharing needles, syringes, or other drug equipment with others
- Exchanging sex for money or drugs
- Having a sexually transmitted disease (STD), such as syphilis
- Having hepatitis or tuberculosis (TB)
- Having sex with anyone who has any of the HIV risk factors listed above

Talk to your health care provider about your risk of HIV infection and how often you should get tested for HIV.

Should Pregnant Women Get Tested for HIV?

CDC recommends that all pregnant women get tested for HIV as early as possible during each pregnancy. Women who are planning to get pregnant should also get tested.

Women with HIV take HIV medicines during pregnancy and childbirth to reduce the risk of mother-to-child transmission of HIV. HIV medicines used as recommended during pregnancy can reduce the risk of mother-to-child transmission of HIV to less than 1%.

What Are the Types of HIV Tests?

There are several HIV tests. Some are used for HIV screening and others for follow-up testing if a screening test result is HIV positive.

HIV screening tests

The **HIV antibody test** is the most common HIV screening test. The test checks for HIV antibodies in blood, urine, or fluids from the mouth. HIV antibodies are disease-fighting proteins that the body produces in response to HIV infection.

The time period from infection with HIV until the body produces enough HIV antibodies to be detected by an HIV antibody test is called the window period. Most people develop HIV antibodies within 3 months after they are infected with HIV. But the window period can vary depending on the HIV test used. In general, anyone who has a negative result on an HIV antibody test within 3 months of a possible exposure to HIV should have the test repeated in 3 months.

The **HIV antigen/antibody test** can detect both HIV antigen (a part of the virus) and HIV antibodies in blood. An antigen/antibody test can detect HIV infection before an HIV antibody test.

Follow-up HIV tests

A positive result on an HIV screening test must always be confirmed by a second HIV blood test. The following tests are used to confirm a positive result on an HIV screening test:

- Antibody differentiation test, which distinguishes HIV-1 from HIV-2

- HIV-1 nucleic acid test, which looks directly for HIV

- Western blot or indirect immunofluorescence assay, which detect antibodies

How Long Does It Take to Get the Results of an HIV Test?

It usually takes a few days to a few weeks to get results of an HIV test. Some rapid HIV antibody tests can produce results within 30 minutes.

Is There an HIV Test for Home Use?

There are two HIV tests approved by the U.S. Food and Drug Administration (FDA) for home use.

The first test is a home collection kit, which involves pricking the finger for a blood sample, sending the sample to a lab for testing, and then calling the lab for results as early as the next business day. If the result is positive for HIV, the lab testing includes a follow-up test to confirm the initial HIV-positive test result. Test results include the follow-up test.

The other approved home use test comes with a test stick and a tube with a testing solution. The test stick is used to swab the gums to get a sample of oral fluids. To get results, the test stick is inserted into the test tube. Test results are ready in 20 minutes. **A positive result on this home HIV test must always be confirmed by additional HIV testing performed in a health care setting.**

Is HIV Testing Confidential?

HIV testing can be confidential or anonymous.

Confidential testing means that your HIV test results will include your name and other identifying information, but only people allowed to see your medical records will see your test results. HIV-positive test results may be reported to local or state health departments to be counted in statistical reports. Health departments remove all personal information (including names and addresses) from HIV test results before sharing the information with CDC. CDC uses this information for reporting purposes and does not share this information with any other organizations.

Anonymous testing means you don't have to give your name when you take an HIV test. When you take the test, you receive a number. To get your HIV test results, you give the number instead of your name.

Where Can I Get Tested for HIV?

Your health care provider can give you an HIV test. HIV testing is also available at many hospitals, medical clinics, community health centers, and AIDS service organizations.

- Use CDC testing locator (gettested.cdc.gov) to find an HIV testing location near you.

Section 14.2

HIV Testing Frequency

Text in this section is excerpted from "HIV Testing Frequency,"
AIDS.gov, June 5, 2015.

Testing Frequency

CDC RECOMMENDS THAT EVERYONE BETWEEN
THE AGES OF 13 AND 64 GET TESTED AT LEAST
ONCE AND THAT HIGH-RISK GROUPS
GET TESTED MORE OFTEN.

USE THE
AIDS.GOV HIV TESTING AND
CARE SERVICES LOCATOR
TO FIND TESTING LOCATIONS NEAR YOU.

THERE ARE MANY PLACES YOU CAN GET AN
HIV TEST, INCLUDING A CLINIC, A DOCTOR'S
OFFICE, OR A MOBILE TESTING VAN.
OR YOU CAN TAKE A HOME HIV TEST.

Figure 14.1. *HIV Testing Frequency*

How often should you take an HIV test? That depends!

The CDC recommends health care providers test everyone between
the ages of 13 and 64 at least once as part of routine health care. One
in seven people in the United States who have HIV do not know they
are infected.

In other words, you should have an HIV test during a medical
check-up—just like you have a blood test or a urine test to be sure
you are healthy.

Behaviors that put you at risk for HIV include having vaginal or
anal sex without a condom or without being on medicines that prevent or treat HIV, or sharing injection drug equipment with someone
who has HIV. If you answer yes to any of the following questions, you
should definitely get an HIV test:

1. Have you had sex with someone who is HIV-positive or whose
    status you didn't know since your last HIV test?

2. Have you injected drugs (including steroids, hormones, or sil-
    icone) and shared equipment (or works, such as needles and
    syringes) with others?

3. Have you exchanged sex for drugs or money?

4. Have you been diagnosed with or sought treatment for a sexually transmitted disease, like syphilis?

5. Have you been diagnosed with or sought treatment for hepatitis or tuberculosis (TB)?

6. Have you had sex with someone who could answer yes to any of the above questions or someone whose history you don't know?

If you continue having unsafe sex or sharing injection drug equipment, you should get tested at least once a year. Sexually active gay and bisexual men may benefit from more frequent testing (e.g., every 3 to 6 months).

You should consult your healthcare provider to see how often you should be tested.

If you or your partner plan to become pregnant, getting an HIV test is very important. All women who are pregnant should be tested during the first trimester of pregnancy. The CDC also recommends another HIV test in the third trimester of pregnancy for women at high risk of HIV, and for women who live in areas where there are high rates of HIV infection among pregnant women or among women aged 15-44.

If you have already been diagnosed with HIV and are pregnant, there are medications and treatment that can lower the chance of passing HIV to your baby. Please contact your doctor or local health department for proper care and information.

Section 14.3

Confidential and Anonymous Testing

Text in this section is excerpted from "Confidential & Anonymous Testing," AIDS.gov, June 5, 2015.

HIV Test Results and Privacy Issues

HIV test results fall under the same privacy rules as all of your medical information. Information about your HIV test cannot be released without your permission. The Health Insurance Portability and Accountability Act of 1996 (HIPAA) ensures that the privacy of individuals' health information is protected while ensuring access to care. However, it is important to note that not all HIV testing sites are bound by HIPAA regulations. **Before you get tested** be sure to inquire about the privacy rules of the HIV test site as well those surrounding your test results.

Available Testing Services

HIV tests can be taken either *confidentially* or *anonymously*. Most states offer both anonymous and confidential testing, however some states only offer confidential testing services.

- **Confidential testing** means that your name and other identifying information will be attached to your test results. The results will go in your medical record and may be shared with your healthcare providers and your insurance company. Otherwise, the results are protected by state and Federal privacy laws.

- **Anonymous testing** means that nothing ties your test results to you. When you take an anonymous HIV test, you get a unique identifier that allows you to get your test results. Not all HIV test sites offer anonymous testing. Contact your local health department or 1-800-CDC-INFO (800-232-4636) to see if there are anonymous test sites in your area.

With confidential testing, if you test positive for HIV or another sexually transmitted infection (STI), the test result and your name will be reported to the state or local health department to help public health officials get better estimates of the rates of HIV in the state. The state health department will then remove all personal information about you (name, address, etc.) and share the remaining non-identifying information with CDC. CDC does not share this information with anyone else, including insurance companies.

If you have concerns regarding who can have access to your tests results, it is important to ask your testing center about their privacy policies and whom they are required to report a positive result to.

Section 14.4

Opt-Out Testing

This section includes excerpts from "Opt-Out Testing,"
AIDS.gov, June 5, 2015; and text from "Pregnant Women, Infants
and Children," Centers for Disease Control and Prevention (CDC),
June 23, 2014.

In 2006, the CDC released its Revised Recommendations for HIV Testing of Adults, Adolescents, and Pregnant Women in Health-Care Settings, which advise providers in *healthcare settings* to:

- Adopt a policy of routine HIV testing for everyone between the ages of **13-64** and all **pregnant women**

- Use *opt-out screening* for HIV—meaning that HIV tests will be done routinely unless a patient explicitly refuses to take an HIV test

- Eliminate the requirements for pretest counseling, *informed consent*, and post-test counseling

"Opt-out testing" does not mean that you MUST take an HIV test. **In general, you have the right to refuse an HIV test.** (Exceptions include blood and organ donors, military applicants and active duty personnel, Federal and state prison inmates under certain circumstances, newborns in some states, and immigrants.)

The CDC believes that opt-out screening for HIV:

- Will help more people find out if they have HIV

- Will help those infected with HIV find out earlier, when treatment works best

- Can further decrease the number of babies born with HIV

- Can reduce stigma associated with HIV testing

- Will enable those who are infected to take steps to protect the health of their partners

An Opt-Out Approach to HIV Screening for Pregnant Women

The chance that HIV infection will be transmitted from an HIV-infected pregnant woman to her child can be reduced to 2% or less (fewer than 2 out of every 100). This is possible because better medicines are available to treat HIV. But first, the pregnant woman and her doctor must know if she is infected with HIV.

What Do We Know?

• Many women across the United States do not get tested for HIV during pregnancy.

• HIV-infected women who do not get tested often transmit HIV to their infants. 2005 CDC data show that among HIV-infected infants born in the 33 states which report HIV-exposed infants, 31% of the mothers of HIV-infected infants had not been tested for HIV until after delivery.

• Studies show that more women are tested when the HIV test is included in the standard group of tests that all pregnant women receive routinely, and when providers recommend HIV testing early in pregnancy to all their pregnant patients.

• Since 1995, CDC has recommended all pregnant women be tested for HIV and, if found to be infected, offered treatment for themselves to improve their health and to prevent passing the virus to their infant.

What Testing Approaches Are Available?

There are two different ways to approach pregnant women about HIV testing:

• **Opt-in:**

  • Pregnant women are given pre-HIV test counseling.

  • They must agree to receiving an HIV test, usually in writing.

• **Opt-out:**

  • Pregnant women are told that an HIV test will be included in the standard group of prenatal tests (that is to say, tests given to all pregnant women), and that they may decline the test.

  • Unless they decline, they will receive an HIV test.

Statistics published in the Nov. 15, 2002, Morbidity Mortality Weekly Report (MMWR) showed that in eight states using the opt-in approach in 1998-1999, testing rates ranged from 25% to 69%. In Tennessee, which uses an opt-out approach, the testing rate was 85%. Other studies support this evidence that, of the voluntary approaches to prenatal HIV testing, more women are tested with the opt-out approach. An evaluation of opt-out testing in Birmingham, Ala. prenatal clinic showed that HIV testing increased from 75% to 88% after opt-out testing was implemented in August 1999. At the Denver Health Medical Center, 98.2% of women who delivered received HIV testing between 1998 and 2001, using opt-out testing.

Which Approach Does CDC Recommend?

In the 2006 *Revised Recommendations for HIV Testing of Adults, Adolescents, and Pregnant Women in Health-Care Settings*, CDC recommended the opt-out approach to testing for all adult and adolescent patients in health-care settings, including pregnant women.

These recommendations emphasize:

- Universal "opt-out" HIV testing for all pregnant women early in every pregnancy;

- A second test in the third trimester in certain geographic areas or for women who are known to be at high risk of becoming infected (e.g., injection-drug users and their sex partners, women who exchange sex for money or drugs, women who are sex partners of HIV-infected persons, and women who have had a new or more than one sex partner during this pregnancy);

- Rapid HIV testing at labor and delivery for women without a prenatal test result; and

- Exploration of reasons that women decline testing.

Studies show that the opt-out approach can:

- Increase testing rates among pregnant women; thereby, increasing the number of pregnant women who know their HIV status;

- Increase the number of HIV-infected women who are offered treatment; and

- Reduce HIV transmission to their babies.

How Is Opt-Out Implemented in the Health Care Setting?

Opt-out has three steps for health-care providers to follow to put this approach into practice (CDC recommends all three steps):

- Tell all pregnant women that an HIV test will be performed as part of the standard group of tests for pregnant women.

- Tell all pregnant women that they may decline this test.

- Give all pregnant women information about how to prevent HIV transmission during pregnancy and provide information about treatment for pregnant women who are HIV-positive.

Chapter 15

HIV Diagnostic Tests

Chapter Contents

Section 15.1

HIV Test Types

Text in this section is excerpted from "HIV Test Types," AIDS.gov,
June 5, 2015.

What Are the Types of HIV Tests and How Do They Work?

The most common HIV test is the **antibody screening test** (immunoassay), which tests for the antibodies that your body makes against
HIV. The immunoassay may be conducted in a lab or as a rapid test at
the testing site. It may be performed on blood or oral fluid (not saliva).
Because the level of antibody in oral fluid is lower than it is in blood,
blood tests tend to find infection sooner after exposure than do oral
fluid tests. In addition, most blood-based lab tests find infection sooner
after exposure than rapid HIV tests.

Several tests are being used more commonly that can detect both
antibodies and antigen (part of the virus itself). These tests can
find recent infection earlier than tests that detect only antibodies.
These antigen/antibody combination tests can find HIV as soon as 3
weeks after exposure to the virus, but they are only available for testing blood, not oral fluid. Not all testing sites offer this test by default;
if you believe you have been recently exposed to HIV, be sure to let
your provider know and ask if this type of test is available.

The **rapid test** is an immunoassay used for screening, and it produces quick results, in 30 minutes or less. Rapid tests use blood or
oral fluid to look for antibodies to HIV. If an immunoassay (lab test
or rapid test) is conducted during the window period (i.e., the period
after exposure but before the test can find antibodies), the test may not
find antibodies and may give a false-negative result. All immunoassays
that are positive need a follow-up test to confirm the result.

Follow-up diagnostic testing is performed if the first immunoassay result is positive. Follow-up tests include: an antibody differentiation test, which distinguishes HIV-1 from HIV-2; an HIV-1 nucleic
acid test, which looks for virus directly, or the Western blot or indirect
immunofluorescence assay, which detect antibodies.

Immunoassays are generally very accurate, but follow-up testing allows you and your health care provider to be sure the diagnosis is right. If your first test is a rapid test, and it is positive, you will be directed to a medical setting to get follow-up testing. If your first test is a lab test, and it is positive, the lab will conduct follow-up testing, usually on the same blood specimen as the first test.

Home HIV Tests

Currently there are only two home HIV tests: the Home Access HIV-1 Test System and the OraQuick In-home HIV test. If you buy your home test online make sure the HIV test is FDA-approved.

The **Home Access HIV-1 Test System** is a home collection kit that involves pricking your finger to collect a blood sample, sending the sample to a licensed laboratory, and then calling in for results as early as the next business day. This test is anonymous. If the test is positive, a follow-up test is performed right away, and the results include the follow-up test. The manufacturer provides confidential counseling and referral to treatment. The tests conducted on the blood sample collected at home find infection later after infection than most lab-based tests using blood from a vein, but earlier than tests conducted with oral fluid.

The **OraQuick In-Home HIV Test** provides rapid results in the home. The testing procedure involves swabbing your mouth for an oral fluid sample and using a kit to test it. Results are available in 20 minutes. If you test positive, you will need a follow-up test. The manufacturer provides confidential counseling and referral to follow-up testing sites. Because the level of antibody in oral fluid is lower than it is in blood, oral fluid tests find infection later after exposure than do blood tests. Up to 1 in 12 people may receive a false negative result with this test.

RNA Tests

RNA tests detect the virus directly (instead of the antibodies to HIV) and thus can detect HIV at about 10 days after infection—as soon as it appears in the bloodstream, before antibodies develop. These tests cost more than antibody tests and are generally not used as a screening test, although your doctor may order one as a follow-up test, after a positive antibody test, or as part of a clinical workup.

Section 15.2

Rapid Oral HIV Tests

Text in this section is excerpted from "Rapid Oral HIV Test," U.S.
Department of Veterans Affairs (VA), July 30, 2015.

Deciding to Get an HIV Test

Deciding whether to get an HIV test may not be easy. Fear and
worry are common feelings. Talking with your health provider can
help you decide if this test is right for you and how to respond to
the results of the test. HIV health educational material can also
explain HIV testing options and answer questions about HIV risk
and transmission.

Delivery of Test Results

Your health provider can explain what your test results mean. He
or she can give you information about how to protect yourself and others from HIV, no matter what the test results are. If your test result
is positive, your health provider can direct you to medical, legal and
emotional support services, as needed.

What Is the Rapid Oral HIV Test?

This test tells if you have HIV, the virus that causes AIDS. With
the rapid test, results take only 20 minutes.

How Does the Rapid Oral HIV Test Work?

When HIV enters the body, antibodies are produced. The test looks
for HIV antibodies in your body.

Who Is at Risk for HIV?

HIV is considered a Sexually Transmitted Disease (STD). Anyone
who has had sex with someone (vaginal, anal or oral), male or female,
should consider having an HIV test.

Other risk factors include:

- Sharing needles or works to inject drugs/vitamins or for tattooing/piercing.

- Having sex with an injection drug user.

- Having been a sex partner with someone who has HIV.

- Being a victim of sexual assault.

- Having a sexually transmitted disease (STD).

What Happens When You Agree to Be Tested?

- The test is explained to you by a health provider.

- A health provider will ask you to rub your gums with a special cotton pad.

- Results are ready in 20 minutes.

- You will learn your results and discuss what they mean.

- Your test result will be confidential (results will only be discussed with you).

What Does a Negative Test Result Mean?

This means that HIV antibodies have not been found at this time in your system.

This could mean one of two things:

1. You do not have HIV **OR**

2. You have HIV but it can take up to 3 months for your system to produce enough antibodies to show on a test result. If you have engaged in activities that have put you at risk for HIV infection in the past 3 months, you should repeat this test in 90 days.

What Does a Positive Test Result Mean?

This means HIV antibodies may be in your system. Positive results must always be confirmed by another test that is sent to the lab.

A confirmed positive test result means:

- You have HIV and can give it to other people during vaginal, anal or oral sex.

- You can give HIV to others if you share needles and works to inject drugs/vitamins or for any other reason.

- A pregnant woman may pass the HIV virus to the fetus in her womb or to the baby during birth or breastfeeding. Medications are available to reduce the risk of transmission.

Why Should You Get Tested?

- Getting diagnosed early can improve your quality of life and improve your treatment options.

- Knowing your HIV status helps you protect yourself and others.

- If you test negative, you may feel less anxious after testing.

- An HIV test is part of routine medical care.

Section 15.3

HIV Home Test Kits

This section includes excerpts from "First Rapid Home-Use HIV Kit Approved for Self-Testing," U.S. Food and Drug Administration (FDA), January 16, 2015; text from "Information regarding the OraQuick In-Home HIV Test," U.S. Food and Drug Administration (FDA), June 18, 2014; and text from "Information regarding the Home Access HIV-1 Test System," U.S. Food and Drug Administration (FDA), October 2, 2012.

First Rapid Home-Use HIV Kit Approved for Self-Testing

On July 3, 2012, the U.S. Food and Drug Administration (FDA) approved the OraQuick In-Home HIV Test, a rapid home-use HIV test kit that does not require sending a sample to a laboratory for analysis. The kit provides a test result in 20-40 minutes, and you can test yourself in your own home.

The kit, which tests a sample of fluid from your mouth, is approved for sale in stores and online to anyone age 17 and older.

FDA wants consumers to know that positive test results using the OraQuick test must be confirmed by follow-up laboratory-based testing. Also, the test can be falsely negative for reasons that include the occurrence of HIV infection within three months before testing. People who engage in behaviors that put them at increased risk of getting HIV— including having unprotected sex with new partners, or injecting illegal drugs—should be re-tested on a regular basis. They should not interpret a negative test to indicate that engaging in high risk behavior is safe.

According to the Centers for Disease Control and Prevention, about 1.2 million people in the U.S. are living with HIV infection, and about 1 in 5 of these people don't know that they are infected, increasing the chance that they will unknowingly spread the infection.

Information regarding the OraQuick In-Home HIV Test

How the OraQuick In-Home HIV Test Works

What Is the OraQuick In-Home HIV Test and How Does It Work?

The OraQuick In-Home HIV Test is a rapid self-administered over-the-counter (OTC) test. The OraQuick In-Home HIV Test kit consists of a test stick (device) to collect the specimen, a test tube (vial) to insert the test stick (device) and complete the test, testing directions, two information booklets ("HIV, Testing and Me" and "What your results mean to you"), a disposal bag and phone numbers for consumer support.

This approved test uses oral fluid to check for antibodies to HIV Type 1 and HIV Type 2, the viruses that cause AIDS. The kit is designed to allow you to take the HIV test anonymously and in private with the collection of an oral fluid sample by swabbing your upper and lower gums with the test device. After collecting the sample, you insert the device into the kit's vial which contains a developer solution, wait 20-40 minutes, and read the test result. A positive result with this test does not mean that an individual is definitely infected with HIV but rather that additional testing should be done in a medical setting to confirm the test result. Additionally, a negative test result does not mean that an individual is definitely not infected with HIV, particularly when exposure may have been within the previous three months. Again an individual should obtain a confirmatory test in a medical setting.

When Should I Take a Test for HIV?

If you actively engage in behavior that puts you at risk for HIV infection, or your partner engages in such behavior, then you should consider testing on a regular basis. It can take some time for the immune system to produce enough antibodies for the test to detect, and this time period can vary from person to person. This timeframe is commonly referred to as the "window period," when a person is infected with HIV but antibodies to the virus cannot be detected, however, the person may be able to infect others. According to the Centers for Disease Control and Prevention, although it can take up to 6 months to develop antibodies for HIV, most people (97%) will develop detectable antibodies in the first 3 months following the time of their infection.

How Reliable Is the OraQuick In-Home HIV Test?

As noted in the package insert, clinical studies have shown that the OraQuick In-Home HIV Test has an expected performance of approximately 92% for test sensitivity (i.e., the percentage of results that will be positive when HIV is present). This means that one false negative result would be expected out of every 12 test results in HIV infected individuals. The clinical studies also showed that the Ora-Quick In-Home HIV Test has an expected performance of 99.98% for test specificity (i.e., the percentage of results that will be negative when HIV is not present). This means that one false positive result would be expected out of every 5,000 test results in uninfected individuals.

It is extremely important for those who self-test using the OraQuick In-Home HIV Test to carefully read and follow all labeled directions. Even when used according to the labeled directions, there will be some false negative results and a small number of false positive results. The OraQuick test package contains step-by-step instructions, and there is also an OraQuick Consumer Support Center to assist users in the testing process.

Results

If the Test Says I'm HIV Positive, What Should I Do?

A positive test result does not necessarily mean that you are infected with HIV. If you test positive for HIV using the OraQuick In-Home Test, you should see your healthcare provider or call the OraQuick Consumer Support Center, which has support center representatives available 24 hours a day/7 days a week to answer your questions and provide referrals to local healthcare providers for follow-up care. You will be advised to obtain confirmatory testing to confirm a positive result or inform you that the initial result was a false positive result. The test kit also contains an information booklet, "What your results mean to You," which is designed to instruct individuals on what to do once they have obtained their test results.

Do I Need a Confirmatory Test?

A positive test result on the OraQuick In-Home HIV Test indicates that you may be infected with HIV. Additional testing in a medical setting will either confirm a positive test result or inform you that the initial result was a false positive result.

What Is a "False Positive" Result?

A "false positive" result occurs when an individual not infected with the HIV virus receives a test result that indicates that he or she is infected with HIV.

If the Test Says I'm HIV Negative, What Should I Do?

A negative result on this test does not necessarily mean that you are not infected with HIV. The OraQuick test kit contains an information booklet, "What your results mean to You," which is designed to instruct individuals on what to do once they have obtained their test results. The test is relatively reliable if there has been sufficient time for HIV antibodies to develop in the infected person. For the OraQuick In-Home HIV Test, that period of time, called the window period, is about three months. If you have recently been engaging in behavior that puts you at high risk for HIV infection, you should take the test again at a later time. Alternatively, you should see your health care provider who can discuss other options for HIV testing.

What Is a "False Negative" Result?

A "false negative" result occurs when an HIV-infected individual receives a test result that incorrectly indicates that he or she is not infected with HIV.

How Quickly Will I Get the Results of the OraQuick Test?

You can read the results of the OraQuick In-Home HIV Test within 20 to 40 minutes.

Information regarding the Home Access HIV-1 Test System

What Is the Home Access HIV-1 Test System?

The Home Access HIV-1 Test System is a laboratory test sold over-the-counter (OTC) that uses fingerstick blood mailed to the testing laboratory. The test kit consists of multiple components, including materials for specimen self-collection, prepaid materials for mailing the specimen to a laboratory for testing, testing directions, an information booklet ("Things you Should Know About HIV and AIDS"), an anonymous registration system and a call center to receive your test results and follow-up counseling by telephone.

This approved system uses a finger prick process for home blood collection which results in dried blood spots on special paper. The dried blood spots are mailed to a laboratory with a confidential and anonymous unique personal identification number (PIN), and are analyzed by trained clinicians in a laboratory using the same tests that are used for samples taken in a doctor's office or clinic. Test results are obtained through a toll free telephone number using the PIN, and post-test counseling is provided by telephone when results are obtained.

When Should I Take a Test for HIV?

If you actively engage in behavior that puts you at risk for HIV infection, or your partner engages in such behavior, then you should consider testing on a regular basis. It may take some time for the immune system to produce sufficient antibodies for the test to detect, and this time period can vary from person to person. This time-frame is commonly referred to as the "window period," when a person is infected with HIV but antibodies to the virus cannot be detected, however, the person may be able to infect others. According to the Centers for Disease Control and Prevention, it can take up to 6 months to develop antibodies to HIV, although most people (97%) will develop detectable antibodies in the first 3 months following the time of their infection.

How Reliable Is the Home Access HIV-1 Test System?

Clinical studies reported to FDA showed that the sensitivity (i.e., the percentage of results that will be positive when HIV is present) was estimated to be greater than 99.9%. The specificity (i.e., the percentage of results that will be negative when HIV is not present) was also estimated to be greater than 99.9%. Results reported as positive have undergone testing using both a screening test and another test to confirm the positive result.

What about Counseling?

The Home Access HIV-1 Test System has a built-in mechanism for pre-test and post-test counseling provided by the manufacturer. This counseling is anonymous and confidential. Counseling, which uses both printed material and telephone interaction, provides the user with an interpretation of the test result. Counseling also provides information on how to keep from getting infected if you are negative, and how to prevent further transmission of disease if you are infected. Counseling provides you with information about treatment options if you are infected, and can even provide referrals to doctors who treat HIV-infected individuals in your area.

If the Test Results Are Positive, What Should I Do?

The counselors can provide you with information about treatment options and referrals to doctors who treat HIV-infected individuals in your area.

Do I Need a Confirmatory Test?

No, a positive result from the Home Access HIV-1 Test System means that antibodies to the HIV-1 virus are present in the blood sample submitted to the testing laboratory. The Home Access HIV-1 Test System includes confirmatory testing for HIV-1, and all confirmation testing is completed before the results are released and available to users of the test system.

How Quickly Will I Get the Results of the Home Access HIV-1 Test System?

You can anonymously call for the results approximately 7 business days (3 business days for the Express System) after shipping your specimen to the laboratory by using the unique PIN on the tear-off label included with your test kit. This label includes both the unique PIN and the toll-free number for the counseling center.

How Are Unapproved Test Systems Different?

The manufacturers of unapproved test systems have not submitted data to FDA to review to determine whether or not their test systems can reliably detect HIV infection. Therefore, FDA cannot give the public any assurance that the results obtained using an unapproved test system are accurate.

How Can I Obtain Additional Information about the Test?

Information on the Home Access HIV-1 Test System can be found on FDA's website (www.fda.gov).

Additionally, information can be obtained from the manufacturer, Home Access Health Corporation.

Chapter 16

Understanding Your Test Results

Chapter Contents

Section 16.1

What Do Your Test Results Mean?

Text in this section is excerpted from "Understanding Your Test
Results," AIDS.gov, June 5, 2015.

What Does a Negative HIV Test Result Mean?

A negative result may not always be accurate. It depends on when
you might have been exposed to HIV and when you took the test.

That's because of the window period—the period of time after you
may have been exposed to HIV, but before a test can detect it. The
window period depends on the type of HIV test that you take. For
antibody tests, if you get a negative result within 3 months of your
most recent possible exposure, you need to get tested again at the
3-month mark. For combination antibody/antigen tests or RNA tests,
that timeframe may be shorter.

Ask your healthcare provider if and when you need to be retested
with a negative test result. And meanwhile, practice abstinence or
mutual monogamy with a trusted partner, use condoms every time
you have sex (and for every sex act—anal, oral, or vaginal) and don't
share needles and other drug equipment (works).

And remember— a negative result is only good for **past exposure**.
If you get a negative test result, but continue to engage in high-risk
behaviors, you are still at risk for HIV infection.

What Does a Positive HIV Test Result Mean?

If your initial HIV test result is positive, follow-up testing is performed. HIV tests are generally very accurate, but follow-up testing
allows you and your health care provider to be sure the diagnosis is
right.

If you had a rapid screening test, the testing site will arrange a
follow-up test to make sure the screening test result was correct. If
your blood was tested in a lab, the lab will conduct a follow-up test on
the same sample. If the confirmatory test is also positive, you will be
diagnosed as "HIV-positive."

At this point, the person giving you your test results will discuss what having HIV means for you and your health. You will be informed about how the virus can affect you and how to protect others from becoming infected. You will also be informed about resources and treatments available to you. Finally, you will be referred to a medical professional for follow-up treatment.

Next Steps If You Are HIV-Positive

The sooner you take steps to protect your health, the better. Early treatment with antiretroviral drugs and a healthy lifestyle can help you stay well. Prompt medical care prevents the onset of AIDS and some life-threatening conditions.

Here are some important steps you can take right away to protect your health:

- See a licensed health care provider, even if you don't feel sick. Your local health department can help you find a health care provider who has experience treating HIV. There are medicines to treat HIV infection and help you stay healthy. It's never too early to start treatment. Current guidelines recommend treatment with antiretroviral therapy (ART) for all people with HIV, including those with early infection.

- Get screened for other sexually transmitted infections (STIs). STIs can cause serious health problems, even when they don't cause symptoms. Using a condom during all sexual contact (anal, vaginal, or oral) can help prevent many STIs.

- Have a TB (tuberculosis) test. You may be infected with TB and not know it. Undetected TB can cause serious illness, but it can be successfully treated if caught early.

- Get help if you smoke cigarettes, drink too much alcohol, or use illegal drugs (such as methamphetamine), which can weaken your immune system. Find substance abuse treatment facilities near you.

To avoid giving HIV to anyone else,

- Tell your partner or partners about your HIV status before you have any type of sexual contact with them (anal, vaginal, or oral).

- Use latex condoms and/or dental dams with every sexual contact. If either partner is allergic to latex, plastic (polyurethane) condoms for either the male or female can be used.

199

- Don't share needles, syringes, or other drug paraphernalia with anyone.

- Stay on ART to keep your virus under control and greatly reduce your ability to spread HIV to others.

- If your steady partner is HIV-negative, discuss whether he or she should consider pre-exposure prophylaxis (PrEP)—medications to prevent HIV.

Section 16.2

Do You Have AIDS?

Text in this section is excerpted from "Newly Diagnosed with HIV:
What You Need to Know," AIDS.gov, April 10, 2015.

What Does "HIV-Positive" Mean?

If you have just been diagnosed with HIV, you may have many questions: What does it mean to be HIV-positive? Does it mean that you have AIDS? Is HIV manageable? What are some of the first things you need to think about and do?

Being diagnosed with HIV means that you have been infected with the Human Immunodeficiency Virus (HIV) and that two HIV tests—a preliminary test and a confirmatory test—have both come back positive.

Once you have been infected with HIV, you will always carry it in your body. There is no cure for HIV. It is a serious, infectious disease that can lead to death if it isn't treated. But there is good news: by getting linked to HIV medical care early, starting antiretroviral therapy (ART), adhering to your medication, and staying in care you can keep the virus under control, and live a healthy life.

Being HIV-positive also means that it is possible for you to pass the virus along to others, including your sexual partners. If you are female, you could also pass it along to your unborn child. Through treatment for HIV disease, you can suppress the virus and reduce the chances of transmitting HIV to others.

Do I Have AIDS?

Being HIV-positive does NOT necessarily mean you have AIDS. AIDS is the most advanced stage of HIV disease. If you are diagnosed early, start treatment, and adhere to your medication, you can stay healthy and prevent the virus from developing into AIDS. Ask your healthcare provider for more specifics about exactly what stage of HIV infection you have.

Is HIV Manageable?

Yes, today HIV is a manageable disease. HIV medications have significantly changed the course of HIV infection since the early days of the epidemic and with the proper care and treatment, you can live a healthy life.

The sooner you take steps to protect your health, the better. Early treatment with antiretroviral drugs and a healthy lifestyle can help you stay well. Prompt medical care prevents the onset of AIDS and some life-threatening AIDS-related conditions.

To view the personal stories of others who have been diagnosed with HIV and learn how they managed their infection and got the virus under control with medication, visit AIDS.gov's Positive Spin (www.positivespin.hiv.gov).

Newly Diagnosed Checklist

Here is a checklist to help you take the first steps toward managing your infection.

- **Don't panic—just breathe.** This is life-changing news but you have options to protect your health. There are HIV medicines to treat HIV infection and help you stay healthy.

- **Find an HIV care provider, even if you don't feel sick.** Your HIV care provider will be the person who partners with you to manage your HIV. He or she will monitor your health on an ongoing basis and work with you to develop a treatment plan. It's never too early to start treatment. Current guidelines recommend treatment with ART for all people with HIV, including those with early infection. If you don't have a regular doctor, your HIV testing location or your local health department can help you find an HIV care provider. Or, you can use the AIDS.gov HIV Testing and Care Services Locator to find a provider near you.

- **Prepare for your first appointment.** Your first appointment with your HIV care provider can cause anxiety. Make a list of questions before you go. Making a list is a good way to organize your thoughts.

- **Do some research.** After you have listed your questions, take some time to understand what it means to have HIV. You can read the information on AIDS.gov, visit other trusted websites, read printed materials (from your testing center or local library), talk with your healthcare provider, or take advantage of community resources.

- **Find a support system.** This is one of the most important pieces of managing a new HIV diagnosis. You can find support among friends, family, or members of your community. If you are not ready to tell other people about your HIV diagnosis, that's ok. Look to community resources and professional organizations that offer support groups for newly diagnosed people, one-on-one counseling, peer counselors, or health educators.

- **Begin thinking about whom you want to tell.** Disclosing can be one of the hardest parts about managing a new diagnosis of HIV. It's important to remember that you do not need to tell everyone all at once, and that there are systems in place to help you. At this time, it is important to disclose your HIV status to your healthcare providers and sexual partners.

Prevent HIV Transmission

You also need to take steps to avoid giving HIV to anyone else:

- **Use ART.** ART reduces the amount of virus (viral load) in your blood and body fluids. ART can keep you healthy for many years, and reduce your chance of transmitting HIV to your sex partners if taken consistently and correctly.

- **If you are taking ART, follow your health care provider's advice.** Visit your health care provider regularly and always take your medication as directed.

- **Use condoms consistently and correctly with every sexual contact.** When used consistently and correctly, condoms are highly effective at preventing HIV.

- **If your steady partner is HIV-negative, talk to him or her about pre-exposure prophylaxis (PrEP),** taking HIV medicines daily to prevent HIV infection. The CDC recommends PrEP be considered for people who are HIV-negative and at substantial risk for HIV infection. This includes HIV-negative individuals who are in an ongoing relationship with an HIV-positive partner, as well as others at high risk.

- **Talk to your partners about post-exposure prophylaxis (PEP) if you think they have had a possible exposure to HIV.** An example of a possible exposure is you have anal or vaginal sex without a condom or the condom breaks and your partner is HIV-negative and not on PrEP. Your partners' chance of exposure to HIV is lower if you are taking ART consistently and correctly, especially if your viral load is undetectable. Your partners should talk to their doctors right away (within 3 days) if they think they have had a possible exposure to HIV. Starting medicine immediately (known as post-exposure prophylaxis, or PEP) and taking it daily for 4 weeks reduces your partners' chance of getting HIV.

- **Don't share needles, syringes, or other drug paraphernalia with anyone.**

- **Choose less risky sexual behaviors.** Oral sex is much less risky than anal or vaginal sex. Anal sex is the highest-risk sexual activity for HIV transmission. If you are HIV-positive, receptive anal sex ("bottoming") is less risky for transmitting HIV than insertive anal sex.

- **Get tested and treated for STDs and encourage your partners to do the same.** If you are sexually active, get tested at least once a year. STDs can have long-term health consequences. They can also increase the chance of getting HIV or transmitting it to others.

Section 16.3

Signs and Symptoms of HIV and AIDS

This section includes excerpts from "Symptoms of HIV," AIDS.gov,
August 27, 2015; and text from "What are the symptoms of HIV/
AIDS?" *Eunice Kennedy Shriver* National Institute of Child Health
and Human Development (NICHD), December 16, 2013.

How Can I Tell If I Have HIV?

You cannot rely on symptoms to tell whether you have HIV. **The
only way to know for sure if you have HIV is to get tested.**

The symptoms of HIV vary, depending on the individual and what
stage of the disease you are in: the early stage, the clinical latency
stage, or AIDS (the late stage of HIV infection). Below are the symptoms that some individuals may experience in these three stages. Not
all individuals will experience these symptoms.

Early Stage of HIV

Within 2-4 weeks after HIV infection, many, but not all, people
experience flu-like symptoms, often described as the "worst flu ever."
This is called acute retroviral syndrome (ARS) and it's the body's natural response to the HIV infection.

Symptoms can include:

- Fever (this is the most common symptom)

- Swollen glands

- Sore throat

- Rash

- Fatigue

- Muscle and joint aches and pains

- Headache

These symptoms can last anywhere from a few days to several
weeks.

You should not assume you have HIV just because you have any of these symptoms. Each of these symptoms can be caused by other illnesses. And some people who have HIV do not show any symptoms at all for 10 years or more.

If you think you may have been exposed to HIV, get an HIV test. Most HIV tests detect antibodies (proteins your body makes against HIV), not HIV itself. But it takes a few weeks for your body to produce these antibodies, so if you test too early, you might not get an accurate test result. A new HIV test is available that can detect HIV directly during this early stage of infection. So be sure to let your testing site know if you think you may have been recently infected with HIV.

You are at high risk of transmitting HIV to others during this early stage, even if you have no symptoms. For this reason, it is very important to take steps to reduce your risk of transmission.

Clinical Latency Stage

After the early stage of HIV infection, the disease moves into a stage called the clinical latency stage. During this stage, people with HIV typically have no symptoms, or only mild ones.

During the clinical latency stage, HIV reproduces at very low levels, although it is still active. If you take *antiretroviral therapy* (ART), you can stay healthy and live in this stage for several decades because treatment helps keep the virus in check. If you are not on ART, this clinical latency stage usually lasts about 10 years, but may be shorter.

You are still able to transmit HIV to others during this stage, even if you have no symptoms.

Progression to AIDS

If you have HIV and you are not on ART, eventually the virus will weaken your body's immune system and you will progress to AIDS (acquired immunodeficiency syndrome), the late stage of HIV infection. Symptoms can include:

- Rapid weight loss

- Recurring fever or profuse night sweats

- Extreme and unexplained tiredness

- Prolonged swelling of the lymph glands in the armpits, groin, or neck

- Diarrhea that lasts for more than a week
- Sores of the mouth, anus, or genitals
- Pneumonia
- Red, brown, pink, or purplish blotches on or under the skin or inside the mouth, nose, or eyelids
- Memory loss, depression, and other neurologic disorders.

Each of these symptoms can also be related to other illnesses. So the only way to know for sure if you have HIV is to get tested.

Many of the severe symptoms and illnesses of HIV disease come from the *opportunistic infections* that occur because your body's immune system has been damaged.

Signs and Symptoms of HIV/AIDS in Infants and Children

HIV infection is often difficult to diagnose in very young children. One the one hand, infants with HIV often appear normal and may show no signs allowing for a clear diagnosis of HIV infection. On the other hand, many infants develop multiple and serious illnesses related to their HIV infection.

Many children with HIV infection do not gain weight or grow normally. If left untreated, HIV-infected children are frequently slow to reach important milestones in motor skills and mental development, such as crawling, walking, and talking. As the disease progresses, many children with untreated HIV develop problems with walking, poor school performance, seizures, and other symptoms of HIV brain encephalopathy (a brain infection).

Children with untreated HIV suffer the usual childhood infections more frequently and more severely than HIV-uninfected children. These infections can cause seizures, fever, pneumonia, recurrent colds, diarrhea, dehydration, and other problems that often result in extended hospital stays and nutritional problems. Like adults with HIV infection, children with HIV are at risk of developing life-threatening opportunistic infections. Pneumocystis pneumonia (PCP), a severe form of pneumonia that strikes people with weakened immune systems, is common and sometimes deadly in infants who do not receive treatment for their HIV infection.

Chapter 17

You and Your HIV/AIDS Healthcare Provider: First Steps

Chapter Contents

Section 17.1

Choosing a Provider

Text in this section is excerpted from "You & Your Provider,"
AIDS.gov, March 25, 2014.

Figure 17.1. *HIV Care Provider*

Finding a Provider: Why It's Important

After you are diagnosed with HIV, it's very important to find an
HIV care provider as soon as possible. HIV treatment has advanced
tremendously in the past decade and with the proper care and treatment, you can stay healthy, live longer, and reduce the chances of
transmitting HIV to others.

Who Provides HIV Care?

HIV care providers are medical professionals who work with you
to manage your HIV care and stay healthy. Many providers will manage your primary health care needs as well. HIV care providers can
include:

- Doctors

- Nurse Practitioners

- Nurses

- Physician Assistants

HIV care providers often work with a team of other healthcare professionals to ensure that you have the best care possible. Other important members of your HIV care team may include:

- Social workers
- Psychologists/psychiatrists
- Pharmacists
- Dieticians
- Dentists
- Case managers and/or other health professionals

These team members will work with you so that you can stay as healthy as possible and live life to the fullest.

How Long Should You Wait before Finding a HIV Provider?

Not long. Mounting scientific evidence has made clear the many benefits of starting *antiretroviral therapy* (ART) as early as possible. The sooner you find an HIV provider, the sooner you can start ART to stay healthy and reduce the risk of transmitting the virus to others.

Before starting you on ART, your HIV provider will want to review your health history, conduct a physical exam, and run some initial lab tests to evaluate your overall health and determine the stage of HIV disease in your body. These lab tests will help you and your provider determine the best treatment plan for you.

Locate a Provider near You

Your HIV testing site can likely provide you with a referral to an HIV provider. Or, if you have a regular doctor, you can also speak with him or her about whether they can lead your HIV care or will refer you to a specialist they work with.

Tips for Choosing a Provider

Here are some tips to keep in mind when choosing a provider:

- You may be referred to an HIV provider by your HIV testing site or your primary healthcare provider. If not, use the Locator above to find an healthcare provider who specializes in HIV care in your area. You can always change your provider later if they are not a good fit for you. The important thing is to get started.

- It's important to remember that not all providers are specialists in HIV. It's perfectly fine for you to ask your provider about his or her training or experience in treating people living with HIV. A good health care provider will not be offended if you ask.

- You are entitled to quality care for your HIV disease. Geography or funding may limit your choices about who your care provider will be, but you have a right to expect treatment from a competent and caring medical professional.

Helping Your Provider Help You

Here are some ways you can help your provider help you:

- Always be open and honest with your provider about things like:

- Medication—Have you missed any doses of your HIV meds? Have you taken them on time and as prescribed?

- Side effects—Are you experiencing any problems with your HIV meds? Have you noticed any changes in your body (e.g., fatigue, weight loss, diarrhea) that might be related to your HIV meds?

- Sexual activity—Are you having sexual contact? Are you protecting yourself and your partner(s)?

- Drug and alcohol use—Are you using illicit drugs and alcohol, and, if so, how much and how frequently? It is important for your provider to know about your substance use because drugs and alcohol may interact with your HIV medications.

- Bring information to go over with your provider. This includes:

- A list of any questions you may have about HIV disease, side effects, HIV medications, or other issues. During an appointment, it can be easy to forget questions you meant to ask. Your best bet is to write them down and show them to your provider. The Department of Veterans Affairs offers a list of sample questions you can bring with you. Remember: There are no stupid questions!

- Any information you may have gotten from friends, the Internet, or other resources that you'd like to discuss.

- A list of all the non-HIV medications you are currently taking (or the medications themselves), including nonprescription ones, like vitamins or other supplements (e.g., Omega-3 fish oil). It is important for your provider to know this information because interactions between different medications in your body can have serious side effects, or make some of your HIV medications less effective.

- A copy of your medical records, if you are seeing a new provider who does not already have them. You have the right to access your medical records and having copies of your records can help you keep track of your lab results, prescriptions, and other key information, and make sure they are complete and accurate.

- Follow up on any lab tests your provider may order and get them done when your provider advises you to do so. Your lab tests need to be done on time so that you and your provider have the information you need to manage your care and keep you healthy. If you don't understand what a lab test is for, ask your provider to explain it to you in everyday terms.

Be Prepared for Your Appointments

Here are some ways you can be prepared for your appointments with your HIV provider:

- Keep track of your appointments the same way you keep track of your other events or activities (phone, paper calendar, online calendar, etc.). If you are concerned about confidentiality, you can try using a code word or activity on your calendar instead.

- If possible, arrive a few minutes before your scheduled appointment time. A patient who is even 10 minutes late can radically disrupt a provider's schedule. Remember—your providers want to give you all the time they possibly can, and it helps if you are there on time.

- Keep in mind you may have to wait when you arrive at your appointment. Providers don't always have control over what happens in their office, and things can change rapidly. There may be someone ahead of you who has an emergency or needs extra attention that day. Be patient—you might be that person some time!

- Before you leave, ask when your next appointment will be and get a written or text reminder from the front desk. This will help you stay on track with your care and protect your health.

211

Always let your providers know when you are going to miss, reschedule, or be late to an appointment. If you have to cancel an appointment, always reschedule at the time you cancel! This will ensure that you don't forget and that you continue to get the care you need to stay healthy.

Section 17.2

Questions to Ask Your Doctor

Text in this section is excerpted from "Doctor, Clinic, & Dental visits," AIDS.gov, April 16, 2015.

Managing Your Appointments

HIV is a treatable condition. If you are diagnosed early, get on antiretroviral therapy (ART), and adhere to your medication, you can stay healthy, live a normal life span, and reduce the chances of transmitting HIV to others. Part of staying healthy is seeing your HIV care provider regularly so that he or she can track your progress and make sure your HIV treatment is working for you.

Your HIV care provider might be a doctor, nurse practitioner, or physician assistant. Some people living with HIV go to an HIV clinic; others see an HIV specialist at a community health center, Veterans Affairs clinic, or other health clinic; and some people see their provider in a private practice.

In addition to seeing your HIV care provider, you may need to see other health care practitioners, including dentists, nurses, case managers, social workers, psychiatrists/psychologists, pharmacists and medical specialists. This may mean juggling multiple appointments, but it is all part of staying healthy. You can help make this easier by preparing a plan for yourself.

Before Your Visit

For many people living with HIV, appointments with their HIV care provider become a routine part of their life. These tips may help

BEFORE VISITING YOUR
HEALTHCARE PROVIDER

Make a list of all of your questions, any symptoms
you have, and any medications you're taking. It's
important to play an active role in your own care.

BE HONEST WITH YOUR
HIV CARE PROVIDER

Your provider isn't there to judge you, but to
provide you the best possible care. Talk openly
with him or her during your visit.

DENTAL CARE IS VERY IMPORTANT
FOR PEOPLE WITH HIV

Make sure you have routine dental check-ups.
And when you notice a problem, see a dentist
right away.

Figure 17.2. *Dental Visits*

you better prepare for your visits to your HIV care provider and get more out of them:

- Start with a list or a notebook. Write down any questions you have before you go.

- Make a list of your health and life goals so that you can talk about them with your HIV provider and how she/he can help you reach them.

- Make a list of any symptoms or problems you are experiencing that you want to talk to your provider about.

- Bring a list of all the HIV and non-HIV medications that you are taking (or the medications themselves), including over-the-counter medications, vitamins, or supplements. Include a list of any HIV medications you may have taken in the past and any problems you had when taking them.

- Bring along a copy of your medical records if you are seeing a new provider who does not already have them. You have the right to access your medical records and having copies of your records can help you keep track of your lab results, prescriptions, and other health information. It can also help your new provider have a better understanding of your health history.

- Be prepared to talk about any changes in your living situation, relationships, insurance, or employment that may affect your ability to keep up with your HIV appointments and treatment or to take care of yourself. Your provider may be able to connect you with resources or services that may assist you.

- Be on time. Most healthcare providers have full appointment schedules—if you are late, you throw the schedule off for everyone who comes after you. If you are late, there is a chance your provider will not be able to see you the same day.

During Your Visit

- If your provider wants to run some lab tests during your visit, make sure you understand what the lab tests are for and what your provider will do with the results. If you don't understand, ask your provider to explain it in everyday terms. Typically, you will be asked to give a sample (blood, urine) during your visit and your provider's office will call you with your results in a few days. Keep track of your results and call your provider back if you have any questions.

- Be honest. Your provider isn't there to judge you, but to make decisions with you based on your particular circumstances. Talk about any HIV medication doses you have missed. Tell your provider about your sexual or alcohol/drug use history. These behaviors can put you at risk of developing drug resistance and getting other sexually transmitted infections (STIs) as well as hepatitis. Your provider will work with you to develop strategies to keep you as healthy as possible.

- Describe any side effects you may be having from your HIV medications. Your provider will want to know how the HIV medications are affecting your body in order to work with you to solve any problems and find the right combination of medications for you.

- Ask your provider about your next visit and what you should bring to that appointment.

- Ask for a list of your upcoming appointments when you check out. Work with your case manager, if you have one, to develop a system to help you remember your appointments, such as a calendar, app, or text/e-mail reminders.

Asking Questions

It's important for you to be an active participant in your own health care and it's your right to ask questions. You may need to direct your questions to different people, depending on what you need/want to know:

- HIV care providers (doctors, nurse practitioners, physician assistants) can answer specific questions about:

- Your prognosis (how your HIV disease is affecting your body)

- How to manage any symptoms you may be experiencing

- Medication issues, including medication changes, new medications, and how the HIV medications may interact with other medications you take.

- Sexual health issues, including questions about any sexual symptoms you may be having, and how you can prevent or treat STIs, and how you can prevent transmitting HIV to your partner(s).

- Family planning considerations, including your goals; birth control options for you and/or your partner, if relevant; your options for having children should you wish to do so; and, if you are an HIV-positive woman who is pregnant or considering getting pregnant, how you can reduce the risk of transmitting HIV to your baby

- Substance use issues, including how alcohol/drug use can affect your HIV treatment and overall health, and whether you should be referred for substance abuse treatment

- Mental health issues, including questions about any mental health symptoms you may be having, and whether you should be referred for mental health treatment

- Referrals for other medical issues you may be experiencing

- The meaning of lab test results

- The need for surgical procedures, if relevant

- Medication adherence strategies (tips for keeping up with your medication and ensuring you take it as scheduled and exactly as prescribed)

- Any clinical trials or research studies that may be relevant for you

- Nurses and case managers often have more time to answer questions about what you discuss with your provider, particularly around:

  - Understanding your HIV treatment plan, including how many pills of each medicine you should take; when to take each medicine; how to take each medicine (for example, with or without food); and how to store each medicine

- Understanding possible side effects from your HIV medication and what you should do if you experience them

- Challenges you may have in taking your medications and/or keeping your medical appointments, and strategies for overcoming these challenges

- Resources to help you better understand lab reports, tests, and procedures

- Mental health and/or substance abuse treatment, housing assistance, food assistance, and other resources that exist in your community

- Insurance and pharmacy benefits, and other aspects of paying for care

- Understanding other medical conditions you may have

- How to quit smoking and resources that are available to assist you

Dental Appointments

Dental visits are an extremely important part of your care when living with HIV. Many signs of HIV infection can begin in the mouth and throat, and people with HIV are more likely to develop some serious dental problems. For these reasons, it is important to see a dentist regularly.
Tips for your dental visit:

- Make sure you have routine dental visits for cleaning and checkups. Preventing problems before they occur is always the best approach.

- Tell your dentist you have HIV. That's not because your dentist will need to take additional precautions—all healthcare professionals use "universal precautions" to prevent the transmission of bloodborne diseases to patients and vice versa. Rather, it will help the dentist know to look for particular oral health problems that you might be at risk for.

- Don't wait for problems in your mouth to get out of hand. When you notice something wrong (such as tooth pain or a mouth sore), call your dentist right away.

- Be on time for your dental visit. Try not to miss your appointment, if you can help it—and if you can't, reschedule it ASAP.

- Keep a record of your dental visits, just like you do with your visits to your HIV care provider. Keep track of when you had dental X-rays (and what was X-rayed), any procedures or treatments you had, and when your next visit is scheduled.

- Bring copies of your recent test results and lab reports. Your dentist may need to have information about your CD4 count and *platelet count* to know how best to treat your dental issue. Also bring a list of any medications you are currently taking, as your dentist needs to know what you are taking to avoid giving you other medications which may have bad interactions.

- Know your rights: Any dentist licensed in the United States should be able to provide at least basic dental care to people living with HIV. If you sense there is discrimination towards you based on your HIV status, there are resources to help you with this.

Frequently Asked Questions

If I am already seeing an HIV provider, do I also need to see a general health care provider?

Usually, your provider will see you for HIV and all of your health care needs and then provide a referral to a specialist if needed. Talk to your HIV provider and ask if this is how he/she will handle your care. Many health centers serve as "patient-centered medical homes" that provide coordinated care and treat the many needs of patients all at once. Ask your provider if this is available.

It has been a while since I saw my HIV care provider, and I am worried that she/he will be upset with me. What should I do?

While staying engaged in care is the best way to ensure healthy outcomes, sometimes people miss appointments or have trouble sticking to their HIV treatment plan for a whole host of reasons. HIV providers are usually concerned when their patients stop going to appointments and happy to see them return to care. If it has been a while since your last HIV medical appointment, you can schedule an appointment with your previous HIV provider or schedule an appointment with a new HIV provider. A new provider can help you ask for your health records to be transferred over from your previous provider. Whether you change providers or not, it may be a good idea to discuss with your provider the reasons you stopped going to your HIV medical appointments in the past so that she/he can help you avoid or address these reasons in the future.

Chapter 18

Navigating the Healthcare System: What You Need to Know

What you need to know to work the system

Here are a few tips and tricks to keep in mind when you are moving through the medical and service system. **IT IS IMPORTANT TO REMEMBER: HIV treatment is most successful for those people who stay engaged and active in their own care.**

- **Know your rights**

  - As a client of HIV/AIDS service providers, you are entitled to the same rights as any other patient in the medical system— and those rights include safety, competent medical care, and confidentiality.

- **Keep track of all the services you access and be knowledgeable about them.**

  - If you are living with HIV, you may work with multiple clinicians, including a primary care provider (doctor, nurse, etc.),

---

Text in this section is excerpted from "Navigating the System," AIDS.gov, June 1, 2012.

as well as a case manager, dietician, dentist, social worker, therapist, and other specialist providers.

• In addition to your medical providers, you may benefit from access to food assistance programs, housing or home health-care programs, or community support groups. It is important to find out what services are available in your local community and, if possible, engage your clinic's staff to help you access these services.

• Keep records of your lab tests and other test results and the name of the provider who ordered them for you.

• Keep a written record of your doctor or provider visits, including your questions (and the answers you receive), tests, plan of care, and next appointment.

• **Communicate with your providers. Be open and honest. Don't be afraid to ask questions.**

  • You always know more about your body and the way you are feeling than your provider does—and your provider can do a better job of helping you if you talk about what you are experiencing.

  • Ask your care providers for copies of your test and lab results

  • What they don't know CAN hurt you. Be open and honest with them about things that might have an impact on your physical and mental health, including your sex life, changes in your personal life or living situation, your medications (side effects and missed doses), new research you may have done, your frustrations or concerns, etc.

  • Let your providers know how they are doing—and be constructive with your criticisms. If you feel your care providers are doing a great job managing your care with you, tell them. Everyone likes to hear positive feedback. And if you are unhappy with your care, try to complain in a constructive way. Give specific examples of things that have made you unhappy with your care—and try to give your provider some positive suggestions on how the two of you can have a more satisfying relationship.

  • Ask about clinical trial options.

  • Always let your providers know when you are going to miss, reschedule, or be late to an appointment. If you have to cancel an appointment, **always reschedule at the time you cancel!** This will ensure that you don't forget and that you continue to get the care you need to stay healthy.

- Remember your provider's receptionist probably isn't a clinician, so if you are calling because you need help with a medical issue, the receptionist is unlikely to be able to help you. You will probably need to wait for your provider to call you back. Be sure you leave the information your provider will need to help you—including a detailed description of any symptoms or problems you may be having.

- **Be prepared—and on time—for your appointments**
  - Keep track of your appointments the same way you keep track of your other events or activities (phone, paper calendar, online calendar, etc.).

  - If you are concerned about confidentiality, you could use a code word or activity on your calendar instead. For example, you could enter "late lunch" for your appointments with your doctor or "go to the grocery store" for your meetings with your HIV case manager.

  - If possible, arrive a few minutes before your scheduled appointment time. A patient who is even 10 minutes late can radically disrupt the schedule of a healthcare provider. Remember—your care providers want to give you all the time they possibly can, and it helps if you are there on time.

  - Keep in mind you may have to wait when you arrive at your appointment. Providers don't always have control over what happens in the healthcare environment, and things can change rapidly. There may be someone ahead of you who has an emergency or needs extra attention that day. Be patient—you might **be** that person some time.

  - Follow up on your labs and get them drawn when your healthcare providers advise you to do so. If they ask you to do a test or a lab before your appointment, try to do so. Providers often ask you do this so they can review your results with you when you come in for your visit.

  - Ask for copies of your labs and tests.

- **Before you leave, ask when your next appointment will be and get a written reminder from the front desk.**

221

- This will help you stay on track with your care and protect your health.

- **Be prepared for life-long learning**

  - HIV research is constantly evolving and changing. It's important to keep up with new advances in care.

  - Learn about your community's resources and become active in your community's HIV services.

  - Learn about politics and HIV and how your government (local, state, and Federal) responds to HIV issues.

  - Read HIV-related publications, including magazines, journals, on-line blogs, and related materials.

Will I have to navigate this complicated HIV care system alone?

There are thousands of community health programs and advocates out there whose exist to help you navigate the HIV care system. Ask your healthcare provider how you can access these services.

Part Four

Treatments and Therapies for HIV/AIDS

Chapter 19

Antiretroviral Treatment

Chapter Contents

Section 19.1

Introduction to HIV and AIDS Treatment

This section includes excerpts from "Overview of HIV Treatments,"
AIDS.gov, August 13, 2015; and text from "HIV Treatment: The
Basics," AIDS*info*, April 28, 2015.

How Is HIV Treated?

HIV is treated using a combination of medicines to fight HIV infection. This is called antiretroviral therapy (ART). ART isn't a cure, but it can control the virus so that you can live a longer, healthier life and reduce the risk of transmitting HIV to others.

ART involves taking a combination of HIV medicines (called an HIV regimen) every day, exactly as prescribed.

These HIV medicines prevent HIV from multiplying (making copies of itself), which reduces the amount of HIV in your body. Having less HIV in your body gives your immune system a chance to recover and fight off infections and cancers. Even though there is still some HIV in the body, the immune system is strong enough to fight off infections and cancers.

By reducing the amount of HIV in your body, HIV medicines also reduce the risk of transmitting the virus to others.

ART is recommended for all people with HIV, regardless of how long they've had the virus or how healthy they are. If left untreated, HIV will attack the immune system and eventually progress to AIDS.

HIV Drug Classes

HIV medicines are grouped into six drug classes according to how they fight HIV. The six drug classes are:

1. Non-nucleoside reverse transcriptase inhibitors (NNRTIs)

2. Nucleoside reverse transcriptase inhibitors (NRTIs)

3. Protease inhibitors (PIs)

4. Fusion inhibitors

5. CCR5 antagonists (CCR5s) (also called entry inhibitors)

6. Integrase strand transfer inhibitors (INSTIs)

The six drug classes include more than 25 HIV medicines that are approved to treat HIV infection. Some HIV medicines are available in combination (in other words, two or more different HIV medicines are combined in one pill.)

The U.S. Department of Health and Human Services (HHS) provides guidelines on the use of HIV medicines to treat HIV infection. The HHS guidelines recommend starting ART with a regimen of three HIV medicines from at least two different drug classes.

NIH AIDS*Info*'s FDA-Approved Medicines provides a complete list of HIV medicines, grouped by class, that are approved by the U.S. Food and Drug Administration (FDA) for the treatment of HIV infection in the United States. In addition, National Institute of Allergy and Infectious Diseases' (NIAID) *Drugs that Fight HIV* is a full-color illustrated guide to approved HIV medications.

Choosing an HIV Regimen

The choice of HIV medicines to include in an HIV regimen depends on a person's individual needs. When choosing an HIV regimen, people with HIV and their health care providers consider the following factors:

- Other diseases or conditions that the person with HIV may have possible side effects of HIV medicines

- Potential interactions between HIV medicines or between HIV medicines and other medicines the person with HIV is taking

- Results of drug-resistance testing (and other tests). Drug-resistance testing identifies which, if any, HIV medicines won't be effective against a person's HIV.

- Convenience of the regimen. For example, a regimen that includes two or more HIV medicines combined in one pill is convenient to follow.

- Any issues that can make it difficult to follow an HIV regimen, such as a busy schedule that changes from day to day.

- Cost of HIV medicines.

There are several recommended HIV regimens, but selecting the best regimen for a particular person depends on the factors listed above.

If you are starting HIV treatment for the first time, NIH AIDS*Info* shares information about selecting a first HIV regimen.

- Antiretroviral therapy (ART) is the use of HIV medicines to treat HIV infection. People on ART take a combination of HIV medicines (called an HIV regimen) every day.

- ART is recommended for everyone infected with HIV. ART can't cure HIV, but HIV medicines help people infected with HIV live longer, healthier lives. ART also reduces the risk of HIV transmission.

- When to start ART and what HIV medicines to take depend on a person's individual needs. People with HIV work closely with their health care providers to make decisions regarding the use of HIV medicines.

What Are Risks of Taking HIV Medicines?

Potential risks of ART include side effects from HIV medicines and drug interactions between HIV medicines or between HIV medicines and other medicines a person is taking. Poor adherence—not taking HIV medicines every day and exactly as prescribed—increases the risk of drug resistance and treatment failure.

Side Effects

Side effects from HIV medicines can vary depending on the medicine and the person taking the medicine. People taking the same HIV medicine can have very different side effects. Some side effects, for example, headache or occasional dizziness, may not be serious. Other side effects, such as swelling of the mouth and tongue or liver damage, can be life-threatening.

Drug Interactions

HIV medicines can interact with other HIV medicines in an HIV regimen. They can also interact with other medicines that a person with HIV is taking. A drug interaction can reduce or increase a medicine's effect on the body. Drug interactions can also cause unwanted side effects.

Drug Resistance

When HIV multiplies in the body, the virus sometimes mutates (changes form) and makes variations of itself. Variations of HIV that develop while a person is taking HIV medicines can lead to drug-resistant strains of HIV. HIV medicines that previously controlled a person's HIV are not effective against the new, drug-resistant HIV. In other words, the person's HIV continues to multiply.

Poor adherence to an HIV regimen increases the risk of drug resistance and treatment failure.

Section 19.2

Starting Anti-HIV Medications

Text in this section is excerpted from "When to Start Antiretroviral Therapy," AIDS*info*, April 28, 2015.

When to Start Antiretroviral Therapy

- Antiretroviral therapy (ART) is the use of HIV medicines to treat HIV infection. ART is recommended for everyone infected with HIV. When to start ART, however, depends on a person's unique needs and circumstances.

- A person's CD4 count is an important factor in the decision to start ART. A low or falling CD4 count indicates that HIV is advancing and damaging the immune system. A rapidly decreasing CD4 count increases the need to start ART.

- The U.S. Department of Health and Human Services (HHS) provides guidelines on the use of HIV medicines to treat HIV infection. The HHS guidelines recommend ART for everyone infected with HIV, but the recommendation is strongest for those with CD4 counts less than 350 cells/mm^3.

- Regardless of CD4 count, ART should be started if a person has a high viral load or any of the following conditions: pregnancy, AIDS, and certain HIV-related illnesses and coinfections.

- ART is a life-long treatment that helps people with HIV live longer, healthier lives. But effective ART depends on medication adherence—taking HIV medicines every day and exactly as prescribed. Before starting ART, it's important to address issues that can make adherence difficult.

When Is It Time to Start Treatment with HIV Medicines?

Treatment with HIV medicines (called antiretroviral therapy or ART for short) is recommended for everyone infected with HIV. ART helps people with HIV live longer, healthier lives and reduces the risk of HIV transmission. When to start ART, however, depends on a person's unique needs and circumstances.

What Factors Influence the Decision to Start ART?

When to start ART depends on the following factors:

- A person's CD4 count and other test results

- Whether the person has any other conditions or diseases, including pregnancy, an HIV-related illness, or AIDS (AIDS is the most advanced stage of HIV infection.)

- The person's ability and willingness to commit to lifelong treatment with HIV medicines

Why Is a Person's CD4 Count an Important Factor in Deciding When to Start ART?

A CD4 count measures the number of CD4 cells in a sample of blood. CD4 cells are infection-fighting cells of the immune system. HIV attacks and destroys CD4 cells, making it hard for the body to fight off infection. A low or falling CD4 count indicates that HIV is advancing and damaging the immune system.

The U.S. Department of Health and Human Services (HHS) provides guidelines on the use of HIV medicines to treat HIV infection. The HHS guidelines recommend ART for everyone with HIV, but the recommendation is strongest for those with CD4 counts less than 350 cells/mm^3. (The CD4 count of a healthy person ranges from 500 to 1,200 cells/mm^3.) The need to start ART is greatest when an HIV-infected person's CD4 count is less than 200 cells/mm^3 or falling rapidly.

Once a person starts taking HIV medicines, an increasing CD4 count is a sign that the immune system is recovering.

What Other Factors Increase the Need to Start ART?

Other factors that increase the need to start ART include high viral loads and conditions such as pregnancy, AIDS, and certain HIV-related illnesses and coinfections.

- **High viral loads**

An HIV viral load test measures the amount of HIV in a person's blood. The need for ART increases when a person's viral load is greater than 100,000 copies/mL.

- **Pregnancy**

Pregnant women with HIV should take HIV medicines to prevent mother-to-child transmission of HIV and to protect their own health. Women who are already taking HIV medicines when they become pregnant should continue taking HIV medicines throughout their pregnancies.

Some women with HIV may not be taking HIV medicines when they become pregnant. In these cases, women who have a high viral load or symptoms of HIV infection should start taking HIV medicines as soon as possible in pregnancy. Women without symptoms of HIV infection and a high viral load may consider waiting until after the first trimester of pregnancy (12 weeks of pregnancy) to begin taking HIV medicines.

- **AIDS**

People whose HIV has advanced to AIDS need to take HIV medicines. A diagnosis of AIDS is based on the following:

- A CD4 count less than 200 cells/mm^3

- The presence of an AIDS-defining condition. AIDS-defining conditions are infections and cancers that are life-threatening when they develop in people with HIV. Certain forms of cervical cancer and tuberculosis are examples of AIDS-defining conditions.

- **HIV-related illnesses and coinfections**

Some illnesses that develop in people infected with HIV increase the need for ART. These illnesses include HIV-related kidney disease and certain opportunistic infections (OIs). OIs are infections that develop more often or are more severe in people with weakened immune systems, such as people with HIV.

Coinfection is when a person has two or more infections at the same time. The need for ART is increased in people who are infected with HIV and certain other infections, such as hepatitis B or hepatitis C virus infection.

How Does a Person's Readiness to Take HIV Medicines Every Day Affect the Decision to Start Treatment?

ART is a life-long treatment that helps people with HIV live longer, healthier lives. But effective treatment depends on medication adherence—taking HIV medicines every day and exactly as prescribed.

Before starting ART, it's important to address issues that can make adherence difficult, such as lack of health insurance to cover the cost of HIV medicines or any issue that can make it hard to take medicines on schedule. Health care providers can recommend resources to help people deal with any issues before they start HIV medicines.

Section 19.3

HIV Treatment Regimens

This section includes excerpts from "What to Start: Selecting a First HIV Regimen," AIDS*info*, April 29, 2015; text from "HIV Treatment – FDA-Approved HIV Medicines," AIDS*info*, May 4, 2015.

Selecting a First HIV Regimen

- The use of HIV medicines to treat HIV infection is called antiretroviral therapy (ART). People on ART take a combination of HIV medicines (called an HIV regimen) every day.
- HIV medicines are grouped into six drug classes according to how they fight HIV. The six drug classes include more than 25 HIV medicines.
- The U.S. Department of Health and Human Services (HHS) provides guidelines on the use of HIV medicines to treat HIV infection. The HHS guidelines recommend starting treatment with a regimen of three HIV medicines from at least two different drug classes.
- The choice of HIV medicines to include in an HIV regimen depends on a person's individual needs. Factors considered when choosing an HIV regimen include possible side effects of HIV medicines, the potential for drug interactions, and the health of the person with HIV.

What is the next step after deciding to start HIV treatment?

The next step is choosing the HIV medicines to take. The use of HIV medicines to treat HIV infection is called antiretroviral therapy (ART). ART helps people with HIV live longer, healthier lives and reduces the risk of HIV transmission. People on ART take a combination of HIV medicines (called an HIV regimen) every day.

There are more than 25 HIV medicines approved to treat HIV infection. Some HIV medicines are available in combination (in other words, two or more different HIV medicines combined in one pill).

The U.S. Department of Health and Human Services (HHS) guidelines on the use of HIV medicines recommend starting ART with a regimen of three HIV medicines from at least two different drug classes.

What are the HIV drug classes?

HIV medicines are grouped into six drug classes according to how they fight HIV. The six drug classes are:

- Non-nucleoside reverse transcriptase inhibitors (NNRTIs)

- Nucleoside reverse transcriptase inhibitors (NRTIs)

- Protease inhibitors (PIs)

- Fusion inhibitors

- CCR5 antagonists (CCR5s) (also called entry inhibitors)

- Integrase strand transfer inhibitors (INSTIs)

In general, a person's first HIV regimen includes two NRTIs in combination with an INSTI, an NNRTI, or a PI boosted with cobicistat (brand name: Tybost) or ritonavir (brand name: Norvir). Cobicistat and ritonavir are given with some HIV medicines to increase (boost) their effectiveness.

What factors are considered when choosing an HIV regimen?

The choice of HIV medicines to include in an HIV regimen depends on a person's individual needs. When choosing an HIV regimen, people with HIV and their health care providers consider the following factors:

- Other diseases or conditions that the person with HIV may have

- Possible side effects of HIV medicines

- Potential interactions between HIV medicines or between HIV medicines and other medicines the person with HIV is taking

- Results of drug-resistance testing (and other tests). Drug-resistance testing identifies which, if any, HIV medicines won't be effective against a person's HIV.

- Convenience of the regimen. For example, a regimen that includes two or more HIV medicines combined in one pill is convenient to follow.

- Any issues that can make it difficult to follow an HIV regimen, such as a busy schedule that changes from day to day

- Cost of HIV medicines

There are several recommended HIV regimens, but selecting the best regimen for a particular person depends on the factors listed above.

What are the recommended regimens for people taking HIV medicines for the first time?

The HHS guidelines recommend the following regimens for people taking HIV medicines for the first time:

INSTI-based regimens

- dolutegravir (brand name: Tivicay) plus Truvada. Truvada is a combination of two HIV medicines—emtricitabine (brand name: Emtriva) and tenofovir disoproxil fumarate (brand name: Viread)—in one pill.

- raltegravir (brand name: Isentress) plus Truvada

- Stribild, which includes the following four medicines combined in one pill: elvitegravir (brand name: Vitekta), cobicistat, a medicine that increases the effectiveness of elvitegravir; emtricitabine; and tenofovir disoproxil fumarate. Stribild is recommended **only** for those with creatinine clearance (CrCl) >70 mL/min before starting ART. (CrCl measures how well the kidneys are working.)

- Triumeq, which includes the following three HIV medicines combined in one pill: abacavir (brand name: Ziagen), dolutegravir, and lamivudine (brand name: Epivir). Because it contains abacavir, Triumeq is recommended **only** for those who are HLA-B*5701 negative. HLA-B*5701 is a gene variation that is linked to a serious allergic reaction to abacavir.

PI-based regimens

darunavir (brand name: Prezista) boosted with ritonavir plus Truvada (Ritonavir increases (boosts) the effectiveness of darunavir.)

Because the needs of people with HIV vary, the regimens recommended for the initial treatment of HIV may not be right for everyone. The HHS guidelines list alternative HIV regimens to use if none of the recommended regimens meet a person's individual needs. An alternative regimen may actually be the preferred regimen for a person.

How long does it take for ART to work?

Viral load is the measure of HIV in a person's blood. A main goal of ART is to reduce a person's viral load to an undetectable level. An undetectable viral load means that the level of HIV in the blood is too low to be detected by a viral load test. An undetectable viral load is the best sign that ART is effective.

Once a person starts taking HIV medicines, it's possible to have an undetectable viral load within 3 to 6 months. Having an undetectable viral load doesn't mean a person's HIV is cured. There is still some HIV in the person's body, but an undetectable viral load is a sign that ART is working effectively. Effective ART helps people with HIV live longer, healthier lives and reduces the risk of HIV transmission.

FDA-Approved HIV Medicines

Treatment with HIV medicines is called antiretroviral therapy (ART). ART is recommended for everyone with HIV. People on ART take a combination of HIV medicines (called an HIV regimen) every day. A person's initial HIV regimen generally includes three HIV medicines from at least two different drug classes.

ART can't cure HIV, but HIV medicines help people with HIV live longer, healthier lives. HIV medicines also reduce the risk of HIV transmission.

The following table lists HIV medicines approved by the U.S. Food and Drug Administration (FDA) for the treatment of HIV infection in the United States. The HIV medicines are listed according to drug class and identified by generic and brand names.

Table 19.1. FDA-Approved HIV Medicines

Drug Class	Generic Name (Other names and acronyms)	Brand Name	FDA Approval Date
Nucleoside Reverse Transcriptase Inhibitors (NRTIs)			
NRTIs block reverse transcriptase, an enzyme HIV needs to make copies of itself.	abacavir (abacavir sulfate, ABC)	Ziagen	December 17, 1998
	didanosine (delayed-release didanosine, dideoxyinosine, enteric-coated didanosine, ddl, ddl EC)	Videx	October 9, 1991
		Videx EC (enteric-coated)	October 31, 2000
	emtricitabine (FTC)	Emtriva	July 2, 2003
	lamivudine (3TC)	Epivir	November 17, 1995
	stavudine (d4T)	Zerit	June 24, 1994
	tenofovir disoproxil fumarate (tenofovir DF, TDF)	Viread	October 26, 2001
	zidovudine (azidothymidine, AZT, ZDV)	Retrovir	March 19, 1987

Table 19.1. Continued

Drug Class	Generic Name (Other names and acronyms)	Brand Name	FDA Approval Date
Non-Nucleoside Reverse Transcriptase Inhibitors (NNRTIs)			
NNRTIs bind to and later alter reverse transcriptase, an enzyme HIV needs to make copies of itself.	delavirdine (delavirdine mesylate, DLV)	Rescriptor	April 4, 1997
	efavirenz (EFV)	Sustiva	September 17, 1998
	etravirine (ETR)	Intelence	January 18, 2008
	nevirapine (extended-release nevirapine, NVP)	Viramune	June 21, 1996
		Viramune XR (extended release)	March 25, 2011
	rilpivirine (rilpivirine hydrochloride, RPV)	Edurant	May 20, 2011
Protease Inhibitors (PIs)			
PIs block HIV protease, an enzyme HIV needs to make copies of itself	atazanavir (atazanavir sulfate, ATV)	Reyataz	June 20, 2003
	darunavir (darunavir ethanolate, DRV)	Prezista	June 23, 2006
	fosamprenavir (fosamprenavir calcium, FOS-APV, FPV)	Lexiva	October 20, 2003
	indinavir (indinavir sulfate, IDV)	Crixivan	March 13, 1996
	nelfinavir (nelfinavir mesylate, NFV)	Viracept	March 14, 1997
	ritonavirn (RTV)	Norvir	March 1, 1996

Table 19.1. Continued

Drug Class	Generic Name (Other names and acronyms)	Brand Name	FDA Approval Date
	saquinavir (saquinavir mesylate, SQV)	Invirase	December 6, 1995
	tipranavir (TPV)	Aptivus	June 22, 2005
Fusion Inhibitors			
Fusion inhibitors block HIV from entering the CD4 cells of the immune system.	enfuvirtide (T-20)	Fuzeon	March 13, 2003
Entry Inhibitors			
Entry inhibitors block proteins on the CD4 cells that HIV needs to enter the cells.	maraviroc (MVC)	Selzentry	August 6, 2007
Integrase Inhibitors			
Integrase inhibitors block HIV integrase, an enzyme HIV needs to make copies of itself.	dolutegravir (DTG)	Tivicay	August 13, 2013
	elvitegravir (EVG)	Vitekta	September 24, 2014
	raltegravir (raltegravir potassium, RAL)	Isentress	October 12, 2007
Pharmacokinetic Enhancers			
Pharmacokinetic enhancers are used in HIV treatment to increase the effectiveness of an HIV medicine included in an HIV regimen.	cobicistat (COBI)	Tybost	September 24, 2014

Table 19.1. Continued

Drug Class	Generic Name (Other names and acronyms)	Brand Name	FDA Approval Date
Combination HIV Medicines			
Combination HIV medicines contain two or more HIV medicines from one or more drug classes.	abacavir and lamivudine (abacavir sulfate / lamivudine, ABC / 3TC)	Epzicom	August 2, 2004
	abacavir, dolutegravir, and lamivudine (abacavir sulfate / dolutegravir sodium / lamivudine, ABC / DTG / 3TC)	Triumeq	August 22, 2014
	abacavir, lamivudine, and zidovudine (abacavir sulfate / lamivudine / zidovudine, ABC / 3TC / ZDV)	Trizivir	November 14, 2000
	atazanavir and cobicistat (atazanavir sulfate / cobicistat, ATV / COBI)	Evotaz	January 29, 2015
	darunavir and cobicistat (darunavir ethanolate / cobicistat, DRV / COBI)	Prezcobix	January 29, 2015

Table 19.1. Continued

Drug Class	Generic Name (Other names and acronyms)	Brand Name	FDA Approval Date
	efavirenz, emtricitabine, and tenofovir disoproxil fumarate (efavirenz / emtricitabine / tenofovir, efavirenz / emtricitabine / tenofovir DF, EFV / FTC / TDF)	Atripla	July 12, 2006
	elvitegravir, cobicistat, emtricitabine, and tenofovir disoproxil fumarate (QUAD, EVG / COBI / FTC / TDF)	Stribild	August 27, 2012
	emtricitabine, rilpivirine, and tenofovir disoproxil fumarate (emtricitabine / rilpivirine hydrochloride / tenofovir disoproxil fumarate, emtricitabine / rilpivirine / tenofovir, FTC / RPV / TDF)	Complera	August 10, 2011
	emtricitabine and tenofovir disoproxil fumarate (emtricitabine / tenofovir, FTC / TDF)	Truvada	August 2, 2004
	lamivudine and zidovudine (3TC / ZDV)	Combivir	September 27, 1997

Table 19.1. Continued

Drug Class	Generic Name (Other names and acronyms)	Brand Name	FDA Approval Date
	lopinavir and ritonavir (ritonavir-boosted lopinavir, LPV/r, LPV / RTV)	Kaletra	September 15, 2000

Section 19.4

Deciding Which Drugs to Take

Text in this section is excerpted from "HIV/AIDS – Treatment," U.S. Department of Veterans Affairs (VA), September 17, 2015.

Once you and your provider have decided that you should start taking drugs for HIV, he or she will come up with a personal treatment plan for you. You will find it easier to understand your plan if you learn about the different drugs available and what they do.

What kinds of drugs are available?

Anti-HIV drugs are also called antiretroviral drugs or antiretrovirals (ARVs). They work because they attack the HIV virus directly. The drugs cripple the ability of the virus to make copies of itself.

There are 6 main classes of anti-HIV drugs:

• Nucleoside Reverse Transcriptase Inhibitors (NRTIs or "nukes")

• Non-Nucleoside Reverse Transcriptase Inhibitors (NNRTIs or "non-nukes")

• Protease Inhibitors (PIs)

• Integrase Inhibitors

- Chemokine Coreceptor Antagonists (CCR5 Antagonists)
- Fusion or Entry Inhibitors

Each group attacks HIV in its own way and helps your body fight the infection. Most of these drugs come as tablets or capsules. Several of these drugs may be combined into one tablet to make it easier to take your medications. These are known as fixed-dose combinations.

The following is a short description of how each group of drugs works and the names of the individual drugs.

Nucleoside Reverse Transcriptase Inhibitors (NRTIs or nukes)

The first group of antiretroviral drugs is the nucleoside reverse transcriptase inhibitors (NRTIs).

NRTIs were the first type of drug available to treat HIV. They remain effective, powerful, and important medications for treating HIV when combined with other drugs. They are better known as nucleoside analogues or "nukes."

When the HIV virus enters a healthy cell, it attempts to make copies of itself. It does this by using an enzyme called reverse transcriptase. The NRTIs work because they block that enzyme. Without reverse transcriptase, HIV can't make new virus copies of itself.

The following is a list of the drugs in the NRTI class:

- Emtriva® (emtricitabine)
- Epivir® (3TC, lamivudine)
- Retrovir® (AZT, zidovudine)
- Videx-EC® (ddI, didanosine)
- Viread® (tenofovir)
- Zerit® (d4T, stavudine)
- Ziagen® (abacavir)

Several of the NRTI drugs may be combined into one tablet to make it easier to take your medications. These drugs are known as fixed-dose combinations:

- Combivir® (Retrovir + Epivir)
- Epzicom® (Epivir + Ziagen)
- Trizivir® (Retrovir + Epivir + Ziagen)
- Truvada® (Viread + Emtriva)

Non-nucleoside Reverse Transcriptase Inhibitors (NNRTIs or non-nukes)

The second type of antiretroviral drugs is the non-nucleoside reverse transcriptase inhibitors (NNRTIs). These drugs are sometimes called non-nucleosides or "non-nukes."

These drugs also prevent HIV from using reverse transcriptase to make copies of itself, but in a different way.

These NNRTIs are available:

- Edurant® (rilpivirine)
- Intelence® (etravirine)
- Rescriptor® (delavirdine)
- Sustiva® (efavirenz)
- Viramune® (nevirapine)

Protease Inhibitors (PIs)

The third group of drugs is the protease inhibitors (PIs).

Once HIV has infected a cell and made copies of itself, it uses an enzyme called protease to process itself correctly so it can be released from the cell to infect other cells. These medicines work by blocking protease.

Nine PIs are available:

- Aptivus® (tipranavir)
- Crixivan® (indinavir)
- Invirase® (saquinavir)
- Kaletra® (lopinavir + ritonavir combined in one tablet)
- Lexiva® (fosamprenavir)
- Norvir® (ritonavir)
- Prezista® (darunavir)
- Reyataz® (atazanavir)
- Viracept® (nelfinavir)

Many PIs are recommended or approved for use only with another drug that "boosts" their effect. One of these is low-dose Norvir®, the other is a non-HIV drug called Tybost® (cobicistat).

Several combination tablets that include a "booster" plus a PI are:

- Evotaz® (Reyataz® + Tybost®)
- Prezcobix® (Prezista® + Tybost®)
- Kaletra® (lopinavir® + Norvir®)

Integrase Inhibitors

This class of anti-HIV drugs works by blocking an enzyme (HIV integrase) that the virus needs in order to splice copies of itself into human DNA.

- Isentress® (raltegravir)
- Tivicay® (dolutegravir)
- Vitekta® (elvitegravir)

(Note: Vitekta must be "boosted" with a pharmacokinetic enhancer, either Tybost® or Norvir®.)

Chemokine Coreceptor Antagonists (CCR5)

To infect a cell, HIV must bind to two types of molecules on the cell's surface. One of these is called a chemokine coreceptor. Drugs known as chemokine coreceptor antagonists block the virus from binding to the coreceptor.

- Selzentry® (maraviroc)

Fusion or Entry Inhibitors

The fusion or entry inhibitors work by stopping the HIV virus from getting into your body's healthy cells in the first place.

Only one fusion inhibitor is available at present, and it needs to be injected:

- Fuzeon® (enfuvirtide, T-20)

Multi-class drug combinations

At present there are four options that combine drugs from two different groups into a complete HIV drug regimen. A patient prescribed one of these combinations takes only one tablet, once a day. Despite the convenience, these combination tablets are not for everyon—each has specific possible side effects or dosing requirements that should be considered. You and your doctor can decide whether these drug combinations are right for you.

- Atripla® (Sustiva + Emtriva + Viread)

- Complera® (Edurant + Emtriva + Viread)

- Stribild® (Vitekta + Tybost + Emtriva + Viread)

- Triumeq® (Tivicay + Epzicom + Ziagin)

Which drugs should you take?

Now that you have learned a little about the types of drugs that are available and how they work, you may be wondering how your health care provider will know which medicines you should take.

Anti-HIV drugs are used in combination with one another in order to get the best results. The goal is to get the viral load as low as possible (to levels that are undetectable by standard laboratory tests) for as long as possible.

Anti-HIV medicines do different things to the virus—they attack it in different ways—so using the different drugs in combination works better than using just one by itself. Combinations usually include three antiretroviral drugs. Except in very special circumstances, anti-HIV drugs should never be used one or two at a time. Using only one or two drugs at a time can fail to control the viral load and let the virus adapt (or become resistant) to the drug. Once the virus adapts to a drug, the drug won't work as well against the virus, and maybe it won't work at all.

There is no one combination of HIV medications that works best for everyone. Each combination has its pluses and minuses.

When drugs are used together, the therapy is called combination therapy [or antiretroviral therapy (ART)].

Questions to ask about each drug

One of the most important things you can do to make sure you take your medicine correctly is to talk with your doctor about your lifestyle, such as your sleeping and eating schedule. If your doctor prescribes a drug, be sure and ask the following questions (and make sure you understand the answers):

- What dose of the drug should be taken? How many pills does this mean?

- How often should the drug be taken?

- Does it matter if it is taken with food, or on an empty stomach?

- Does the drug have to be kept in a refrigerator?

- What are the side effects of the drug?

- What should be done to deal with the side effects?

- How severe do side effects have to be before a doctor is called?

During every visit to your doctor, you should talk about whether you are having trouble staying on your treatment plan. Studies show that patients who take their medicine in the right way get the best results: their viral loads stay down, their CD4 counts stay up, and they feel healthier.

Section 19.5

Prevention Benefits

Text in this section is excerpted from "HIV/AIDS – Prevention Benefits of HIV Treatment," Centers for Disease Control and Prevention (CDC), April 15, 2013.

To realize the full prevention benefit of treating HIV infection, we should keep in mind four overarching tenets:

- HIV testing is the foundation for both prevention and care efforts.
- Early identification of infection empowers individuals to take action that benefits both their own health and the public health.
- Early treatment of infected persons substantially reduces their risk of transmitting HIV to others.
- The prevention benefit of treatment can only be realized with effective treatment, which requires linkage to and retention in care, and adherence to antiretroviral therapy.

The advent in 1996 of potent combination antiretroviral therapy (ART), sometimes called HAART (highly active antiretroviral therapy) or cART (effective combination antiretroviral therapy), changed the course of the HIV epidemic. These "cocktails" of three or more antiretroviral drugs used in combination gave patients and scientists new hope for fighting the epidemic, and have significantly improved life expectancy—to decades rather than months.

For many years, scientists believed that treating HIV-infected persons also significantly reduced their risk of transmitting the infection to sexual and drug-using partners who did not have the virus. The circumstantial evidence was substantial, but no one had conducted a randomized clinical trial—the gold standard for proving an intervention works. That changed in 2011 with the publication of findings from the HIV Prevention Trials Network (HPTN) 052 study, a randomized clinical trial designed in part to evaluate whether the early initiation of ART can prevent the sexual transmission of HIV among heterosexual couples in which one partner is HIV-infected and the other is not. This landmark study validated that early HIV treatment has a profound prevention benefit: results showed that the risk of transmitting HIV to an uninfected partner was reduced by 96%.

As a concept and a strategy, treating HIV-infected persons to improve their health and to reduce the risk of onward transmission— sometimes called *treatment as prevention*—refers to the personal and public health benefits of using ART to continuously suppress HIV viral load in the blood and genital fluids, which decreases the risk of transmitting the virus to others. The practice has been used since the mid-1990s to prevent mother-to-child, or perinatal, transmission of the virus. Research published in 1994 showed that zidovudine, more commonly known as AZT, when given to HIV-infected pregnant women and to their newborns reduced the risk of perinatal transmission from about 25% to 8%. Since then, routinely testing pregnant women and treating infected mothers with ART during pregnancy, delivery, and while breastfeeding, when practiced according to recommendations, has reduced the mother's risk of transmitting HIV to her child by 90%. In one study, women who received at least 14 days of ART reduced the risk of transmitting HIV to their babies to less than 1%.

Putting Treatment as Prevention in Perspective

Treatment by itself is not going to solve the global HIV epidemic. On the domestic front, controlling and ultimately ending the epidemic will require a combination of scientifically proven HIV prevention tools as highlighted in the National HIV/AIDS Strategy, including

- Focusing on science-based HIV prevention efforts by supporting and expanding targeted use of high-impact HIV prevention approaches.

- Making better investments by intensifying HIV prevention in the communities where HIV is most heavily concentrated.

- Increasing access to HIV screening and medical care, including through

  - boosting federal investments for AIDS Drug Assistance Programs (ADAPs) to expand access to life-saving medications, and

  - implementing the Affordable Care Act, which will increase health coverage for thousands of Americans living with HIV.

- Sustaining a shared response to the domestic epidemic through the support of HIV prevention efforts across all levels of society, including federal, state, and local governments, faith-based communities, and the private sector.

Providing treatment to people living with HIV infection to improve their health must always be the first priority. Getting an HIV test is the first step to identifying persons with HIV infection and the pivotal entry point into the medical care system for both treatment and prevention. More than 1.1 million persons in the United States are living with HIV, and almost 1 in 5 (18.1%) do not know they are infected. By lowering the level of virus in the body, early ART helps people with HIV live longer, healthier lives and also lowers their chances of transmitting HIV to others. Although observational data had suggested that ART significantly reduces viral load and the risk of sexual transmission of HIV in heterosexual couples where one partner is infected and the other is not, it was the HPTN 052 study that definitively showed that early treatment of HIV-infected persons dramatically cuts the rate of new infections. Studies of communities with high concentrations of injection drug users (IDUs) and men who have sex with men (MSM) have shown that as ART use increased within the community, the community's viral load declined, as did rates of new HIV diagnoses. However, it is critical to remember that the prevention benefit of treatment is not 100%, and there has been at least one report of HIV transmission from a person with suppressed viral load to an uninfected sexual partner.

For persons living with or at risk for HIV infection, emphasizing these fundamental safeguards will continue to be crucial:

- Knowing their HIV status through routine testing.

- Getting into care soon after HIV diagnosis and starting antiretroviral treatment.

- Remaining in care and staying on HIV treatment.

- Modifying behaviors that reduce the probability of getting or spreading HIV—such as using condoms properly and consistently, reducing numbers of partners, and avoiding sharing needles and syringes.

Test and Treat

The ability of antiretroviral drugs to prevent secondary transmission of HIV from an infected person to an uninfected sexual or drug-using partner has led to several proposed "test-and-treat" strategies. Test-and-treat programs are based on the premise that the rate of new HIV infections will be maximally reduced by using aggressive methods to test and diagnose all people living with HIV infection, treat them with ART regardless of CD4 cell count or viral load at diagnosis, and link them to care. In one study, mathematical modeling suggested that a universal test-and-treat-strategy in which all adults aged 15 years or older are tested annually could control the South African epidemic, reducing both HIV incidence and mortality to less than 1 case per 1,000 people per year within 10 years of full implementation of the strategy—and reducing prevalence of HIV infection to less than 1% within 50 years. Other investigators have not been as optimistic about the ultimate benefits of this strategy. Only 50% of persons in the United States with HIV remain in care, and about 18% do not know they are infected; these persons may contribute to the onward transmission of HIV. In addition to expanding testing and treating HIV infection earlier, overcoming the challenges of undiagnosed infection and poor engagement in care will result in better care of HIV-infected populations and reduced numbers of new HIV infections.

Challenges and the Future of HIV Prevention

The landmark HPTN 052 clinical trial was conducted almost solely among heterosexual couples who, as part of the study, received frequent counseling related to HIV, sexually transmitted diseases (STDs), and family planning. Results of a recent observational study of more than 38,000 serodiscordant heterosexual couples across China showed that treating the HIV-infected partner reduced the risk of transmitting HIV to the uninfected partner by 26%—a much more modest effect than that found in the HPTN 052 study couples. Unlike the couples enrolled in HPTN 052, the couples in China were not part of an intensive study, and data were not available on sexual risk factors, adherence to antiretroviral treatment, or virological treatment outcome measures. Additional data are needed to estimate the prevention benefit of treatment for other populations, such as MSM, IDUs, and persons with acute or primary HIV infection, and in other settings such as North America and during routine clinical care.

As HIV treatment has evolved from a complicated regimen of numerous pills taken several times a day with severe side effects to a now once-daily pill with few side effects, some persons living with HIV may have become complacent about maintaining safer sex and safer injection use practices. Since HIV treatment became widely available in developed countries, several studies have shown a resurgence of HIV infections and increases in STDs, in particular syphilis, and especially among MSM. Some studies have cautioned that the prevention benefits of effective ART would be offset by risk compensation, meaning that increases in risky sexual and injection-drug-use behavior might be observed as effective ART is widely disseminated. However, results of one meta-analysis demonstrated that HIV-positive persons receiving ART, compared with those not receiving ART, did not show increased sexual risk behavior, even when therapy resulted in an undetectable viral load. Yet, persons with HIV who believe that using ART or having a suppressed viral load protects them against transmitting HIV may be more likely to engage in unprotected sex or other risky behaviors. These behaviors might be amenable to change through prevention messages and other effective approaches. Making sure that preventive behaviors are sustained in communities facing higher risk of HIV infection is crucial.

The future of HIV prevention will be shaped by operational and implementation research on the efficacy of combination prevention strategies, of which treatment may be one component. Providing treatment to all HIV-infected persons will be an important step—a recommendation that is included in the current *Guidelines for the Use of Antiretroviral Agents in HIV-1-Infected Adults and Adolescents*. The Department of Health and Human Services panel based its recommendations primarily on mounting evidence showing the harmful impact of ongoing HIV replication on AIDS and non-AIDS disease progression. In addition, the updated recommendations reflect emerging data showing the benefit of effective ART in preventing secondary transmission of HIV. Although the panel agrees that this public health benefit of ART is significant, its recommendations on when to begin ART are based primarily on the benefit of treatment to the HIV-infected individual. If treatment is to achieve its full prevention potential, current gaps in the HIV prevention, treatment, and care continuum must be narrowed or closed. Considerable changes in the US health care delivery system will be required to accommodate the increased demand for services that expanded testing, treatment, and linkage and retention in care will bring.

Now that early ART of HIV-infected persons has been shown to be very effective at preventing secondary transmission of HIV among individuals, the current goal is to determine the extent to which ART can be used broadly and effectively to reduce the spread of HIV within a population. At least two community randomized trials that use ART as their basis are planned, and the results could determine the conclusive benefit of this successful intervention.

Still, resource constraints, logistical hurdles, emergence of drug-resistant viral strains, adherence to therapy regimens, and risk compensation remain concerns that scientists, health care providers, policy makers, and communities must confront if the individual and public health benefits of treatment are to be fully realized.

Chapter 20

HIV/AIDS Medication Adherence

Key Points

- Medication adherence means sticking firmly to an HIV regimen—taking HIV medicines every day and exactly as prescribed.

- HIV medicines prevent HIV from multiplying, which protects the immune system and reduces the risk of drug resistance and HIV treatment failure. Medication adherence lets HIV medicines do their job!

- Adherence can be difficult for many reasons. For example, side effects from HIV medicines can make it hard to stick to an HIV regimen.

- Strategies to help maintain adherence include using a 7-day pill box and setting daily pill reminders on a smartphone.

Text in this chapter is excerpted from "HIV Medication Adherence," AIDS*info*, April 29, 2015.

What is medication adherence?

Adherence means "to stick firmly." So for people with HIV, medication adherence means sticking firmly to an HIV regimen—taking HIV medicines every day and exactly as prescribed.

Why is adherence to an HIV regimen important?

Adherence to an HIV regimen gives HIV medicines the chance to do their job: to prevent HIV from multiplying and destroying the immune system. HIV medicines help people with HIV live longer, healthier lives. HIV medicines also reduce the risk of HIV transmission.

Poor adherence to an HIV regimen allows HIV to destroy the immune system. A damaged immune system makes it hard for the body to fight off infections and certain cancers. Poor adherence also increases the risk of drug resistance and HIV treatment failure.

What is drug resistance?

Drug resistance can develop as HIV multiplies in the body. When HIV multiplies, the virus sometimes mutates (changes form) and makes variations of itself. Variations of HIV that develop while a person is taking HIV medicines can lead to new, drug-resistant strains of HIV. HIV medicines that used to suppress the person's HIV are not effective against the new drug-resistant HIV. In other words, the person's HIV continues to multiply.

Once drug-resistant HIV develops, it remains in the body. Drug resistance limits the number of HIV medicines available to include in a current or future HIV regimen.

What is the connection between medication adherence and drug resistance?

Taking HIV medicines every day prevents HIV from multiplying, which reduces the risk that HIV will mutate and produce drug-resistant HIV. Skipping HIV medicines allows HIV to multiply, which increases the risk of drug-resistant HIV developing.

Research shows that a person's first HIV regimen offers the best chance for long-term treatment success. So adherence is important from the start—when a person first begins taking HIV medicines.

Why is medication adherence sometimes difficult?

Adherence to an HIV regimen can be difficult for several reasons. For example, side effects from HIV medicines, such as nausea or diarrhea, can make it hard to follow an HIV regimen. When an HIV regimen includes several HIV medicines, it's easy to forget how many pills to take and when to take them.

The following factors can also make medication adherence difficult:

- Side effects from interactions between HIV medicines and other medicines a person may take

- Trouble swallowing pills or other difficulty taking medicines

- A busy schedule, shift work, or travel away from home that makes it hard to take medicines on time

- Illness or depression

- Alcohol or drug use that interferes with the activities of daily life

- Fear of disclosing one's HIV-positive status to others

- Lack of health insurance to cover the cost of HIV medicines

Before starting HIV medicines, it helps to have strategies in place to maintain adherence. Strategies may include using a 7-day pill box or using an app (for example, the AIDS*info* Drug Database app) to set daily pill reminders.

Chapter 21

HIV/AIDS Treatment Interruptions

Discontinuation or Interruption of Antiretroviral Therapy

Discontinuation of antiretroviral therapy (ART) may result in viral rebound, immune decompensation, and clinical progression. Thus, planned interruptions of ART are not generally recommended. However, unplanned interruption of ART may occur under certain circumstances as discussed below.

Short-Term Therapy Interruptions

Reasons for short-term interruption (days to weeks) of ART vary and may include drug toxicity; intercurrent illnesses that preclude oral intake, such as gastroenteritis or pancreatitis; surgical procedures; or interrupted access to drugs. Stopping ART for a short time (i.e., less than 1 to 2 days) because of a medical/surgical procedure can usually be done by holding all drugs in the regimen. Recommendations for some other scenarios are listed below:

Unanticipated Short-Term Therapy Interruption

When a Patient Experiences a Severe or Life-Threatening Toxicity or Unexpected Inability to Take Oral Medications:

Text in this chapter is excerpted from "Management of the Treatment-Experienced Patient," AIDS*info*, April 8, 2015.

- All components of the drug regimen should be stopped simultaneously, regardless of drug half-life.

Planned Short-Term Therapy Interruption (Up to 2 Weeks)

When All Regimen Components Have Similar Half-Lives and Do Not Require Food for Proper Absorption:

- All drugs may be given with a sip of water, if allowed; otherwise, all drugs should be stopped simultaneously. All discontinued regimen components should be restarted simultaneously.

When All Regimen Components Have Similar Half-Lives and Require Food for Adequate Absorption, and the Patient Cannot Take Anything by Mouth for a Short Time:

- Temporary discontinuation of all drug components is indicated. The regimen should be restarted as soon as the patient can resume oral intake.

When the ARV Regimen Contains Drugs with Different Half-Lives:

- Stopping all drugs simultaneously may result in functional monotherapy with the drug with the longest half-life (typically a non-nucleoside reverse transcriptase inhibitor [NNRTI]), which may increase the risk of selection of NNRTI-resistant mutations. Some experts recommend stopping the NNRTI first and the other ARV drugs 2 to 4 weeks later. Alternatively, the NNRTI may be replaced with a ritonavir (or cobicistat)-boosted protease inhibitor (PI/r or PI/c) for 4 weeks. The optimal time sequence for staggered discontinuation of regimen components, or replacement of the NNRTI with a PI/r (or PI/c), has not been determined.

Planned Long-Term Therapy Interruptions

Planned long-term therapy interruptions are **not recommended** outside of controlled clinical trials **(AI).** Several research studies are evaluating approaches to a functional (virological control in the absence of therapy) or sterilizing (virus eradication) cure of HIV infection. Currently, the only way to reliably test the effectiveness of these strategies may be to interrupt ART and closely monitor viral rebound over time in the setting of a clinical trial.

If therapy must be discontinued, patients should be aware of and understand the risks of viral rebound, acute retroviral syndrome, increased risk of HIV transmission, decline of CD4 count, HIV disease progression, development of minor HIV-associated manifestations such as oral thrush or serious non-AIDS complications (e.g., renal, cardiac, hepatic, or neurologic complications), development of drug resistance, and the need for chemoprophylaxis against opportunistic infections as a result of CD4 decline. Patients should be counseled about the need for close clinical and laboratory monitoring during therapy interruptions.

Chapter 22

Monitoring HIV/AIDS Treatment Success

Chapter Contents

Section 22.1

Viral Load Test

Text in this section is excerpted from "Viral Load," AIDS.gov,
September 3, 2015.

What Is "Viral Load"?

The term "viral load" refers to the amount of HIV in a sample of
your blood. When your viral load is high, you have more HIV in your
body, and that means your immune system is not fighting HIV as
well.

What Is a Viral Load Test and Why Is It Important?

A viral load test is a lab test that measures the number of HIV virus
particles in a milliliter of your blood. These particles are called "copies."

A viral load test helps provide information on your health status
and how well antiretroviral therapy (ART – treatment with HIV medicines) is controlling the virus.

ART involves taking a combination of HIV medicines (called an
HIV regimen) every day. ART can't cure HIV, but it can help you live
a longer, healthier life and reduce your risk of HIV transmission.

The goal of ART is to move your viral load down, ideally to undetectable levels. In general, your viral load will be declared "undetectable" if
it is under 40 to 75 copies in a sample of your blood. The exact number
depends on the lab that analyzes your test.

Having an "undetectable" viral load doesn't mean that the virus
is completely gone from your body, just that it is below what a lab
test can find. You still have HIV and need to stay on ART to remain
healthy.

What Is a Normal Viral Load?

There is really no such thing as a "normal" viral load. People who
aren't infected with HIV have no viral load at all, so there's no "normal"
range for reference, as there is for many other HIV lab tests (such as
CD4 counts.)

When and How Often Do I Need a Viral Load Test?

Your HIV care provider will order a viral load test at your first visit to determine your viral load. A viral load test will:

- Show how well your HIV treatment is controlling the virus, and

- Provide health information on your health status.

After that, you should have a viral load test every 3 to 6 months before you start taking a new HIV medicine, and 2 to 8 weeks after starting or changing HIV medicines until your viral load is suppressed.

Can I Transmit HIV If I Have an Undetectable Viral Load?

As noted above, the goal of ART is to reduce your viral load, ideally to an undetectable level. If your viral load goes down after starting ART, the treatment is working.

Having an undetectable viral load greatly lowers your chance of transmitting the virus to your sexual and drug-using partners who are HIV-negative. However, even when your viral load is undetectable, HIV can still exist in semen, vaginal and rectal fluids, breast milk, and other parts of your body. For this reason, you should continue to take steps to prevent HIV transmission. For example:

1. HIV may still be found in your genital fluids (semen or vaginal fluids). The viral load test only measures the amount of HIV in your blood. Although ART also lowers viral load in genital fluids, HIV can sometimes be present in your genital fluids even when it is undetectable in your blood.

2. Your viral load may go up between tests. When this happens, you may be more likely to transmit HIV to your partner(s). Your viral load may go up without you knowing it because you may not feel any different.

3. Sexually transmitted diseases (STDs) can increase your viral load in your genital fluids. This means that if you are living with HIV and also have an STD, you may be able to transmit HIV to your partner(s) even if your viral load is undetectable.

Researchers are studying how much you can lower your chances of transmitting HIV when your viral load is undetectable. One large multinational study indicates that ART that consistently suppresses HIV is highly effective at preventing sexual transmission of the virus in heterosexual couples where one person is HIV-infected and the other is not. In fact, that study found that ARTreduces the risk of heterosexual HIV transmission by 93% or more if viral suppression is achieved and maintained. Researchers did not observe any HIV transmission during this study when the HIV-infected partner's virus was stably suppressed by ART.

If you are taking ART, follow your HIV care provider's advice. Visit your HIV care provider regularly and always take your HIV meds as directed. This will give you the greatest chance of having an undetectable viral load. Taking other actions, like using a condom consistently and correctly, can lower your chances of transmitting HIV or contracting an STD even more.

Section 22.2

CD4 Count

Text in this section is excerpted from "CD4 Count," AIDS.gov,
September 9, 2015.

What Is a CD4 Count and why Is It Important?

A CD4 count is a lab test that measures the number of CD4 T lymphocytes (CD4 cells) in a sample of your blood. In people with HIV, it is the most important laboratory indicator of how well your immune system is working and the strongest predictor of HIV progression.

To understand why it's important, it's helpful to know what CD4 cells are. CD4 cells (often called T-cells or T-helper cells) are a type of white blood cells that play a major role in protecting your body from infection. They send signals to activate your body's immune response when they detect "intruders," like viruses or bacteria.

Once a person is infected with HIV, the virus begins to attack and destroy the CD4 cells of the person's immune system. HIV uses the machinery of the CD4 cells to multiply (make copies of itself) and spread throughout the body. This process is called the HIV life cycle.

So, during your regular check-ups, your HIV care provider will want to know your CD4 count to help keep track of how healthy you are and whether the virus has progressed in your body:

- The CD4 count of an uninfected adult/adolescent who is generally in good health ranges from 500 cells/mm3 to 1,200 cells/mm3.

- A very low CD4 count (less than 200 cells/mm3) is one of the ways to determine whether a person living with HIV has progressed to stage 3 infection (AIDS).

Your CD4 count is also used to help you and your HIV care provider decide when to start antiretroviral therapy (ART).

ART involves taking a combination of HIV medicines (called an HIV regimen) every day. It prevents HIV from multiplying and destroying your infection-fighting CD4 cells. ART can't cure HIV, but it can help you live a longer, healthier life and reduce your risk of HIV transmission.

ART is recommended for everyone with HIV, but the urgency to start ART is greater in people with low or rapidly falling CD4 counts. A falling CD4 count indicates that HIV is advancing and damaging your immune system.

After you start ART, your HIV care provider will use your CD4 count as one way to check how well your medication is working to monitor the effectiveness of your HIV regimen. Your HIV care provider will also monitor your CD4 count to determine whether it has fallen to a level at which you might be at risk for certain opportunistic infections. In that case, your HIV care provider may prescribe some additional medications to prevent other infections.

> When the amount of HIV in your blood is lowered by ART, it allows the CD4 cells to reproduce and increase in number. The higher your CD4 count, the better able you are to fight HIV and other infections.

When and How Often Do I Need a CD4 Count?

Your HIV care provider will order a CD4 count at your first visit after you are diagnosed in order to establish a baseline level.

After that, current HIV treatment guidelines recommend that your HIV care provider order a CD4 test every 3 to 6 months when you are starting ART to see how well you are responding to treatment. Depending on your health status, your HIV care provider may switch to every 6 to 12 months once treatment has increased your CD4 levels to higher levels and your viral load is suppressed. If your CD4 count reaches normal levels and your *viral load* remains suppressed, your HIV care provider may not check your CD4 count unless there is a change in your health or viral load.

Your CD4 count can vary from day to day. It can also vary depending on the time of day your blood is drawn and on whether you have other infections or illnesses, like the flu or sexually transmitted infections (STIs). The trend of your CD4 count (whether it's rising or falling) over time is what's really important—not an individual test result.

CD4 Count: A Summary

- A CD4 count ranges from 500–1,200 cells/mm3 in healthy adults/adolescents.

- A CD4 count of fewer than 200 cells/mm3 is one of the qualifications for a diagnosis of stage 3 infection (AIDS).

- ART is recommended for everyone with HIV, but the urgency to start ART is greater in people with low or rapidly falling CD4 counts.

- Your CD4 count can vary from day to day. It can also vary depending on the time of day your blood is drawn and on whether you have other infections or illnesses, like the flu or STIs.

- Typically, your HIV care provider will check your CD4 count every 3 to 6 months when you are starting ART. Once your CD4 level rebounds and your viral load is suppressed, your provider may check your CD4 count less frequently.

Section 22.3

Drug Resistance Test

This section includes excerpts from "Drug Resistance," AIDS.gov,
June 1, 2012; and text from "Drug-Resistance Testing," AIDS*info*,
May 1, 2014.

HIV Drug Resistance Basics

When you are first diagnosed with HIV infection, your blood is full
of copies of the HIV virus, all looking for CD4 cells that they can attach
themselves to. This virus is called "wild type," because it has never
been challenged by the HIV medications that can control it.

Once you start treatment, the goal is to keep HIV from reproducing.
When HIV isn't fully controlled by HIV drugs, the virus makes copies
of itself at a very rapid rate. Because this *replication* is occurring so
fast, HIV often makes mistakes in the copies. If these "mistaken copies"
are able to reproduce themselves, they are called **mutations**—which
creates new forms of the virus.

Mutations may not respond to existing HIV drugs—a characteristic
known as resistance. This means that the drugs are less effective and do
not stop the virus from multiplying. If your healthcare provider suspects
that you have a drug-resistant virus, he or she can do drug resistance
testing (called **genotyping** or **phenotyping**) to find out if you have
drug-resistant HIV and which of your meds may have stopped working.

Reducing Drug Resistance

- You can help reduce the chances that you will develop drug-resistant forms of HIV by taking a few simple steps:

- Work with your healthcare provider to find a drug combination
  that is effective and that you can tolerate.

- Take every dose of every medication every day, missing as few
  as possible.

- Keep your appointments with your HIV clinician and have your
  CD4 count and viral load checked every 3-4 months. Those

267

tests will help detect resistance so that, if necessary, you can make changes to your treatment plan and keep your HIV under control.

• Keep a record of which combinations of HIV medications you've taken.

Genotypic and Phenotypic Resistance Assays

Genotypic and phenotypic resistance assays are used to assess viral strains and inform selection of treatment strategies. Standard assays provide information on resistance to nucleoside reverse transcriptase inhibitors (NRTIs), non-nucleoside reverse transcriptase inhibitors (NNRTIs), and protease inhibitors (PIs). Testing for integrase and fusion inhibitor resistance can also be ordered separately from several commercial laboratories. Co-receptor tropism assays should be performed whenever the use of a CCR5 antagonist is being considered. Phenotypic co-receptor tropism assays have been used in clinical practice. A genotypic assay to predict co-receptor use is now commercially available.

Chapter 23

HIV/AIDS Treatment Side Effects

Chapter Contents

Section 23.1

Common Side Effects

This section includes excerpts from "HIV Medicines and Side Effects," AIDSinfo, December 22, 2014; and text from "Side Effects Guide to HIV Treatment," U.S. Department of Veterans Affairs (VA), July 30, 2015.

- HIV medicines help people with HIV live longer, healthier lives. Sometimes HIV medicines can also cause side effects. Most side effects from HIV medicines are manageable, but a few can be very serious.

- Different HIV medicines can cause different side effects. In addition, people taking the same HIV medicine can have very different side effects.

- If you are taking HIV medicines, tell your health care provider about any side effects that you are having. Some side effects, for example headaches or occasional dizziness, may not be serious. Other side effects, such as swelling of the mouth and tongue or damage to the liver, can be life-threatening. **However, do NOT cut down on, skip, or stop taking your HIV medicines unless your health care provider tells you to.**

- When side effects from HIV medicines become unbearable or life-threatening, it's time to change medicines. Fortunately, there are many HIV medicines available to include in an HIV regimen. The choice of HIV medicines to replace those causing side effects will depend on a person's individual needs.

Can HIV medicines cause side effects?

HIV medicines help people with HIV live longer, healthier lives. Sometimes HIV medicines can also cause side effects. Most side effects from HIV medicines are manageable, but a few can be very serious.

If you are taking HIV medicines, tell your health care provider about any side effects that you are having.

Different HIV medicines can cause different side effects. In addition, people taking the same HIV medicine can have very different side effects.

Some side effects, for example headaches or occasional dizziness, may not be serious. Other side effects, such as swelling of the mouth and tongue or damage to the liver, can be life threatening.

Side effects from HIV medicines can last only a few days or weeks or continue for a much longer time. Some side effects may not appear until many months or even years after starting an HIV medicine.

What are common short-term side effects from HIV medicines?

When starting an HIV medicine for the first time, it's common to have side effects that last a couple of weeks. These short-term side effects can include:

- Feeling tired

- Nausea (upset stomach)

- Vomiting

- Diarrhea

- Headache

- Fever

- Muscle pain

- Occasional dizziness

Sometimes, side effects that may not seem serious, such as fever, rash, nausea, or fatigue, can be a sign of a life-threatening condition. Any swelling of the face, eyes, lips, or tongue is considered a life-threatening side effect that requires immediate medical attention. If you are taking HIV medicines, tell your health care provider about any side effects that you are having. **Do NOT cut down on, skip, or stop taking your HIV medicines unless your health care provider tells you to.** Stopping HIV medicines allows HIV to multiply and damage the immune system. This increases the risk of infections and cancer. Stopping HIV medicines also increases the risk of drug resistance.

Anemia

Anemia means you have a low red blood cell count. The red blood cells take oxygen to different parts of the body, and when your body is short of oxygen, you feel tired.

Many people with HIV have anemia at some point. HIV can cause it; so can some of the anti-HIV drugs.

To see if you have anemia (a symptom of anemia is feeling tired, fatigued, or short of breath), your health care provider can do a simple blood test. If you are anemic, food or other medicines can help.

Quick Tips: Anemia

- First, find out if you have anemia. If you are short of breath or tired and the tiredness doesn't go away after getting rest, ask your doctor whether you should get tested for anemia.

- If you find out you have anemia, your doctor will prescribe a treatment according to the cause of the anemia. Some of these treatments may include:

- changing medications

- taking iron, folate, or vitamin B12

- changing your diet

Diarrhea

Diarrhea is common in people with HIV, and it can be caused by a variety of things including some anti-HIV medicines. Diarrhea can range from being a small hassle to being a serious medical problem. Talk to your health care provider if diarrhea goes on for a long time, if it is bloody, if it is accompanied by fever, or if it worries you.

When you have diarrhea, always be sure to replace the fluids you have lost by drinking ginger ale, broth, herbal tea, or water.

You can also ask your doctor about taking medicines to help with your diarrhea.

Dry mouth

Certain HIV medicines can cause dry mouth, making it difficult to chew, swallow, and talk.

Quick Tips: Diarrhea

What to try:

- Try the BRATT diet (bananas, rice, applesauce, tea, and toast).
- Eat foods high in soluble fiber. This kind of fiber can slow the diarrhea by soaking up liquid. Soluble fiber is found in oatmeal, grits, and soft bread (but not in whole grain).
- Try psyllium husk fiber bars (another source of soluble fiber). You can find these at health food stores and many groceries. Eating two of these bars and drinking a big glass of water before bedtime may help your diarrhea.
- Ask your doctor about taking calcium pills.
- Drink plenty of clear liquids.

What to avoid:

- Stay away from foods high in insoluble fiber, such as whole grains, brown rice, bran, or the skins of vegetables and fruits. These kinds of foods can make diarrhea worse.
- Avoid milk products.
- Don't eat too many greasy, high-fiber, or very sweet foods.
- Don't take in too much caffeine.
- Avoid raw or undercooked fish, chicken, and meat.

Treating dry mouth can be simple—start by drinking plenty of liquids during or between meals. If your dry mouth is severe or doesn't go away, talk to your doctor about prescribing a treatment for you.

Quick Tips: Dry Mouth

- Rinse your mouth throughout the day with warm, salted water.
- Carry sugarless candies, lozenges, or crushed ice with you to cool the mouth and give it moisture.
- Try slippery elm or licorice tea (available in health food stores). They can moisten the mouth, and they taste great!
- Ask your doctor about mouth rinse and other products to treat your dry mouth.

Fatigue

Many people feel tired, especially when they are stressed or their lives are busier than usual. Symptoms of being tired can include: having a hard time getting out of bed, walking up stairs, or even concentrating on something for very long.

If the tiredness (or fatigue) doesn't go away, even after you have given your body and mind time to rest, this tiredness can become a problem. It can get worse if you don't deal with it.

Talk with your health care provider if your fatigue is not going away or is becoming too hard to deal with. The more information you can give your doctor about how you are feeling, the more likely the two of you will be able to come up with the right treatment for your fatigue.

Quick Tips: Fatigue

- Get plenty of rest.
- Go to sleep and wake up at the same time every day. Changing your sleeping habits too much can actually make you feel tired.
- Try to get some exercise.
- Keep prepackaged or easy-to-make food in the kitchen for times when you're too tired to cook.
- Follow a healthy, balanced diet. Your health care provider may be able to help you create a meal plan.
- Talk to your doctor about the possibility that you have anemia or other medical problems. Anemia means that you have a low red blood cell count, and it can make you feel tired.

Headaches

The most common cause of headaches is tension or stress, something we all have from time to time. Medications, including anti-HIV drugs, can cause them, too.

Headaches usually can be taken care of with drugs you can buy without a prescription, such as ibuprofen or acetaminophen. You can also help to prevent future headaches by reducing stress.

Quick Tips: Headache

For on-the-spot headache relief, try some of these suggestions:

- Lie down and rest in a quiet, dark room.
- Take a hot, relaxing bath.
- Give yourself a "scalp massage"—massage the base of your skull with your thumbs and massage both temples gently.
- Check with your doctor about taking an over-the-counter pain reliever, such as aspirin.

To prevent headaches from happening again, try the following:

- Avoid things that can cause headaches, like chocolate, red wine, onions, hard cheese, and caffeine.
- Reduce your stress level.

Nausea and vomiting

Certain medications used to treat HIV can cause nausea. They make you feel sick to your stomach and want to throw up. This usually goes away a few weeks after starting a new medication.

Call your doctor if you vomit repeatedly throughout the day, or if nausea or vomiting keeps you from taking your medication.

Quick Tips: Nausea and Vomiting

What to try:

- Eat smaller meals and snack more often.
- The BRATT Diet (bananas, rice, applesauce, tea, and toast) can help with nausea and diarrhea.
- Keep dry crackers by your bed. Before getting out of bed in the morning, eat a few and stay in bed for a few minutes. This can help reduce nausea.
- Try some herbal tea—such as peppermint or ginger tea.
- Sip cold, carbonated drinks such as ginger ale or Sprite.
- Open your windows when cooking so the smell of food won't be too strong.

- Talk with your health care provider about whether you should take medicine for your nausea.
- If you do vomit, be sure to "refuel" your body with fluids such as broth, carbonated beverages, juice, or popsicles.

What to avoid:

- Avoid things that can upset the stomach, such as alcohol, aspirin, caffeine, and smoking.
- Avoid hot or spicy foods.
- Don't eat too many greasy or fried foods.
- Don't lie down immediately after eating.

Pain and nerve problems

HIV itself and some medications for HIV can cause damage to your nerves. This condition is called peripheral neuropathy. When these nerves are damaged, your feet, toes, and hands can feel like they're burning or stinging. It can also make them numb or stiff.

You should talk to your doctor if you have pain like this.

Quick Tips: Pain and Nerve Problem

- Massaging your feet can make the pain go away for a while.
- Soak your feet in ice water to help with the pain.
- Wear loose-fitting shoes and slippers.
- When you're in bed, don't cover your feet with blankets or sheets. The bedding can press down on your feet and toes and make the pain worse.
- Ask your doctor about taking an over-the-counter pain reliever to reduce the pain and swelling.

Rash

Some medications can cause skin problems, such as rashes. Most rashes come and go, but sometimes they signal that you are having a bad reaction to the medication.

It's important that you check your skin for changes, especially after you start a new medication. Be sure to report any changes to your health care provider.

Quick Tips: Rash

- Avoid very hot showers or baths. Water that is too hot can irritate the skin.
- Avoid being in the sun. Sun exposure can make your rash worse.
- Try using unscented, non-soapy cleansers for bathing or showering.
- A rash that blisters, or involves your mouth, the palms of your hands, or the soles of your feet, or one that is accompanied by shortness of breath, can be dangerous: contact your doctor right away.

Weight Loss

Weight loss goes along with some of these other side effects. It can happen because of vomiting, nausea, fatigue, and other reasons.

Talk with your health care provider if you're losing weight without trying, meaning that you're not on a reducing diet.

Quick Tips: Weight Loss

- Be sure to keep track of your weight, by weighing yourself on scales and writing down how much you weigh. Tell your doctor if there are any changes.
- Create your own high-protein drink by blending together yogurt, fruit (for sweetness), and powdered milk, whey protein, or soy protein.
- Between meals, try store-bought nutritional beverages or bars (such as Carnation Instant Breakfast, Benefit, Ensure, Scandishake, Boost High Protein, NuBasics). Look for ones that are high in proteins, not sugars or fats.

- Spread peanut butter on toast, crackers, fruit, or vegetables.
- Add cottage cheese to fruit and tomatoes.
- Add canned tuna to casseroles and salads.
- Add shredded cheese to sauces, soups, omelets, baked potatoes, and steamed vegetables.
- Eat yogurt on your cereal or fruit.
- Eat hard-boiled (hard-cooked) eggs. Use them in egg-salad sandwiches or slice and dice them for tossed salads.
- Add diced or chopped meats to soups, salads, and sauces.
- Add dried milk powder, whey protein, soy protein or egg white powder to foods (for example, scrambled eggs, casseroles, and milkshakes).

What are some long-term side effects from HIV medicines?

Some side effects from HIV medicines appear months or even years after starting a medicine and continue for a long time. Examples of long-term side effects include:

- Changes in how the body uses and stores fat (lipodystrophy)
- An increase in fat levels in the blood (hyperlipidemia)
- Thinning of the bones (osteoporosis)

What are ways to manage side effects from HIV medicines?

When taking HIV medicines, it helps to plan ahead. If you are starting HIV medicines, talk to your health care provider about possible side effects. Tell your health care provider about your lifestyle and point out any possible side effects that would be especially hard for you to manage. The information will help your health care provider recommend medicines best suited to your needs.

Depending on the HIV medicines you take, your health care provider will:

- Tell you which specific side effects to look out for.
- Offer you suggestions on how to deal with those side effects. For example, to manage nausea and vomiting, eat smaller meals more often and avoid spicy foods.

- Tell you about the signs of life-threatening side effects (for example, swelling of the mouth and tongue) that require immediate medical attention.

When side effects from HIV medicines become unbearable or life-threatening, it's time to change medicines. Fortunately, there are many HIV medicines available to include in an HIV regimen. The choice of HIV medicines to replace those causing side effects will depend on a person's individual needs.

Section 23.2

Adverse Effects of Antiretroviral (ARV) Drugs

Text in this section is excerpted from "Limitations to Treatment Safety and Efficacy – Adverse Effects of Antiretroviral Agents," AIDS*info*, April 8, 2015.

Adverse effects have been reported with the use of all antiretroviral (ARV) drugs and are among the most common reasons cited for switching or discontinuing therapy and for medication non-adherence. Fortunately, newer ARV regimens are less toxic than regimens used in the past. Generally less than 10% of antiretroviral therapy (ART)-naive patients enrolled in randomized trials have treatment-limiting adverse events. However, because most clinical trials have a relatively short follow-up duration, the longer term complications of ART can be underestimated. In the Swiss Cohort study during a median of 6 years of follow-up, the presence of laboratory adverse events probably or certainly related to ART was associated with higher rates of mortality, which highlights the importance of monitoring for adverse events in overall patient management.

Several factors may predispose individuals to adverse effects of ARV medications. For example, compared with men, women (especially ART-naive women with CD4 T lymphocyte cell counts >250 cells/mm^3) seem to have a higher propensity to develop Stevens-Johnson

279

syndrome, rashes, and hepatotoxicity from nevirapine (NVP) and have higher rates of lactic acidosis due to nucleoside reverse transcriptase inhibitors. Other factors may also contribute to the development of adverse events:

- Concomitant use of medications with overlapping and additive toxicities;

- Comorbid conditions that increase the risk of or exacerbate adverse effects (e.g., alcoholism or coinfection with viral hepatitis increases the risk of hepatotoxicity);

- Drug-drug interactions that may lead to an increase in drug toxicities (e.g., interactions that result from concomitant use of statins with protease inhibitors); or

- Genetic factors that predispose patients to abacavir (ABC) hypersensitivity reaction.

The therapeutic goals of ART are to safely achieve and maintain viral suppression and improve immune function. To accomplish these goals, the clinician must consider the toxicity potential of an ARV regimen, as well as the individual patient's underlying conditions, concomitant medications, and prior history of drug intolerances. In addition, it should be appreciated that, in general, the overall benefits of ART outweigh its risks and that some non-AIDS related conditions (e.g., anemia, cardiovascular disease, renal impairment) may be more likely in the absence of ART.

N/A indicates either that there are no reported cases for the particular side effect or that data for the specific ARV drug class are not available.

Switching Antiretroviral Therapy because of Adverse Effects

Most patients do not experience treatment-limiting ART-associated toxicities; however, some patients do, and in these cases, ART must be modified. ART-associated adverse events can range from acute and potentially life threatening to chronic and insidious. Acute life-threatening events (e.g., acute hypersensitivity reaction due to ABC, lactic acidosis due to stavudine [d4T] and didanosine [ddI], liver and/or severe cutaneous toxicities due to NVP) usually require the immediate discontinuation of all ARV drugs and re-initiation of an alternative regimen without overlapping toxicity. Non-life threatening toxicities (e.g., urolithiasis with atazanavir [ATV], renal tubulopathy with

Table 23.1. Antiretroviral Therapy-Associated Common and/or Severe Adverse Effects

Adverse Effect	NRTIs	NNRTIs	PIs	INSTI	EI
Bleeding Events	N/A	N/A	Spontaneous bleeding, hematuria in hemophilia. TPV: Intracranial hemorrhage associated with CNS lesions, trauma, alcohol abuse, hypertension, coagulopathy, anti-coagulant or anti-platelet agents, vitamin E	N/A	N/A
Bone Density Effects	TDF: Associated with greater loss of BMD than other NRTIs. Osteomalacia has been reported in association with proximal renal tubulopathy.	Decreases in BMD observed after the initiation of any ART regimen.			N/A
Bone Marrow Suppression	ZDV: Anemia, neutropenia	N/A	N/A	N/A	N/A

Table 23.1. Continued

Adverse Effect	NRTIs	NNRTIs	PIs	INSTI	EI
Cardiovascular Disease	ABC and ddI: Associated with an increased risk of MI in some cohort studies. Absolute risk greatest in patients with traditional CVD risk factors.	N/A	Associated with MI and stroke in some cohorts. SQV/r, ATV/r, and LPV/r: PR prolongation. Risks include pre-existing heart disease, other medications. SQV/r: QT prolongation. Obtain ECG before administering SQV.	N/A	N/A
Cholelithiasis	N/A	N/A	ATV: Cholelithiasis and kidney stones may present concurrently. Median onset is 42 months.	N/A	N/A
Diabetes Mellitus / Insulin Resistance	ZDV, d4T, and ddI	N/A	Reported for some (IDV, LPV/r), but not all PIs	N/A	N/A
Dyslipidemia	d4T > ZDV > ABC: ↑LDL and TG	EFV↑TG,↑LDL,↑HDL	All RTV-boosted PIs:↑LDL,↑TG,↑HDL LPV/r = FPV/r and LPV/r > DRV/r and ATV/r: ↑TG	EVG/c/TDF/FTC:↑ TG,↑LDL,↑HDL	N/A

Table 23.1. Continued

Adverse Effect	NRTIs	NNRTIs	PIs	INSTI	EI
Gastrointestinal Effects	Nausea and vomiting: ddI and ZDV > other NRTIs Pancreatitis: ddI	N/A	GI intolerance (e.g., diarrhea, nausea, vomiting) Diarrhea: Common with LPV/r, more frequent than DRV/r andATV/r	Nausea and diarrhea: EVG/c/TDF/FTC	N/A
Hepatic Effects	Reported with most NRTIs. Steatosis most common with ZDV, d4T, or ddI. ddI: Prolonged exposure linked to non-cirrhotic portal hypertension, esophageal varices. Flares: HIV/HBV-co-infected patients may develop severe hepatic flares when TDF, 3TC, and FTC are withdrawn or when HBV resistance develops.	NVP > other NNRTIs NVP: Severe hepatotoxicity associated with skin rash or hypersensitivity. 2-week NVP dose escalation may reduce risk. Risk is greater for women with pre-NVP CD4 count >250 cells/mm³ and men with pre-NVP CD4 count >400 cells/mm³. NVP should **never** be used for post-exposure prophylaxis, or in patients with hepatic insufficiency (Child-Pugh B or C).	All PIs: Drug-induced hepatitis and hepatic decompensation have been reported; greatest frequency with TPV/r. IDV, ATV: Jaundice due to indirect hyperbilirubinemia TPV/r: **Contraindicated** in patients with hepatic insufficiency (Child-Pugh B or C)	N/A	MVC: Hepatotoxicity with or without rash or HSRs reported

Table 23.1. Continued

Adverse Effect	NRTIs	NNRTIs	PIs	INSTI	EI
Hypersensitivity Reaction Excluding rash alone or Stevens-Johnson syndrome	ABC:**Contraindicated** if HLA-B*5701 positive. Median onset 9 days; 90% of reactions occur within first 6 weeks of treatment. HSR symptoms (in order of descending frequency): fever, rash, malaise, nausea, headache, myalgia, chills, diarrhea, vomiting, abdominal pain, dyspnea, arthralgia, and respiratory symptoms. Symptoms worsen with continuation of ABC. Patients, regardless of HLA-B*5701 status, should not be re-challenged with ABC if HSR is suspected.	NVP: Hypersensitivity syndrome of hepatotoxicity and rash that may be accompanied by fever, general malaise, fatigue, myalgias, arthralgias, blisters, oral lesions, conjunctivitis, facial edema, eosinophilia, renal dysfunction, granulocytopenia, or lymphadenopathy. Risk is greater for ARV-naive women with pre-NVP CD4 count >250 cells/mm^3 and men with pre-NVP CD4 count >400 cells/mm^3. Overall, risk is higher for women than men. 2-week dose escalation of NVP reduces risk.	N/A	RAL: HSR reported when RAL given in combination with other drugs known to cause HSR. All ARVs should be stopped if HSR occurs. DTG: Reported in <1% of patients in clinical development program	MVC: Reported as part of a syndrome related to hepatotoxicity

Table 23.1. Continued

Adverse Effect	NRTIs	NNRTIs	PIs	INSTI	EI
Lactic Acidosis	Reported with NRTIs, especially d4T, ZDV, and ddI: Insidious onset with GI prodrome, weight loss, and fatigue. May rapidly progress with tachycardia, tachypnea, jaundice, weakness, mental status changes, pancreatitis, and organ failure. Mortality high if serum lactate >10 mmol/L. Women and obese patients at increased risk.	N/A	N/A	N/A	N/A
Lipodystrophy	Lipoatrophy: d4T > ZDV. May be more likely when NRTIs combined with EFV than with an RTV-boosted PI.	Lipohypertophy: Trunk fat increase observed with EFV-, PI-, and RAL-containing regimens; however, causal relationship has not been established.	N/A	N/A	N/A
Myopathy/Elevated Creatine Phosphokinase	ZDV: Myopathy	N/A	N/A	RAL: ↑CPK, weakness and rhabdomyolysis	N/A

Table 23.1. Continued

Adverse Effect	NRTIs	NNRTIs	PIs	INSTI	EI
Nervous System/ Psychiatric Effects	Peripheral neuropathy: d4T > ddl and ddC (can be irreversible). d4T: Associated with rapidly progressive, ascending neuro-muscular weakness resembling Guil-lain-Barré syndrome (rare)	EFV: Somnolence, insomnia, abnormal dreams, dizziness, impaired concentra-tion, depression, psy-chosis, and suicidal ideation. Symptoms usually subside or diminish after 2-4 weeks. Bedtime dos-ing may reduce symp-toms. Risks include psychiatric illness, concomitant use of agents with neuropsy-chiatric effects, and increased EFV con-centrations because of genetic factors or increased absorption with food. An associ-ation between EFV and suicidal ideation, suicide, and attempt-ed suicide (especially among younger patients and those with history of mental illness or substance abuse) was found in a retrospective analysis of comparative trials.	N/A	All INSTIs: Insomnia RAL: Depression and suicidal ideation (un-common)	N/A

Table 23.1. Continued

Adverse Effect	NRTIs	NNRTIs	PIs	INSTI	EI
Rash	FTC: Hyperpigmentation	All NNRTIs	ATV, DRV, FPV, LPV/r, TPV	RAL, EVG/c/TDF/FTC	MVC
Renal Effects/ Urolithiasis	TDF: ↑SCr, proteinuria, hypophosphatemia, urinary phosphate wasting, glycosuria, hypokalemia, non-anion gap metabolic acidosis Concurrent use with PI appears to increase risk.	N/A	ATV and LPV/r: Increased chronic kidney disease risk in a large cohort study. IDV: ↑SCr, pyuria, renal atrophy or hydronephrosis IDV, ATV: Stone, crystal formation; adequate hydration may reduce risk.	COBI (in EVG/c/ TDF/FTC) and DTG: Inhibits Cr secretion without reducing renal glomerular function.	N/A
Stevens-Johnson Syndrome/Toxic Epidermal Necrosis	ddl, ZDV: Reported cases	NVP > DLV, EFV, ETR, RPV	FPV, DRV, IDV, LPV/r, ATV: Reported cases	RAL	N/A

Key to Abbreviations: *3TC = lamivudine; ABC = abacavir; ALT= alanine amionotransferase; ARV = antiretroviral; ATV = atazanavir; ATV/r = atazanavir/ritonavir; BMD = bone mineral density; Cr = creatinine; CrCl = creatinine clearance; CNS = central nervous system; COBI or c = cobicistat; CPK = creatine phosphokinase; CVD = cardiovascular disease; d4T = stavudine; ddC = zalcitabine; ddl = didanosine; DLV = delavirdine; DRV = darunavir; DRV/r = darunavir/ritonavir; DTG = dolutegravir; ECG = electrocardiogram; EFV = efavirenz; EI = entry inhibitor; ETR = etravirine; EVG = elvitegravir; FPV = fosamprenavir; FPV/r = fosamprenavir/ritonavir; FTC = emtricitabine; GI = gastrointestinal; HBV = hepatitis B virus; HDL = high-density lipoprotein; HSR = hypersensitivity reaction; IDV = indinavir; INSTI = integrase strand transfer inhibitor; LDL = low-density lipoprotein; LPV/r = lopinavir/ritonavir; MI = myocardial infarction; MVC = maraviroc; NFV = nelfinavir; NNRTI = non-nucleoside reverse transcriptase inhibitor; NRTI = nucleoside reverse transcriptase inhibitor; NVP = nevirapine; PI = protease inhibitor; PT= prothrombin time; RAL = raltegravir; RPV = rilpivirine; RTV = ritonavir; SCr = serum creatinine; SQV = saquinavir; SQV/r = saquinavir/ritonavir; TDF = tenofovir disoproxil fumarate; TG = triglyceride; TPV = tipranavir; TPV/r = tipranavir/ritonavir; ZDV = zidovudine* tenofovir [TDF]) can usually be managed by substituting another ARV agent for the presumed causative agent without interruption of ART. Other, chronic, non-life threatening adverse events (e.g., dyslipidemia) can be addressed either by switching the potentially causative agent for another agent or by managing the adverse event with additional pharmacological or non-pharmacological interventions. Management strategies must be individualized for each patient.

Switching from an effective ARV regimen to a new regimen must be done carefully and only when the potential benefits of the change outweigh the potential complications of altering treatment. The fundamental principle of regimen switching is to maintain viral suppression. When selecting a new agent or regimen, providers should be aware that resistance mutations selected for, regardless of whether previously or currently identified by genotypic resistance testing, are archived in HIV reservoirs, and even if absent from subsequent resistance test results, may reappear under selective pressure. It is critical that providers review the following before implementing any treatment switch:

- the patient's medical and complete ARV history including prior virologic responses to ART;
- resistance test results;
- viral tropism (when maraviroc [MVC] is being considered);
- HLA B*5701 status (when ABC is being considered);
- co-morbidities;
- adherence history;
- prior intolerances to any medications; and
- concomitant medications and supplements and their potential for drug interactions with ARVs.

Patient acceptance of new food or dosing requirements must also be assessed. In some cases, medication costs may also be a factor to consider before switching treatment. Signs and symptoms of ART-associated adverse events may mimic those of comorbidities, adverse effects of concomitant medications, or HIV infection itself. Therefore, concurrent with ascribing a particular clinical event to ART, alternative causes for the event should be investigated. In the case of a severe adverse event, it may be necessary to discontinue or switch ARVs pending the outcome of such an investigation. For the first few months after an ART switch, the patient should be closely monitored for any new adverse events. The patient's viral load should also be monitored to assure continued viral suppression.

Table 23.2. lists several major ART-associated adverse events and potential options to appropriately switch agents in an ARV regimen. The table focuses on the ARVs most commonly used in the United States and lists substitutions that are supported by ARV switch studies, findings of comparative ARV trials and observational cohort studies, or expert opinion. Switching a successful ARV regimen should be done carefully and only when the potential benefits of the change outweigh the potential complications of altering treatment.

Table 23.2. Antiretroviral Therapy-Associated Adverse Events That Can Be Managed with Substitution of Alternative Antiretroviral Agent

Adverse Event	ARV Agent(s)/Drug Class		Comments
	Switch from	Switch to	
Bone Density Effects	TDFa	ABCb	Declines in BMD have been observed with the start of most ART regimens. Switching from TDF to alternative ARV agents has been shown to increase bone density, but the clinical significance of this increase remains uncertain.
Bone Marrow Suppression	ZDV	TDF or ABCb	ZDV has been associated with neutropenia and macrocytic anemia.
Central Nervous System/ Neuropsychiatric Side Effects Dizziness, suicidal ideation, abnormal dreams, depression	EFV	Alternative NNRTI (RPV, ETR, NVP), a PI/c or PI/r, or an INSTI	In most patients, EFV-related CNS effects subside within 4 weeks after initiation of the drug. Persistent or intolerable effects should prompt substitution of EFV.
Dyslipidemia Hypertriglyceridemia (with or without elevated low-density LDL level)	RTV- or CO-BI-boosted regimens or EFV	RAL, DTG, RPV, NVP, or unboosted ATVc	Elevated TG and LDL levels are more common with LPV/r and FPV/r than with other RTV-boosted PIs. Improvements in TG and LDL levels observed with switch from LPV/r to ATV or ATV/r.c

Table 23.2. Continued

Adverse Event	ARV Agent(s)/Drug Class		Comments
	Switch from	**Switch to**	
Gastrointestinal Effects Nausea, diarrhea	LPV/r	ATV/c, ATV/r, DRV/c, DRV/r, RAL, DTG, DRV/c, EVG/c/TDF/FTC	GI intolerance is common with boosted PIs and is linked to the total dose of RTV. More GI toxicity is seen with LPV/r than with ATV/r or DRV/r. GI effects are often transient, and do not warrant substitution unless persistent and intolerable.
	Other RTV- or COBI-boosted regimens	RAL, DTG, unboosted ATV,c NNRTIs	In a trial of treatment-naive patients, rates of diarrhea and nausea were similar for EVG/c/TDF/FTC and ATV/r plus TDF/FTC.
Hypersensitivity Reaction	ABC	TDF	Never re-challenge with ABC following a suspected HSR, regardless of the patient's HLA B*5701 status.
	NVP, EFV, ETR, RPV	Non-NNRTI ART	Risk of HSR with NVP is higher for women and those with high CD4 cell counts.
	DTG, RAL MVC	Non-INSTI ART Suitable alternative ART	Reactions to NVP, ETR, RAL, DTG and MVC may be accompanied by elevated liver transaminases.
Insulin Resistance	LPV/r, FPV/r	NNRTI (NVP or RPV), INSTI, unboosted ATVc	Results of switch studies have been inconsistent. Studies in HIV-negative patients suggest a direct causal effect of LPV/r (and IDV) on insulin resistance. However, traditional risk factors may be stronger risk factors for insulin resistance than use of any PI.

Table 23.2. Continued

Adverse Event	ARV Agent(s)/Drug Class		Comments
	Switch from	**Switch to**	
Jaundice and Icterus	ATV, ATV/c, ATV/r	DRV/c, DRV/r, INSTI, or NN-RTI	Increases in unconjugated bilirubin are common with ATV and generally do not require modification of therapy unless resultant symptoms are distressing to the patient.
Lipoatrophy Subcutaneous fat wasting of limbs, face, buttocks	d4T, ZDV	TDF or ABCb	Peripheral lipoatrophy is a legacy of prior thymidine analog (d4T and ZDV) use. Switching from these ARVs prevents worsening lipoatrophy, but fat recovery is typically slow (may take years) and incomplete.
Lipohypertrophy	Accumulation of visceral, truncal, dorso-cervical, and breast fat has been observed during ART, particularly during use of older PI-based regimens (e.g., IDV), but whether ART directly causes increased fat deposits remains unclear. There is no clinical evidence that switching to another first line regimen will reverse weight or visceral fat gain.		
Rash	NNRTIs (especially NVP and EFV)	PI- or INSTI-based regimen	Mild rashes developing after initiation of NNRTIs other than NVP rarely require treatment switch. When serious rash develops due to any NNRTI, switch to another drug class.
	DRV/c, DRV/r	ATV/c, ATV/r or another drug class (e.g., INSTI)	Mild rashes following DRV/r may resolve with close follow-up only. For more severe reactions, change to an alternative boosted PI or an agent from another drug class.
Renal Effects Including proximal renal tubulopathy, elevated creatinine	TDFa	ABCb	TDF may cause tubulopathy.

Table 23.2. Continued

Adverse Event	ARV Agent(s)/Drug Class		Comments
	Switch from	Switch to	
	ATV/c, ATV/r, LPV/r	DTG, RAL, or NNRTI	COBI and DTG, and to a lesser extent RPV can increase SCr through inhibition of creatinine secretion. This effect does not affect glomerular filtration. However, assess for renal dysfunction if SCr increases by >0.4 mg/dL.
Stones Nephrolithiasis and cholelithiasis	ATV, ATV/c, ATV/r	DRV/c, DRV/r, INSTI, or NN-RTI	Assuming that ATV/r is believed to cause the stones.

a In patients with chronic active HBV infection, another agent active against HBV should be substituted for TDF.

b ABC should be used only in patients known to be HLA-B*5701 negative.

c TDF reduces ATV levels; therefore, unboosted ATV should not be coadministered with TDF. Long term data for unboosted ATV are unavailable.

Key to Abbreviations: ABC = abacavir; ART = antiretroviral therapy; ARV = antiretroviral; ATV = atazanavir; ATV/c = atazanavir/cobicistat; ATV/r = atazanavir/ritonavir; BMD = bone mineral density; CD4 = CD4 T lymphocyte; CNS = central nervous system; COBI or c = cobicistat; d4T = stavudine; DRV/c = darunavir/cobicistat; DRV/r = darunavir/ritonavir; DTG = dolutegravir; EFV = efavirenz; ETR = etravirine; EVG = elvitegravir; FPV/r = fosamprenavir/ritonavir; FTC = emtricitabine; GI = gastrointestinal; HBV = hepatitis B virus; HSR = hypersensitivity reaction; IDV = indinavir; INSTI = integrase strand transfer inhibitor; LDL = low-density lipoprotein; LPV/r = lopinavir/ritonavir; MVC = maraviroc; NNRTI = non-nucleoside reverse transcriptase inhibitor; NVP = nevirapine; PI = protease inhibitor; PI/c = protease inhibitor/cobicistat; PI/r = protease inhibitor/ritonavir; RAL = raltegravir; RPV = rilpivirine; RTV = ritonavir; SCr = serum creatinine; TDF = tenofovir disoproxil fumarate; TG = triglycerides; ZDV = zidovudine

Section 23.3

Hepatotoxicity

Text in this section is excerpted from "Side Effects of HIV Medicines -
HIV and Hepatotoxicity," AIDS*info*, December 15, 2014.

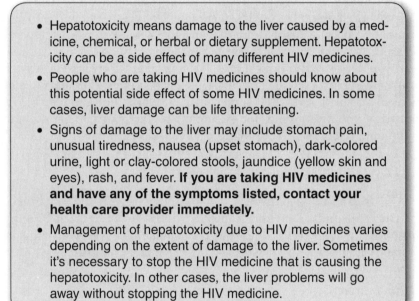

- Hepatotoxicity means damage to the liver caused by a medicine, chemical, or herbal or dietary supplement. Hepatotoxicity can be a side effect of many different HIV medicines.

- People who are taking HIV medicines should know about this potential side effect of some HIV medicines. In some cases, liver damage can be life threatening.

- Signs of damage to the liver may include stomach pain, unusual tiredness, nausea (upset stomach), dark-colored urine, light or clay-colored stools, jaundice (yellow skin and eyes), rash, and fever. **If you are taking HIV medicines and have any of the symptoms listed, contact your health care provider immediately.**

- Management of hepatotoxicity due to HIV medicines varies depending on the extent of damage to the liver. Sometimes it's necessary to stop the HIV medicine that is causing the hepatotoxicity. In other cases, the liver problems will go away without stopping the HIV medicine.

What is hepatotoxicity?

Hepatotoxicity means damage to the liver caused by a medicine, chemical, or herbal or dietary supplement. Hepatotoxicity can be a side effect of many different HIV medicines.

People taking HIV medicines should know about this potential side effect of some HIV medicines. In some cases, damage to the liver can be life threatening.

What HIV medicines can cause hepatotoxicity?

HIV medicines in the following drug classes can cause hepatotoxicity:

Nucleoside reverse transcriptase inhibitors (NRTIs)

Hepatotoxicity is a risk with most NRTIs.

Non-nucleoside reverse transcriptase inhibitors (NNRTIs)

Among NNRTIs, the risk of hepatotoxicity is greatest with nevirapine (brand name: Viramune). The risk is greater in the first few months of treatment and greater for women than for men. The risk is greatest for women who have CD4 counts above 250 cells/mm^3 before starting nevirapine.

Treatment with nevirapine starts on a gradual schedule. The schedule gives the person taking the medicine 2 weeks to reach the full recommended dose of nevirapine. During the 2-week period, the person is carefully monitored for signs of hepatotoxicity due to nevirapine.

If you are starting nevirapine, it's important to work closely with your health care provider during this 2-week period. Don't miss any medical appointments. Tell your health care provider about any symptoms that you are having (for example, stomach pain, upset stomach, or unusual tiredness). Your symptoms could be a sign of liver damage.

Protease inhibitors (PIs)

All PIs can increase the risk of hepatotoxicity, but the risk is greatest with tipranavir (brand name: Aptivus) boosted with ritonavir (brand name: Norvir). (When the HIV medicines are given together, ritonavir increases or "boosts" the effectiveness of tipranavir.)

CCR5 antagonists

Maraviroc (brand name: Selzentry) has been reported to cause hepatotoxicity.

The AIDS*info* drug database includes information on HIV medicines, including medicines in the NRTI, NNRTI, and PI drug classes.

Are there other factors that can increase the risk of hepatotoxicity?

The following factors may increase the risk of hepatotoxicity due to HIV medicines:

- Being over 50 years of age

- Also having hepatitis B and/or hepatitis C infection

- Taking other medicines that can cause liver damage
- Alcohol or drug abuse
- Obesity
- Past history of liver damage

What are the symptoms of hepatotoxicity?

Symptoms of hepatotoxicity include the following:

- Stomach pain
- Nausea (upset stomach)
- Unusual tiredness
- Dark-colored urine
- Light or clay-colored stools
- Jaundice (yellow skin and eyes)
- Fever
- Rash

In addition to these symptoms, the liver may be enlarged (bigger than usual).

If you are taking HIV medicines and have any of these symptoms, contact your health care provider immediately. However, do NOT cut down on, skip, or stop taking your HIV medicines unless your health care provider tells you to.

How is hepatotoxicity detected?

Liver function tests (LFTs) are a group of blood tests used to check for damage to the liver. Before treatment with HIV medicines is started, LFTs are done to check for already-existing liver damage. The risk of hepatotoxicity is greater in people who have liver damage before they start taking HIV medicines. If LFT results show pre-existing liver damage, HIV medicines that may cause hepatotoxicity should be avoided. There are many other HIV medicines available to use instead.

Once treatment with HIV medicines begins, LFTs are done to monitor for signs of hepatotoxicity.

How is hepatotoxicity managed?

Management of hepatotoxicity due to HIV medicines varies depending on the extent of damage to the liver. Sometimes it's necessary to stop the HIV medicine that is causing the hepatotoxicity. However, the decision to stop taking an HIV medicine should only be done in consultation with a health care provider. **If you are taking HIV medicines, do NOT cut down on, skip, or stop taking your HIV medicines unless your health care provider tells you to.**

If you are taking or plan to take HIV medicines, talk to your health care provider about the risk of hepatotoxicity.

Section 23.4

Hyperlipidemia

Text in this section is excerpted from "Side Effects of HIV Medicines – HIV and Hyperlipidemia," AIDS*info*, December 22, 2014.

- Hyperlipidemia refers to high levels of fat in the blood, including cholesterol and triglycerides. Hyperlipidemia increases the risk of heart disease, gall bladder disease, and pancreatitis (inflammation of the pancreas).
- HIV infection and treatment with some HIV medicines can increase the risk of hyperlipidemia. Other risk factors for hyperlipidemia include a family history of hyperlipidemia, a high-fat diet, and smoking.
- Eating foods that are low in saturated fat, trans fat, and cholesterol and being active on most days of the week can help control blood fat levels. Medicines are also used to reduce high blood fat levels.
- In people with HIV, treatment for hyperlipidemia may include changing an HIV regimen to avoid taking HIV medicines that can increase blood fat levels.

What is hyperlipidemia?

Hyperlipidemia is the medical term for high levels of fat in the blood. Fats in the blood (also called lipids) include cholesterol and triglycerides. The body makes cholesterol and triglycerides. The fats also come from some of the foods we eat.

The body needs cholesterol and triglycerides to function properly but having too much can cause problems. High levels of cholesterol and triglycerides increase the risk of heart disease, gall bladder disease, and pancreatitis (inflammation of the pancreas).

What are the symptoms of hyperlipidemia?

Usually hyperlipidemia has no symptoms. A blood test is used to measure levels of fat in the blood and to detect hyperlipidemia.

Testing for hyperlipidemia is recommended both before and after a person starts taking HIV medicines. If blood fat levels are normal, testing is recommended once a year. If blood fat levels are too high, more frequent testing is recommended.

What are risk factors for hyperlipidemia in people with HIV?

HIV infection and treatment with some HIV medicines can increase the risk of hyperlipidemia.

The following HIV medicines can raise blood fat levels:

- All HIV medicines in the protease inhibitor (PI) drug class. (HIV medicines are grouped into drug classes according to how they fight HIV.) The AIDS*info* drug database includes information for all HIV medicines, including those in the PI drug class.

- Efavirenz (brand name: Sustiva), which belongs to the non-nucleoside reverse transcriptase inhibitor (NNRTI) drug class. Efavirenz is one of the components of the combination medicine Atripla. Combination medicines include two or more different HIV medicines in one pill.

- Abacavir (brand name: Ziagen), stavudine (brand name: Zerit), and zidovudine (brand name: Retrovir), which belong to the nucleoside reverse transcriptase inhibitor (NRTI) drug class. Abacavir is a component of the combination medicines Epzicom, Triumeq, and Trizivir. Zidovudine is included in the combination medicines Combivir and Trizivir.

- Stribild, which is a combination medicine that includes three HIV medicines: elvitegravir (brand name: Vitekta), emtricitabine (brand name: Emtriva), and tenofovir disoproxil fumarate (brand name: Viread). Stribild also includes cobicistat (brand name: Tybost), a medicine that increases the effectiveness of elvitegravir.

Are there other risk factors for hyperlipidemia?

The following are additional risk factors for hyperlipidemia:

- Family history of hyperlipidemia
- Other medical conditions, including high blood pressure, diabetes, and an underactive thyroid gland
- A high-fat, high-carbohydrate diet
- Being overweight or obese
- Smoking
- Alcohol use
- Lack of physical activity

Many of these risk factors for hyperlipidemia can be controlled by lifestyle choices. For example, maintaining a healthy weight is one way to reduce the risk of hyperlipidemia.

What are other steps a person can take to prevent hyperlipidemia?

Here are additional steps to take to reduce the risk of hyperlipidemia.

- **Eat foods low in saturated fat, trans fat, and cholesterol.** Eat less full-fat dairy products, fatty meats, and desserts high in fat and sugar. Limit foods that are high in cholesterol, such as egg yolks, fatty meats, and organ meat (like liver and kidney). Instead, choose low-fat or fat-free milk, cheese, and yogurt; eat more foods that are high in fiber, like oatmeal, oat bran, beans, and lentils; and eat more vegetables and fruits.

- **Get active.** Get at least 30 minutes of aerobic physical activity on most days of the week. Aerobic activities include walking quickly, biking slowly, and gardening.

- **If you smoke, quit.** Nicotine gum, patches, and lozenges can make it easier to quit.

- **Drink in moderation.** Men should have no more than two alcoholic drinks a day; women no more than one drink. One drink is a glass of wine, a bottle of beer, or a shot of hard liquor.

People who already have hyperlipidemia can also follow these steps to lower their blood fat levels.

What is the treatment for hyperlipidemia?

Lifestyle changes may not be enough to reduce blood fat levels.

In people with HIV, treatment for hyperlipidemia may include changing an HIV regimen to avoid taking HIV medicines that can increase blood fat levels.

There are also medicines that can help control blood fat levels. The most common medicines used to reduce cholesterol levels are called statins. Fibrates are a type of medicine used to lower triglycerides.

HIV medicines can interact with medicines that lower blood fat levels. If you have HIV and need medicine to control hyperlipidemia, your health care provider can recommend medicines that are safe to take with your HIV regimen.

Section 23.5

Lactic Acidosis

Text in this section is excerpted from "Side Effects of HIV Medicines –
HIV and Lactic Acidosis," AIDS*info*, December 15, 2014.

- Lactic acidosis is a condition caused by the buildup of lactic acid in the blood. The condition is a rare but serious side effect of some HIV medicines.
- All HIV medicines in the nucleoside reverse transcriptase inhibitor (NRTI) drug class may cause lactic acidosis, but the risk is greatest with didanosine (brand name: Videx), stavudine (brand name: Zerit), and zidovudine (brand

name: Retrovir). Zidovudine is one of the HIV medicines in the combination drugs Combivir and Trizivir. (Combination drugs include two or more different HIV medicines in one pill.)

- Early signs of lactic acidosis can include fatigue, loss of appetite, nausea and vomiting, stomach pain, and weight loss. Although these symptoms may not seem serious, they can be the first signs of life-threatening lactic acidosis. If you are taking HIV medicines, always tell your health care provider about any symptoms that you are having— even symptoms that may not seem serious.

- Signs of life-threatening lactic acidosis can include above normal heart rate, rapid breathing, jaundice (yellowing of the skin and the whites of the eyes), and muscle weakness. **If you are taking HIV medicines and have these signs of lactic acidosis, get medical help immediately.**

- Treatment for lactic acidosis involves stopping the HIV medicine that is causing the condition. In the rare cases when lactic acidosis becomes life-threatening, immediate treatment in a hospital is necessary.

What is lactic acidosis?

Lactic acidosis is a condition caused by the buildup of lactic acid in the blood. The condition is a rare but serious side effect of some HIV medicines.

HIV medicines in the nucleoside reverse transcriptase inhibitor (NRTI) drug class can cause the body to produce too much lactic acid. NRTIs can also damage the liver so that it can't break down lactate in the blood.

All medicines in the NRTI drug class have been linked to lactic acidosis, but the link is strongest for the following NRTIs:

- didanosine (brand name: Videx)

- stavudine (brand name: Zerit)

- zidovudine (brand name: Retrovir). Zidovudine is one of the HIV medicines in the combination drugs Combivir and Trizivir. (Combination drugs include two or more different HIV medicines in one pill.)

If you are taking NRTIs, it's important to know about lactic acidosis. Although lactic acidosis is a rare side effect of NRTIs, the condition can be life-threatening.

Are there other risk factors for lactic acidosis?

In addition to use of some HIV medicines, risk factors for lactic acidosis include the following:

- Pregnancy

- Obesity

- Older age

- Lower CD4 count

What are the symptoms of lactic acidosis?

Lactic acidosis often develops gradually. Early signs of lactic acidosis can include fatigue, loss of appetite, nausea and vomiting, stomach pain, and weight loss. These symptoms may not seem serious, but they can be the first signs of life-threatening lactic acidosis. If you are taking HIV medicines, always tell your health care provider about any symptoms that you are having—even symptoms that may not seem serious.

Lactic acidosis can advance rapidly. Signs of dangerously high levels of lactate in blood include:

- Above normal heart rate

- Rapid breathing

- Jaundice (yellowing of the skin and the whites of the eyes)

- Muscle weakness

If you are taking HIV medicines and have any of these symptoms, get medical help immediately.

What tests are used to detect lactic acidosis?

Tests used to diagnose lactic acidosis include:

- A test to measure the level of lactate in the blood

- Other blood tests to check the functioning of the liver

- An ultrasound or CT scan of the liver

301

What is the treatment for lactic acidosis?

An HIV medicine that is causing lactic acidosis should be discontinued. However, stopping an HIV medicine because of lactic acidosis doesn't mean stopping HIV treatment. There are many HIV medicines to include in an HIV regimen.

But if you are taking HIV medicines, do NOT cut down on, skip, or stop taking your medicines unless your health care provider tells you to.

In the rare cases when lactic acidosis becomes life-threatening, immediate treatment in a hospital is necessary.

Section 23.6

Lipodystrophy

Text in this section is excerpted from "Side Effects of HIV Medicines – HIV and Lipodystrophy," AIDS*info*, December 15, 2014.

- Lipodystrophy refers to the changes in body fat that affect some people with HIV. Lipodystrophy can include buildup or loss of body fat.

- A person with HIV can have fat loss or fat buildup or both. Whether the changes are obvious to see or not noticeable depends on the degree of fat loss or fat buildup.

- The exact cause of lipodystrophy is unknown. It may be due to HIV infection or medicines used to treat HIV. Newer HIV medicines are less likely to cause the condition than HIV medicines developed in the past. Many people with HIV never develop lipodystrophy.

- There isn't a cure for lipodystrophy, but switching HIV medicines may help. Other ways to manage lipodystrophy include liposuction (surgical removal of fat) and injections of fat or a fat-like substance as a filler to make up for fat loss in the face.

What is lipodystrophy?

Lipodystrophy refers to the changes in body fat that affect some people with HIV. Lipodystrophy can include:

- Buildup of body fat
- Loss of body fat

What causes lipodystrophy?

The exact cause of lipodystrophy is unknown. It may be due to HIV infection or medicines used to treat HIV.
Other risk factors for lipodystrophy include:

- **Age:** Older people are at higher risk.
- **Race:** Whites have the highest risk.
- **Gender:** Men are more likely to have fat loss in the arms and legs. Women are more likely to have buildup of breast and abdominal fat.
- **Length and severity of HIV infection:** The risk is higher with longer and more severe HIV infection.

Lipodystrophy can't be cured, but switching HIV medicines may help. Newer HIV medicines are less likely to cause lipodystrophy than HIV medicines developed in the past.
Many people with HIV never develop lipodystrophy.

What parts of the body are affected by lipodystrophy?

Fat buildup (also called lipohypertrophy) can occur:

- Around the organs in the belly (also called the abdomen)
- On the back of the neck between the shoulders (called buffalo hump)
- In the breasts
- In the face
- Just under the skin. (The fatty bumps are called lipomas.)

Fat loss (also called lipoatrophy) tends to occur:

- In the arms and legs
- In the buttocks
- In the face

A person with HIV can have fat loss or fat buildup or both. Whether the changes are obvious to see or not noticeable depends on the degree of fat loss or fat buildup.

Which HIV medicines are linked to lipodystrophy?

Although more research is needed to prove that there is a link between HIV medicines and lipodystrophy, some HIV medicines have been associated with the condition.

Fat loss may be associated with use of the following HIV medicines in the nucleoside reverse transcriptase inhibitor (NRTI) drug class. (HIV medicines are grouped into drug classes according to how they fight HIV.)

- Stavudine (brand name: Zerit).

- Zidovudine (brand name: Retrovir). Zidovudine is also a component of the combination medicines Combivir and Trizivir. Combination medicines include more than one HIV medicine in a single pill.

Fat gain may be linked to HIV regimens that include the following HIV medicines:

- HIV medicines in the protease inhibitor (PI) drug class. The AIDS*info* drug database includes easy-to-understand information on HIV medicines in the PI drug class.

- Efavirenz (brand name: Sustiva), which is an HIV medicine in the non-nucleoside reverse transcriptase inhibitor (NNRTI) drug class. Efavirenz is one of the components of Atripla, a combination HIV medicine.

- Raltegravir (brand name: Isentress), an HIV medicine in the integrase inhibitor (INSTI) drug class.

Is lipodystrophy a serious health problem?

It can be. Too much fat gain in the abdominal cavity can increase the risk of heart attack and diabetes.

Fat gain in the breasts can be painful. Buffalo humps may cause headaches and problems with breathing.

The changes in appearance caused by lipodystrophy can be upsetting and affect a person's self-esteem. Because of lipodystrophy, a person may decide to stop taking HIV medicines. However, the decision to stop taking HIV medicines (or cut down on the dose of a medicine) should be made only in consultation with a health care provider. Stopping HIV medicines allows HIV to multiply and damage the immune system, which increases the risk of HIV-related infections and cancer. Stopping HIV medicines also increases the risk of drug resistance.

Can lipodystrophy be cured?

Unfortunately, there isn't a cure for lipodystrophy. More research is needed to understand the cause of lipodystrophy in people with HIV and to find a cure for the condition. However, there are ways to manage lipodystrophy.

In some people, changing HIV medicines may lessen the effects of lipodystrophy. Newer HIV medicines are less likely to cause lipodystrophy than HIV medicines developed in the past.

But, if you are taking HIV medicines, do NOT cut down on, skip, or stop taking your medicines unless your health care provider tells you to.

Liposuction (surgical removal of fat) is sometimes used to reduce a buffalo hump. This procedure is not recommended to remove abdominal fat because of possible damage to surrounding organs. Fat or a fat-like substance can be used as a filler to make up for fat loss in the face. The filler is injected in the cheeks or around the eyes and mouth.

Medicines may help lessen the effects of lipodystrophy. For example, tesamorelin (brand name: Egrifta) is a medicine used to reduce the buildup of abdominal fat due to lipodystrophy.

A healthy diet and daily exercise may help to build muscle and reduce fat buildup.

Section 23.7

Osteoporosis

Text in this section is excerpted from "Side Effects of HIV Medicines –
HIV and Osteoporosis," AIDS*info*, July 31, 2015.

- Osteoporosis is a disease that causes bones to become weak and easy to break. Osteoporosis increases the risk of fractures of the hip, spine, and wrist.

- The main risk factor for osteoporosis is advancing age beyond 30. Anyone can get osteoporosis, but it's most common in older women.

- Factors that may increase the risk of osteoporosis in people living with HIV include HIV infection itself and some HIV medicines (for example, tenofovir [brand name: Viread]). Also, HIV medicines are helping people with HIV live longer, and advancing age increases the risk of osteoporosis.

- Other risk factors for osteoporosis include a poor diet, physical inactivity, and smoking. These risk factors can be managed by lifestyle changes. For example, eating a healthy diet that includes foods rich in calcium and vitamin D and doing weight-bearing exercises can make bones stronger and help slow the rate of bone loss.

What is osteoporosis?

The human body is made up of more than 200 bones, from the skull to the bones of the toes. We depend on bones to hold us up, help us move, and protect our internal organs, such as the heart, kidneys, and liver. Osteoporosis is a disease that causes bones to become weak and easy to break. Osteoporosis increases the risk of fractures of the hip, spine, and wrist.

The main risk factor for osteoporosis is advancing age beyond 30. Anyone can get osteoporosis, but it's most common in older women.

Are people with HIV at risk of osteoporosis?

Yes. Experts are not sure why, but bone loss occurs faster in people living with HIV. Factors that increase the rate of bone loss in people with HIV may include:

- HIV infection itself.

- Some HIV medicines. For example, in several studies, bone loss has been linked to the use of tenofovir (brand name: Viread). Atripla, Complera, Stribild, and Truvada are combination medicines that include tenofovir. (Combination medicines contain two or more different HIV medicines in one pill.)

- Taking other medicines for a long time (for example, steroids or antacids) can also increase the risk of osteoporosis.

- Older age. HIV medicines, are helping people with HIV live longer, and advancing age increases the risk of osteoporosis.

Staying healthy with HIV includes taking steps to prevent osteoporosis.

What are other risk factors for osteoporosis?

There are many risk factors for osteoporosis. Some risk factors, such as HIV infection, can't be changed. Other risk factors, for example a poor diet or lack of exercise, can be managed with lifestyle choices.
Risk factors for osteoporosis that can't be changed include:

- **Age:** The risk of osteoporosis increases as people get older and the bones become thinner and weaker.

- **Gender:** Compared with men, women have smaller bones, and after menopause, women lose bone more rapidly than men do.

- **Race/ethnicity:** The risk of osteoporosis is greatest for white and Asian women. However, even though African-American women tend to have higher bone density than white women, they are still at risk for osteoporosis. Factors that increase the risk of osteoporosis in African-American women include a low-calcium diet, intolerance to lactose (the main sugar in milk), and diseases such as sickle cell anemia and lupus that are more common in African Americans. African-American women are also more likely to die from osteoporosis-related fractures than white women.

- **Family history:** Osteoporosis tends to run in families.

The following risk factors for osteoporosis can be controlled by life-style choices:

- **Poor diet:** A diet low in calcium and vitamin D increases the risk of osteoporosis.

- **Physical inactivity:** Bones become stronger with exercise, so physical inactivity increases the risk of osteoporosis.

- **Smoking:** Smoking is bad for the bones.

- **Drinking:** Too much alcohol can cause bone loss and broken bones.

How does osteoporosis develop?

To maintain healthy bones, our body constantly replaces old bone tissue with new bone tissue. Up to about age 30, bone tissue is replaced faster than it is lost. But beyond age 30, the reverse is true: more bone is broken down than is replaced.

Osteoporosis develops when bone loss is so great that bones can break easily.

There is no cure for osteoporosis. However, once the disease develops, there are medicines that can slow down bone loss or increase bone formation.

What are the symptoms of osteoporosis?

Osteoporosis is often called a silent disease because bone loss occurs without symptoms. The first sign of osteoporosis is often a broken bone.

A bone density test is used to measure bone strength and diagnose osteoporosis. The test takes about 15 minutes and is safe, painless, and requires no preparation. The U.S. Preventive Services Task Force recommends all women above the age of 65 have a bone density test to screen for osteoporosis. There are currently no recommendations for routine screening for osteoporosis in people living with HIV, but individuals infected with HIV may wish to discuss bone density testing with their health care providers.

What are steps to take to prevent osteoporosis?

Preventing osteoporosis means making lifestyle choices to reduce the risk of the disease.

- **Eat a healthy diet rich in calcium and vitamin D.** Foods high in calcium include dairy products, such as milk, yogurt, and cheese. Milk is also fortified with vitamin D. Other foods high in calcium include broccoli, sardines, tofu, and oranges. If needed, heath care providers can offer guidance on taking calcium and vitamin D supplements.

- **Stay active.** Weight-bearing exercises, such as walking, jogging, and dancing, can make bones stronger and help slow the rate of bone loss.

- **Don't smoke.**

- **Cut down on alcohol.** Drinking too much can lead to bone loss and increase the risk of fractures due to both bone loss and falling. If you drink alcohol, drink in moderation—no more than one drink a day for women and up to two drinks a day for men. One drink is a bottle of beer, a glass of wine, or a shot of liquor.

Section 23.8

Skin Rash

Text in this section is excerpted from "Side Effects of HIV Medicines – HIV and Rash," AIDS*info*, December 9, 2014.

- A rash is an irritated area of the skin that is sometimes itchy, red, and painful.
- Possible causes of rash in people with HIV include HIV infection itself, other infections, HIV medicines, and other medicines.
- Rash is among the most common side effects of HIV medicines. Rash due to HIV medicines is often not serious and goes away in several days to weeks without treatment. Sometimes it may be necessary to switch to another HIV medicine. In rare cases, a rash caused by an HIV medicine can be a sign of a serious, life-threatening condition.
- If you have HIV, tell your health care provider if you have a rash. A rash that may not seem serious can be a sign of a life-threatening condition that requires immediate medical attention.

Why do people with HIV develop rash?

A rash is an irritated area of the skin that is sometimes itchy, red, and painful. Possible causes of rash in people with HIV include:

- HIV infection itself
- Other infections
- HIV and other medicines

HIV infection

A rash may be the first sign that a person is infected with HIV. This earliest stage of HIV infection is called acute HIV infection. A rash may also be a symptom of HIV infection at any stage of the disease.

Other infections

Rash may be a symptom of other infections. HIV destroys the infection-fighting cells of the immune system. Damage to the immune system puts people with HIV at risk of infections, and rash is a symptom of many infections.

HIV and other Medicines

Many medicines, including medicines used to treat HIV and other infections, can cause a rash.

Rash is among the most common side effects of HIV medicines. HIV medicines in all HIV drug classes can cause a rash. (HIV medicines are grouped into drug classes according to how they fight HIV.)

Rash due to HIV medicines is often not serious and goes away in several days to weeks without treatment. Sometimes it may be necessary to switch to another HIV medicine. If you are taking HIV medicines, tell your health care provider if you have a rash. In rare cases, a rash caused by an HIV medicine can be a sign of a serious, life-threatening condition.

What are serious rash-related conditions?

Rash can be a sign of a serious hypersensitivity reaction. A hypersensitivity reaction is an unusual allergic reaction to a medicine. In addition to rash, signs of a hypersensitivity reaction can include fever, fatigue, difficulty breathing, and kidney damage.

Stevens-Johnson syndrome (SJS) is a rare but life-threatening hypersensitivity reaction reported with use of some HIV medicines. (When SJS affects at least 30% of the total surface area of the skin, the condition is called toxic epidermal necrolysis [TEN].) People taking HIV medicines need to know about this condition. It rarely occurs, but when it does, it can cause death.

Symptoms of SJS include fever; pain or itching of the skin; swelling of the tongue and face; blisters that develop on the skin and mucous membranes, especially around the mouth, nose, and eyes; and a rash that starts quickly and may spread.

A severe hypersensitivity reaction can be life threatening and requires immediate medical attention. SJS must be treated immediately. Go to the emergency room or call 911 if you have symptoms of SJS. However, do NOT cut down on, skip, or stop taking your HIV medicines unless your health care provider tells you to.

What HIV medicines can cause a hypersensitivity reaction?

Nevirapine (brand name: Viramune) and abacavir (brand name: Ziagen) are two HIV medicines that can cause a hypersensitivity reaction.

Nevirapine

To reduce the risk of a hypersensitivity reaction due to nevirapine, the medicine is started on a gradual schedule. The schedule allows the person taking the medicine 2 weeks to reach the full recommended dose of nevirapine. During the 2-week period, the person is carefully monitored for signs of a hypersensitivity reaction to nevirapine.

Abacavir

Hypersensitivity reaction to abacavir has been linked to the HLA-B*5701 molecule. Testing for HLA-B*5701 is done before starting treatment with abacavir. People who test positive for HLA-B*5701 should not use abacavir. People who are taking abacavir and develop signs of hypersensitivity reaction to abacavir must stop the medicine immediately. They can never take abacavir again. In addition, they can never take the combination medicines Epzicom, Triumeq, and Trizivir, which contain abacavir. (Combination medicines include two or more different HIV medicines in one pill.)

Cases of hypersensitivity reaction have also been reported with use of dolutegravir (brand name: Tivicay), maraviroc (brand name: Selzentry), and raltegravir (brand name: Isentress).

311

Chapter 24

HIV/AIDS Treatment Complications—Drug Interactions

Overview

Pharmacokinetic (PK) drug-drug interactions between antiretroviral (ARV) drugs and concomitant medications are common, and may lead to increased or decreased drug exposure. In some instances, changes in drug exposure may increase toxicities or affect therapeutic responses. When prescribing or switching one or more drugs in an ARV regimen, clinicians must consider the potential for drug-drug interactions—both those that affect ARVs and those that ARVs affect on other drugs a patient is taking. A thorough review of concomitant medications in consultation with a clinician with expertise in ARV pharmacology can help in designing a regimen that minimizes undesirable interactions. Recommendations for managing a particular drug interaction may differ depending on whether a new ARV is being initiated in a patient on a stable concomitant medication or a new concomitant medication is being initiated in a patient on a stable ARV regimen. The magnitude and significance of interactions are difficult to predict when several drugs

---

Text in this chapter is excerpted from "Drug Interactions," AIDS*info*, April 8, 2015.

with competing metabolic pathways are prescribed concomitantly. When prescribing interacting drugs is necessary, clinicians should be vigilant in monitoring for therapeutic efficacy and/or concentration-related toxicities.

Mechanisms of Pharmacokinetic Interactions

PK interactions may occur during absorption, metabolism, or elimination of the ARV and/or the interacting drugs. The most common mechanisms of interactions are described below and listed for each ARV drug in Table 24.1.

Pharmacokinetic Interactions Affecting Drug Absorption

The extent of oral absorption of drugs can be affected by the following mechanisms:

- Acid reducing agents, such as proton pump inhibitors, H2 antagonists, or antacids, can reduce the absorption of ARVs that require gastric acidity for optimal absorption (i.e., atazanavir [ATV] and rilpivirine [RPV]).

- Products that contain polyvalent cations, such as aluminum, calcium, magnesium-containing antacids, supplements, or iron products, can bind to integrase inhibitors (INSTI) and reduce absorption of these ARV agents.

- Drugs that induce or inhibit the enzyme CYP3A4 or efflux transporter p-glycoprotein in the intestines may reduce or promote the absorption of other drugs.

Pharmacokinetic Interactions Affecting Hepatic Metabolism

Two major enzyme systems are most frequently responsible for clinically significant drug interactions.

1. The cytochrome P450 enzyme system is responsible for the metabolism of many drugs, including the non-nucleoside reverse transcriptase inhibitors (NNRTI), protease inhibitors (PI), CCR5 antagonist maraviroc (MVC), and the INSTI elvitegravir (EVG). Cytochrome P450 3A4 (CYP3A4) is the most common enzyme responsible for drug metabolism, though

314

multiple enzymes may be involved in the metabolism of a drug. ARVs and concomitant medications may be inducers, inhibitors, and/or substrates of these enzymes.

2. The uridine diphosphate (UDP)-glucuronosyltransferase (UGT) 1A1 enzyme is the primary enzyme responsible for the metabolism of the INSTIs dolutegravir (DTG) and raltegravir (RAL). Drugs that induce or inhibit the UGT enzyme can affect the PKs of these INSTIs.

Pharmacokinetic Enhancers (Boosters)

PK enhancing is a strategy used to increase exposure of an ARV by concomitantly administering a drug that inhibits the enzymes that metabolize the ARV. Currently in clinical practice, two agents are used as PK enhancers: ritonavir (RTV) and cobicistat (COBI). Both of these agents are potent inhibitors of the CYP3A4 enzyme, resulting in higher drug exposures of the co-administered ARV metabolized by this pathway. Importantly, RTV and COBI may have different effects on other CYP or UGT metabolizing enzymes and drug transporters. Complex or unknown mechanisms of PK-based interactions preclude extrapolation of RTV drug interactions to certain COBI interactions, such as interactions with warfarin, phenytoin, voriconazole, oral contraceptives, certain HMG-CoA reductase inhibitors (or statins), and other drugs.

Other Mechanisms of Pharmacokinetic Interactions

Knowledge of drug transporters is evolving, elucidating additional drug interaction mechanisms. For example, DTG decreases the renal clearance of metformin by inhibiting organic anion transporters in renal tubular cells. Similar transporters aid hepatic, renal, and biliary clearance of drugs and may be susceptible to drug interactions. ARVs and concomitant medications may be inducers, inhibitors, and/ or substrates of these drug transporters.

Drugs That Should Not Be Used with Antiretroviral Agents

This table only lists drugs that should not be coadministered at any dose and regardless of RTV or COBI enhancing.

Table 24.1. Drugs That Should Not Be Used With Antiretroviral Agents

ARV Agentsa,b	Cardiac Agents	Lipid-Lowering Agents	Antimy-co-bac-terial Agents	Antie-pileptic Agents	Neurolog-ic Agents	Herbs	HCV Agentsc	Other Agents
ATV +/- RTV or COBI	Dronedarone Ranolazine	Lovastatin Simvastatin	Rifampin Rifapentined	None	Lurasidone Midazolame Pimozide Triazolam	St. John's wort	Boceprevir Simeprevir	Alfuzosin Cisapridef Ergot derivatives Irinotecan Salmeterol Sildenafil for PAH
DRV/c or DRV/r	Dronedarone Ranolazine	Lovastatin Simvastatin	Rifampin Rifapentined	None	Lurasidone Midazolame Pimozide Triazolam	St. John's wort	Boceprevir Dasabuvir Ombitasvir Paritaprevir Simeprevir	Alfuzosin Cisapridef Ergot derivatives Salmeterol Sildenafil for PAH
FPV +/- RTV	Dronedarone Flecainide Propafenone Ranolazine	Lovastatin Simvastatin	Rifampin Rifapentined	None	Lurasidone Midazolame Pimozide Triazolam	St. John's wort	Boceprevir Dasabuvir Ombitasvir Paritaprevir Simeprevir	Alfuzosin Cisapridef Ergot derivatives Salmeterol Sildenafil for PAH

Table 24.1. Continued

ARV Agentsa,b	Cardiac Agents	Lipid-Lowering Agents	Antimyco-bacterial Agents	Antiepileptic Agents	Neurologic Agents	Herbs	HCV Agentsc	Other Agents
LPV/r	Dronedarone Ranolazine	Lovastatin Simvastatin	Rifamping Rifapentined	None	Lurasidone Midazolame Pimozide Triazolam	St. John's wort	Boceprevir Dasabuvir Ombitasvir Paritaprevir Simeprevir	Alfuzosin Cisapridef Ergot derivatives Salmeterol Sildenafil for PAH
SQV/r	Amiodarone Dofetilide Dronedarone Flecainide Lidocaine Propafenone Quinidine Ranolazine	Lovastatin Simvastatin	Rifamping Rifapentined	None	Lurasidone Midazolame Pimozide Trazodone Triazolam	Garlic supplements St. John's wort	Boceprevir Dasabuvir Ombitasvir Paritaprevir Simeprevir	Alfuzosin Cisapridef Ergot derivatives Salmeterol Sildenafil for PAH
TPV/r	Amiodarone Dronedarone Flecainide Propafenone Quinidine Ranolazine	Lovastatin Simvastatin	Rifampin Rifapentined	None	Lurasidone Midazolame Pimozide Triazolam	St. John's wort	Boceprevir Dasabuvir Ledipasvir Ombitasvir Paritaprevir Simeprevir Sofosbuvir	Alfuzosin Cisapridef Ergot derivatives Salmeterol Sildenafil for PAH

317

Table 24.1. Continued

ARV Agentsa,b	Cardiac Agents	Lipid-Lowering Agents	Antimyco-bacterial Agents	Antiepileptic Agents	Neurologic Agents	Herbs	HCV Agentsc	Other Agents
EFV	None	None	Rifapentined	None	None	St. John's wort	Boceprevir Dasabuvir Ombitasvir Paritaprevir Simeprevir	None
ETR	None	None	Rifampin Rifapentined	Carbamazepine Phenobarbital Phenytoin	None	St John's wort	Dasabuvir Ombitasvir Paritaprevir Simeprevir	Clopidogrel
NVP	None	None	Rifapentined	None	None	St. John's wort	Dasabuvir Ombitasvir Paritaprevir Simeprevir	Keto-conazole
RPV	None	None	Rifampin Rifapentined	Carbamazepine Oxcarbazepine Phenobarbital Phenytoin	None	St. John's wort	Dasabuvir Ombitasvir Paritaprevir	Proton pump inhibitors

Table 24.1. Continued

ARV Agents[a,b]	Cardiac Agents	Lipid-Lowering Agents	Antimyco-bacterial Agents	Antie-pileptic Agents	Neurolog-ic Agents	Herbs	HCV Agents[c]	Other Agents
MVC	None	None	Rifapentine[d]	None	None	St. John's wort	Dasabuvir Ombitasvir Paritaprevir	None
EVG/c/TDF/FTC or EVG + PI/r	Ranolazine	Lovastatin Simvastatin	Rifampin Rifapentine[d]	None	Lurasidone Pimozide Midazolame Triazolam	St. John's wort	EVG/c/TDF/FTC: Boceprevir Dasabuvir Ledipasvir Ombitasvir Paritaprevir Simeprevir EVG + PI/r: Refer to agents listed for the selected PI	Alfuzosin Cisapridef Ergot derivatives Salmeterol Sildenafil for PAH
DTG	Dofetilide	None	Rifapentine[d]	None	None	St. John's wort	None	None

[a] DLV, IDV, NFV, and RTV (as sole PI) are not included in this table. Refer to the appropriate FDA package insert for information regarding DLV-, IDV-, NFV-, and RTV (as sole PI)-related drug interactions.

Table 24.1. Continued

[b]Certain listed drugs are contraindicated on the basis of theoretical considerations. Thus, drugs with narrow therapeutic indices and suspected metabolic involvement with CYP450 3A, 2D6, or unknown pathways are included in this table. Actual interactions may or may not occur in patients.

[c]HCV agents listed include only those that are commercially available at the publication of these guidelines.

[d]HIV-infected patients who received rifapentine as part of a treatment regimen for TB had a higher rate of TB relapse and acquired rifamycin resistance than those treated with other rifamycin-based regimens. Therefore an alternative agent to rifapentine is recommended for TB treatment.

[e]Use of oral midazolam is contraindicated. Single-dose parenteral midazolam can be used with caution and can be given in a monitored situation for procedural sedation.

[f]The manufacturer of cisapride has a limited-access protocol for patients who meet specific clinical eligibility criteria.

[g]A high rate of Grade 4 serum transaminase elevation was seen when a higher dose of RTV was added to LPV/r or SQV or when double-dose LPV/r was used with rifampin to compensate for rifampin's induction effect; therefore, these dosing strategies should not be used. Suggested alternatives to:

Lovastatin, simvastatin: Fluvastatin, pitavastatin, and pravastatin (except for pravastatin with DRV/r) have the least potential for drug-drug interactions . Use atorvastatin and rosuvastatin with caution; start with the lowest possible dose and titrate based on tolerance and lipid-lowering efficacy.

Rifampin: Rifabutin

Midazolam, triazolam: temazepam, lorazepam, oxazepam

Key to Acronyms: ARV = antiretroviral; ATV = atazanavir; COBI = cobicistat; CYP = cytochrome P; DLV = delavirdine; DRV/c = darunavir/cobicistat; DRV/r = darunavir/ritonavir; DTG = dolutegravir; EFV = efavirenz; ETR = etravirine; EVG = elvitegravir; EVG/c/TDF/FTC = elvitegravir/cobicistat/tenofovir/emtricitabine; FDA = Food and Drug Administration; FPV = fosamprenavir; FTC = emtricitabine; HCV = hepatitis C virus; IDV = indinavir; LPV/r = lopinavir/ritonavir; MVC = maraviroc; NFV = nelfinavir; NVP = nevirapine; PAH = pulmonary arterial hypertension; PI = protease inhibitor; PI/r = ritonavir-boosted protease inhibitor; PK = pharmacokinetic; RPV = rilpivirine; RTV = ritonavir; SQV = saquinavir; SQV/r = saquinavir/ritonavir; TB = tuberculosis; TDF = tenofovir disoproxil fumarate; TPV/r = tipranavir/ritonavir

Chapter 25

Complementary and Alternative (CAM) Therapies for HIV/AIDS

Overview

Many people use complementary (sometimes known as alternative) health treatments to go along with the medical care they get from their doctor.

These therapies are called "complementary" therapies because usually they are used alongside the more standard medical care you receive (such as your doctor visits and the anti-HIV drugs you might be taking).

They are sometimes called "alternative" because they don't fit into the more mainstream, Western ways of looking at medicine and health care. These therapies may not fit in with what you usually think of as "health care."

Some common complementary therapies include:

• Physical (body) therapies, such as yoga, massage, and acupuncture

• Relaxation techniques, such as meditation and visualization

• Herbal medicine (from plants)

Text in this chapter is excerpted from "Alternative (Complementary) Therapies for HIV/AIDS," U.S. Department of Veterans Affairs (VA), September 17, 2015.

With most complementary therapies, your health is looked at from a holistic (or "whole picture") point of view. Think of your body as working as one big system. From a holistic viewpoint, everything you do—from what you eat to what you drink to how stressed you are—affects your health and well-being.

Do alternative therapies work?

Healthy people use these kinds of therapies to try to make their immune systems stronger and to make themselves feel better in general. People who have diseases or illnesses, such as HIV, use these therapies for the same reasons. They also can use these therapies to help deal with symptoms of the disease or side effects from the medicines that treat the disease.

Many people report positive results from using complementary therapies. In most cases, however, there is not enough research to tell if these treatments really help people with HIV.

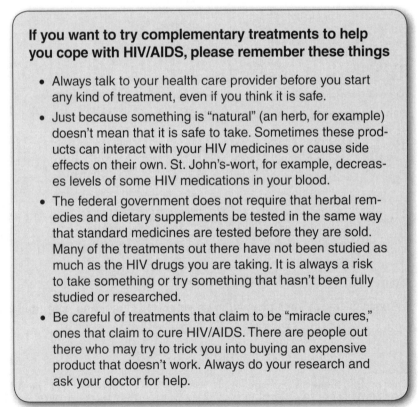

If you want to try complementary treatments to help you cope with HIV/AIDS, please remember these things

- Always talk to your health care provider before you start any kind of treatment, even if you think it is safe.

- Just because something is "natural" (an herb, for example) doesn't mean that it is safe to take. Sometimes these products can interact with your HIV medicines or cause side effects on their own. St. John's-wort, for example, decreases levels of some HIV medications in your blood.

- The federal government does not require that herbal remedies and dietary supplements be tested in the same way that standard medicines are tested before they are sold. Many of the treatments out there have not been studied as much as the HIV drugs you are taking. It is always a risk to take something or try something that hasn't been fully studied or researched.

- Be careful of treatments that claim to be "miracle cures," ones that claim to cure HIV/AIDS. There are people out there who may try to trick you into buying an expensive product that doesn't work. Always do your research and ask your doctor for help.

- Complementary therapies are not substitutes for the treatment and drugs you receive from your doctor. Never stop taking your anti-HIV drugs just because you've started another therapy.
- The federal government is funding studies of how well some alternative therapies work to treat disease, so keep your eyes open for news about these studies.

Here you can read about some of the more common complementary therapies that people with HIV use. Sometimes these are used alone, but often they are used in combination with one another. For example, some people combine yoga with meditation.

Physical (Body) therapies

Physical, or body, therapies include such activities as yoga, massage, and aromatherapy. These types of therapies focus on using a person's body and senses to promote healing and well-being. Here you can learn about examples of these types of therapies.

Yoga

Yoga is a set of exercises that people use to improve their fitness, reduce stress, and increase flexibility.

Yoga can involve breathing exercises, certain stretches and poses, and meditation.

Many people, including people with HIV, use yoga to reduce stress and to become more relaxed and calm. Some people think that yoga helps make them healthier in general, because it can make a person's body stronger.

If you would like to try yoga, talk to your health care provider. There are many different types of yoga and various classes you can take. You can also try out yoga by following a program on videotape.

Before you begin any kind of exercise program, always talk with your doctor.

Massage

Many people believe that massage therapy is an excellent way to deal with the stress and side effects that go along with having an illness, including HIV.

During massage therapy, a trained therapist moves and rubs your body tissues (such as your muscles). There are many kinds of massage therapy.

You can try massage therapy for reducing muscle and back pain, headaches, and soreness. Massages also can improve your blood flow (your circulation) and reduce tension. Some people think that massages might even make your immune system stronger.

If you are interested in learning more about massage, you should ask your doctor to recommend a trained therapist. Your doctor may have a list of trained massage therapists, so if you want to learn more about massage, ask.

Acupuncture

Acupuncture is part of a whole healing system known as traditional Chinese medicine. During acupuncture treatment, tiny needles (about as wide as a hair) are inserted into certain areas of a person's body. Most people say that they don't feel any pain at all from the needles.

Many people with HIV use acupuncture. Some people think that acupuncture can help treat symptoms of HIV and side effects from the medicine, like fatigue and stomach aches.

Some people say that acupuncture can be used to help with neuropathy (body pain caused by nerve damage from HIV or the medicines used to treat HIV).

Others report that acupuncture gives them more energy.

If you are interested in trying it out, ask your doctor to recommend an expert. At the end of this guide are links to Web sites where you can read more about the history of acupuncture and how it works.

Aromatherapy

Aromatherapy is based on the idea that certain smells can change the way you feel. The smells used in aromatherapy come from plant oils, and they can be inhaled (breathed in) or used in baths or massages.

People use aromatherapy to help them deal with stress or to help with fatigue. For example, some people report that lavender oil calms them down and helps them sleep better.

You can also ask friends or family if they've tried aromatherapy or know someone who has. At the end of this guide are links to Web sites where you can learn more about aromatherapy.

Please remember! The oils used in aromatherapy can be very strong and even harmful. Always talk with an expert before buying and using these oils yourself.

Relaxation techniques

Relaxation therapies, such as meditation and visualization, focus on how a person's mind and imagination can promote overall health and well-being. In this section, you can read about some examples of how you can use relaxation therapies to reduce stress and relax.

Meditation

Meditation is a certain way of concentrating that allows your mind and body to become very relaxed. Meditation helps people to focus and be quiet.

There are many different forms of meditation. Most involve deep breathing and paying attention to your body and mind.

Sometimes people sit still and close their eyes to meditate. Meditation also can be casual. For instance, you can meditate when you are taking a walk or watching a sunrise.

People with HIV can use meditation to relax. It can help them deal with the stress that comes with any illness. Meditation can help you to calm down and focus if you are feeling overwhelmed.

If you are interested in learning more about meditation, you should ask your health care provider for more information. There may be meditation classes you can take. At the end of this guide are links to Web sites where you can learn more.

Visualization

Visualization is another method people use to feel more relaxed and less anxious. People who use visualization imagine that they are in a safe, relaxing place (such as the beach). Most of us use visualization without realizing it–for example, when we daydream or remember a fun, happy time in our lives.

Focusing on a safe, comfortable place can help you to feel less stress, and sometimes it can lessen the pain or side effects from HIV or the medicines you are taking.

You can ask your doctor where you can learn more about visualization. There are classes you can take, and there are self-help tapes that you can listen to that lead you through the process. See the links at the end of this guide.

Herbal medicines

Herbal medicines are substances that come from plants, and they work like standard medicine. They can be taken from all parts of a plant, including the roots, leaves, berries, and flowers.

People with HIV sometimes take these medicines to help deal with side effects from anti-HIV medicines or with symptoms from the illness.

An important note about St. John's wort: St. John's wort has become a popular herbal medicine for treating depression. It interacts with the liver and can change how some drugs work in your body, including some anti-HIV drugs (for example, protease inhibitors and NNRTIs). If you are taking antiviral drugs for your HIV, you should NOT take St. John's wort. Be sure you tell you doctor if you are using St. John's wort. You should also not take St. John's wort if you are taking other antidepressants.

- It is important to remember to always use herbs carefully. Learn the proper dosage and use. Don't take too much of anything.
- Always ask your doctor before taking anything new. Just because something is "natural" or "non-drug" doesn't mean that it is safe.
- Finally, learn about the possible side effects of an herbal therapy. Remember: Some herbs can interfere with your HIV medications.

Chapter 26

HIV and AIDS Treatment for Children and Pregnant Women

The Use of HIV Medicines during Pregnancy

- Pregnant women with HIV take HIV medicines to reduce the risk of mother-to-child transmission of HIV and to protect their own health.

- Women who are already taking HIV medicines when they become pregnant should continue taking the medicines during pregnancy. Women with HIV who are not taking HIV medicines when they become pregnant should consider starting HIV medicines as soon as possible.

- Pregnant women with HIV can safely use many HIV medicines during pregnancy. Pregnant women and their health care providers carefully consider the benefits and the risks of specific HIV medicines when choosing an HIV regimen to use during pregnancy.

This chapter includes excerpts from "The Use of HIV Medicines During Pregnancy," AIDS*info*, August 17, 2015; and text from "Guidelines for the Use of Antiretroviral Agents in Pediatric HIV Infection – Treatment Recommendations," AIDS*info*, March 5, 2015.

- Because pregnancy affects how the body processes medicine, the dose of an HIV medicine may change during pregnancy. But women should always talk to their health care providers before making any changes.

The goal of HIV care during pregnancy is to protect the health of HIV-infected women and their babies. All pregnant women with HIV should take HIV medicines to reduce the risk of mother-to-child transmission of HIV. The HIV medicines will also protect the health of the pregnant women.

What is mother-to-child transmission of HIV?

Mother-to-child transmission of HIV is the spread of HIV from a woman to her child during pregnancy or childbirth (also called labor and delivery) or in breast milk. Mother-to-child transmission is the most common way that children become infected with HIV.

HIV medicines work in several ways to prevent mother-to-child transmission of HIV—both during pregnancy and after birth.

During pregnancy

The goal of HIV medicines is to reduce the amount of HIV in the body to an undetectable level (called an undetectable viral load) throughout a woman's pregnancy. By reducing the amount of HIV in the body, HIV medicines reduce the chances that an HIV-infected woman will pass HIV to her baby during pregnancy and childbirth.

HIV medicine also passes from a pregnant woman to her baby across the placenta (also called the afterbirth). This transfer of HIV medicine prevents mother-to-child transmission of HIV, especially near delivery when a baby is most exposed to any HIV in the mother's blood and other fluids.

After birth

After birth, babies born to HIV-infected women receive HIV medicines to protect against infection from any HIV that passed from mother to child during childbirth.

Are HIV medicines safe to use during pregnancy?

Pregnant women with HIV can safely use many HIV medicines during pregnancy. Pregnant women and their health care providers carefully consider the benefits and the risks of specific HIV medicines when choosing an HIV regimen to use during pregnancy.

When recommending HIV medicines for use in pregnancy, health care providers consider the potential short- and long-term effects of HIV medicines on babies born to women with HIV. No HIV medicines have been clearly linked to birth defects, but some HIV medicines have raised concerns. Women who take HIV medicines during pregnancy are encouraged to enroll in the Antiretroviral Pregnancy Registry. The registry monitors prenatal (before birth) exposures to HIV medicines to detect any potential increase in the risk of drug-related birth defects. Pregnant women exposed to HIV medicines voluntarily enroll in the Registry through their health care providers.

Health care providers also consider the following factors when recommending HIV medicines to use during pregnancy:

- Pregnancy-related changes in the body that can affect how the body processes HIV medicines. Because of these changes, the dose of an HIV medicine may change during pregnancy.

- The risk of certain side effects from HIV medicines during pregnancy.

- A woman's medical history, including any past use of HIV medicines.

- Possible drug interactions between HIV medicines and other medicines a woman may be taking.

- Drug-resistance test results. Drug-resistance testing identifies which, if any, HIV medicines won't be effective against a person's HIV.

- A woman's ability to take HIV medicines as instructed.

When should a pregnant woman with HIV begin to take HIV medicines?

Some women with HIV may already be taking HIV medicines when they become pregnant. They should continue taking the HIV medicines throughout their pregnancies. The HIV medicines will continue to protect the women's health **and** prevent mother-to-child transmission of HIV.

A woman's HIV regimen may change during pregnancy. For example, some HIV medicines may not be recommended during pregnancy because of the increased risk of side effects. Because pregnancy affects how the body processes medicine, the dose of an HIV medicine may change. But women should always talk to their health care providers before making any changes.

Women with HIV who are not taking HIV medicines when they become pregnant should consider starting HIV medicines as soon as possible. HIV medicines reduce the amount of HIV in the body (HIV viral load). Having less HIV in the body reduces the risk of mother-to-child transmission of HIV and protects a woman's health.

What HIV medicines should an HIV-infected pregnant woman take?

When recommending HIV medicines for use in pregnancy, health care providers follow the same guidelines used for women who are not pregnant. They also consider what is known about the use of specific HIV medicines in pregnancy, including the risk of side effects that could harm a pregnant woman or her baby.

For women who have never taken HIV medicines, the preferred HIV regimen should include two nucleoside reverse transcriptase inhibitors (NRTIs) plus an integrase strand transfer inhibitor (INSTI), a non-nucleoside reverse transcriptase inhibitor (NNRTI), or a protease inhibitor (PI) with low-dose ritonavir (brand name: Norvir).

The regimen generally should include at least one of the following NRTIs that pass easily across the placenta:

- abacavir (brand name: Ziagen)
- emtricitabine (brand name: Emtriva)
- lamivudine (brand name: Epivir)
- tenofovir disoproxil fumarate (brand name: Viread)
- zidovudine (brand name: Retrovir)

Do women with HIV take HIV medicines during and after childbirth?

During childbirth, women with HIV take HIV medicines to reduce the risk of mother-to-child transmission of HIV.

Babies born to women with HIV receive HIV medicines for 6 weeks after birth to prevent mother-to-child transmission of HIV. The HIV medicines protect the babies from any HIV that may have passed from mother to child during childbirth.

Women discuss with their health care providers whether to continue taking HIV medicines after childbirth. HIV medicines are recommended for everyone infected with HIV. HIV medicines prevent HIV from advancing to AIDS and reduce the risk of sexual transmission of HIV.

General Considerations

Antiretroviral (ARV) treatment of pediatric HIV infection has steadily improved since the introduction of potent combination drug regimens that effectively suppress viral replication in most patients, resulting in a lower risk of virologic failure due to development of drug resistance. Combination antiretroviral therapy (cART) regimens including at least three drugs from at least two drug classes are recommended; such regimens have been associated with enhanced survival, reduction in opportunistic infections and other complications of HIV infection, improved growth and neurocognitive function, and improved quality of life in children. In the United States and the United Kingdom, significant declines in morbidity, mortality, and hospitalizations have been reported in HIV-infected children between 1994 and 2006, concomitant with increased use of highly active combination regimens. As a result, perinatally HIV-infected children are now living into the third and fourth decades of life, and potentially beyond.

The increased survival of HIV-infected children is associated with challenges in selecting successive new ARV drug regimens. In addition, therapy is associated with short- and long-term toxicities, which can be recognized in childhood or adolescence.

ARV drug-resistant virus can develop during cART because of poor adherence, subtherapeutic drug levels, a regimen that is not potent, or a combination of these factors which results in incomplete viral suppression. In addition, primary drug resistance may be seen in ARV-naive children who have become infected with a resistant virus. Thus, decisions about when to start therapy, what drugs to choose in ARV-naive children and how to best treat ARV-experienced children remain complex. Whenever possible, decisions regarding the management of pediatric HIV infection should be directed by or made in consultation with a specialist in pediatric and adolescent HIV infection. Treatment of ARV-naive children, when to change therapy, and treatment of ARV-experienced children will be discussed in separate sections of the guidelines.

Several factors need to be considered in making decisions about initiating and changing cART in children, including:

- Severity of HIV disease and risk of disease progression, as determined by age, presence or history of HIV-related illnesses, degree of CD4 T lymphocyte (CD4) immunosuppression, and level of HIV plasma viremia;

- Availability of appropriate (and palatable) drug formulations and pharmacokinetic (PK) information on appropriate dosing in a child's age/weight group;

- Potency, complexity (e.g., dosing frequency, food and fluid requirements), and potential short- and long-term adverse effects of the cART regimen;

- Effect of initial regimen choice on later therapeutic options;

- A child's cART history;

- Presence of ARV drug-resistant virus;

- Presence of comorbidity, such as tuberculosis, hepatitis B or C virus infection, or chronic renal or liver disease, that could affect decisions about drug choice and the timing of initiation of therapy;

- Potential ARV drug interactions with other prescribed, over-the-counter, or complementary/alternative medications taken by a child; and

- The anticipated ability of the caregiver and child to adhere to the regimen.

The following recommendations provide general guidance for decisions related to treatment of HIV-infected children, and flexibility should be exercised according to a child's individual circumstances. Guidelines for treatment of HIV-infected children are evolving as new data from clinical trials become available. Although prospective, randomized, controlled clinical trials offer the best evidence for formulation of guidelines, most ARV drugs are approved for use in pediatric patients based on efficacy data from clinical trials in adults, with supporting PK and safety data from Phase I/II trials in children. In addition, efficacy has been defined in most adult trials based on surrogate marker data, as opposed to clinical endpoints. For the development of these guidelines, the Panel reviewed relevant clinical trials published in peer-reviewed journals or in abstract form, with attention to data from pediatric populations when available.

Goals of Antiretroviral Treatment

Although there was a single case report of a period of prolonged remission in an HIV-infected child treated with a cART regimen initiated at age 30 hours, viremia returned in this child after more than 2 years of undetectable HIV RNA levels following discontinuation of cART. Current cART has not been shown to eradicate HIV infection in perinatally infected infants due to persistence of HIV in CD4 lymphocytes and other cells. Some data suggest that the half-life of intracellular HIV proviral DNA is even longer in infected children than in adults (median 14 months vs. 5–10 months, respectively). Thus, based on currently available data, HIV causes a chronic infection likely requiring treatment for life once a child starts therapy. The goals of cART for HIV-infected children and adolescents include:

- Preventing and reducing HIV-related morbidity and mortality;
- Restoring and/or preserving immune function as reflected by CD4 cell measures;
- Maximally and durably suppressing viral replication;
- Preventing emergence of viral drug-resistance mutations;
- Minimizing drug-related toxicity;
- Maintaining normal physical growth and neurocognitive development;
- Improving quality of life;
- Reducing the risk of sexual transmission to discordant partners in adolescents who are sexually active; and
- Reducing the risk of perinatal transmission in adolescent females who become pregnant.

Strategies to achieve these goals require a complex balance of potentially competing considerations.

Use and Selection of Combination Antiretroviral Therapy

The treatment of choice for HIV-infected children is a regimen containing at least three drugs from at least two classes of ARV drugs. The Panel has recommended several preferred and alternative regimens. The most appropriate regimen for an individual child depends on multiple factors as noted above. A regimen that is characterized as an alternative choice may be a preferred regimen for some patients.

333

Drug Sequencing and Preservation of Future Treatment Option

The choice of ARV treatment regimens should include consideration of future treatment options, such as the presence of or potential for drug resistance. Multiple changes in ARV drug regimens can rapidly exhaust treatment options and should be avoided. Appropriate sequencing of drugs for use in initial and second-line therapy can preserve future treatment options and is another strategy to maximize long-term benefit from therapy. Current recommendations for initial therapy are to use two classes of drugs, thereby sparing three classes of drugs for later use.

Maximizing Adherence

As discussed in Adherence to Antiretroviral Therapy in HIV-Infected Children and Adolescents, poor adherence to prescribed regimens can lead to subtherapeutic levels of ARV medications, which increases the risk of development of drug resistance and likelihood of virologic failure. Issues related to adherence to therapy should be fully assessed, discussed, and addressed with a child's caregiver and the child (when age appropriate) before the decision to initiate therapy is made. Participation by the caregiver and child in the decision-making process is crucial. Potential problems should be identified and resolved before starting therapy, even if this delays initiation of therapy. In addition, frequent follow-up is important to assess virologic response to therapy, drug intolerance, viral resistance, and adherence. Finally, in patients who experience virologic failure, it is critical to fully assess adherence and possible viral resistance before making changes to the cART regimen.

Chapter 27

Medical Marijuana

What is Medical Marijuana?

The term *medical marijuana* refers to using the whole unprocessed marijuana plant or its basic extracts to treat a disease or symptom. The U.S. Food and Drug Administration (FDA) has not recognized or approved the marijuana plant as medicine.

However, scientific study of the chemicals in marijuana, called *cannabinoids,* has led to two FDA-approved medications that contain cannabinoid chemicals in pill form. Continued research may lead to more medications.

Because the marijuana plant contains chemicals that may help treat a range of illnesses or symptoms, many people argue that it should be legal for medical purposes. In fact, a growing number of states have legalized marijuana for medical use.

Why isn't the marijuana plant an FDA-approved medicine?

The FDA requires carefully conducted studies (clinical trials) in hundreds to thousands of human subjects to determine the benefits and risks of a possible medication. So far, researchers have not conducted enough large-scale clinical trials that show that the benefits of the marijuana plant (as opposed to its cannabinoid ingredients) outweigh its risks in patients it is meant to treat.

Text in this chapter is excerpted from "DrugFacts: Is Marijuana Medicine?" National Institute on Drug Abuse (NIDA), July 2015.

What are cannabinoids?

Cannabinoids are chemicals related to *delta-9-tetrahydrocannab-inol* (THC), marijuana's main mind-altering ingredient. Other than THC, the marijuana plant contains more than 100 other cannabinoids. Scientists as well as illegal manufacturers have produced many cannabinoids in the lab. Some of these cannabinoids are extremely powerful and have led to serious health effects when abused.

The body also produces its own cannabinoid chemicals. They play a role in regulating pleasure, memory, thinking, concentration, body movement, awareness of time, appetite, pain, and the senses (taste, touch, smell, hearing, and sight).

What is CBD?

There is growing interest in the marijuana chemical cannabidiol (CBD) to treat certain conditions such as childhood epilepsy, a disorder that causes a child to have violent seizures. Therefore, scientists have been specially breeding marijuana plants and making CBD in oil form for treatment purposes. These drugs may be less desirable to recreational users because they are not intoxicating.

How might cannabinoids be useful as medicine?

Currently, the two main cannabinoids from the marijuana plant that are of medical interest are THC and CBD.

THC increases appetite and reduces nausea. The FDA-approved THC-based medications are used for these purposes. THC may also decrease pain, inflammation (swelling and redness), and muscle control problems.

CBD is a cannabinoid that does not affect the mind or behavior. It may be useful in reducing pain and inflammation, controlling epileptic seizures, and possibly even treating mental illness and addictions.

NIH-funded and other researchers are continuing to explore the possible uses of THC, CBD, and other cannabinoids for medical treatment.

Scientists are also conducting preclinical and clinical trials with marijuana and its extracts to treat numerous diseases and conditions, including AIDS.

Are People with Health- and Age-Related Problems More Vulnerable to Marijuana's Risks?

Regular medicinal use of marijuana is a fairly new practice. For that reason, its effects on people who are weakened because of age or illness are still relatively unknown. Older people and those suffering from AIDS could be more vulnerable to the drug's harmful effects. Scientists need to conduct more research to determine if this is the case.

What medications contain cannabinoids?

Two FDA-approved drugs, dronabinol and nabilone, contain THC. They treat nausea caused by chemotherapy and increase appetite in patients with extreme weight loss caused by AIDS.

Points to Remember

- The term *medical marijuana* refers to treating a disease or symptom with the whole unprocessed marijuana plant or its basic extracts.
- The FDA has not recognized or approved the marijuana plant as medicine.
- However, scientific study of the chemicals in marijuana called *cannabinoids* has led to two FDA-approved medications in pill form.
- Cannabinoids are chemicals related to *delta-9-tetrahydrocannabinol* (THC), marijuana's main mind-altering ingredient.
- The body also produces its own cannabinoid chemicals.
- Currently, the two main cannabinoids from the marijuana plant that are of interest for medical treatment are THC and *cannabidiol* (CBD).
- Scientists are conducting preclinical and clinical trials with marijuana and its extracts to treat numerous diseases and conditions.

Part Five

Common Co-Occurring Infections and Complications of HIV/AIDS

Chapter 28

Opportunistic Infections and Their Relationship to HIV/AIDS

Opportunistic infections (OIs) are infections that occur more frequently and are more severe in individuals with weakened immune systems, including people with HIV. OIs are less common now than they were in the early days of HIV and AIDS because better treatments reduce the amount of HIV in a person's body and keep a

PEOPLE WITH HEALTHY IMMUNE SYSTEMS CAN BE EXPOSED TO CERTAIN VIRUSES AND HAVE NO REACTION TO THEM,

BUT PEOPLE LIVING WITH HIV CAN FACE SERIOUS THREATS FROM OPPORTUNISTIC INFECTIONS.

These infections are called "OPPORTUNISTIC" because they take advantage of your weakened immune system, and they can cause devastating illnesses.

ANTIRETROVIRAL THERAPY CAN HELP BY INCREASING YOUR NUMBER OF CD4 CELLS, WHICH WILL HELP PROTECT YOU FROM OIS

YOU MAY ALSO TAKE MEDICATIONS USED TO PREVENT DISEASE FROM OCCURRING. (PROPHYLAXIS)

Figure 28.1. *Opportunistic Infections*

Text in this chapter is excerpted from "Opportunistic Infections," Centers for Disease Control and Prevention (CDC), January 16, 2015.

person's immune system stronger. However, many people with HIV still develop OIs because they may not know of their HIV infection, they may not be on treatment, or their treatment may not be keeping their HIV levels low enough for their immune system to fight off infections.

For those reasons, it is important for individuals with HIV to be familiar with the most common OIs so that they can work with their healthcare provider to prevent them or to obtain treatment for them as early as possible.

Most Common Opportunistic Infections

When a person living with HIV gets certain infections (called opportunistic infections, or OIs), he or she will get a diagnosis of AIDS, the most serious stage of HIV infection. AIDS is also diagnosed if a type of blood cell that fights infection (known as CD4 cells) falls below a certain level in persons with HIV. These blood cells are a critical part of a person's immune system.

CDC has developed a list of OIs that indicate a person has AIDS. It does not matter how many CD4 cells a person has, receiving a diagnosis with any of these OIs means HIV infection has progressed to AIDS. HIV treatment can help restore the person's immune system.

Following is a list of the most common OIs for individuals living in the United States. Additionally, CDC, the National Institutes of Health, the HIV Medicine Association of the Infectious Disease Society of America (HIVMA/IDSA), and other experts in infectious disease have published Guidelines for the Prevention and Treatment of Opportunistic Infections in HIV-Infected Adults and Adolescents. While the guidelines are intended for healthcare professionals, some consumers may find them useful.

Table 28.1. Most Common Opportunistic Infections

Candidiasis of bronchi, trachea, esophagus, or lungs	This illness is caused by infection with a common (and usually harmless) type of fungus called *Candida*. Candidiasis, or infection with *Candida*, can affect the skin, nails, and mucous membranes throughout the body. Persons with HIV infection often have trouble with *Candida*, especially in the mouth and vagina. However, candidiasis is only considered an OI when it infects the esophagus (swallowing tube) or lower respiratory tract, such as the trachea and bronchi (breathing tube), or deeper lung tissue.

Table 28.1. Continued

Invasive cervical cancer	This is a cancer that starts within the cervix, which is the lower part of the uterus at the top of the vagina, and then spreads (becomes invasive) to other parts of the body. This cancer can be prevented by having your care provider perform regular examinations of the cervix
Coccidioidomycosis	This illness is caused by the fungus *Coccidioides immitis*. It most commonly acquired by inhaling fungal spores, which can lead to a pneumonia that is sometimes called desert fever, San Joaquin Valley fever, or valley fever. The disease is especially common in hot, dry regions of the southwestern United States, Central America, and South America.
Cryptococcosis	This illness is caused by infection with the fungus *Cryptococcus neoformans*. The fungus typically enters the body through the lungs and can cause pneumonia. It can also spread to the brain, causing swelling of the brain. It can infect any part of the body, but (after the brain and lungs) infections of skin, bones, or urinary tract are most common.
Cryptosporidiosis, chronic intestinal (greater than one month's duration)	This diarrheal disease is caused by the protozoan parasite *Cryptosporidium*. Symptoms include abdominal cramps and severe, chronic, watery diarrhea.
Cytomegalovirus diseases (particularly retinitis) (CMV)	This virus can infect multiple parts of the body and cause pneumonia, gastroenteritis (especially abdominal pain caused by infection of the colon), encephalitis (infection) of the brain, and sight-threatening retinitis (infection of the retina at the back of eye). People with CMV retinitis have difficulty with vision that worsens ever time. CMV retinitis is a medical emergency because it can cause blindness if not treated promptly.
Encephalopathy, HIV-related	This brain disorder is a result of HIV infection. It can occur as part of acute HIV infection or can result from chronic HIV infection. Its exact cause is unknown but it is thought to be related to infection of the brain with HIV and the resulting inflammation.
Herpes simplex (HSV): chronic ulcer(s) (greater than one month's duration); or bronchitis, pneumonitis, or esophagitis	Herpes simplex virus (HSV) is a very common virus that for most people never causes any major problems. HSV is usually acquired sexually or from an infected mother during birth. In most people with healthy immune systems, HSV is usually latent (inactive). However, stress, trauma, other infections, or suppression of the immune system (such as by HIV), can reactivate the latent virus and symptoms can return. HSV can cause

Table 28.1. Continued

	painful cold sores (sometime called fever blisters) in or around the mouth, or painful ulcers on or around the genitals or anus. In people with severely damaged immune systems, HSV can also cause infection of the bronchus (breathing tube), pneumonia (infection of the lungs) and esophagitis (infection of the esophagus, or swallowing tube).
Histoplasmosis	This illness is caused by the fungus *Histoplasma capsulatum*. *Histoplasma* most often infects the lungs and produces symptoms that are similar to those of influenza or pneumonia. People with severely damaged immune systems can get a very serious form of the disease called progressive disseminated histoplasmosis. This form of histoplasmosis can last a long time and involves organs other than the lungs.
Isosporiasis, chronic intestinal (greater than one month's duration)	This infection is caused by the parasite *Isospora belli*, which can enter the body through contaminated food or water. Symptoms include diarrhea, fever, headache, abdominal pain, vomiting, and weight loss.
Kaposi's sarcoma (KS)	This cancer, also known as KS, is caused by a virus called Kaposi's sarcoma herpesvirus (KSHV) or human herpesvirus 8 (HHV-8). KS causes small blood vessels, called capillaries, to grow abnormally. Because capillaries are located throughout the body, KS can occur anywhere. KS appears as firm pink or purple spots on the skin that can be raised or flat. KS can be life-threatening when it affects organs inside the body, such the lung, lymph nodes or intestines.
Lymphoma, multiple forms	Lymphoma refers to cancer of the lymph nodes and other lymphoid tissues in the body. There are many different kinds of lymphomas. Some types, such as non-Hodgkin lymphoma and Hodgkin lymphoma, are associated with HIV infection.
Tuberculosis (TB)	Tuberculosis (TB) infection is caused by the bacteria *Mycobacterium tuberculosis*. TB can be spread through the air when a person with active TB coughs, sneezes, or speaks. Breathing in the bacteria can lead to infection in the lungs. Symptoms of TB in the lungs include cough, tiredness, weight loss, fever, and night sweats. Although the disease usually occurs in the lungs, it may also affect other parts of the body, most often the larynx, lymph nodes, brain, kidneys, or bones.

Table 28.1. Continued

Mycobacterium avium **complex (MAC) or** *Mycobacterium kansasii,* **disseminated or extrapulmonary. Other** *Mycobacterium,* **disseminated or extrapulmonary.**	MAC is caused by infection with different types of mycobacterium: *Mycobacterium avium, Mycobacterium intracellulare,* or *Mycobacterium kansasii.* These mycobacteria live in our environment, including in soil and dust particles. They rarely cause problems for persons with healthy immune systems. In people with severely damaged immune systems, infections with these bacteria spread throughout the body and can be life-threatening.
Pneumocystis carinii **pneumonia (PCP)**	This lung infection, also called PCP, is caused by a fungus, which used to be called *Pneumocystis carinii,* but now is named *Pneumocystis jirovecii.* PCP occurs in people with weakened immune systems, including people with HIV. The first signs of infection are difficulty breathing, high fever, and dry cough.
Pneumonia, recurrent	Pneumonia is an infection in one or both of the lungs. Many germs, including bacteria, viruses, and fungi can cause pneumonia, with symptoms such as a cough (with mucous), fever, chills, and trouble breathing. In people with immune systems severely damaged by HIV, one of the most common and life-threatening causes of pneumonia is infection with the bacteria *Streptococcus pneumoniae,* also called *Pneumococcus.* There are now effective vaccines that can prevent infection with *Streptococcus pneumoniae* and all persons with HIV infection should be vaccinated.
Progressive multifocal leukoencephalopathy	This rare brain and spinal cord disease is caused by the JC virus. It is seen almost exclusively in persons whose immune systems have been severely damaged by HIV. Symptoms may include loss of muscle control, paralysis, blindness, speech problems, and an altered mental state. This disease often progresses rapidly and may be fatal.
Salmonella **septicemia, recurrent**	*Salmonella* are a kind of bacteria that typically enter the body through ingestion of contaminated food or water. Infection with salmonella (called salmonellosis) can affect anyone and usually causes a self-limited illness with nausea, vomiting, and diarrhea. *Salmonella* septicemia is a severe form of infection in which the bacteria circulate through the whole body and exceeds the immune system's ability to control it.

Table 28.1. Continued

Toxoplasmosis of brain	This infection, often called toxo, is caused by the parasite *Toxoplasma gondii.* The parasite is carried by warm-blooded animals including cats, rodents, and birds and is excreted by these animals in their feces. Humans can become infected with it by inhaling dust or eating food contaminated with the parasite. *Toxoplasma* can also occur in commercial meats, especially red meats and pork, but rarely poultry. Infection with toxo can occur in the lungs, retina of the eye, heart, pancreas, liver, colon, testes, and brain. Although cats can transmit toxoplasmosis, litter boxes can be changed safely by wearing gloves and washing hands thoroughly with soap and water afterwards. All raw red meats that have not been frozen for at least 24 hours should be cooked through to an internal temperature of at least 150°F.
Wasting syndrome due to HIV	Wasting is defined as the involuntary loss of more than 10% of one's body weight while having experienced diarrhea or weakness and fever for more than 30 days. Wasting refers to the loss of muscle mass, although part of the weight loss may also be due to loss of fat.

Preventing Opportunistic Infections

The best ways to prevent getting an OI are to get into and stay on medical care and to take HIV medications as prescribed. Sometimes, your health care provider will also prescribe medications specifically to prevent certain OIs. By staying on HIV medications, you can keep the amount of HIV in your body as low as possible and keep your immune system healthy. It is especially important that you get regular check-ups and take all of your medications as prescribed by your care giver. Taking HIV medications is a life-long commitment.

In addition to taking HIV medications to keep your immune system strong, there are other steps you can take to prevent getting an OI.

- Use condoms consistently and correctly to prevent exposure to sexually transmitted infections.

- Don't share drug injection equipment. Blood with hepatitis C in it can remain in syringes and needles after use and the infection can be transmitted to the next user.

- Get vaccinated—your doctor can tell you what vaccines you need. If he or she doesn't, you should ask.

- Understand what germs you are exposed to (such as tuberculosis or germs found in the stools, saliva, or on the skin of animals) and limit your exposure to them.

- Don't consume certain foods, including undercooked eggs, unpasteurized (raw) milk and cheeses, unpasteurized fruit juices, or raw seed sprouts.

- Don't drink untreated water such as water directly from lakes or rivers. Tap water in foreign countries is also often not safe. Use bottled water or water filters.

- Ask your doctor to review with you the other things you do at work, at home, and on vacation to make sure you aren't exposed to an OI.

Treating Opportunistic Infections

If you do develop an OI, there are treatments available, such as antibiotics or antifungal drugs. Having an OI may be a very serious medical situation and its treatment can be challenging. The development of an OI likely means that your immune system is weakened and that your HIV is not under control. That is why it is so important to be on medication, take it as prescribed, see your care provider regularly, and undergo the routine monitoring he or she recommends to ensure your viral load is reduced and your immune system is healthy.

Chapter 29

Strategies for Managing Opportunistic Infections

Opportunistic infections can be caused by viruses, bacteria, and fungus, even parasites. One way to avoid these infections is to reduce your risk of exposure to these germs. Here are some practical suggestions.

Sexual exposures

- Use condoms every time you have sex.

- Avoid oral-anal sex.

- Use waterproof gloves if you're going to insert your finger into your partner's anus.

- Frequently wash hands and genitals with warm soapy water after any sex play that brings them in contact with feces.

Injection drug use

- Do not inject drugs.

Text in this chapter is excerpted from "Preventing Opportunistic Infections (OIs)," U.S. Department of Veterans Affairs (VA), September 17, 2015.

- If you cannot stop using, avoid sharing needles and other equipment.

- Get vaccinated against hepatitis A and hepatitis B.

Job exposure

Certain type of jobs or facilities can put an HIV-positive person at risk of OIs. These include work in:

- health care facilities

- homeless shelters

- day-care centers

- prisons

- places that involved work with animals (such as farms, veterinary clinics, pet stores)

Pet exposure

Pets can carry diseases that don't affect a healthy person but can pose a serious risk to someone with HIV. For that reason, if you have a pet, follow these suggestions.

General

- Wash your hands after handling your pet (especially before eating).

- Avoid contact with your pet's feces. If your pet has diarrhea, ask a friend or family member to take care of it.

- If you are getting a new pet, try not to get one that is younger than a year old, especially if it has diarrhea. (Young animals are more likely to carry certain germs like Salmonella.) Avoid stray animals.

Cats

- Keep your cat indoors. It should not be allowed to hunt, and should not be fed raw or undercooked meat.

- Have a friend or family member clean the litter box daily. If you have to do it yourself, wash your hands thoroughly afterward.

- Control fleas (ask your vet how to do this).

- Avoid playing with your cat in ways that may result in scratches or bites. If you do get scratched or bitten, wash the area right away. Don't let your cat lick your cuts or wounds.

Birds

- Avoid areas where there are bird droppings. Do not disturb soil underneath bird-roosting sites.

Others

- Avoid touching reptiles, such as snakes, lizards, iguanas, and turtles.
- Wear gloves if you are cleaning an aquarium.

Cautions about food and water

- Avoid raw or undercooked eggs (including hollandaise sauce, Caesar salad dressing, some mayonnaises, eggnog, cake and cookie batter).
- Avoid raw or undercooked poultry, meat, and seafood (especially raw seafood). Use a meat thermometer. Cook poultry to 180° F, and other meats to 165° F. If you don't have a meat thermometer, cook meat until no traces of pink remain.
- Avoid unpasteurized dairy products and fruit juice.
- Avoid raw seed sprouts (such as alfalfa, mung beans).
- Thoroughly wash fruits and vegetables before eating.
- Don't let uncooked meats come into contact with other uncooked foods. (Wash thoroughly hands, cutting boards, counters, knives, and other utensils after contact with uncooked meats.)
- Do not drink water directly from lakes or rivers. Filtered water is preferable, particular if your immune system is weak.

HIV-positive people whose immune systems are severely weakened may want to:

- Avoid soft cheeses (feta, brie, camembert, blue-veined, and Mexican-style cheeses, such as queso fresco).
- Cook leftover foods or ready-to-eat foods, such as hot dogs, until they are steaming hot.

351

- Avoid food from delicatessens, such as prepared meats, salads, and cheeses—or heat these foods until steaming before eating.

Cautions about travel

Before you travel to other countries, particularly developing countries, talk to your doctor about ways you can avoid getting sick on your trip.

When traveling in developing countries, people who are HIV positive have to be especially cautious of food and water that may be contaminated. It is best to avoid:

- raw fruits and vegetables (unless you peel them first)

- raw or undercooked seafood or meat

- tap water (or ice made with tap water)

- unpasteurized milk or dairy products

- swallowing water when swimming

Talk to your health care provider about whether you need to get vaccinated before your trip and whether you need to take drugs to prevent diseases that are common in the country you are going to visit.

Chapter 30

HIV/AIDS and Co-Occurring Bacterial Infections

Chapter Contents

Section 30.1

Mycobacterium Avium Complex (MAC)

Text in this section is excerpted from "Mycobacterium Avium Complex (MAC)," U.S. Department of Veterans Affairs (VA), September 17, 2015.

This condition is caused by bacteria present everywhere in the environment—in soil, food, and animals. It is difficult to avoid exposure because MAC is in so many places. In general, avoid handling soil, and carefully handle and prepare food.

Symptoms of MAC can include:

- fever
- night sweats
- weight loss
- loss of appetite
- chronic diarrhea
- weakness
- fatigue
- abdominal pain

HIV drugs, by helping your immune system stay strong, can help your body fight the infection. Antibiotics given over a long period of time can control the infection, and be stopped once the disease is cured and the immune system is strong enough. Call your doctor if you have vision changes or abdominal discomfort while being treated for MAC.

Food Safety Tips

What should I know about food safety?

Paying attention to food and water safety is important when you have HIV, because your immune system is already weakened and working hard to fight off infections.

If food is not handled or prepared in a safe way, germs from the food can be passed on to you. These germs can make you sick.

You need to handle and cook food properly to keep those germs from getting to you.

Here are some food safety guidelines:

- Keep everything clean. Clean your counters and utensils often.

- Wash your hands with soap and warm water before and after preparing and eating food.

- Check expiration dates on food packaging. Do not eat foods that have a past expiration date.

- Rinse all fresh fruits and vegetables with clean water.

- Thaw frozen meats and other frozen foods in the refrigerator or in a microwave. Never thaw foods at room temperature. Germs that grow at room temperature can make you very sick.

- Clean all cutting boards and knives (especially those that touch chicken and meat) with soap and hot water before using them again.

- Make sure you cook all meat, fish, and poultry "well-done." You might want to buy a meat thermometer to help you know for sure that it is done. Put the thermometer in the thickest part of the meat and not touching a bone. Cook the meat until it reaches 165 to 212 degrees Fahrenheit on your thermometer.

- Do not eat raw, soft-boiled, or "over easy" eggs, or Caesar salads with raw egg in the dressing.

- Do not eat sushi, raw seafood, or raw meats, or unpasteurized milk or dairy products.

- Keep your refrigerator cold, set no higher than 40 degrees. Your freezer should be at 0 degrees.

- Refrigerate leftovers at temperatures below 40 degrees F. Do not eat leftovers that have been sitting in the refrigerator for more than 3 days.

- Keep hot items heated to over 140 degrees F, and completely reheat leftovers before eating.

- Throw away any foods (like fruit, vegetables, and cheese) that you think might be old. If food has a moldy or rotten spot, throw it out. When in doubt, throw it out.

- Some germs are spread through tap water. If your public water supply isn't totally pure, drink bottled water.

Section 30.2

Tuberculosis

Text in this section is excerpted from "Tuberculosis," AIDS.gov,
March 21, 2013.

Tuberculosis (TB) is a disease that is caused by a specific type
of bacterial infection called Mycobacterium tuberculosis. TB usually
affects the lungs, but it can also affect the brain, kidneys, spine or
other organ systems. TB can cause serious health problems, including
death, if left untreated.

TUBERCULOSIS REMAINS A SERIOUS THREAT FOR PEOPLE LIVING WITH HIV/AIDS BECAUSE TB AND HIV INFECTION CAN WORK TOGETHER TO MAKE YOU VERY SICK.   WORLDWIDE TUBERCULOSIS IS THE LEADING CAUSE OF DEATH AMONG PEOPLE LIVING WITH HIV.   THERE ARE A NUMBER OF TREATMENT OPTIONS FOR PEOPLE LIVING WITH HIV WHO HAVE EITHER LATENT TB INFECTION OR ACTIVE TB DISEASE.

Figure 30.1. *Tuberculosis and HIV*

According to the Centers for Disease Control and Prevention (CDC),
fewer people in the U.S. have TB disease than in past years. However,
despite a decrease in reported TB cases, the disease remains a serious
threat, especially for people living with HIV/AIDS. That's because TB
infection and HIV infection can work together to make you very sick.
Worldwide, TB is the leading cause of death among people living with HIV.

TB is an issue for people living with HIV/AIDS in the U.S. because:

- It is estimated that about 4.2% of Americans (13 million individuals) are infected with TB bacteria.

- As of 2011, CDC estimated 6% of all TB cases and 10% of TB cases among people aged 25–44 occurred among people who were HIV-positive.

Because of the serious health risks for *coinfection* with TB and
HIV, the CDC recommends that **all HIV-positive people should be**

tested for TB. Those who test positive for TB should begin treatment immediately.

How TB Is Spread

TB is primarily an airborne disease. When a person with active TB disease coughs, sneezes, speaks, or sings, TB germs spread through the air. These germs can float in the air for several hours. If you breathe in the air containing these TB germs, you can become infected.

TB is NOT spread by:

- Shaking someone's hand

- Sharing food or drink

- Touching bed linens or toilet seats

- Sharing toothbrushes

- Kissing

Two Types of TB Infection

There are two types of TB infection **latent** and **active**. People with **latent** TB infection (LTBI) don't have any signs or symptoms of the disease and don't feel sick. They are not infectious and cannot spread TB infection to others. However, these people could develop TB disease in the future, especially if they have HIV infection. That's because people with TB infection and HIV infection have a **very high risk** of developing TB disease. Fortunately, people with LTBI can take medicine to prevent them from developing active, severe TB disease.

When people are clinically ill with TB, they are said to have "**active**" TB disease. People with active TB disease can spread the illness to others. Medicines which can cure TB are usually given to these people.

Symptoms

Symptoms of TB can vary from person to person. People who have LTBI will have no symptoms. People with active TB infection can experience persistent coughing (including coughing up blood), night sweats, fever, weight loss, chills, and fatigue. If you are experiencing any of these symptoms, you should consult your healthcare provider right a way.

Testing

There are two types of tests to determine if you have TB infection—a **skin test** and a **blood test**.

You can get a skin test at the health department or at your doctor's office. A healthcare worker will use a small needle to inject some testing fluid (called tuberculin) just under the skin on the lower part of your arm. After 2–3 days, you must return to have your skin test checked by a healthcare worker. A "positive" reaction usually means that you have TB infection.

There are also tests that use a small amount of your blood to check for TB. The advantage of the blood test is that only one visit is required to draw blood for the test and you don't have to wait 2–3 days for the result. However, not all healthcare providers offer these tests.

A positive TB skin test or TB blood test can only show that you have been infected with TB bacteria. **It does not tell whether or not you have progressed to TB disease**. You will need to take other tests, such as a chest x-ray, and give a sample of *sputum*, to see whether you have TB disease and whether the strain of TB is *drug-resistant*. These tests will help you and your healthcare provider choose the best course of treatment.

How Often Should I Be Tested

In general, CDC recommends that all people who are newly diagnosed with HIV infection should be tested for TB as soon as possible. In addition, people living with HIV and at risk for TB exposure should be tested annually to find out if they have LTBI. You should also be retested for TB if you are just beginning *antiretroviral therapy* for your HIV disease.

Treatment

There are a number of treatment options for people living with HIV who have either LTBI or active TB disease. Treatment consists of long-term (9–12 months) antibiotic therapy for both LTBI and active disease. If you are taking antiretrovirals for your HIV disease, the treatment period may be even longer.

Treatment for TB can be as challenging as treatment for HIV. There are some risks involved, mainly because the treatments can cause liver damage in some people. If you have both HIV and TB, it is important to be closely monitored by a healthcare provider during your treatment to make sure you are not hurt by side effects from taking TB and HIV medicines together.

Also, if you begin antibiotic therapy for TB, it's important to take ALL your medication, on time and in the way your health-care provider recommends. Like HIV, TB can become resistant to medications quickly if you miss doses of your meds.

Drug-Resistant TB

Unfortunately, some strains of TB bacteria have stopped responding to medications regularly used to treat TB disease. Drug resistance is more common in people who:

- Do not take their TB medicine regularly

- Do not take all of their TB medicine as directed by their health-care provider

- Develop active TB disease again, after having taken TB medicine in the past

- Come from areas of the world where drug-resistant TB is common

- Have spent time with someone known to have drug-resistant TB disease

Multidrug-resistant TB (MDR TB) is TB that is resistant to at least two of the best anti-TB drugs—isoniazid and rifampin. MDR TB is extremely difficult to treat and can be fatal.

Although the number of cases in the United States remained steady since 1998, MDR TB has now been reported in nearly all states and the District of Columbia.

Extensively Drug-Resistant Tuberculosis (XDR TB) is resistant to the most powerful first-line and second-line drugs. Patients with XDR TB have fewer, less-effective treatment options and often have worse treatment outcomes.

People living with HIV infection or with AIDS are at greater risk of dying of MDR TB and XDR TB.

Chapter 31

HIV/AIDS and Co-Occurring Fungal Infections

Chapter Contents

Section 31.1

HIV/AIDS and Fungal Infections: An Overview

Text in this section is excerpted from "Who Gets Fungal Infections –
HIV/AIDS and Fungal Infections," Centers for Disease Control and
Prevention (CDC), February 13, 2014.

As a person living with HIV/AIDS, you have many opportunities
for a healthy and full life. You may also have some health challenges.
One of those challenges is avoiding infections.

Many fungal infections are called opportunistic infections, which
means that they usually affect people with weak immune systems.
Because HIV weakens the immune system, you have a greater
chance of getting some types of fungal infections, like cryptococcosis,
coccidioidomycosis, histoplasmosis, and pneumocystis pneumonia
(PCP).

What you need to know about fungal infections

Your CD4 count is important. You're at greatest risk for fungal
infection when your CD4 count is less than 200. Keeping your CD4
count above 200 may help you avoid serious illness.

Anti-retroviral therapy (ART) is important. Starting ART
helps slow the progress of HIV and can reduce your chances of getting
a fungal infection.

Fungal infections can range from mild to life-threatening.
Some fungal infections are mild skin rashes, but others can be deadly,
like fungal meningitis. Because of this, it's important to seek treatment
as soon as possible to try to avoid serious infection.

Fungal infections can look like bacterial or viral infections.
If you're taking medicine to fight an infection and you aren't getting
better, ask your doctor about testing you for a fungal infection.

Where you live (geography) matters. Some disease-causing
fungi are more common in certain parts of the world. If you have

HIV/AIDS and live in or visit these areas, you're more likely to get these infections than the general population.

Your activities matter. Disease-causing fungi can be found in air, dust, and soil, especially soil that contains bird or bat droppings. Doing activities that disturb the soil, like gardening, cleaning chicken coops, construction, demolition, and visiting caves can cause you to inhale more fungi and increases your chance of infection.

Some fungal infections can interfere with taking your medications. Thrush, an infection in the mouth and throat, is sometimes seen among people living with HIV/AIDS. This infection is not usually life-threatening, but can be painful, make it difficult to eat, or interfere with taking your medications. Your nutrition is an important part of staying healthy, so it's important to seek care for this infection.

Preventing fungal infections in people living with HIV/AIDS

Fungi are difficult to avoid because they are a natural part of the environment. Fungi live outdoors in soil, on plants, trees, and other vegetation. They are also on many indoor surfaces and on your skin. However, there may be some ways for you to lower your chances of getting a serious fungal infection.

Learn about fungal infections. There are different types of fungal infections. Learning about them can help you and your healthcare provider recognize the symptoms early, which may prevent serious illness.

Find out about your risk. The danger of getting a fungal infection can change depending on your location and your CD4 count. Learning what things can put you at risk may prevent serious illness.

Get additional medical care if necessary. Fungal infections often resemble other illnesses. Visiting your healthcare provider may help with faster diagnosis and may prevent serious illness.

Antifungal medication. Your healthcare provider may prescribe medication to prevent fungal infections. For example, they may recommend medication (TMP-SMX, also called Bactrim, Septra, or Cotrim) to prevent a type of fungal pneumonia called *Pneumocystis jirovecii* pneumonia (PCP).

Protect yourself from the environment. There may be some ways to lower your chances of getting a serious fungal infection by trying to avoid disease-causing fungi in the environment. It's important to note that although these actions are recommended, they have not been proven to prevent fungal infections.

- Try to avoid areas with a lot of dust like construction or excavation sites.

- Stay inside during dust storms.

- Stay away from areas with bird and bat droppings. This includes places like chicken coops and caves.

- Wear gloves when handling materials such as soil, moss, or manure.

- Wear shoes, long pants, and a long-sleeved shirt when doing outdoor activities such as gardening, yard work, or visiting wooded areas.

Testing for early fungal infection. In areas of the world with high rates of HIV/AIDS and where cryptococcosis is common, high-risk HIV patients can be tested for this infection before symptoms appear. If the test detects early cryptococcal infection, treatment can prevent it from becoming deadly.

Section 31.2

Candidiasis

This section includes excerpts from "Candidiasis," Centers for Disease Control and Prevention (CDC), June 12, 2015; and text from "Candidiasis (thrush)," U.S. Department of Veterans Affairs (VA), July 30, 2015.

Candidiasis is a fungal infection caused by yeasts that belong to the genus *Candida*. There are over 20 species of *Candida* yeasts that can cause infection in humans, the most common of which is *Candida albicans*. *Candida* yeasts normally live on the skin and mucous membranes without causing infection; however, overgrowth of these organisms can cause symptoms to develop. Symptoms of candidiasis vary depending on the area of the body that is infected.

Candidiasis that develops in the mouth or throat is called "thrush" or oropharyngeal candidiasis. Candidiasis in the vagina is commonly referred to as a "yeast infection." Invasive candidiasis occurs when *Candida* species enter the bloodstream and spread throughout the body.

Some people show no symptoms, but for those who have them, symptoms can include:

- white patches on the tongue

- smooth red areas on the back of the tongue

- painful areas in the mouth

- changes in taste

- sensitivity to spicy foods

- decreased appetite

- pain or difficulty swallowing

- yeast infection of the vagina (vaginal itching and white discharge)

Treatments for thrush include oral drugs (suspensions) that you swish around in your mouth and swallow as well as oral antifungal medications. If you are taking drugs for thrush or a yeast infection, be sure to:

- brush your teeth after each meal;

- rinse your mouth of all food before using either lozenges or suspension;

- avoid hurting your mouth: use a soft toothbrush, avoid foods and drinks that are too hot or too spicy.

Section 31.3

Cryptococcal Meningitis

Text in this section is excerpted from "Preventing Deaths from
Cryptococcal Meningitis," Centers for Disease Control and
Prevention (CDC), September 30, 2014.

What is cryptococcal meningitis?

Cryptococcus neoformans is a fungus that lives in the environment
throughout the world. Most people likely breathe in this microscopic
fungus when they are children but never get sick from it, but in people
with weakened immune systems such as those living with HIV/AIDS,
Cryptococcus can stay hidden in the body and later become a serious
(but not contagious) brain infection called cryptococcal meningitis.

Why is cryptococcal meningitis a problem?

Most cases of cryptococcal meningitis occur in people who have HIV/
AIDS. The widespread availability of antiretroviral therapy (ART)
in developed countries has helped improve the immune systems of
many HIV patients so that they don't become vulnerable to infection
with *Cryptococcus*. However, cryptococcal meningitis is still a major
problem in resource-limited countries where HIV prevalence is high
and access to healthcare is limited. Worldwide, nearly 1 million new
cases of cryptococcal meningitis occur each year, resulting in 625,000
deaths, most of which occur in sub-Saharan Africa.

Strategies to prevent deaths from cryptococcal meningitis

Although it's not possible to prevent the initial exposure to *Cryptococcus*, diagnosing and treating early cryptococcal infections in people
at high risk for developing cryptococcal meningitis can prevent associated deaths. Therefore, CDC is working to improve diagnosis and treatment of cryptococcal meningitis in countries with large populations of
people living with HIV/AIDS. In these areas, CDC is helping implement targeted cryptococcal screening programs and build laboratory
capacity to detect cryptococcal infections early. This allows for more

timely treatment, reduced mortality due to cryptococcal meningitis, and overall improved quality of life.

- **Targeted screening for early cryptococcal infection**

Cryptococcal antigen, a chemical marker for cryptococcal infection, can be detected in the body weeks to months before symptoms of meningitis appear. In a targeted screening program, people who have advanced HIV infection are tested for cryptococcal antigen before starting ART. A patient who tests positive for cryptococcal antigen can take antifungal medication to help the body fight the early stage of the infection, which has been shown to prevent deaths due to cryptococcal meningitis.

- **Improved access to diagnostics**

In order to screen people living with HIV for early cryptococcal infection and to diagnose other patients with cryptococcal meningitis, healthcare facilities and laboratories must have access to the right diagnostic tests. Currently, these tests are unavailable in many district and provincial laboratories in sub-Saharan Africa. Equipping these facilities with the ability to perform these tests is an important step in reducing deaths from cryptococcal meningitis.

A new lateral flow assay for detecting cryptococcal antigen is simple to use on a small sample of blood or spinal fluid. The test accurately detects both early and advanced cryptococcal infections more than 95% of the time. In addition, the test is inexpensive, rapid, and doesn't require costly laboratory equipment and expertise, making it ideal for resource-limited settings.

- **Improved access to antifungal medications Doctor holding bottle of pills**

Essential medications for the treatment of cryptococcal infections are often unavailable in areas of the world that are most in need. Amphotericin B and flucytosine are two antifungal medications that have been shown to improve survival in patients with cryptococcal meningitis. Although these drugs are the standard-of-care in developed countries, they are widely unavailable in sub-Saharan Africa and Asia.

Section 31.4

Pneumocystis Carinii Pneumonia (PCP)

Text in this section is excerpted from "Pneumocystis
pneumonia," Centers for Disease Control and Prevention (CDC),
February 13, 2014.

Pneumocystis pneumonia (PCP) is a serious illness caused by the
fungus *Pneumocystis jirovecii.* PCP is one of the most frequent and
severe opportunistic infections in people with weakened immune systems, particularly people with HIV/AIDS. Although people with HIV/
AIDS are less likely to get PCP today than in recent years, PCP is still
a significant public health problem.

Symptoms

The symptoms of PCP are fever, dry cough, shortness of breath, and
fatigue. In people with weakened immune systems, PCP can be very
serious, so it is important to see a doctor if you have these symptoms.

In HIV-infected patients, PCP usually presents sub-acutely, and
symptoms include a low-grade fever. In HIV-uninfected patients,
symptoms of PCP tend to develop more quickly and patients typically
experience a high fever.

Risk and Prevention

Who gets pneumocystis pneumonia (PCP)?

PCP is extremely rare in healthy people. Most people who get PCP
have weakened immune systems due to HIV/AIDS, cancer treatments,
or organ transplants. Other groups of people who are at risk for PCP
include:

- HIV-exposed but uninfected children

- People who are receiving immunosuppressive therapies, such as
  organ transplant patients

- People with connective tissue diseases or chronic lung diseases

How can I prevent pneumocystis pneumonia (PCP)?

There is no vaccine to prevent PCP. Some groups of people who are at high risk of developing PCP may need to take a medication called TMP-SMX to prevent the illness from occurring. If your doctor thinks you are at risk for developing PCP, he or she might prescribe this medicine for you. TMP-SMX prophylaxis is currently recommended for:

- All HIV-infected patients with CD4 < 350 cells / μL
- Infants born to HIV-infected mothers
- Children with a history of PCP
- Stem cell transplant patients

Sources

Scientists are still learning about how people get PCP. Studies have shown that many people are exposed to the fungus as children, but they do not get sick because their immune systems are strong. Some healthy adults carry the fungus in their lungs and never develop symptoms of PCP. However, if a person's immune system stops working normally, the fungus can start causing symptoms.

Diagnosis and Testing

PCP is diagnosed by using a microscope to identify *P. jirovecii* organisms in a sample of lung fluid or tissue. The sample is usually induced sputum or bronchoalveolar lavage (BAL) material. It may be necessary to get the sample through transbronchial biopsy or open-lung biopsy—these diagnostic techniques are more sensitive and specific, but they are also more invasive.

Polymerase chain reaction (PCR) is also used to detect *P. jirovecii* DNA in clinical specimens. PCR can be particularly helpful in detecting silent *P. jirovecii* infections in HIV-infected patients.

Treatment and Outcomes

PCP requires treatment with prescription medicine that must be taken for three weeks. The best form of treatment for PCP is trimethoprim sulfamethoxazole (TMP-SMX), which is also known by the brand names Bactrim, Septra, and Cotrim. This medicine is given orally or through a vein.

TMP-SMX can cause negative side effects such as a rash and nausea, but the benefits of treating the PCP usually outweigh the risks of these side effects. Without treatment, PCP can be fatal.

Chapter 32

HIV/AIDS and Co-Occurring Parasitic Infections

Chapter Contents

Section 32.1

Cryptosporidiosis

This section includes excerpts from "Cryptosporidium," Centers for
Disease Control and Prevention (CDC), April 20, 2015; and text
from "Cryptosporidium – Prevention & Control," Centers for Disease
Control and Prevention (CDC), July 17, 2015.

What is cryptosporidiosis?

Cryptosporidiosis is a disease that causes watery diarrhea. It is
caused by microscopic germs—parasites called *Cryptosporidium*.
Cryptosporidium, or "Crypto" for short, can be found in water, food,
soil or on surfaces or dirty hands that have been contaminated with
the feces of humans or animals infected with the parasite. During
2001–2010, Crypto was the leading cause of waterborne disease outbreaks, linked to recreational water in the United States. The parasite is found in every region of the United States and throughout
the world.

How is cryptosporidiosis spread?

Crypto lives in the gut of infected humans or animals. An infected
person or animal sheds Crypto parasites in their poop. An infected
person can shed 10,000,000 to 100,000,000 Crypto germs in a single
bowel movement. Shedding of Crypto in poop begins when symptoms
like diarrhea begin and can last for weeks after symptoms stop. Swallowing as few as 10 Crypto germs can cause infection.

Crypto can be spread by:

- Swallowing recreational water (for example, the water in swimming pools, fountains, lakes, rivers) contaminated with Crypto

  - Crypto's high tolerance to chlorine enables the parasite to
    survive for long periods of time in chlorinated drinking and
    swimming pool water

- Drinking untreated water from a lake or river that is contaminated with Crypto

- Swallowing water, ice, or beverages contaminated with poop from infected humans or animals
- Eating undercooked food or drinking unpasteurized/raw apple cider or milk that gets contaminated with Crypto
- Touching your mouth with contaminated hands
  - Hands can become contaminated through a variety of activities, such as touching surfaces or objects (e.g., toys, bathroom fixtures, changing tables, diaper pails) that have been contaminated by poop from an infected person, changing diapers, caring for an infected person, and touching an infected animal
- Exposure to poop from an infected person through oral-anal sexual contact

Crypto is **not** spread through contact with blood.

What are the symptoms of cryptosporidiosis, when do they begin, and how long do they last?

Symptoms of Crypto generally begin 2 to 10 days (average 7 days) after becoming infected with the parasite. Symptoms include:

- Watery diarrhea
- Stomach cramps or pain
- Dehydration
- Nausea
- Vomiting
- Fever
- Weight loss

Symptoms usually last about 1 to 2 weeks (with a range of a few days to 4 or more weeks) in people with healthy immune systems.

The most common symptom of cryptosporidiosis is **watery diarrhea**. Some people with Crypto will have no symptoms at all.

Who is most at risk for cryptosporidiosis?

People who are most likely to become infected with *Cryptosporidium* include:

- Children who attend childcare centers, including diaper-aged children

- Childcare workers
- Parents of infected children
- People who take care of other people with Crypto
- International travelers
- Backpackers, hikers, and campers who drink unfiltered, untreated water
- People who drink from untreated shallow, unprotected wells
- People, including swimmers, who swallow water from contaminated sources
- People who handle infected calves or other ruminants like sheep
- People exposed to human poop through sexual contact

Contaminated water might include water that has not been boiled or filtered, as well as contaminated recreational water sources (e.g., swimming pools, lakes, rivers, ponds, and streams). Several community-wide outbreaks have been linked to drinking tap water or recreational water contaminated with *Cryptosporidium*. Crypto's high tolerance to chlorine enables the parasite to survive for long periods of time in chlorinated drinking and swimming pool water. This means anyone swallowing contaminated water could get ill.

Note: Although Crypto can infect all people, some groups are likely to develop more serious illness.

- **Young children and pregnant women** may be more likely to get dehydrated because of their diarrhea so they should drink plenty of fluids while ill.
- People with **severely weakened immune systems** are at risk for more serious disease. Symptoms may be more severe and could lead to serious or life-threatening illness. Examples of people with weakened immune systems include those with AIDS; those with inherited diseases that affect the immune system; and cancer and transplant patients who are taking certain immunosuppressive drugs.

What should I do if I think I might have cryptosporidiosis?

For diarrhea whose cause has not been determined, the following actions may help relieve symptoms: Individuals who have health concerns should talk to their healthcare provider.

- Drink plenty of fluids to remain well hydrated and avoid dehydration. Serious health problems can occur if the body does not maintain proper fluid levels. For some people, diarrhea can be severe resulting in hospitalization due to dehydration.

- Maintain a well-balanced diet. Doing so may help speed recovery.

- Avoid beverages that contain caffeine, such as tea, coffee, and many soft drinks.

- Avoid alcohol, as it can lead to dehydration.

Contact your healthcare provider if you suspect that you have cryptosporidiosis.

How is cryptosporidiosis diagnosed?

Cryptosporidiosis is a diarrheal disease that is spread through contact with the stool of an infected person or animal. The disease is diagnosed by examining stool samples. People infected with Crypto can shed the parasite irregularly in their poop (for example, one day they shed parasite, the next day they don't, the third day they do) so patients may need to give three samples collected on three different days to help make sure that a negative test result is accurate and really means they do not have Crypto. Healthcare providers should specifically request testing for Crypto. Routine ova and parasite testing does not normally include Crypto testing.

What is the treatment for cryptosporidiosis?

Most people with healthy immune systems will recover from cryptosporidiosis without treatment. The following actions may help relieve symptoms. Individuals who have health concerns should talk to their healthcare provider.

- Drink plenty of fluids to remain well hydrated and avoid dehydration. Serious health problems can occur if the body does not maintain proper fluid levels. For some people, diarrhea can be severe resulting in hospitalization due to dehydration.

- Maintain a well-balanced diet. Doing so may help speed recovery.

- Avoid beverages that contain caffeine, such as tea, coffee, and many soft drinks.

- Avoid alcohol, as it can lead to dehydration.

Over-the-counter anti-diarrheal medicine might help slow down diarrhea, but a healthcare provider should be consulted before such medicine is taken.

A drug called nitazoxanide has been FDA-approved for treatment of diarrhea caused by *Cryptosporidium* in people with healthy immune systems and is available by prescription. Consult with your healthcare provider for more information about potential advantages and disadvantages of taking nitazoxanide.

Note: Infants, young children, and pregnant women may be more likely than others to suffer from dehydration. Losing a lot of fluids from diarrhea can be dangerous—and especially life-threatening in infants. These people should drink extra fluids when they are sick. Severe dehydration may require hospitalization for treatment with fluids given through your vein (intravenous/IV fluids). If you are pregnant or a parent and you suspect you or your child are severely dehydrated, contact a healthcare provider about fluid replacement options.

How should I clean my house to help prevent the spread of cryptosporidiosis?

No cleaning method is guaranteed to be completely effective against Crypto. However, you can lower the chance of spreading Crypto by taking the following precautions:

- **Wash linens, clothing, dishwasher- or dryer-safe soft toys, etc. soiled with poop or vomit as soon as possible.**
  - Flush excess vomit or poop on clothes or objects down the toilet.
  - Use laundry detergent, and wash in hot water: 113°F or hotter for at least 20 minutes or at 122°F or hotter for at least 5 minutes.
  - Machine dry on the highest heat setting.
- For other household object and surfaces (for example, diaper-change areas):
  - Remove all visible poop.
  - Clean with soap and water.
  - Let dry completely for at least 4 hours.
  - If possible, expose to direct sunlight during the 4 hours.

- Wash your hands with soap and water after cleaning objects or surfaces that could be contaminated with Crypto.

Note: The best way to prevent the spread of *Cryptosporidium* in the home is by practicing good hygiene. Wash your hands frequently with soap and water, especially after using the toilet, after changing diapers, and before eating or preparing food. **Alcohol-based hand sanitizers are not effective against Crypto.**

Prevention and Control – General Public

Practice Good Hygiene

Everywhere

- Wet hands with clean, running water and apply soap. Lather all surfaces of hands and scrub for at least 20 seconds.
- Rinse with clean, running water and dry with a clean towel or air:
  - before preparing or eating food,
  - after using the toilet,
  - after changing diapers or cleaning up a child who has used the toilet,
  - before and after caring for someone who is ill with diarrhea,
  - after handling an animal, particularly young livestock, or its stool,
  - after gardening, even if wearing gloves.

Note: Alcohol-based hand sanitizers do not effectively kill *Cryptosporidium*.

At child care facilities

- Exclude children who are ill with diarrhea from child care settings until the diarrhea has stopped.

At the pool

- Protect others by not swimming if ill with diarrhea.
  - If cryptosporidiosis is diagnosed, do not swim for at least 2 weeks after diarrhea stops.

- Do not swallow the water.

- Take young children on bathroom breaks every 60 minutes or check their diapers every 30—60 minutes.

Avoid Water That Might Be Contaminated

- Do not drink untreated water from lakes, rivers, springs, ponds, streams, or shallow wells.

- Follow advice given during local drinking water advisories.

- If the safety of drinking water is in doubt (e.g., during an outbreak, or if water treatment is unknown) use at least one of the following:

  - Commercially bottled water,

  - Water that has been previously boiled for 1 minute and left to cool. At elevations above 6,500 feet (1,981 meters), boil for 3 minutes.

  - Use a filter designed to remove *Cryptosporidium*.

  - The label might read 'NSF 53' or 'NSF 58'.

  - Filter labels that read "absolute pore size of 1 micron or smaller" are also effective.

- If the safety of drinking water is in doubt (e.g., during an outbreak or if water treatment is unknown), use bottled, boiled, or filtered water to wash fruits and vegetables that will be eaten raw.

Practice Extra Caution while Traveling

- Do not use or drink inadequately treated water or use ice when traveling in countries where the water might be unsafe.

- Avoid eating uncooked foods when traveling in countries where the food supply might be unsafe.

Prevent Contact and Contamination with Feces during Sex

- Use barriers (e.g., condoms, natural rubber latex sheets, dental dams, or cut-open non-lubricated condoms) between the mouth and a partner's genitals or rectum.

- Wash hands immediately after handling a condom or other barrier used during anal sex and after touching the anus or rectal area.

Section 32.2

Toxoplasmosis

Text in this section is excerpted from "Toxoplasmosis Frequently Asked Questions (FAQs)," Centers for Disease Control and Prevention (CDC), January 10, 2013.

What is toxoplasmosis?

A single-celled parasite called *Toxoplasma gondii* causes a disease known as toxoplasmosis. While the parasite is found throughout the world, more than 60 million people in the United States may be infected with the *Toxoplasma* parasite. Of those who are infected, very few have symptoms because a healthy person's immune system usually keeps the parasite from causing illness. However, pregnant women and individuals who have compromised immune systems should be cautious; for them, a *Toxoplasma* infection could cause serious health problems.

How do people get toxoplasmosis?

A *Toxoplasma* infection occurs by:

- Eating undercooked, contaminated meat (especially pork, lamb, and venison).

- Accidental ingestion of undercooked, contaminated meat after handling it and not washing hands thoroughly (*Toxoplasma* cannot be absorbed through intact skin).

- Eating food that was contaminated by knives, utensils, cutting boards and other foods that have had contact with raw, contaminated meat.

- Drinking water contaminated with *Toxoplasma gondii*.

- Accidentally swallowing the parasite through contact with cat feces that contain *Toxoplasma*. This might happen by

  - cleaning a cat's litter box when the cat has shed *Toxoplasma* in its feces

  - touching or ingesting anything that has come into contact with cat feces that contain *Toxoplasma*

  - accidentally ingesting contaminated soil (e.g., not washing hands after gardening or eating unwashed fruits or vegetables from a garden)

- Mother-to-child (congenital) transmission.

- Receiving an infected organ transplant or infected blood via transfusion, though this is rare.

What are the signs and symptoms of toxoplasmosis?

Symptoms of the infection vary.

- Most people who become infected with *Toxoplasma gondii* are not aware of it.

- Some people who have toxoplasmosis may feel as if they have the "flu" with swollen lymph glands or muscle aches and pains that last for a month or more.

- Severe toxoplasmosis, causing damage to the brain, eyes, or other organs, can develop from an acute *Toxoplasma* infection or one that had occurred earlier in life and is now reactivated. Severe cases are more likely in individuals who have weak immune systems, though occasionally, even persons with healthy immune systems may experience eye damage from toxoplasmosis.

- Signs and symptoms of ocular toxoplasmosis can include reduced vision, blurred vision, pain (often with bright light), redness of the eye, and sometimes tearing. Ophthalmologists sometimes prescribe medicine to treat active disease. Whether or not medication is recommended depends on the size of the eye lesion, the location, and the characteristics of the lesion (acute active, versus chronic not progressing). An ophthalmologist will provide the best care for ocular toxoplasmosis.

- Most infants who are infected while still in the womb have no symptoms at birth, but they may develop symptoms later in life. A small percentage of infected newborns have serious eye or brain damage at birth.

Who is at risk for developing severe toxoplasmosis?

People who are most likely to develop severe toxoplasmosis include:

- Infants born to mothers who are newly infected with *Toxoplasma gondii* during or just before pregnancy.
- Persons with severely weakened immune systems, such as individuals with AIDS, those taking certain types of chemotherapy, and those who have recently received an organ transplant.

What should I do if I think I am at risk for severe toxoplasmosis?

If you are planning to become pregnant, your health care provider may test you for *Toxoplasma gondii*. If the test is positive it means you have already been infected sometime in your life. There usually is little need to worry about passing the infection to your baby. If the test is negative, take necessary precautions to avoid infection.

If you are already pregnant, you and your health care provider should discuss your risk for toxoplasmosis. Your health care provider may order a blood sample for testing.

If you have a weakened immune system, ask your doctor about having your blood tested for *Toxoplasma*. If your test is positive, your doctor can tell you if and when you need to take medicine to prevent the infection from reactivating. If your test is negative, it means you need to take precautions to avoid infection.

What should I do if I think I may have toxoplasmosis?

If you suspect that you may have toxoplasmosis, talk to your health care provider. Your provider may order one or more varieties of blood tests specific for toxoplasmosis. The results from the different tests can help your provider determine if you have a *Toxoplasma gondii* infection and whether it is a recent (acute) infection.

What is the treatment for toxoplasmosis?

Once a diagnosis of toxoplasmosis is confirmed, you and your health care provider can discuss whether treatment is necessary. In an otherwise healthy person who is not pregnant, treatment usually is not needed. If symptoms occur, they typically go away within a few weeks to months. For pregnant women or persons who have weakened immune systems, medications are available to treat toxoplasmosis.

How can I prevent toxoplasmosis?

There are several general sanitation and food safety steps you can take to reduce your chances of becoming infected with *Toxoplasma gondii*.

- Cook food to safe temperatures. A food thermometer should be used to measure the internal temperature of cooked meat. Do not sample meat until it is cooked. USDA recommends the following for meat preparation.

  For Whole Cuts of Meat (excluding poultry)

  - Cook to at least 145° F (63° C) as measured with a food thermometer placed in the thickest part of the meat, then allow the meat to rest* for three minutes before carving or consuming.

  For Ground Meat (excluding poultry)

  - Cook to at least 160° F (71° C); ground meats do not require a rest* time.

  For All Poultry (whole cuts and ground)

  - Cook to at least 165° F (74° C), and for whole poultry allow the meat to rest* for three minutes before carving or consuming.

According to USDA, "A 'rest time' is the amount of time the product remains at the final temperature, after it has been removed from a grill, oven, or other heat source. During the three minutes after meat is removed from the heat source, its temperature remains constant or continues to rise, which destroys pathogens."

- Freeze meat for several days at sub-zero (0° F) temperatures before cooking to greatly reduce chance of infection.

- Peel or wash fruits and vegetables thoroughly before eating.

- Do not eat raw or undercooked oysters, mussels, or clams (these may be contaminated with *Toxoplasma* that has washed into sea water).

- Do not drink unpasteurized goat's milk.

- Wash cutting boards, dishes, counters, utensils, and hands with hot soapy water after contact with raw meat, poultry, seafood, or unwashed fruits or vegetables.

- Wear gloves when gardening and during any contact with soil or sand because it might be contaminated with cat feces that contain *Toxoplasma*. Wash hands with soap and warm water after gardening or contact with soil or sand.

- Teach children the importance of washing hands to prevent infection.

If I am at risk, can I keep my cat?

Yes, you may keep your cat if you are a person at risk for a severe infection (e.g., you have a weakened immune system or are pregnant); however, there are several safety precautions to avoid being exposed to *Toxoplasma gondii* :

- Ensure the cat litter box is changed daily. The *Toxoplasma* parasite does not become infectious until 1 to 5 days after it is shed in a cat's feces.

- If you are pregnant or immunocompromised:
  - Avoid changing cat litter if possible. If no one else can perform the task, wear disposable gloves and wash your hands with soap and warm water afterwards.
  - Keep cats indoors.
  - Do not adopt or handle stray cats, especially kittens. Do not get a new cat while you are pregnant.

- Feed cats only canned or dried commercial food or well-cooked table food, not raw or undercooked meats.

- Keep your outdoor sandboxes covered.

Your veterinarian can answer any other questions you may have regarding your cat and risk for toxoplasmosis.

Once infected with Toxoplasma is my cat always able to spread the infection to me?

No, cats only spread *Toxoplasma* in their feces for a few weeks following infection with the parasite. Like humans, cats rarely have

383

symptoms when infected, so most people do not know if their cat has been infected. The *Toxoplasma* shedding in feces will go away on its own; therefore it does not help to have your cat or your cat's feces tested for *Toxoplasma*.

Chapter 33

HIV/AIDS and Co-Occurring Viral Infections

Chapter Contents

Section 33.1

Cytomegalovirus (CMV)

This section includes excerpts from "Cytomegalovirus (CMV)," U.S.
Department of Veterans Affairs (VA), September 17, 2015; text from
"Pregnancy – Preventing Infections," Centers for Disease Control
and Prevention (CDC), May 1, 2013; and text from "CDC Features –
Diseases & Conditions," Centers for Disease Control and Prevention
(CDC), June 29, 2015.

Cytomegalovirus (or CMV) is passed by close contact through sex
and through saliva, urine, and other body fluids. It can be passed
from mother to child during pregnancy and by breast-feeding. If
you are not infected, using condoms during sex may help prevent
infection.

Many people are infected with this virus, though they have no
symptoms. In HIV-positive people, the infection can be extremely serious. Symptoms can include:

- blind spots in vision, loss of peripheral vision

- headache, difficulty concentrating, sleepiness

- mouth ulcers

- pain in the abdomen, bloody diarrhea

- fever, fatigue, weight loss

- shortness of breath

- lower back pain

- confusion, apathy, withdrawal, personality changes

Drugs are available to keep symptoms of the infection under control.
Anti-HIV drugs can improve the condition, too. If you have CMV and
haven't started taking drugs for HIV, it may be best to wait until you
have been on treatment for CMV for a few weeks.

Treatment can prevent further loss of vision but cannot reverse
existing damage. If you experience any vision problems, tell your provider immediately.

Cytomegalovirus (CMV) and Pregnancy

CMV, or cytomegalovirus, is a common virus that infects people of all ages. Once CMV is in a person's body, it stays there for life. Most infections with CMV are "silent," meaning most people who are infected with CMV have no signs or symptoms. However, CMV can cause disease in unborn babies.

CMV is spread through:

- Person to person contact (such as, kissing, sexual contact, and getting saliva or urine on your hands and then touching your eyes, or the inside of your nose or mouth)

- Breast milk of an infected woman who is breast feeding

- Infected pregnant women can pass the virus to their unborn babies

- Blood transfusions and organ transplantations

> Contact with the saliva or urine of young children is a major cause of CMV infection among pregnant women.

Prevention

Pregnant women may want to take steps to reduce their risk of exposure to CMV and so reduce the risk of CMV infection of their fetus. Here are a few simple steps you can take to avoid exposure to saliva and urine that might contain CMV:

- Wash your hands often with soap and water for 15–20 seconds, especially after

    - changing diapers

    - feeding a young child

    - wiping a young child's nose or drool

    - handling children's toys

- Do not share food, drinks, or eating utensils used by young children

- Do not put a child's pacifier in your mouth

- Do not share a toothbrush with a young child

Table 33.1. Examples of symptoms or disabilities caused by congenital (meaning present at birth) CMV

Temporary Symptoms	Permanent Symptoms or Disabilities
Liver problems	Hearing Loss
Spleen problems	Vision loss
Jaundice (yellow skin and eyes)	Mental disability
Purple skin splotches	Small head
Lung problems	Lack of coordination
Small size at birth	Seizures
Seizures	Death

- Avoid contact with saliva when kissing a child

- Clean toys, countertops, and other surfaces that come into contact with children's urine or saliva

People who work closely with children in settings, such as child care facilities, may be at greater risk of CMV infection than persons who do not work in such settings. If you are pregnant and work with children, follow standard handwashing procedures after contact with body fluids, such as urine and saliva, that could contain CMV.

Symptoms

Most healthy children and adults infected with CMV have no symptoms and may not even know that they have been infected. Others may develop a mild illness. Symptoms may include fever, sore throat, fatigue, and swollen glands. These symptoms are similar to those of other illnesses, so most people are not aware that they are infected with CMV.

Most babies born with CMV (in other words, "congenital" CMV) never develop symptoms or disabilities. When babies do have symptoms, some can go away but others can be permanent.

Treatment

Currently, no treatment is recommended for CMV infection in healthy pregnant women. Vaccines for preventing CMV infection are still in the research and development stage.

Help Children with Congenital CMV Live Healthy

Some children with congenital cytomegalovirus (CMV) infection may have hearing or vision loss, or other health problems.

Parents can help children with congenital CMV have healthy, full lives by having specific health checks and treatments.

CMV is a virus that pregnant women can be infected with and pass to their unborn babies. This is called congenital CMV. About 1 in 150 children is born with congenital CMV infection. Most babies who get congenital CMV will not have signs or symptoms. However, about 20 out of 100 babies born with CMV infection will have symptoms or long-term health issues. These can include developmental disabilities, hearing and vision loss, problems with the liver, spleen or lungs, and seizures.

Early Treatment May Help

Babies who have symptoms from CMV when they are born have had moderate benefits for long-term hearing and brain development when they get antiviral medicine beginning in the first month of their lives. But this medicine has side effects, and babies who get it should be closely monitored by their doctor. Antiviral medicine has not been studied in babies with congenital CMV who do not show any symptoms, or only have hearing loss as a symptom.

Get Hearing Checks and Therapies

Symptoms of congenital CMV infection will be different for each child. The symptoms can range from mild to severe.

Parents can help children with congenital CMV infection live a healthy, full life by

- Having your child's hearing checked regularly.
    - Hearing loss can affect your child's ability to develop communication, language, and social skills. The earlier your child's hearing loss is diagnosed, the sooner you can get them the services they need.
- Bringing your child to services such as speech, occupational, and physical therapy.
    - Access to these services early in life will often help children with congenital CMV infection to develop to their full potential.

Signs of Congenital CMV

Babies may be diagnosed with congenital CMV while they are still in their mother's womb, or after they are born. Signs that a baby might have congenital CMV infection when they are born are:

- jaundice (yellowish coloring of the skin)

- enlarged liver

- enlarged spleen

- petechiae (skin rash resulting from bleeding in the skin)

- pneumonia

- central nervous system damage with small head size, brain abnormalities, eye problems or hearing loss

---

How CMV Spreads

CMV is passed from infected people to others through direct contact with body fluids such as blood, urine, saliva, blood, breast milk, or semen. Common ways people become infected with CMV differ by age group:

- Infants usually get infection from breast milk
- Children typically get infection through contact with other children
- Teenagers or adults mostly get infection through contact with saliva or urine of young children or through sexual contact.

Pregnant women can pass CMV to their unborn baby if they were infected before or during pregnancy. It is not known what factors lead to a woman with CMV giving birth to a baby with congenital CMV.

Blood, urine or saliva tests are done to confirm a diagnosis of congenital CMV. Some babies with congenital CMV infection are identified after they are diagnosed with hearing loss.

Talk with your doctor if you suspect your child might have congenital CMV infection.

Section 33.2

Genital Herpes

This section includes excerpts from "Herpes simplex virus," U.S. Department of Veterans Affairs (VA), September 17, 2015; and text from "Genital Herpes – CDC Fact Sheet (Detailed)," Centers for Disease Control and Prevention (CDC), September 24, 2015.

Herpes simplex is caused by a virus. Symptoms include red, painful sores on the mouth ("fever blisters"), genitals, or anal area. Genital herpes is passed through sexual contact. Herpes on the mouth is easily spread through kissing. It can be spread to the genitals through oral sex. Although less common, the virus can be spread even if you don't have blisters. Using latex barrier protection during sex can decrease the risk of infection.

Drugs are available to help herpes blisters heal, but there's no cure. Outbreaks may occur periodically for the rest of your life. Suppressive therapy with daily antiviral treatment can help reduce the number of outbreaks.

What is genital herpes?

Genital herpes is a sexually transmitted disease (STD) caused by the herpes simplex viruses type 1 (HSV-1) or type 2 (HSV-2).

How common is genital herpes?

Genital herpes infection is common in the United States. CDC estimates that, annually, 776,000 people in the United States get new herpes infections. Nationwide, 15.5 % of persons aged 14 to 49 years have HSV-2 infection. The overall prevalence of genital herpes is likely higher than 15.5% because an increasing number of genital herpes infections are caused by HSV-1. HSV-1 is typically acquired in childhood; as the prevalence of HSV-1 infection has declined in recent decades, people may have become more susceptible to genital herpes from HSV-1.

HSV-2 infection is more common among women than among men (20.3% versus 10.6% in 14 to 49 year olds). Infection is more easily transmitted from men to women than from women to men. HSV-2 infection is more common among non-Hispanic blacks (41.8%) than among non-Hispanic whites (11.3%). This disparity remains even among persons with similar numbers of lifetime sexual partners. For example, among persons with 2–4 lifetime sexual partners, HSV-2 is still more prevalent among non-Hispanic blacks (34.3%) than among non-Hispanic whites (9.1%) or Mexican Americans (13%). Most infected persons are unaware of their infection. In the United States, an estimated 87.4% of 14–49 year olds infected with HSV-2 have never received a clinical diagnosis.

The percentage of persons in the United States who are infected with HSV-2 decreased from 21.2% in 1988–1994 to 15.5% in 2007-2010.

How do people get genital herpes?

Infections are transmitted through contact with lesions, mucosal surfaces, genital secretions, or oral secretions. HSV-1 and HSV-2 can also be shed from skin that looks normal. Generally, a person can only get HSV-2 infection during sexual contact with someone who has a genital HSV-2 infection. Transmission most commonly occurs from an infected partner who does not have visible sores and who may not know that he or she is infected. In persons with asymptomatic HSV-2 infections, genital HSV shedding occurs on 10% of days, and on most of those days the person has no signs or symptoms.

What are the symptoms of genital herpes?

Most individuals infected with HSV-1 or HSV-2 are asymptomatic or have very mild symptoms that go unnoticed or are mistaken for another skin condition. As a result, 87.4% of infected individuals remain unaware of their infection. When symptoms do occur, they typically appear as one or more vesicles on or around the genitals, rectum or mouth. The average incubation period after exposure is 4 days (range, 2 to 12). The vesicles break and leave painful ulcers that may take two to four weeks to heal. Experiencing these symptoms is referred to as having an "outbreak" or episode.

Clinical manifestations of genital herpes differ between the first and recurrent outbreaks of HSV. The first outbreak of herpes is often associated with a longer duration of herpetic lesions, increased viral shedding (making HSV transmission more likely) and systemic symptoms including fever, body aches, swollen lymph nodes, or headache. Recurrent outbreaks of genital herpes are common, in particular during the first year of infection. Approximately half of patients who recognize recurrences have prodromal symptoms, such as mild tingling or shooting pains in the legs, hips or buttocks, which occur hours to days before the eruption of herpetic lesions. Symptoms of recurrent outbreaks are typically shorter in duration and less severe than the first outbreak of genital herpes. Although the infection can stay in the body indefinitely, the number of outbreaks tends to decrease over time. Recurrences and subclinical shedding are much less frequent for genital HSV-1 infection than for genital HSV-2 infection.

What are the complications of genital herpes?

Genital herpes may cause painful genital ulcers that can be severe and persistent in persons with suppressed immune systems, such as HIV-infected persons. Both HSV-1 and HSV-2 can also cause rare but serious complications such as blindness, encephalitis (inflammation of the brain), and aseptic meningitis (inflammation of the linings of the brain). Development of extragenital lesions in the buttocks, groin, thigh, finger, or eye may occur during the course of infection.

Some persons who contract genital herpes have concerns about how it will impact their overall health, sex life, and relationships. There can be can be considerable embarrassment, shame, and stigma associated with a herpes diagnosis that can substantially interfere with a patient's relationships. Clinicians can address these concerns by encouraging patients to recognize that while herpes is not curable, it is a manageable condition. Three important steps that providers can take for their newly-diagnosed patients are: giving information, providing support resources, and helping define options. Since a diagnosis of genital herpes may affect perceptions about existing or future sexual relationships, it is important for patients to understand how to talk to sexual partners about STDs.

What is the link between genital herpes and HIV?

Genital ulcerative disease caused by herpes make it easier to transmit and acquire HIV infection sexually. There is an estimated 2- to 4-fold increased risk of acquiring HIV, if exposed to HIV when genital herpes is present. Ulcers or breaks in the skin or mucous membranes (lining of the mouth, vagina, and rectum) from a herpes infection may compromise the protection normally provided by the skin and mucous membranes against infections, including HIV. Herpetic genital ulcers can bleed easily, and when they come into contact with the mouth, vagina, or rectum during sex, they may increase the risk of HIV transmission.

How does genital herpes affect a pregnant woman and her baby?

Neonatal herpes is one of the most serious complications of genital herpes. Healthcare providers should ask all pregnant women if they have a history of genital herpes. Herpes infection can be passed from mother to child during pregnancy, childbirth, or in the newborn period, resulting in a potentially fatal neonatal herpes infection. During pregnancy there is a higher risk of perinatal transmission during the first outbreak than with a recurrent outbreak, thus it is important that women avoid contracting herpes during pregnancy. Women should be counseled to abstain from intercourse during the third trimester with partners known to have or suspected of having genital herpes.

A woman with genital herpes may be offered antiviral medication from 36 weeks gestation through delivery to reduce the risk of a recurrent outbreak. Routine HSV screening of pregnant women is not recommended. However, at onset of labor, all women should undergo careful examination and questioning to evaluate for presence of prodromal symptoms or herpetic lesions. If herpes symptoms are present, a cesarean delivery is recommended to prevent HSV transmission to the infant.

How is genital herpes diagnosed?

The preferred HSV tests for patients with active genital ulcers include viral culture or detection of HSV DNA by polymerase chain reaction (PCR). HSV culture requires collection of a sample from the sore and, once viral growth is seen, specific cell staining to differentiate between HSV-1 and HSV-2. However, culture sensitivity is low, especially for recurrent lesions, and declines as lesions heal. PCR is more sensitive, allows for more rapid and accurate results, and is increasingly being used. Because viral shedding is intermittent, failure to detect HSV by culture or PCR does not indicate and absence of HSV infection. Tzanck preparations are insensitive and nonspecific and should not be used.

Serologic tests are blood tests that detect antibodies to the herpes virus. Several ELISA-based serologic tests are FDA approved and available commercially. Older assays that do not accurately distinguish HSV-1 from HSV-2 antibody remain on the market, so providers should specifically request serologic type-specific assays when blood tests are performed for their patients. The sensitivities of type-specific serologic tests for HSV-2 vary from 80-98%; false-negative results might be more frequent at early stages of infection. Additionally, false positive results may occur at low index values and should be confirmed with another test such as Biokit or the Western Blot. Negative HSV-1 results should be interpreted with caution because some ELISA-based serologic tests are insensitive for detection of HSV-1 antibody.

For the symptomatic patient, testing with both virologic and serologic assays can determine whether it is a new infection or a newly-recognized old infection. A primary infection would be supported by a positive virologic test and a negative serologic test, while the diagnosis of recurrent disease would be supported by positive virologic and serologic test results.

CDC does not recommend screening for HSV-1 or HSV-2 in the general population. Several scenarios where type-specific serologic HSV tests may be useful include

- Patients with recurrent genital symptoms or atypical symptoms and negative HSV PCR or culture;

- Patients with a clinical diagnosis of genital herpes but no laboratory confirmation;

- Patients who report having a partner with genital herpes;

- Patients presenting for an STD evaluation (especially those with multiple sex partners);

- Persons with HIV infection; and

- MSM at increased risk for HIV acquisition.

Is there a cure or treatment for herpes?

There is no cure for herpes. Antiviral medications can, however, prevent or shorten outbreaks during the period of time the person takes the medication. In addition, daily suppressive therapy (i.e. daily use of antiviral medication) for herpes can reduce the likelihood of transmission to partners.

Several clinical trials have tested vaccines against genital herpes infection, but there is currently no commercially available vaccine that is protective against genital herpes infection. One vaccine trial showed efficacy among women whose partners were HSV-2 infected, but only among women who were not infected with HSV-1. No efficacy was observed among men whose partners were HSV-2 infected. A subsequent trial testing the same vaccine showed some protection from genital HSV-1 infection, but no protection from HSV-2 infection.

How can herpes be prevented?

Correct and consistent use of latex condoms can reduce the risk of genital herpes. However, outbreaks can occur in areas that are not covered by a condom.

The surest way to avoid transmission of sexually transmitted diseases, including genital herpes, is to abstain from sexual contact, or to be in a long-term mutually monogamous relationship with a partner who has been tested and is known to be uninfected.

Persons with herpes should abstain from sexual activity with partners when sores or other symptoms of herpes are present. It is important to know that even if a person does not have any symptoms, he or she can still infect sex partners. Sex partners of infected persons should be advised that they may become infected and they should use condoms to reduce the risk. Sex partners can seek testing to determine if they are infected with HSV.

Section 33.3

Shingles (Herpes Zoster Virus)

Text in this section is excerpted from "Shingles (Herpes zoster)," Centers for Disease Control and Prevention (CDC), May 1, 2014.

Almost 1 out of every 3 people in the United States will develop shingles, also known as zoster or herpes zoster, in their lifetime. There are an estimated 1 million cases of shingles each year in this country. Anyone who has recovered from chickenpox may develop shingles; even children can get shingles. However the risk of shingles increases as you get older. About half of all cases occur in men and women 60 years old or older.

Some people have a greater risk of getting shingles. This include people who

- have medical conditions that keep their immune systems from working properly, such as certain cancers like leukemia and lymphoma, and human immunodeficiency virus (HIV), and

- people who receive immunosuppressive drugs, such as steroids and drugs that given after organ transplantation.

People who develop shingles typically have only one episode in their lifetime. However, a person can have a second or even a third episode.

Cause

Shingles is caused by the varicella zoster virus (VZV), the same virus that causes chickenpox. After a person recovers from chickenpox, the virus stays dormant (inactive) in the body. For reasons that are not fully known, the virus can reactivate years later, causing shingles. Shingles is not caused by the same virus that causes genital herpes, a sexually transmitted disease.

Signs and Symptoms

Shingles is a painful rash that develops on one side of the face or body. The rash forms blisters that typically scab over in 7 to 10 days and clears up within 2 to 4 weeks.

Before the rash develops, people often have pain, itching, or tingling in the area where the rash will develop. This may happen anywhere from 1 to 5 days before the rash appears.

Most commonly, the rash occurs in a single stripe around either the left or the right side of the body. In other cases, the rash occurs on one side of the face. In rare cases (usually among people with weakened immune systems), the rash may be more widespread and look similar to a chickenpox rash. Shingles can affect the eye and cause loss of vision.

Other symptoms of shingles can include

- Fever

- Headache

- Chills

- Upset stomach

Transmission

Shingles cannot be passed from one person to another. However, the virus that causes shingles, the varicella zoster virus, can be spread from a person with active shingles to another person who has never had chickenpox. In such cases, the person exposed to the virus might develop chickenpox, but they would not develop shingles.

The virus is spread through direct contact with fluid from the rash blisters caused by shingles.

A person with active shingles can spread the virus when the rash is in the blister-phase. A person is not infectious before the blisters appear. Once the rash has developed crusts, the person is no longer contagious.

Shingles is less contagious than chickenpox and the risk of a person with shingles spreading the virus is low if the rash is covered.

If you have shingles

- Keep the rash covered.

- Avoid touching or scratching the rash.

- Wash your hands often to prevent the spread of varicella zoster virus.

- Until your rash has developed crusts, avoid contact with

  - pregnant women who have never had chickenpox or the chickenpox vaccine;

  - premature or low birth weight infants; and

  - people with weakened immune systems, such as people receiving immunosuppressive medications or undergoing chemotherapy, organ transplant recipients, and people with human immunodeficiency virus (HIV) infection.

Complications

The most common complication of shingles is a condition called post-herpetic neuralgia (PHN). People with PHN have severe pain in the areas where they had the shingles rash, even after the rash clears up.

The pain from PHN may be severe and debilitating, but it usually resolves in a few weeks or months in most patients. Some people can have pain from PHN for many years.

As people get older, they are more likely to develop PHN, and the pain is more likely to be severe. PHN occurs rarely among people under 40 years of age but can occur in up to a third of untreated people who are 60 years of age and older.

Shingles may lead to serious complications involving the eye. Very rarely, shingles can also lead to pneumonia, hearing problems, blindness, brain inflammation (encephalitis) or death.

Prevention and Treatment

The only way to reduce the risk of developing shingles and the long-term pain from post-herpetic neuralgia (PHN) is to get vaccinated. CDC recommends that people aged 60 years and older get one dose of shingles vaccine. Shingles vaccine is available in pharmacies and doctor's offices. Talk with your healthcare professional if you have questions about shingles vaccine.

Several antiviral medicines—acyclovir, valacyclovir, and famciclovir—are available to treat shingles. These medicines will help shorten the length and severity of the illness. But to be effective, they must be started as soon as possible after the rash appears. Thus, people who have or think they might have shingles should call their healthcare provider as soon as possible to discuss treatment options.

Analgesics (pain medicine) may help relieve the pain caused by shingles. Wet compresses, calamine lotion, and colloidal oatmeal baths may help relieve some of the itching.

Section 33.4

Human Papillomavirus (HPV)

Text in this section is excerpted from "Human Papillomavirus
(HPV)," Centers for Disease Control and Prevention (CDC),
July 31, 2015.

What is HPV?

HPV is short for human papillomavirus and is a group of more
than 150 related viruses. Each HPV virus in this large group is given
a number which is called its HPV type. HPV is named for the warts
(papillomas) some HPV types can cause. Some other HPV types can
lead to cancer, especially cervical cancer. There are more than 40 HPV
types that can infect the genital areas of males and females. But there
are vaccines that can prevent infection with the most common types
of HPV.

How Do People Get HPV?

HPV is transmitted through intimate skin-to-skin contact. You
can get HPV by having vaginal, anal, or oral sex with someone
who has the virus. It is most commonly spread during vaginal or
anal sex. HPV is the most common sexually transmitted infection
(STI). Anyone who is sexually active can get HPV, even if you have
had sex with only one person. HPV is so common that nearly all
sexually active men and women get it at some point in their lives.
HPV can be passed even when an infected person has no signs or
symptoms. You can develop symptoms years after you have sex
with someone who is infected, making it hard to know when you
first became infected.

HPV Vaccines

HPV vaccines are given as a series of three shots over 6 months
to protect against HPV infection and the health problems that HPV
infection can cause. There are three HPV vaccines (Cervarix, Gardasil,

and Gardasil 9). Girls and young women should get any of these HPV vaccines to prevent cervical cancer.

Two of the HPV vaccines (Gardasil and Gardasil 9) also protect against genital warts and anal cancer in both females and males. Boys should get one of these HPV vaccines to prevent anal cancer and genital warts. Girls can get either of these vaccines to prevent cervical cancer, vulvar cancer, vaginal cancer, anal cancer and genital warts.

HPV vaccines offer the best protection to girls and boys who receive all three vaccine doses and have time to develop an immune response before being sexually active with another person. That's why HPV vaccination is recommended for preteen girls and boys at age 11 or 12 years.

Who else should get the HPV vaccine?

All kids who are 11 or 12 years old should get the three-dose series of HPV vaccine to protect against HPV. Teen boys and girls who did not start or finish the HPV vaccine series when they were younger should get it now. Young women can get HPV vaccine through age 26, and young men can get vaccinated through age 21. The vaccine is also recommended for any man who has sex with men through age 26, and for men with compromised immune systems (including HIV) through age 26, if they did not get HPV vaccine when they were younger.

HPV Vaccine Safety

The human papillomavirus (HPV) vaccines are safe, effective, and offer long-lasting protection against cancers caused by HPV.

Each HPV vaccine—Gardasil® 9, Gardasil®, and Cervarix®—went through years of extensive safety testing before they were licensed by the U.S. Food and Drug Administration (FDA). Gardasil® 9 was studied in clinical trials with more than 15,000 females and males; Gardasil® was studied in clinical trials with more than 29,000 females and males, and Cervarix® was studied in trials with more than 30,000 females.

Research from before and after the vaccines were licensed show that HPV vaccines are safe. As with all approved vaccines, CDC and the FDA closely monitor the safety of HPV vaccines after they are licensed. Any problems detected with these vaccines will be reported to health officials, health care providers, and the public.

Like any vaccine or medicine, HPV vaccines can cause side effects. The most common side effects are pain, redness, or swelling in the arm where the shot was given; dizziness, fainting, nausea, and headache. HPV vaccination is typically not associated with any serious side effects. The benefits of HPV vaccination far outweigh any potential risk of side effects.

How can people prevent HPV?

There are several ways that people can lower their chances of getting HPV:

Vaccines can protect males and females against some of the most common types of HPV. HPV vaccines are safe and effective. They are given in three doses over six months. HPV vaccines are most effective when given at 11 or 12 years old.

- Girls and women: Two vaccines (Cervarix and Gardasil) are available to protect females against the types of HPV that cause most cervical cancers. One of these vaccines (Gardasil) also protects against most genital warts. This vaccine has also been shown to protect against anal, vaginal and vulvar cancers. Both vaccines are recommended for 11 or 12 year-old girls, and for females through 26 years of age, who did not get any or all of the doses when they were younger.

- Boys and men: One vaccine (Gardasil) protects males against most genital warts and anal cancers. This vaccine is recommended for boys aged 11 or 12 years, and for males aged through 21 years of age, who did not get any or all doses when they were younger. The vaccine is also recommended for gay and bisexual young men (or any young man who has sex with men) and also for young men with compromised immune systems (including HIV) through age 26, if they did not get HPV vaccine when they were younger.

For those who are sexually active, condoms may lower the risk of HPV infection. To be most effective, they should be used with every sex act, from start to finish. Condoms may also lower the risk of developing HPV-related diseases, such as genital warts and cervical cancer. But HPV can infect areas that are not covered by a condom—so condoms may not fully protect against HPV.

People can also lower their chances of getting HPV by being in a faithful relationship with one partner; limiting their number of sex partners; and being with a partner who has had no or few prior sex partners. But even people with only one lifetime sex partner can get HPV. And it may not be possible to determine if a partner who has been sexually active in the past is currently infected. Not having sex is the only sure way to avoid HPV.

How can people prevent HPV-related diseases?

There are ways to prevent the possible health effects of HPV, including two common problems: genital warts and cervical cancer.

- **Preventing Genital Warts:** One vaccine (Gardasil) protects against most genital warts in men and women.

- **Preventing Cervical Cancer:** Two vaccines (Cervarix and Gardasil) protect against most cervical cancers in women. Cervical cancer can also be prevented with routine cervical cancer screening (Pap test) and follow-up of abnormal results. The Pap test can find abnormal cells on the cervix so that they can be removed before cancer develops. Abnormal cells often become normal over time, but can sometimes turn into cancer. These cells can usually be treated, depending on their severity and on the woman's age, past medical history, and other test results. An HPV DNA test, which can find certain HPV types on a woman's cervix, may also be used with a Pap test in certain cases (called co-testing). Even women who were vaccinated when they were younger need regular cervical cancer screening because the vaccines do not protect against all cervical cancers.

- **Preventing Anal and Penile Cancers:** One vaccine (Gardasil) protects against most anal cancers. There is no routinely recommended screening test for anal or penile cancer because more information is still needed to find out if those tests are effective. There are no data on efficacy of the vaccine to prevent cancers of the penis, but most HPV-related cancers of the penis are caused by the HPV types prevented by the vaccines. Both vaccines are likely to prevent HPV-16- and HPV-18-related cancers of the anus and penis; systems that monitor cancer rates through time will help clarify the impact of vaccine on these cancers.

- **Preventing Cancers of the Oropharynx (also called oropharyngeal cancer; cancers of the back of the throat, including the base of the tongue and tonsils):** There is no approved test to find early signs of oropharyngeal cancer because more information is still needed to find out if those tests are effective. There are no data on efficacy of the vaccine to prevent cancers of the oropharynx, but most HPV-associated cancers of the oropharynx are caused by the HPV types prevented by the vaccines. Smoking is also a risk factor for cancers of the oropharynx, so not smoking or quitting can help reduce your risk.

- **Preventing Juvenile-Onset Recurrent Respiratory Papillomatosis (JORRP):** Cesarean ("C-section") delivery is not recommended for women with genital warts to prevent JORRP in their babies. This is because it is not clear that cesarean delivery prevents JORRP in infants and children. There are no data on efficacy of the vaccine to prevent recurrent respiratory papillomatosis but most cases are caused by the HPV types prevented by the one of the vaccines (Gardasil). Gardasil is likely to prevent HPV-6 and HPV-11 related RRP.

Although there is no routine screening test for HPV-associated diseases other than cervical cancer, you should visit your doctor regularly for checkups.

What are the signs, symptoms and health consequences of HPV?

In most cases, HPV goes away on its own and does not cause any health problems. But when HPV does not go away, it can cause health problems like genital warts and cancer.

Genital warts usually appear as a small bump or groups of bumps in the genital area. They can be small or large, raised or flat, or shaped like a cauliflower. A healthcare provider can usually diagnose warts by looking at the genital area.

Cervical cancer usually does not have symptoms until it is quite advanced, very serious and hard to treat. For this reason, it is important for women to get regular screening for cervical cancer. Screening tests can find early signs of disease so that problems can be treated early, before they ever turn into cancer.

Other HPV-related cancers might not have signs or symptoms until they are advanced and hard to treat. These include cancers of the vulva, vagina, penis, anus, and oropharynx (cancers of the back of the throat, including the base of the tongue and tonsils).

Is there a treatment for HPV or related problems?

There is no treatment for the virus itself, but there are treatments for the problems that HPV can cause:

- **Visible genital warts** may remain the same, grow more numerous, or go away on their own. They can be removed by the patient with medications. They can also be treated by a health care provider. Some people choose not to treat warts. No one treatment is better than another.

- **Abnormal cervical cells** (found on a Pap test) often become normal over time, but they can sometimes turn into cancer. If they remain abnormal, these cells can usually be treated to prevent cervical cancer from developing. This may depend on the severity of the cell changes, the woman's age and past medical history, and other test results. It is critical to follow up with testing and treatment, as recommended by a doctor.

- **Cervical cancer** is most treatable when it is diagnosed and treated early. Problems found can usually be treated, depending on their severity and on the woman's age, past medical history, and other test results. Most women who get routine cervical cancer screening and follow up as told by their provider can find problems before cancer even develops. Prevention is always better than treatment.

- **Other HPV cancers** are also more treatable when diagnosed and treated early. Although there is no routine screening test for these cancers, you should visit your doctor regularly for checkups.

- **Recurrent Respiratory Papillomatosis (RRP)**, a rare condition in which warts grow in the throat, can be treated with surgery or medicines. It can sometimes take many treatments or surgeries over a period of years.

Section 33.5

Progressive Multifocal Leukoencephalopathy (PML)

This section includes excerpts from "Progressive multifocal leukoencephalopathy (PML)," U.S. Department of Veterans Affairs (VA), July 30, 2015; and text from "NINDS Progressive Multifocal Leukoencephalopathy Information Page," National Institute of Neurological Disorders and Stroke (NINDS), September 11, 2015.

This disease is caused by a virus called the JC virus. Most people probably already are infected, but in HIV-positive people the virus can cause disease. The virus is possibly spread through sexual contact, or from mother to child.

Symptoms can include:

- difficulty in speaking

- difficulty in walking

- weakness in arms or legs

- personality changes

- seizures

- changes in vision

- headache

- shaky hands

There is no specific treatment for Progressive Multifocal Leukoencephalopathy (PML), but some HIV drug combinations can reverse the symptoms and keep the JC virus under control. People with PML should have a good support system. Friends, roommates, or family members can help make sure that HIV medications are taken on time, in the right combination, and at the right dose. The disease is extremely serious and can lead to death.

What is Progressive Multifocal Leukoencephalopathy?

Progressive multifocal leukoencephalopathy (PML) is a disease of the white matter of the brain, caused by a virus infection that targets cells that make myelin—the material that insulates nerve cells (neurons). Polyomavirus JC (often called JC virus) is carried by a majority of people and is harmless except among those with lowered immune defenses.

The disease is rare and occurs in patients undergoing chronic corticosteroid or immunosuppressive therapy for organ transplant, or individuals with cancer (such as Hodgkin's disease or lymphoma). Individuals with autoimmune conditions such as multiple sclerosis, rheumatoid arthritis, and systemic lupus erythematosis—some of whom are treated with biological therapies that allow JC virus reactivation—are at risk for PML as well.

PML is most common among individuals with HIV-1 infection / acquired immune deficiency syndrome (AIDS). Studies estimate that prior to effective antiretroviral therapy, as many as 5 percent of persons infected with HIV-1 eventually develop PML that is an AIDS-defining illness. However, current HIV therapy using antiretroviral drugs (ART), which effectively restores immune system function, allows as many as half of all HIV-PML patients to survive, although they may sometimes have an inflammatory reaction in the regions of the brain affected by PML. The symptoms of PML are diverse, since they are related to the location and amount of damage in the brain, and may evolve over the course of several weeks to months.

The most prominent symptoms are clumsiness; progressive weakness; and visual, speech, and sometimes personality changes. The progression of deficits leads to life-threatening disability and (frequently) death. A diagnosis of PML can be made following brain biopsy or by combining observations of a progressive course of the disease, consistent white matter lesions visible on a magnetic resonance imaging (MRI) scan, and the detection of the JC virus in spinal fluid.

Is there any treatment?

Currently, the best available therapy is reversal of the immune-deficient state, since there are no effective drugs that block virus infection without toxicity. Reversal may be achieved by using plasma exchange to accelerate the removal of the therapeutic agents that put patients at risk for PML. In the case of HIV-associated PML, immediately beginning anti-retroviral therapy will benefit most individuals. Several new drugs that laboratory tests found effective against infection are being used in PML patients with special permission of the U.S. Food and Drug Administration. Hexadecyloxypropyl-Cidofovir (CMX001) is currently being studied as a treatment option for JVC because of its ability to suppress JVC by inhibiting viral DNA replication.

What is the prognosis?

In general, PML has a mortality rate of 30-50 percent in the first few months following diagnosis but depends on the severity of the underlying disease and treatment received. Those who survive PML can be left with severe neurological disabilities.

Section 33.6

Viral Hepatitis

This section includes excerpts from "HIV and Viral Hepatitis,"
Centers for Disease Control and Prevention (CDC), March 2014; and
text from "Viral Hepatitis – Information for Gay and Bisexual Men,"
Centers for Disease Control and Prevention (CDC), October 2013.

Overview

Hepatitis means inflammation of the liver. This condition is most often caused by a virus. In the United States, the most common causes of viral hepatitis are hepatitis A virus (HAV), hepatitis B virus (HBV), and hepatitis C virus (HCV). HBV and HCV are common among people who are at risk for, or living with, HIV.

You can get some forms of viral hepatitis the same way you get HIV—through unprotected sexual contact and injection drug use. HAV, which causes a short-term but occasionally severe illness, is usually spread when the virus is ingested from contact with food, drinks, or objects (including injection drug equipment), contaminated by feces (or stool) of an infected person.

Coinfection

People with HIV infection are often affected by viral hepatitis; about one-third are coinfected with either HBV or HCV, which can cause long-term illness and death. More people living with HIV have HCV than HBV. Viral hepatitis progresses faster and causes more liver-related health problems among people with HIV than among those who do not have HIV. Although drug therapy has extended the life expectancy of people with HIV, liver disease—much of which is related to HCV and HBV—has become the leading cause of non-AIDS-related deaths in this population.

People with HIV who are coinfected with either HBV or HCV are at increased risk for serious, life- threatening complications. As a result, anyone living with HIV should be tested for HBV and HCV. Coinfection with hepatitis may also complicate the management of HIV infection. To prevent coinfection for those who are not already infected with HBV, the Advisory Committee on Immunization Practices recommends HAV and/or HBV vaccination of high-risk patients (including those who are gay, bisexual, and other men who have sex with men [MSM], injection drug users) with HIV infection or AIDS.

The Numbers

- Of people with HIV in the United States, about 25% are coinfected with HCV, and about 10% are coinfected with HBV.

- About 80% of people with HIV who inject drugs also have HCV.

- HIV coinfection more than triples the risk for liver disease, liver failure, and liver-related death from HCV.

- About 20% of all new HBV infections and 10% of all new HAV infections in the United States are among MSM. In the United States, HCV is twice as prevalent among blacks as among whites.

Transmission

People can be infected with the three most common types of hepatitis in these ways:

- **HAV:** Ingestion of contaminated fecal matter, even in tiny amounts, from close person-to-person contact with an infected person, sexual contact with an infected person, or contaminated food, drink, or objects, including injection equipment.

- **HBV:** Contact with infectious blood, semen, or other body fluids; sexual contact with an infected person; sharing of contaminated needles, syringes, or other injection drug equipment; and needlesticks or other sharp-instrument injuries. In addition, an infected woman can pass the virus to her newborn.

- **HCV:** Contact with blood of an infected person, primarily through sharing contaminated needles, syringes, or other injection drug equipment, and, less commonly, sexual contact with an infected person, birth to an infected mother, and needlesticks or other sharp-instrument injuries from an infected person.

- Chronic HCV is often "silent," and many people can have the infection for decades without having symptoms or feeling sick. Compared with other age groups, people aged 46 to 64 are 4 to 5 times as likely to be infected with HCV.

- Any sexual activity with an infected person increases the risk of contracting hepatitis. In particular, unprotected anal sex increases the risk for both HBV and HIV among MSM, and direct anal-oral contact increases the risk for HAV.

- New data suggest that sexual transmission of HCV among MSM with HIV occurs more commonly than previously believed.

Symptoms

Many people with viral hepatitis do not have symptoms and do not know they are infected. For acute hepatitis, symptoms usually appear within several weeks to several months of exposure and can last up to 6 months. Symptoms of chronic viral hepatitis can take decades to develop and people can live with an infection for years and not feel sick. When symptoms do appear with chronic hepatitis, they often are a sign of advanced liver disease.

Symptoms for both acute and chronic viral hepatitis can include: fever, fatigue, loss of appetite, nausea, vomiting, abdominal pain, dark urine, grey-colored stools, joint pain, and jaundice.

Prevention

If you have HIV infection, you can lower your risk of contracting hepatitis and other bloodborne viruses by not sharing toothbrushes, razors, or other personal items that may come into contact with an infected person's blood. Do not get tattoos or body piercings from an unlicensed facility or in an informal setting, which may use dirty needles or other instruments. Just as HIV-positive individuals would not want to engage in behaviors that would put them at risk for hepatitis, these same behaviors would also put others at risk for HIV.

- **HAV:** The best way to prevent HAV infection is to get vaccinated. The Centers for Disease Control and Prevention (CDC) recommends vaccination for HAV for people who are at risk for HIV infection, including MSM; users of recreational drugs, whether injected or not; and sex partners of infected people.

- **HBV:** The best way to prevent HBV infection is to get vaccinated. CDC recommends vaccination against HBV for people who have or are at risk for HIV infection, including MSM; people who inject drugs; sex partners of infected people; people with multiple sex partners; anyone with a sexually transmitted infection; and health care and public safety workers exposed to blood on the job.

- **HCV:** There is no vaccine for HCV. CDC estimates that people born during 1945 through 1965 account for nearly 75% of all HCV infections in the United States. The best way to prevent HCV infection is to never inject drugs or to stop injecting drugs if you currently do so by getting into and staying in a drug treatment program. If you continue injecting drugs, always use new, sterile syringes and never reuse or share syringes, needles, water, or other drug preparation equipment.

Testing and Treatment

Health care providers use blood tests to detect viral hepatitis in their patients. The virus can be detected even if a person has no symptoms. In the case of HBV, the test result can help determine if a person has been infected and, if not, whether he or she would benefit from vaccination. If an antibody test is positive for HCV, a follow-up test must be done to confirm current infection.

Treatment for viral hepatitis varies. There is no treatment for HAV infection, but almost all people who get HAV recover completely and do not have any lasting liver damage, although they may feel sick for months. Both chronic HBV and HCV can be treated with antiviral medications. For HBV, treatment can delay or limit the effects of liver damage. Many people infected with HCV experience clearance of the virus as a result of treatment. Newly approved treatments are shorter, have fewer side effects, and may be more effective.

Coinfection with viral hepatitis may also complicate the treatment and management of HIV infection. Because viral hepatitis infection is often serious in people with HIV infection and may lead to liver damage more quickly, CDC recommends that all people with HIV infection be tested for HBV and HCV, CDC also recommends that everyone born during 1945-1965 should be tested at least once for HCV.

HIV/HBV and HIV/HCV coinfections can be effectively treated in many people, but treatment is complex, and people with coinfection should look for health care providers with expertise in the management of both HIV infection and viral hepatitis.

Are gay and bisexual men at risk for viral hepatitis?

Yes. Among adults, an estimated 10% of new Hepatitis A cases and 20% of new Hepatitis B cases occur in gay or bisexual men. Gay and bisexual men are at increased risk for Hepatitis C if they are involved in high-risk behaviors.

Sharing needles or other equipment used to inject drugs puts a person at risk for Hepatitis B, Hepatitis C, and HIV. Of people with HIV infection, 10% also have Hepatitis B and 25% also have Hepatitis C. New research shows that gay men who are HIV-positive and have multiple sex partners may increase their risk for Hepatitis C.

Should gay and bisexual men be vaccinated?

Yes. Experts recommend that all gay and bisexual men be vaccinated for Hepatitis A and B. The Hepatitis A and B vaccines can be given separately or as a combination vaccine. The vaccines are safe, effective, and require 2-3 shots given over a period of 6 months depending on the type of vaccine. A person should complete all shots in the series for long-term protection.

There is no vaccine for Hepatitis C. The best way to prevent Hepatitis C is by avoiding behaviors that can spread the disease, especially sharing needles or other equipment to inject drugs.

Should gay and bisexual men get tested for viral hepatitis?

It depends upon the type of hepatitis and a person's risk factors. Testing is not recommended for Hepatitis A.

CDC recommends gay and bisexual men get tested for Hepatitis B. Getting tested can determine if a person is or has been infected with Hepatitis B and if he will need the vaccine series for protection.

Testing for Hepatitis C is not recommended for gay and bisexual men unless they were born from 1945 through 1965, have HIV, or are engaging in risky behaviors.

Chapter 34

HIV/AIDS and Co-Occurring Cancer

Chapter Contents

Section 34.1

HIV Infection and Cancer Risk

Text in this section is excerpted from "Cancer," AIDS.gov June 1, 2012.

HIV doesn't cause cancer, but it can increase your risk.

Having HIV disease can put you at risk for many types of *opportunistic infections* and other diseases—including certain types of cancer that are more common or more aggressive in people with HIV.

HIV-related cancers include certain types of immune-system cancers *(lymphomas)*, *Kaposi's sarcoma*, and cancers that affect the *anus* and the *cervix*. You may also see these cancers referred to as "AIDS-related cancers."

A low *CD4 count* appears to be the primary risk factor for many of these cancers. *HPV infection* is another major risk factor.

Lymphoma

Lymphoma is a specific type of cancer that involves the *lymph nodes* and the lymph system. If you have HIV and a low CD4 count, you are at risk for several types of lymphoma.

The most common HIV-related lymphoma is called *Non-Hodgkin's Lymphoma* (NHL). This type of cancer occurs most often in patients with an average CD4 count of **100 cells/mm**^{3} or less. Patients with NHL can have a range of symptoms including:

- Painless, swollen lymph nodes in the neck, chest, underarm, or groin

- Night sweats

- Weight loss

- Fever

(Other conditions may cause the same symptoms. Consult your healthcare provider if you have any of these symptoms.)

It usually takes multiple tests to diagnose NHL, including blood tests, a *biopsy*, and imaging studies (*MRI, CT scan, or PET scan*). Treatment for this condition is complex and involves treating both the cancer and your HIV infection.

Primary Central Nervous System (CNS) Lymphoma

Your *central nervous system* consists of your brain, spinal cord, and spinal nerves. This system controls all the workings of your body. HIV can infect and damage parts of it.

Primary CNS lymphoma is a type of cancer that typically occurs in people with CD4 counts less than **50 cells/mm**^{3}. This type of cancer affects the lymph system in your brain and spinal cord. Symptoms of this type of cancer can include:

- Headache

- Memory loss

- Confusion

- Other neurological changes

(Other conditions may cause the same symptoms. Consult your healthcare provider if you have any of these symptoms.)

Diagnosis includes many of the same types of tests as those for Non-Hodgkin's lymphoma—but because CNS lymphoma affects the brain directly, your healthcare provider may want to do a brain biopsy as well. *Radiation therapy* is the most common treatment for AIDS-related CNS lymphoma.

Kaposi's Sarcoma

Kaposi's Sarcoma (KS) is a cancer of the connective tissue that is caused by a strain of human herpesvirus (HHV-8). KS occurs most often in people with CD4 counts below **200-300/mm**^{3}. Before the AIDS epidemic, Kaposi's sarcoma was found mainly in elderly Italian and Jewish men, for whom it was a slow-growing and mild form of cancer.

For people living with HIV/AIDS, however, KS can develop very quickly. KS appears as purplish/reddish spots (called lesions) which generally develop first on the skin, or inside the mouth. Lesions can develop anywhere on the body—including on internal organs.

While KS is treatable with *chemotherapy*, the best way to combat it is to improve CD4 count by using *antiretroviral therapy*.

417

Anal Cancer

Anal cancer occurs when *malignant* cells form in the tissues of the *anus*. Anal cancer is rare in otherwise healthy people—but since the mid-1990s, the number of cases of anal cancer has increased dramatically and continues to rise.

Anal cancer is caused by the *human papilloma virus (HPV)*. If you have HPV and/or HIV disease, you have a much greater risk of developing anal cancer.

Men who have sex with men (MSM) are particularly at risk for developing anal cancer, whether or not they have HIV. But MSM who are HIV-positive are up to 40 times more likely to get anal cancer.

Symptoms of anal cancer can include:

- Bleeding from the anus or rectum

- Pain or pressure in the area around the anus

- Itching or discharge from the anus

- A lump near the anus

- A change in bowel habits

(Other conditions may cause the same symptoms. Consult your healthcare provider if you have any of these symptoms.)

Some experts recommend that men who are at risk for anal cancer have an anal *Pap test* each year. CDC has not yet recommended this as the standard of care, but if you are at risk, you should talk with your healthcare provider about the potential benefits of getting an anal Pap test.

Invasive Cervical Cancer

Cervical cancer forms in tissues of the *cervix* (the organ connecting the *uterus* and *vagina*). It is usually a slow-growing cancer that may not have symptoms. *HPV infection* is the main cause of cervical cancer.

Invasive cervical cancer occurs when cancerous cells spread from the surface of the cervix to other parts of the body. Although any woman, regardless of her HIV status, may develop cervical cancer, there is an increased risk of developing cervical cancer if you are female and HIV-positive. Invasive cervical cancer is an *AIDS-defining condition* for women.

In its early stages (when it is most likely to respond to treatment), cervical cancer rarely has symptoms, but women with cervical cancer can experience:

- Abnormal bleeding between periods

- Pelvic pain

- Pain during sex

- Abnormal vaginal bleeding

(Other conditions may cause the same symptoms. Consult your healthcare provider if you have any of these symptoms.)

Early detection is important to prevent invasive cervical cancer. Regular *Pap tests* are the key—these tests can show abnormal cell changes (*cervical dysplasia*) before they become cancerous. When cell changes are found and treated early, almost all women can avoid getting cervical cancer.

An abnormal Pap test does NOT mean you have cervical cancer—but, if you have an abnormal or unclear result, you need to talk with your healthcare provider about follow-up tests and care.

If you do have cervical cancer, it is important to treat it early, before it becomes invasive. Treatment methods can include surgery, radiation therapy, or chemotherapy.

Section 34.2

Kaposi Sarcoma

Text in this section is excerpted from "Kaposi Sarcoma Treatment (PDQ®)," National Cancer Institute (NCI), August 12, 2015.

Kaposi sarcoma is a disease in which malignant tumors (cancer) can form in the skin, mucous membranes, lymph nodes, and other organs.

Kaposi sarcoma is a cancer that causes lesions (abnormal tissue) to grow in the skin; the mucous membranes lining the mouth, nose, and throat; lymph nodes; or other organs. The lesions are usually purple and are made of cancer cells, new blood vessels, red blood cells, and white blood cells. Kaposi sarcoma is different from other cancers in that lesions may begin in more than one place in the body at the same time.

Human herpesvirus-8 (HHV-8) is found in the lesions of all patients with Kaposi sarcoma. This virus is also called Kaposi sarcoma herpesvirus (KSHV). Most people infected with HHV-8 do not get Kaposi sarcoma. Those infected with HHV-8 who are most likely to develop Kaposi sarcoma have immune systems weakened by disease or by drugs given after an organ transplant.

There are several types of Kaposi sarcoma, including:

- Classic Kaposi sarcoma.

- African Kaposi sarcoma.

- Immunosuppressive therapy-related Kaposi sarcoma.

- Epidemic Kaposi sarcoma.

- Nonepidemic Kaposi sarcoma.

Tests that examine the skin, lungs, and gastrointestinal tract are used to detect (find) and diagnose Kaposi sarcoma.

The following tests and procedures may be used:

- **Physical exam and history :** An exam of the body to check general signs of health, including checking skin and lymph nodes for signs of disease, such as lumps or anything else that seems unusual. A history of the patient's health habits and past illnesses and treatments will also be taken.

- **Chest X-ray :** An X-ray of the organs and bones inside the chest. An X-ray is a type of energy beam that can go through the body and onto film, making a picture of areas inside the body. This is used to find Kaposi sarcoma in the lungs.

- **Biopsy :** The removal of cells or tissues so they can be viewed under a microscope by apathologist to check for signs of cancer.

    One of the following types of biopsies may be done to check for Kaposi sarcoma lesions in the skin:

    - **Excisional biopsy :** A scalpel is used to remove the entire skin growth.

- **Incisional biopsy :** A scalpel is used to remove part of a skin growth.

- **Core biopsy :** A wide needle is used to remove part of a skin growth.

- **Fine-needle aspiration (FNA) biopsy :** A thin needle is used to remove part of a skin growth.

An endoscopy or bronchoscopy may be done to check for Kaposi sarcoma lesions in the gastrointestinal tract or lungs.

- **Endoscopy for biopsy**: A procedure to look at organs and tissues inside the body to check for abnormal areas. An endoscope is inserted through an incision(cut) in the skin or opening in the body, such as the mouth. An endoscope is a thin, tube-like instrument with a light and a lens for viewing. It may also have a tool to remove tissue or lymph node samples, which are checked under a microscope for signs of disease. This is used to find Kaposi sarcoma lesions in the gastrointestinal tract.

- **Bronchoscopy for biopsy**: A procedure to look inside the trachea and large airways in the lung for abnormal areas. A bronchoscope is inserted through the nose or mouth into the trachea and lungs. A bronchoscope is a thin, tube-like instrument with a light and a lens for viewing. It may also have a tool to remove tissue samples, which are checked under a microscope for signs of disease. This is used to find Kaposi sarcoma lesions in the lungs.

After Kaposi sarcoma has been diagnosed, tests are done to find out if cancer cells have spread to other parts of the body.

The following tests and procedures may be used to find out if cancer has spread to other parts of the body:

- **Blood chemistry studies :** A procedure in which a blood sample is checked to measure the amounts of certain substances released into the blood by organs and tissues in the body. An unusual (higher or lower than normal) amount of a substance can be a sign of disease.

- **CT scan (CAT scan):** A procedure that makes a series of detailed pictures of areas inside the body, such as the lung, liver, and spleen, taken from different angles. The pictures are made by a computer linked to an x-ray machine. A dye may be injecte-dinto a vein or swallowed to help the organs or tissues show up more clearly. This procedure is also called computed tomography, computerized tomography, or computerized axial tomography.

- **PET scan (positron emission tomography scan):** A procedure to find malignanttumor cells in the body. A small amount of radioactive glucose (sugar) is injected into a vein. The PET scanner rotates around the body and makes a picture of where glucose is being used in the body. Malignant tumor cells show up brighter in the picture because they are more active and take up more glucose than normal cells do. Thisimaging test checks for signs of cancer in the lung, liver, and spleen.

- **CD34 lymphocyte count:** A procedure in which a blood sample is checked to measure the amount of CD34 cells (a type of white blood cell). A lower than normal amount of CD34 cells can be a sign the immune system is not working well.

Certain factors affect prognosis (chance of recovery) and treatment options.

The prognosis (chance of recovery) and treatment options depend on the following:

- The type of Kaposi sarcoma.
- The general health of the patient, especially the patient's immune system.
- Whether the cancer has just been diagnosed or has recurred (come back).

Classic Kaposi Sarcoma

Classic Kaposi sarcoma is found most often in older men of Italian or Eastern European Jewish origin.

Classic Kaposi sarcoma is a rare disease that gets worse slowly over many years.

Signs of classic Kaposi sarcoma may include slow-growing lesions on the legs and feet.

Patients may have one or more red, purple, or brown skin lesions on the legs and feet, most often on the ankles or soles of the feet. Over time, lesions may form in other parts of the body, such as the stomach, intestines, or lymph nodes. The lesions usually don't cause any symptoms, but may grow in size and number over a period of 10 years or more. Pressure from the lesions may block the flow of lymph and blood in the legs and cause painful swelling. Lesions in the digestive tract may cause gastrointestinal bleeding.

Another cancer may develop.

Some patients with classic Kaposi sarcoma may develop another type of cancer before the Kaposi sarcoma lesions appear or later in life. Most often, this second cancer is non-Hodgkin lymphoma. Frequent follow-up is needed to watch for these second cancers.

African Kaposi Sarcoma

African Kaposi sarcoma is a fairly common form of the disease found in young adult males who live near the equator in Africa. Signs of African Kaposi sarcoma can be the same as classic Kaposi sarcoma. However, African Kaposi sarcoma can also be found in a much more aggressive form that may cause sores on the skin and spread from the skin to the tissues to the bone. Another form of Kaposi sarcoma that is common in young children in Africa does not affect the skin but spreads through the lymph nodes to vital organs, and quickly becomes fatal.

This type of Kaposi sarcoma is not common in the United States and treatment information is not included in this summary.

Immunosuppressive Therapy-Related Kaposi Sarcoma

Immunosuppressive therapy-related Kaposi sarcoma is found in patients who have had an organ transplant (for example, a kidney, heart, or liver transplant). These patients take drugs to keep their immune systems from attacking the new organ. When the body's immune system is weakened by these drugs, diseases like Kaposi sarcoma can develop.

Immunosuppressive therapy-related Kaposi sarcoma often affects only the skin, but may also occur in the mucous membranes or certain other organs of the body.

This type of Kaposi sarcoma is also called transplant-related or acquired Kaposi sarcoma.

Epidemic Kaposi Sarcoma

Epidemic Kaposi sarcoma is found in patients who have AIDS.

Epidemic Kaposi sarcoma occurs in patients who have acquired immunodeficiency syndrome (AIDS). AIDS is caused by the human immunodeficiency virus (HIV), which attacks and weakens the immune system. When the body's immune system is weakened by HIV; infections and cancers such as Kaposi sarcoma can develop.

Most cases of epidemic Kaposi sarcoma in the United States have been diagnosed in homosexual or bisexual men infected with HIV.

Signs of epidemic Kaposi sarcoma can include lesions that form in many parts of the body.

The signs of epidemic Kaposi sarcoma can include lesions in different parts of the body, including any of the following:

- Skin

- Lining of the mouth

- Lymph nodes

- Stomach and intestines

- Lungs and lining of the chest

- Liver

- Spleen

Kaposi sarcoma is sometimes found in the lining of the mouth during a regular dental check-up.

In most patients with epidemic Kaposi sarcoma, the disease will spread to other parts of the body over time. Fever, weight loss, or diarrhea can occur. In the later stages of epidemic Kaposi sarcoma, life-threatening infections are common.

The use of drug therapy called HAART (highly active antiretroviral therapy) reduces the risk of epidemic Kaposi sarcoma in patients infected with HIV.

HAART (highly active antiretroviral therapy) is a combination of several drugs that block HIV and slow down the development of AIDS and AIDS-related Kaposi sarcoma.

Nonepidemic Gay-related Kaposi Sarcoma

There is a type of nonepidemic Kaposi sarcoma that develops in homosexual men who have no signs or symptoms of HIV infection. This type of Kaposi sarcoma progresses slowly, with new lesions appearing every few years. The lesions are most common on the arms, legs, and genitals, but can develop anywhere on the skin.

This type of Kaposi sarcoma is rare and treatment information is not included in this section.

Section 34.3

AIDS-Related Lymphoma

Text in this section is excerpted from "AIDS-Related Lymphoma Treatment (PDQ®)," National Cancer Institute (NCI), September 17, 2015.

AIDS-related lymphoma is a disease in which malignant (cancer) cells form in the lymph system of patients who have AIDS.

AIDS is caused by the human immunodeficiency virus (HIV), which attacks and weakens the body's immune system. The immune system is then unable to fight infection and diseases that invade the body. People with HIV disease have an increased risk of developing infections, lymphoma, and other types of cancer. A person with HIV disease who develops certain types of infections or cancer is then diagnosed with AIDS. Sometimes, people are diagnosed with AIDS and AIDS-related lymphoma at the same time.

Lymphomas are cancers that affect the white blood cells of the lymph system, part of the body's immune system. The lymph system is made up of the following:

- **Lymph**: Colorless, watery fluid that travels through the lymph system and carries white blood cells called lymphocytes. Lymphocytes protect the body against infections and the growth of tumors.

425

- **Lymph vessels**: A network of thin tubes that collect lymph from different parts of the body and return it to the bloodstream.

- **Lymph nodes**: Small, bean-shaped structures that filter lymph and store white blood cells that help fight infection and disease. Lymph nodes are located along the network of lymph vessels found throughout the body. Clusters of lymph nodes are found in the underarm, pelvis, neck, abdomen, and groin.

- **Spleen**: An organ that makes lymphocytes, filters the blood, stores blood cells, and destroys old blood cells. The spleen is on the left side of the abdomen near the stomach.

- **Thymus**: An organ in which lymphocytes grow and multiply. The thymus is in the chest behind the breastbone.

- **Tonsils**: Two small masses of lymph tissue at the back of the throat. The tonsils make lymphocytes.

- **Bone marrow**: The soft, spongy tissue in the center of large bones. Bone marrow makes white blood cells, red blood cells, and platelets.

There are many different types of lymphoma.

Lymphomas are divided into two general types: Hodgkin lymphoma and non-Hodgkin lymphoma. Both Hodgkin lymphoma and non-Hodgkin lymphoma may occur in AIDS patients, but non-Hodgkin lymphoma is more common. When a person with AIDS has non-Hodgkin lymphoma, it is called an AIDS-related lymphoma.

AIDS-related lymphomas grow and spread quickly.

Non-Hodgkin lymphomas are grouped by the way their cells look under a microscope. They may be indolent (slow-growing) or aggressive (fast-growing). AIDS-related lymphoma is usually aggressive. There are three main types of AIDS-related lymphoma:

- Diffuse large B-cell lymphoma.
- B-cell immunoblastic lymphoma.
- Small non-cleaved cell lymphoma.

Signs of AIDS-related lymphoma include weight loss, fever, and night sweats.

These and other signs and symptoms may be caused by AIDS-related lymphoma or by other conditions. Check with your doctor if you have any of the following:

- Weight loss or fever for no known reason.
- Night sweats.
- Painless, swollen lymph nodes in the neck, chest, underarm, or groin.
- A feeling of fullness below the ribs.

Tests that examine the body and lymph system are used to help detect (find) and diagnose AIDS-related lymphoma.

The following tests and procedures may be used:

- **Physical exam and history** : An exam of the body to check general signs of health, including checking for signs of disease, such as lumps or anything else that seems unusual. A history of the patient's health habits and past illnesses and treatments will also be taken.
- **Complete blood count (CBC)**: A procedure in which a sample of blood is drawn and checked for the following:
  - The number of red blood cells, white blood cells, and platelets.
  - The amount of hemoglobin (the protein that carries oxygen) in the red blood cells.
  - The portion of the sample made up of red blood cells.
- **Lymph node biopsy**: The removal of all or part of a lymph node. A pathologist views the tissue under a microscope to look for cancer cells. One of the following types of biopsies may be done:
  - **Excisional biopsy** : The removal of an entire lymph node.
  - **Incisional biopsy** : The removal of part of a lymph node.
  - **Core biopsy** : The removal of tissue from a lymph node using a wide needle.
  - **Fine-needle aspiration (FNA) biopsy** : The removal of tissue from a lymph node using a thin needle.

- **Bone marrow aspiration and biopsy** : The removal of bone marrow, blood, and a small piece of bone by inserting a hollow needle into the hipbone or breastbone. A pathologist views the bone marrow, blood, and bone under a microscope to look for signs of cancer.

- **HIV test** : A test to measure the level of HIV antibodies in a sample of blood. Antibodies are made by the body when it is invaded by a foreign substance. A high level of HIV antibodies may mean the body has been infected with HIV.

- **Chest X-ray** : An X-ray of the organs and bones inside the chest. An X-ray is a type of energy beam that can go through the body and onto film, making a picture of areas inside the body.

Certain factors affect prognosis (chance of recovery) and treatment options.

The prognosis (chance of recovery) and treatment options depend on the following:

- The stage of the cancer.

- The number of CD4 lymphocytes (a type of white blood cell) in the blood.

- Whether the patient has ever had AIDS-related infections.

- The patient's ability to carry out regular daily activities.

Stages of AIDS-Related Lymphoma

After AIDS-related lymphoma has been diagnosed, tests are done to find out if cancer cells have spread within the lymph system or to other parts of the body.

The process used to find out if cancer cells have spread within the lymph system or to other parts of the body is called staging. The information gathered from the staging process determines the stage of the disease. It is important to know the stage in order to plan treatment, but AIDS-related lymphoma is usually advanced when it is diagnosed. The following tests and procedures may be used in the staging process:

- **Blood chemistry studies** : A procedure in which a blood sample is checked to measure the amounts of certain substances released into the blood by organs and tissues in the body. An unusual (higher or lower than normal) amount of a substance can be a sign of disease. The blood sample will be checked for the level of LDH (lactate dehydrogenase).

- **CT scan (CAT scan)**: A procedure that makes a series of detailed pictures of areas inside the body, such as the lung, lymph nodes, and liver, taken from different angles. The pictures are made by a computer linked to an x-ray machine. A dye may be injected into a vein or swallowed to help the organs or tissues show up more clearly. This procedure is also called computed tomography, computerized tomography, or computerized axial tomography.

- **PET scan (positron emission tomography scan)**: A procedure to find malignant tumor cells in the body. A small amount of radioactive glucose (sugar) is injected into a vein. The PET scanner rotates around the body and makes a picture of where glucose is being used in the body. Malignant tumor cells show up brighter in the picture because they are more active and take up more glucose than normal cells do.

- **MRI (magnetic resonance imaging)**: A procedure that uses a magnet, radio waves, and a computer to make a series of detailed pictures of areas inside the body. A substance called gadolinium is injected into the patient through a vein. The gadolinium collects around the cancer cells so they show up brighter in the picture. This procedure is also called nuclear magnetic resonance imaging (NMRI).

- **Lumbar puncture** : A procedure used to collect cerebrospinal fluid (CSF) from the spinal column. This is done by placing a needle between two bones in the spine and into the CSF around the spinal cord and removing a sample of the fluid. The sample of CSF is checked under a microscope for signs that the cancer has spread to the brain and spinal cord. This procedure is also called an LP or spinal tap.

There are three ways that cancer spreads in the body.

Cancer can spread through tissue, the lymph system, and the blood:

- Tissue. The cancer spreads from where it began by growing into nearby areas.

- Lymph system. The cancer spreads from where it began by getting into the lymph system. The cancer travels through the lymph vessels to other parts of the body.

- Blood. The cancer spreads from where it began by getting into the blood. The cancer travels through the blood vessels to other parts of the body.

Stages of AIDS-related lymphoma may include E and S.

AIDS-related lymphoma may be described as follows:

- E: "E" stands for extranodal and means the cancer is found in an area or organ other than the lymph nodes or has spread to tissues beyond, but near, the major lymphatic areas.

- S: "S" stands for spleen and means the cancer is found in the spleen.

The following stages are used for AIDS-related lymphoma:

Stage I

Stage I AIDS-related lymphoma is divided into stage I and stage IE.

- **Stage I**: Cancer is found in one lymphatic area (lymph node group, tonsils and nearby tissue, thymus, or spleen).

- **Stage IE**: Cancer is found in one organ or area outside the lymph nodes.

Stage II

Stage II AIDS-related lymphoma is divided into stage II and stage IIE.

- **Stage II**: Cancer is found in two or more lymph node groups either above or below the diaphragm (the thin muscle below the lungs that helps breathing and separates the chest from the abdomen).

- **Stage IIE**: Cancer is found in one or more lymph node groups either above or below the diaphragm. Cancer is also found outside the lymph nodes in one organ or area on the same side of the diaphragm as the affected lymph nodes.

Stage III

Stage III AIDS-related lymphoma is divided into stage III, stage IIIE, stage IIIS, and stage IIIE+S.

- **Stage III**: Cancer is found in lymph node groups above and below the diaphragm (the thin muscle below the lungs that helps breathing and separates the chest from the abdomen).
- **Stage IIIE**: Cancer is found in lymph node groups above and below the diaphragm and outside the lymph nodes in a nearby organ or area.
- **Stage IIIS**: Cancer is found in lymph node groups above and below the diaphragm, and in the spleen.
- **Stage IIIE+S**: Cancer is found in lymph node groups above and below the diaphragm, outside the lymph nodes in a nearby organ or area, and in the spleen.

Stage IV

In stage IV AIDS-related lymphoma, the cancer:

- is found throughout one or more organs that are not part of a lymphatic area (lymph node group, tonsils and nearby tissue, thymus, or spleen) and may be in lymph nodes near those organs; or
- is found in one organ that is not part of a lymphatic area and has spread to organs or lymph nodes far away from that organ; or
- is found in the liver, bone marrow, cerebrospinal fluid (CSF), or lungs (other than cancer that has spread to the lungs from nearby areas).

Patients who are infected with the Epstein-Barr virus or whose AIDS-related lymphoma affects the bone marrow have an increased risk of the cancer spreading to the central nervous system (CNS).

For treatment, AIDS-related lymphomas are grouped based on where they started in the body, as follows:

Peripheral / systemic lymphoma

Lymphoma that starts in lymph nodes or other organs of the lymph system is called peripheral/systemic lymphoma. The lymphoma may spread throughout the body, including to the brain or bone marrow.

Primary CNS lymphoma

Primary CNS lymphoma starts in the central nervous system (brain and spinal cord). Lymphoma that starts somewhere else in the body and spreads to the central nervous system is not primary CNS lymphoma.

Treatment Option Overview

There are different types of treatment for patients with AIDS-related lymphoma.

Different types of treatment are available for patients with AIDS-related lymphoma. Some treatments are standard (the currently used treatment), and some are being tested in clinical trials. A treatment clinical trial is a research study meant to help improve current treatments or obtain information on new treatments for patients with cancer. When clinical trials show that a new treatment is better than the standard treatment, the new treatment may become the standard treatment. Patients may want to think about taking part in a clinical trial. Some clinical trials are open only to patients who have not started treatment.

Treatment of AIDS-related lymphoma combines treatment of the lymphoma with treatment for AIDS.

Patients with AIDS have weakened immune systems and treatment can cause further damage. For this reason, patients who have AIDS-related lymphoma are usually treated with lower doses of drugs than lymphoma patients who do not have AIDS.

Highly-active antiretroviral therapy (HAART) is used to slow progression of HIV (which is a retrovirus). Treatment with HAART may allow some patients to safely receive anticancer drugs in standard or higher doses. Medicine to prevent and treat infections, which can be serious, is also used.

AIDS-related lymphoma usually grows faster than lymphoma that is not AIDS-related and it is more likely to spread to other parts of the body. In general, AIDS-related lymphoma is harder to treat.

Three types of standard treatment are used:

Chemotherapy

Chemotherapy is a cancer treatment that uses drugs to stop the growth of cancer cells, either by killing the cells or by stopping them from dividing. When chemotherapy is taken by mouth or injected into a vein or muscle, the drugs enter the bloodstream and can reach cancer cells throughout the body (systemic chemotherapy). When chemotherapy is placed directly into the cerebrospinal fluid (intrathecal chemotherapy), an organ, or a body cavity such as the abdomen, the drugs mainly affect cancer cells in those areas (regional chemotherapy). Combination chemotherapy is treatment using more than one anticancer drug. The way the chemotherapy is given depends on the type and stage of the cancer being treated.

Intrathecal chemotherapy may be used in patients who are more likely to have lymphoma in the central nervous system (CNS).

Colony-stimulating factors are sometimes given together with chemotherapy. This helps lessen the side effects chemotherapy may have on the bone marrow.

Radiation therapy

Radiation therapy is a cancer treatment that uses high-energy x-rays or other types of radiation to kill cancer cells or keep them from growing. There are two types of radiation therapy. External radiation therapy uses a machine outside the body to send radiation toward the cancer. Internal radiation therapy uses a radioactive substance sealed in needles, seeds, wires, or catheters that are placed directly into or near the cancer. The way the radiation therapy is given depends on the type and stage of the cancer being treated.

High-dose chemotherapy with stem cell transplant

High-dose chemotherapy with stem cell transplant is a way of giving high doses of chemotherapy and replacing blood-forming cells destroyed by the cancer treatment. Stem cells (immature blood cells) are removed from the blood or bone marrow of the patient or a donor and are frozen and stored. After the chemotherapy is completed, the stored stem cells are thawed and given back to the patient through an infusion. These reinfused stem cells grow into (and restore) the body's blood cells.

New types of treatment are being tested in clinical trials.

Targeted therapy

Targeted therapy is a type of treatment that uses drugs or other substances to identify and attack specific cancer cells without harming normal cells. Monoclonal antibody therapy is one type of targeted therapy being studied in the treatment of AIDS-related lymphoma.

Monoclonal antibody therapy is a cancer treatment that uses antibodies made in the laboratory from a single type of immune system cell. These antibodies can identify substances on cancer cells or normal substances that may help cancer cells grow. The antibodies attach to the substances and kill the cancer cells, block their growth, or keep them from spreading. Monoclonal antibodies are given by infusion. These may be used alone or to carry drugs, toxins, or radioactive material directly to cancer cells.

Patients may want to think about taking part in a clinical trial.

For some patients, taking part in a clinical trial may be the best treatment choice. Clinical trials are part of the cancer research process. Clinical trials are done to find out if new cancer treatments are safe and effective or better than the standard treatment.

Many of today's standard treatments for cancer are based on earlier clinical trials. Patients who take part in a clinical trial may receive the standard treatment or be among the first to receive a new treatment.

Patients who take part in clinical trials also help improve the way cancer will be treated in the future. Even when clinical trials do not lead to effective new treatments, they often answer important questions and help move research forward.

Patients can enter clinical trials before, during, or after starting their cancer treatment.

Some clinical trials only include patients who have not yet received treatment. Other trials test treatments for patients whose cancer has not gotten better. There are also clinical trials that test new ways to stop cancer from recurring (coming back) or reduce the side effects of cancer treatment.

Clinical trials are taking place in many parts of the country.

Follow-up tests may be needed.

Some of the tests that were done to diagnose the cancer or to find out the stage of the cancer may be repeated. Some tests will be repeated in order to see how well the treatment is working. Decisions about whether to continue, change, or stop treatment may be based on the results of these tests.

Some of the tests will continue to be done from time to time after treatment has ended. The results of these tests can show if your condition has changed or if the cancer has recurred (come back). These tests are sometimes called follow-up tests or check-ups.

Chapter 35

Other AIDS-Related Health Concerns

Chapter Contents

Section 35.1

Neurological Complications of AIDS

Text in this section is excerpted from "Neurological Complications of AIDS," National Institute of Neorological Disorders and Stroke (NINDS), August 20, 2015.

How does AIDS affect the nervous system?

The virus does not appear to directly invade nerve cells but it jeopardizes their health and function. The resulting inflammation may damage the brain and spinal cord and cause symptoms such as confusion and forgetfulness, behavioral changes, headaches, progressive weakness, and loss of sensation in the arms and legs. Cognitive motor impairment or damage to the peripheral nerves is also common. Research has shown that the HIV infection can significantly alter the size of certain brain structures involved in learning and information processing.

Other nervous system complications that occur as a result of the disease or the drugs used to treat it include pain, seizures, shingles, spinal cord problems, lack of coordination, difficult or painful swallowing, anxiety disorder, depression, fever, vision loss, gait disorders, destruction of brain tissue, and coma. These symptoms may be mild in the early stages of AIDS but can become progressively severe.

In the United States, neurological complications are seen in more than 50 percent of adults with AIDS. Nervous system complications in children may include developmental delays, loss of previously achieved milestones, brain lesions, nerve pain, smaller than normal skull size, slow growth, eye problems, and recurring bacterial infections.

What are some of the neurological complications that are associated with AIDS?

AIDS-related disorders of the nervous system may be caused directly by the HIV virus, by certain cancers and opportunistic infections (illnesses caused by bacteria, fungi, and other viruses that would not otherwise affect people with healthy immune systems), or by toxic effects of the drugs used to treat symptoms. Other neuro-AIDS disorders of unknown origin may be influenced by but are not caused directly by the virus.

AIDS dementia complex (ADC), or HIV-associated dementia (HAD), occurs primarily in persons with more advanced HIV infection. Symptoms include encephalitis (inflammation of the brain), behavioral changes, and a gradual decline in cognitive function, including trouble with concentration, memory, and attention. Persons with ADC also show progressive slowing of motor function and loss of dexterity and coordination. When left untreated, ADC can be fatal. It is rare when anti-retroviral therapy is used. Milder cognitive complaints are common and are termed HIV-associated neurocognitive disorder (HAND). Neuropsychologic testing can reveal subtle deficits even in the absence of symptoms.

Central nervous system (CNS) lymphomas are cancerous tumors that either begin in the brain or result from a cancer that has spread from another site in the body. CNS lymphomas are almost always associated with the Epstein-Barr virus (a common human virus in the herpes family). Symptoms include headache, seizures, vision problems, dizziness, speech disturbance, paralysis, and mental deterioration. Individuals may develop one or more CNS lymphomas. Prognosis is poor due to advanced and increasing immunodeficiency, but is better with successful HIV therapy.

Cryptococcal meningitis is seen in about 10 percent of untreated individuals with AIDS and in other persons whose immune systems have been severely suppressed by disease or drugs. It is caused by the fungus *Cryptococcus neoformans*, which is commonly found in dirt and bird droppings. The fungus first invades the lungs and spreads to the covering of the brain and spinal cord, causing inflammation. Symptoms include fatigue, fever, headache, nausea, memory loss, confusion, drowsiness, and vomiting. If left untreated, patients with cryptococcal meningitis may lapse into a coma and die.

Cytomegalovirus (CMV) infections can occur concurrently with other infections. Symptoms of CMV encephalitis include weakness in the arms and legs, problems with hearing and balance, altered mental states, dementia, peripheral neuropathy, coma, and retinal disease that may lead to blindness. CMV infection of the spinal cord and nerves can result in weakness in the lower limbs and some paralysis, severe lower back pain, and loss of bladder function. It can also cause pneumonia and gastrointestinal disease. This is rarely seen in HIV-treated individuals since advanced immunity is required for CMV to emerge.

Herpes virus infections are often seen in people with AIDS. The *herpes zoster virus*, which causes chickenpox and shingles, can infect the brain and produce encephalitis and myelitis (inflammation of the spinal cord). It commonly produces shingles, which is an eruption of blisters and intense pain along an area of skin supplied by an infected nerve. In people exposed to herpes zoster, the virus can lay dormant in the nerve tissue for years until it is reactivated as shingles. This reactivation is common in persons with AIDS because of their weakened immune systems. Signs of shingles include painful blisters (like those seen in chickenpox), itching, tingling, and pain in the nerves.

People with AIDS may suffer from several different forms of *neuropathy*, or nerve pain, each strongly associated with a specific stage of active immunodeficiency disease. *Peripheral neuropathy* describes damage to the peripheral nerves, the vast communications network that transmits information between the brain and spinal cord to every other part of the body. Peripheral nerves also send sensory information back to the brain and spinal cord. HIV damages the nerve fibers that help conduct signals and can cause several different forms of neuropathy. *Distal sensory polyneuropathy* causes either a numbing feeling or a mild to painful burning or tingling sensation that normally begins in the legs and feet. These sensations may be particularly strong at night and may spread to the hands. Affected persons have a heightened sensitivity to pain, touch, or other stimuli. Onset usually occurs in the later stages of the HIV infection and may affect the majority of advanced-stage HIV patients.

Neurosyphilis, the result of an insufficiently treated syphilis infection, seems more frequent and more rapidly progressive in people with HIV infection. It may cause slow degeneration of the nerve cells and nerve fibers that carry sensory information to the brain. Symptoms, which may not appear for some decades after the initial infection and vary from person to person, include weakness, diminished reflexes, unsteady gait, progressive degeneration of the joints, loss of coordination, episodes of intense pain and disturbed sensation, personality changes, dementia, deafness, visual impairment, and impaired response to light. The disease is more frequent in men than in women. Onset is common during mid-life.

Progressive multifocal leukoencephalopathy (PML) primarily affects individuals with suppressed immune systems (including nearly 5 percent of people with AIDS). PML is caused by the JC virus, which travels to the brain, infects multiple sites, and destroys the cells that make myelin – the fatty protective covering for many of the body's nerve and brain cells. Symptoms include various types of mental deterioration, vision loss, speech disturbances, ataxia (inability to coordinate movements), paralysis, brain lesions, and, ultimately, coma. Some individuals may also have compromised memory and cognition, and seizures may occur. PML is relentlessly progressive and death usually occurs within 6 months of initial symptoms. However, immune reconstitution with highly active antiretroviral therapy allows survival of more than half of HIV-associated PML cases in the current treatment era.

Psychological and neuropsychiatric disorders can occur in different phases of the HIV infection and AIDS and may take various and complex forms. Some illnesses, such as AIDS dementia complex, are caused directly by HIV infection of the brain, while other conditions may be triggered by the drugs used to combat the infection. Individuals may experience anxiety disorder, depressive disorders, increased thoughts of suicide, paranoia, dementia, delirium, cognitive impairment, confusion, hallucinations, behavioral abnormalities, malaise, and acute mania.

Toxoplasma encephalitis, also called cerebral toxoplasmosis, occurs in about 10 percent of untreated AIDS patients. It is caused by the parasite *Toxoplasma gondii*, which is carried by cats, birds, and other animals and can be found in soil contaminated by cat feces and sometimes in raw or undercooked meat. Once the parasite invades the immune system, it remains there; however, the immune system in a healthy person can fight off the parasite, preventing disease. Symptoms include encephalitis, fever, severe headache that does not respond to treatment, weakness on one side of the body, seizures, lethargy, increased confusion, vision problems, dizziness, problems with speaking and walking, vomiting, and personality changes. Not all patients show signs of the infection. Antibiotic therapy, if used early, will generally control the complication.

Vacuolar myelopathy causes the protective myelin sheath to pull away from nerve cells of the spinal cord, forming small holes called vacuoles in nerve fibers. Symptoms include weak and stiff legs and unsteadiness when walking. Walking becomes more difficult as the disease progresses and many patients eventually require a wheelchair.

Some people also develop AIDS dementia. Vacuolar myelopathy may affect up to 30 percent of untreated adults with AIDS and its incidence may be even higher in HIV-infected children.

How are these disorders diagnosed?

Based on the results of the individual's medical history and a general physical exam, the physician will conduct a thorough neurological exam to assess various functions: motor and sensory skills, nerve function, hearing and speech, vision, coordination and balance, mental status, and changes in mood or behavior. The physician may order laboratory tests and one or more of the following procedures to help diagnose neurological complications of AIDS.

Brain imaging can reveal signs of brain inflammation, tumors and CNS lymphomas, nerve damage, internal bleeding or hemorrhage, white matter irregularities, and other brain abnormalities. Several painless imaging procedures are used to help diagnose neurological complications of AIDS.

- *Computed tomography* (also called a CT scan) uses X-rays and a computer to produce two-dimensional images of bone and tissue, including inflammation, certain brain tumors and cysts, brain damage from head injury, and other disorders. It provides more details than an X-ray alone.

- *Magnetic resonance imaging* (MRI) uses a computer, radio waves, and a powerful magnetic field to produce either a detailed three-dimensional picture or a two-dimensional "slice" of body structures, including tissues, organs, bones, and nerves. It does not use ionizing radiation (as does an X-ray) and gives physicians a better look at tissue located near bone.

- *Functional MRI* (fMRI) uses the blood's magnetic properties to pinpoint areas of the brain that are active and to note how long they stay active. It can assess brain damage from head injury or degenerative disorders such as Alzheimer's disease and can identify and monitor other neurological disorders, including AIDS dementia complex.

- *Magnetic resonance spectroscopy* (MRS) uses a strong magnetic field to study the biochemical composition and concentration of hydrogen-based molecules, some of which are very specific to nerve cells, in various brain regions. MRS is being used experimentally to identify brain lesions in people with AIDS.

Electromyography, or EMG, is used to diagnose nerve and muscle dysfunction (such as neuropathy and nerve fiber damage caused by the HIV virus) and spinal cord disease. It records spontaneous muscle activity and muscle activity driven by the peripheral nerves.

Biopsy is the removal and examination of tissue from the body. A brain biopsy, which involves the surgical removal of a small piece of the brain or tumor, is used to determine intracranial disorders and tumor type. Unlike most other biopsies, it requires hospitalization. Muscle or nerve biopsies can help diagnose neuromuscular problems, while a brain biopsy can help diagnose a tumor, inflammation, or other irregularity.

Cerebrospinal fluid analysis can detect any bleeding or brain hemorrhage, infections of the brain or spinal cord (such as neurosyphilis), and any harmful buildup of fluid. It can also be used to sample viruses that may be affecting the brain. A sample of the fluid is removed by needle, under local anesthesia, and studied to detect any irregularities.

How are these disorders treated?

No single treatment can cure the neurological complications of AIDS. Some disorders require aggressive therapy while others are treated symptomatically.

Neuropathic pain is often difficult to control. Medicines range from analgesics sold over the counter to antiepileptic drugs, opiates, and some classes of antidepressants. Inflamed tissue can press on nerves, causing pain. Inflammatory and autoimmune conditions leading to neuropathy may be treated with corticosteroids, and procedures such as plasmapheresis (or plasma exchange) can clear the blood of harmful substances that cause inflammation.

Treatment options for AIDS- and HIV-related neuropsychiatric or psychotic disorders include antidepressants and anticonvulsants. Psychostimulants may also improve depressive symptoms and combat lethargy. Antidementia drugs may relieve confusion and slow mental decline, and benzodiazepines may be prescribed to treat anxiety. Psychotherapy may also help some individuals.

Aggressive antiretroviral therapy is used to treat AIDS dementia complex, vacuolar myopathy, progressive multifocal leukoencephalopathy, and cytomegalovirus encephalitis. HAART, or highly active antiretroviral therapy, combines at least three drugs to reduce the amount of virus circulating in the blood and may also delay the start of some infections.

Other neuro-AIDS treatment options include physical therapy and rehabilitation, radiation therapy and/or chemotherapy to kill or shrink cancerous brain tumors that may be caused by the HIV virus, antifungal or antimalarial drugs to combat certain bacterial infections associated with the disorder, and penicillin to treat neurosyphilis.

What research is being done?

Within the federal government, the National Institute of Neurological Disorders and Stroke (NINDS), one part of the National Institutes of Health (NIH), supports research on the neurological consequences of AIDS. The NINDS works closely with its sister agency, the National Institute of Allergy and Infectious Diseases (NIAID), which has primary responsibility for research related to HIV and AIDS.

Several NINDS-funded projects are studying the role of virally infected brain macrophages (cells that normally work to protect against infection) in causing disease in the central nervous system of adult macaques. The focus of these projects includes gene analyses and the study of key neuroimmune regulatory molecules that are turned on in the brain during the course of viral infection at levels that have been shown to be toxic.

Several animal-based models of HIV (including mouse, rat, and simian models) are used by scientists to study disease mechanisms and the course of AIDS, and NINDS grantees are working to develop new models of HIV. Several projects rely on a mouse model of severe combined immunodeficiency (a group of inherited disorders that are characterized by a lack of or severe defect in cells responsible for protecting the immune system). This model allows researchers to transplant developing human brain tissue from culture into the brains of the mice to monitor and assess neurologic damage caused by HIV infection. Other studies use mice bred to carry symptoms of HIV, and NINDS grantees are using these animals to see if the brain can function as a sanctuary for HIV-infected cells that can migrate to and infect peripheral lymph tissue.

The NINDS also supports research into the mechanisms of neurological illnesses related to immunodeficiency in AIDS patients. Several different investigators are studying the JC virus, which can reproduce in the brains of immunosuppressed patients and cause PML, and one study identified a novel receptor for the JC virus. Other studies of infectious agents include an investigation of the interaction of the fungal agent *Cryptococcus* with the blood vessels of the brain, and an analysis of neurosyphilis in people with AIDS. Scientists are also studying the effect of neurotoxic proteins and antiviral therapies directly on nerve cells as the cause for distal sensory peripheral neuropathy.

Several researchers are studying AIDS dementia and cognitive changes in HIV. NINDS-sponsored scientists are using fMRI and MRS to assess brain function and any behavioral deficits in HIV-affected individuals. Investigators hope to better understand how progressive neuronal cell death contributes to cognitive dysfunction and AIDS dementia. The National NeuroAIDS Tissue Consortium, a project supported jointly by the NINDS and its sister agency, the National Institute of Mental Health, is collecting tissues from people with AIDS who have suffered from dementia and other neurological complications of HIV infection for distribution to researchers around the globe.

The Neurological AIDS Research Consortium was established by the NINDS in 1993 to design and conduct clinical trials on HIV-associated neurologic disease. To date, the Consortium has supported studies of neurological function in advanced AIDS and the treatment of HIV-associated peripheral neuropathy, PML, and CMV infection. Current studies are optimizing therapy for painful neuropathy using methadone and duloxetine. Recent studies evaluated minocycline for dementia treatment and are studying the effects of salvage HAART (using drug therapies to treat HIV strains that have become resistant to drug combination therapy) in the nervous system.

Section 35.2

Oral Health Issues

This section begins with excerpts from "Oral Health Issues," AIDS.
gov, May 7, 2014; and text from "Mouth Problems and HIV,"
National Institute of Dental and Craniofacial Research (NIDCR),
August 1, 2014.

Your Mouth, Your Health

When you are focused on your overall health and well-being—and
especially when you are dealing with a chronic health condition like
HIV—it can be easy to overlook dental issues and oral health care.

But good dental hygiene is an important part of managing your HIV
disease. If you wait until you are having problems with your teeth and
gums to see a dentist, you can end up with an infection, pain, and/or
tooth loss.

Figure 35.1. *Oral Health*

Poor oral health can even lead to malnutrition. If you can't chew or
swallow because your mouth hurts, you may not eat enough to keep
yourself healthy. This also can affect how your body absorbs your HIV
medication. In addition, any infection can stimulate the virus to grow,
resulting in loss of viral suppression and higher viral loads.

HIV and Oral Health

Your mouth may be the first part of your body to show signs of HIV
infection. Oral opportunistic infections, such as *candidiasis* (thrush),
are sometimes the first indicator that your immune system is not
working properly—and oral health can be an important indicator of
how HIV is affecting your body.

446

Anyone can have oral health problems, but HIV disease can make you more susceptible to:

- Oral warts, which can also progress to oral cancer
- Fever blisters
- *Oral hairy leukoplakia*
- Thrush
- Canker sores
- Cavities
- Gum disease (periodontitis and gingivitis)

In addition, bacterial infections that begin in the mouth, such as tooth decay, can become more serious and, if not treated, spread into your bloodstream and harm your heart and other organs. This is particularly dangerous for people living with HIV/AIDS who may have compromised immune systems.

People with HIV/AIDS may also experience dry mouth, which increases the risk of tooth decay and can make chewing, eating, swallowing, and even talking difficult. Some HIV medications can cause dry mouth.

The best ways to avoid these problems include:

- See your dentist regularly for cleanings and ask about the best way to care for your mouth and teeth.
- Brush your teeth at least twice a day. (After every meal is better!)
- Floss every day. Flossing cleans parts of your teeth that your toothbrush can't reach.
- Take all your HIV medications on schedule—this will protect your immune system and prevent oral opportunistic infections.
- Let your doctor know if your HIV meds are causing you to have dry mouth. There are remedies.
- Examine your mouth often and tell your primary care provider if you notice any unusual changes in the way your mouth looks or feels.
- If you do not have a dentist, ask your regular clinic or provider to refer you to one.

Mouth Problems Can Be Treated

Remember, with the right treatment, your mouth can feel better. And that's an important step toward living well, not just longer, with HIV.

Table 35.1. Mouth Problems

Description	It could be:	What & where?	Painful?	Contagious?	Treatment
Red sores *ulcers*	Aphthous ulcers. Also known as Canker Sores	Red sores that might also have a yellow-gray film on top. They are usually on the moveable parts of the mouth such as the tongue or inside of the cheeks and lips.	Yes	No	Mild cases – Over-the-counter cream or prescription mouthwash that contains corticosteroids; More severe cases – corticosteroids in a pill form
	OR				
	Herpes A viral infection	Red sores usually on the roof of the mouth. They are sometimes on the outside of the lips, where they are called fever blisters.	Sometimes	Yes	Prescription pill can reduce healing time and frequency of outbreaks.
White hairlike growth	Hairy Leukoplakia caused by the Epstein-Barr virus	White patches that do not wipe away; sometimes very thick and "hairlike." Usually appear on the side of the tongue or sometimes inside the cheeks and lower lip.	Not usually	No	Mild cases – not usually required; More severe cases – a prescription pill that may reduce severity of symptoms. In some severe cases, a pain reliever might also be required.

Table 35.1. Continued

Description	It could be:	What & where?	Painful?	Contagious?	Treatment
White creamy or bumpy patcheslike cottage cheese	Candidiasis, a fungal (yeast) infection – Also known as thrush	White or yellowish patches (or can sometimes be red). If wiped away, there will be redness or bleeding underneath. They can appear anywhere in the mouth.	Sometimes, a burning feeling	No	Mild cases – prescription antifungal lozenge or mouthwash; More severe cases – prescription antifungal pills.
Warts		Small, white, gray, or pinkish rough bumps that look like cauliflower. They can appear inside the lips and on other parts of the mouth.	Not usually	Possibly	Inside the mouth – a doctor can remove them surgically or use "cryosurgery" – a way of freezing them off; On the lips – a prescription cream that will wear away the wart. Warts can return after treatment.

Section 35.3

Wasting Syndrome

Text in this section is excerpted from "HIV wasting syndrome," U.S. Department of Veterans Affairs (VA), October 7, 2015.

Wasting syndrome refers to unwanted weight loss that is equal to more than 10 percent of their body weight. For a 150-pound man, this means a loss of 15 pounds or more. Weight loss can result in loss of both fat and muscle. Once lost, the weight is difficult to regain.

The condition may occur in people with advanced HIV disease, and can be caused by many things: HIV, inflammation, or opportunistic infections. The weight loss may be accompanied by low-grade fever, and sometimes diarrhea. The person may get full easily, or have no appetite at all.

The most important treatment for wasting syndrome is effective treatment of HIV with antiretrovirals. In addition, the condition may be controlled, to some degree, by eating a good diet. A "good diet" for an HIV-positive person may not be the low-fat, low-calorie diet recommended for healthy people. Compared with other people, you may need to take in more calories and protein to keep from losing muscle mass. To do this, you can add to your meals:

- peanut butter
- legumes (dried beans and peas)
- cheeses
- eggs
- instant breakfast drinks
- milkshakes
- sauces

You can also maintain or increase muscle mass through exercise, especially with progressive strength-building exercises. These include resistance and weight-lifting exercise.

Section 35.4

Kidney Disease

Text in this section is excerpted from "Kidney Disease," AIDS.gov, August 9, 2013.

Kidney Function and Disease

Your kidneys filter extra water and wastes out of your blood and make *urine*. They also help control your blood pressure and make hormones that your body needs to stay healthy.

If your kidneys don't work properly, harmful waste products can build up in your body and cause serious health problems.

UP TO 30% OF PEOPLE LIVING WITH HIV HAVE ABNORMAL KIDNEY FUNCTION. UNTREATED KIDNEY PROBLEMS CAN BE FATAL.

THE SIDE EFFECTS OF HIV MEDICATION CAN CAUSE KIDNEY DISEASE. WORK CLOSELY WITH HEALTHCARE PROVIDERS TO ENSURE YOUR KIDNEY'S HEALTH.

HIV CAN DAMAGE YOUR KIDNEYS; BUT THIS IS EXTREMELY UNCOMMON IN PEOPLE LIVING WITH HIV WHO HAVE A SUPPRESSED VIRAL LOAD.

Figure 35.2. *Kidney Disease*

Kidney disease (also known as "renal disease") is an important complication of HIV infection. Up to 30 percent of people living with HIV have abnormal kidney function, which can lead to end-stage renal disease (ESRD), the complete or almost complete failure of the kidneys to work. This can require dialysis or a kidney transplant. Untreated kidney problems can be fatal.

Are you at risk?

If you have HIV, you are more likely to develop kidney disease if you:

• Are African American

• Have *diabetes*

- Have high blood pressure

- Are older

- Have a lower *CD4 count* (below 200 cells/mm³)

- Have a higher *viral load*

- Have *Hepatitis B* or *Hepatitis C*

Signs and Symptoms

Unfortunately, early kidney disease has no symptoms. If your kidneys are not working properly, they may suffer serious damage before you begin experiencing problems. That's why it's so important for your healthcare provider to test your kidney function on a regular basis.

A *urinalysis* is the most common test used to check kidney function. Your healthcare provider will order this test to check your urine for a number of things, including protein, *ketones,* and sugar. Protein in your urine is a sign that your kidneys are not working the way they should. Ketones and sugar in your urine are markers for diabetes—a major cause of kidney disease.

What role does HIV play in kidney disease?

Kidney disease is common in people living with HIV/AIDS—up to 30% have abnormal kidney function. HIV can affect your kidneys in many different ways, but the most common are HIV-associated nephropathy and nephrotoxicity.

HIV Associated Nephropathy (HIVAN)

HIVAN is damage to your kidneys caused by the *Human Immuno-deficiency Virus* (HIV) itself. African American men with HIV/AIDS seem to be most at risk for developing HIVAN. It is most common in patients with CD4 counts less than 200 cells/mm³, but it can occur at any CD4 count.

HIVAN is extremely uncommon in individuals with HIV who have a suppressed viral load (a low amount of HIV in their blood). There-fore, if you have HIVAN, it is very important to be started on *antiret-roviral therapy* (ART) at the earliest sign of kidney problems—and to stay on it—no matter what your CD4 count is. Research shows that people who have HIVAN can stay healthy and live longer by staying on ART.

Nephrotoxicity

"Nephrotoxicity" is a term that means "toxicity or injury to the kidneys." For people living with HIV/AIDS, nephrotoxicity can be an adverse side effect of certain HIV medications, including *protease inhibitors* and *nucleoside reverse transcriptase inhibitors* (NRTIs— commonly called "nukes").

Your kidneys clear many medications from your body, so if your kidneys aren't working properly, your healthcare provider may need to adjust the HIV meds that you are taking. Sometimes that means changing which HIV meds you take; other times it means changing your dosage. Work with your healthcare provider to find a treatment regimen that works for you.

HIV Treatment and Kidney Disease

Thanks to scientific advances in effective ART, people with HIV are living longer. But as people with HIV live longer, kidney problems may increase. While widespread access to and earlier initiation of ART has led to a decrease in HIVAN, other causes of kidney disease persist and, in some cases, are on the rise.

For example, in the U.S., people who are infected with HIV are three times more likely to develop hypertension (high blood pressure) and are four times more likely to develop diabetes than uninfected individuals. Both hypertension and diabetes are common causes of end-stage renal disease.

In addition, about 25% of people living with HIV in the United States are co-infected with hepatitis C virus (HCV), an inflammation of the liver that causes a chronic infection. HCV is associated with several types of kidney disease.

People living with HIV can also develop kidney disease caused by side effects of medication, including some antiretroviral (ARV) medications, as noted above.

For these reasons, it is very important to work closely with your healthcare provider to monitor your HIV treatment and ensure your kidneys stay healthy.

Part Six

Living with HIV Infection

Chapter 36

Coping with an HIV/AIDS Diagnosis

Coping with an HIV/AIDS Diagnosis

Your next steps

Finding out that you have HIV can be scary and overwhelming. If you feel overwhelmed, try to remember that you can get help and that these feelings will get better with time.

Testing positive for HIV is a serious matter but one that you *can* deal with. This chapter will take you through the steps you need to take to protect your health:

- Understand your diagnosis

- Find support

- Work with your doctor

- Monitor your health

- Be aware of possible complications

- Protect others

Text in this chapter is excerpted from "Getting an HIV Diagnosis – Your Next Steps: Entire Lesson," U.S. Department of Veterans Affairs (VA), September 27, 2015.

- Consider treatment
- Move forward with your life

There are some things that you should know about HIV that may ease some of the stress or confusion you are feeling.

Remember:

- You are not alone. Many people are living with HIV, even if you don't know that they are.
- HIV does not equal death: Having HIV does not mean that you are going to die of it. Most people with HIV can live long heal thy lives if they get medical treatment and take care of themselves.
- A diagnosis of HIV does not automatically mean that you have AIDS.
- Don't freeze: Learning how to live with HIV and getting in touch with a health care team that knows how to manage HIV will help you to feel better and get on with your life.

Understand your diagnosis

When your medical provider tells you that you are HIV positive, it means that you have been infected with the Human Immunodeficiency Virus (HIV). However, the HIV test does not tell you if you have AIDS or how long you have been infected or how sick you might be.

Soon after your diagnosis, your provider will run other tests to determine your overall health, and the condition of your immune system.

Learn about HIV and AIDS

The more you know about HIV and how to treat it, the less confused and anxious you will be about your diagnosis. The more you learn, the better you will be at making decisions about your health. You don't have to learn it all at once, however. It is important to go at a pace you are comfortable with. This may be fast, slow, or in-between. You may want to go over the same information several times.

There are many ways to learn about HIV and AIDS:

- Read information online. Remember that there is a lot of internet information that can be inaccurate or misleading- be sure to look for reputable sites whose content can be trusted. Check out government or nonprofit educational organizations that deal with HIV and AIDS issues.

- Use your local library: The most current information will be in the library's collection of newspapers and magazines.

- Check with your local medical center to see if there's an on-site library where you can find patient materials on HIV and AIDS.

Find support

Talk with others who have been diagnosed with HIV and AIDS. Ask your doctors if they know of any support groups. Or you can go online, where you can find message boards and chat rooms. Always discuss what you learn from these sources with your provider. The information may not be accurate; and even if it is, it may not be right for your particular situation.

Finding support means finding people who are willing to help you through the emotional and physical issues you are going to face. If you let the right people in your life know that you are HIV positive, they can:

- offer you support and understanding;

- provide you with assistance, such as running errands and helping with child care, doctor visits, and work;

- learn from you how HIV is spread and work with you to prevent the virus from spreading.

Telling others

Deciding to tell others that you are HIV positive is an important personal choice. It can make a big difference in how you cope with the disease. It can also affect your relationships with people.

If you decide to share information about your diagnosis, it is best to tell people you trust or people who are directly affected. These include:

- family members;

- people you spend a lot of time with, such as good friends; and

- all your health care providers, such as doctors, nurses, and dentists.

You don't have to tell everyone about your HIV status right away. You might want to talk with a counselor or social worker first.

Join a support group

Some VA Medical Centers have a support group for veterans with HIV, so you may want to ask your provider if your center has one that you can join for support and for more information about living with HIV.

Joining a group of people who are facing the same challenges you are facing can have important benefits. These include feeling better about yourself, finding a new life focus, making new friendships, improving your mood, and better understanding your needs and those of your family. People in support groups often help each other deal with common experiences associated with being HIV positive.

Support groups are especially helpful if you live alone or don't have family and friends nearby.

There are different types of support groups, from hotlines to face-to-face encounter groups. Here are descriptions of some of the most popular types, and suggestions about how to find them.

Hotlines

Find a hotline in your area by talking to a social worker in your hospital. Or look in the telephone book, in the yellow pages under "Social Service Organizations." Ask the hotline to "match" you with another person with a history like yours. He or she can give you practical advice and emotional support over the telephone.

Professional help

Veterans with HIV can get referrals to mental health professionals, such as psychologists, nurse therapists, clinical social workers, or psychiatrists. You also will likely have a social worker who is part of the HIV clinic where you will receive care. You can also get help for drug abuse.

Self-help organizations

Self-help groups enable people to share experiences and pool their knowledge to help each other and themselves. They are run by members, not by professionals (though professionals are involved). Because members face similar challenges, they feel an instant sense of community. These groups are volunteer, nonprofit organizations, with no fees (though sometimes there are small dues).

Work with your provider

HIV is the virus that causes AIDS. If ignored, it can lead to illness and death. This is why it is so important to get medical care if you find out you have HIV. Do not be afraid to seek a doctor or nurse practitioner with experience in treating HIV-infected patients—he or she can help you to stay well. Most doctors who treat HIV are specialists in infectious disease. They work with a team of other health professionals who focus on HIV as a chronic, or lifelong, disease.

Treatments for HIV are not perfect (no medicine is), but are very effective for most people. They also work very well to decrease the chance that you will transmit HIV to sex partners (for pregnant women they also decrease the risk of infecting the baby). A doctor or other health care provider can explain the best options for you.

If you work with your health care provider in planning your care, you can deal with the disease in a way that is best for you.

Before appointments

Start with a list or notebook. Prepare for your appointment with your doctor by writing down:

- any questions that you have
- any symptoms or problems you want to tell the doctor about (include symptoms such as poor sleep, trouble concentrating, feeling tired)
- a list of the medications that you are taking (include herbs and vitamins), including a list of any HIV medications you have taken in the past and any HIV-related problems you have had when taking them.
- upcoming tests or new information you've heard about
- changes in your living situation, such as a job change

That way you won't forget anything during the appointment.

You may want to ask a friend or family member to come with you and take notes. It can be difficult for you to take notes and pay attention to what your doctor is saying at the same time.

461

During appointments

Go over your lab work, and keep track of your results. If your doctor wants you to have some medical tests, make sure you understand what the test is for and what your doctor will do with the results. If you don't understand what your doctor is saying, ask the doctor to explain it in everyday terms.

If you feel your doctor has forgotten something during the appointment, it is better to ask about it than to leave wondering whether something was supposed to happen that didn't. It's your right to ask questions of your doctor. You also have a legal right to see your medical records. After all, it's your body.

Be honest. Your doctor isn't there to judge you, but to make decisions based on your particular circumstances. Tell your doctor about your sexual or drug use history. These behaviors can put you at risk of getting other sexually transmitted diseases as well as hepatitis. If your body is fighting off these other diseases, it will not be able to fight off HIV as effectively. You may get sicker, faster.

> If you have sex with someone of the same sex or someone other than your spouse, it's OK to tell your doctor. You cannot get kicked out of the medical center or lose your benefits if you have sex with someone of your same sex, or someone other than your spouse.

Monitor your health

Once you have been diagnosed with HIV, you need to pay closer attention to your health than you did before.

You can keep track of your immune system in two ways. First, have regular lab tests done. Lab tests often can show signs of illness before you have any noticeable symptoms.

Second, listen to what your body is telling you, and be on the alert for signs that something isn't right. Note any change in your health—good or bad. And don't be afraid to call a doctor.

Have regular lab tests

Your doctor will use laboratory tests to check your health. Some of these tests will be done soon after you learn you are HIV positive.

The lab tests look at several things:

- how well your immune system is functioning
- how rapidly HIV is progressing
- certain basic body functions (tests look at your kidneys, liver, cholesterol, and blood cells)
- whether you have other diseases that are associated with HIV

For your first few doctor visits, be prepared to have a lot of blood drawn. Don't worry. You are not going to have so much blood drawn at every appointment.

Be aware of possible complications

By weakening your immune system, HIV can leave you vulnerable to certain cancers and infections. These infections are called "opportunistic" because they take the opportunity to attack you when your immune system is weak.

In addition, HIV is recognized to be an inflammatory disease that affects many parts of the body, not just the immune system. That means that HIV can affect organs like the brain, kidneys, liver and heart and may increase the risk of some cancers.

Certain changes can happen to HIV-positive people who are living longer and taking HIV medicines. Some people who were treated with older HIV medicines have experienced visible changes in body shape and appearance. Sometimes these changes can raise the risk of heart disease and diabetes.

Know when to call a medical provider

You don't need to panic every time you have a headache or get a runny nose. But if a symptom is concerning you or is not going away, it is always best to have a provider check it out even if it doesn't feel like a big deal. The earlier you see a provider when you have unusual symptoms, the better off you are likely to be.

Protect others

Once you have HIV, you can give the virus to others by having unprotected sex or by sharing needles (or, if you are pregnant and not on HIV medications, you can pass HIV to the baby during pregnancy, delivery or by breast-feeding). This is true even if you are feeling

The following symptoms may or may not be serious, but don't wait until your next appointment before calling a doctor if you are experiencing them.

Breathing problems:

- persistent cough
- wheezing or noisy breathing
- sharp pain when breathing
- difficulty catching your breath

Skin problems:

- Appearance of brownish, purple or pink blotches on the skin
- Onset of rash—especially important if you are taking medication

Eye or vision problems:

- blurring, wavy lines, sudden blind spots
- eye pain
- sensitivity to light

Aches and pains:

- numbness, tingling, or pain in hands and feet
- headache, especially when accompanied by a fever
- stiffness in neck
- severe or persistent cough
- persistent cramps
- pain in lower abdomen, often during sex (women in particular)

Other symptoms:

- mental changes—confusion, disorientation, loss of memory or balance
- appearance of swollen lymph nodes, especially when larger on one side of the body
- diarrhea—when severe, accompanied by fever, or lasting more than 3 days
- weight loss
- high or persistent fever
- fatigue
- frequent urination

perfectly fine. Using condoms and clean needles can prevent infecting other people. It can also protect you from getting other sexually transmitted diseases. Taking HIV medications that suppress HIV also greatly reduces the likelihood of transmitting HIV infection to another person.

Sometimes it can be difficult to explain that you have HIV to people you have had sex with or shared needles with in the past. However, it is important that they know so that they can decide whether to get tested. If you need help telling people that you may have exposed them to HIV, many city or county health departments will tell them for you, without using your name. Ask your provider about this service.

> Before telling your partner that you have HIV, take some time alone to think about how you want to bring up the subject.
>
> - Decide when and where would be the best time and place to have a conversation. Choose a time when you expect that you will both be comfortable, rested, and as relaxed as possible.
> - Think about how your partner may react to stressful situations. If there is a history of violence in your relationship, consider your safety first and plan the situation with a case manager or counselor.

Consider treatment

Whether or not to start treatment for HIV is a decision that each person must make with his or her providers. HIV medication (known as antiretrovirals) is recommended for all HIV infected people, and more urgently for anyone who has evidence of immune suppression (a CD4+ cell count of less than 350–500) or an AIDS diagnosis (an infection or cancer associated with HIV). It also is more urgently recommended for anyone who has a sex partner who is not infected with HIV, and for women who may become pregnant. Current guidelines recommend starting HIV treatment because HIV is known to affect many parts of the body even early on in infection, and some damage caused by HIV can be irreversible.

In general, you and your provider will need to consider:

- how healthy your immune system is (this is usually measured by your CD4 count)

- whether or not you have AIDS

- whether you can stick to a treatment plan

- what your other medical problems are

- whether you have sex partners who may be at risk of becoming infected

- if you are a woman, whether you plan to become pregnant

Move forward with your life

Life does not end with a diagnosis of HIV. In fact, with proper treatment, people with HIV can live long healthy lives. HIV can be a manageable chronic disease, like diabetes or heart disease. Taking care of your overall health can help you deal with HIV:

- Get regular medical and dental checkups

- Eat a healthy diet

- Exercise regularly

- Avoid smoking and recreational drug use

- Go easy on alcohol

- Use condoms during sex (it can protect others from getting HIV, and can protect you from other sexually transmitted diseases)

Chapter 37

Staying Healthy with HIV/AIDS

Chapter Contents

Section 37.1

HIV and Nutrition

Text in this section is excerpted from "Diet and Nutrition and
HIV: Entire Lesson," U.S. Department of Veterans Affairs (VA),
September 17, 2015.

Why is nutrition important?

Nutrition is important for everyone because food gives our bodies
the nutrients they need to stay healthy, grow, and work properly.
Foods are made up of six classes of nutrients, each with its own special
role in the body:

- Protein builds muscles and a strong immune system.

- Carbohydrates (including vegetables, fruits, grains) give you
  energy.

- Fat gives you extra energy.

- Vitamins regulate body processes.

- Minerals regulate body processes and also make up body tissues.

- Water gives cells shape and acts as a medium where body processes can occur.

Having good nutrition means eating the right types of foods in the
right amounts so you get these important nutrients.

Do I need a special diet?

There are no special diets, or particular foods, that will boost your
immune system. But there are things you can do to keep your immunity up.

When you are infected with HIV, your immune system has to
work very hard to fight off infections—and this takes energy (measured in calories). This means you may need to eat more food than
you used to.

If you are underweight—or you have advanced HIV disease, high viral loads, or opportunistic infections—you should include more protein as well as extra calories (in the form of carbohydrates and fats). You'll find tips for doing this in the next section.

If you are overweight, keep in mind, you may need to eat more food to meet your extra needs.

How do I keep from losing weight?

Weight loss can be a common problem for people with relatively advanced stages of HIV infection, and it should be taken very seriously. It usually improves with effective antiretroviral therapy (ART). Losing weight can be dangerous because it makes it harder for your body to fight infections and to get well after you're sick.

People with HIV often do not eat enough because:

- HIV may reduce your appetite, make food taste bad, and prevent the body from absorbing food in the right way. Some HIV medicines may also cause these symptoms (if this is so, tell your HIV specialist—you may be able to change to medications that do not have these side effects).

- symptoms like a sore mouth, nausea, and vomiting make it difficult to eat

- fatigue from HIV or medicines may make it hard to prepare food and eat regularly

To keep your weight up, you will need to take in more protein and calories. What follows are ways to do that.

To add protein to your diet

Protein-rich foods include meats, fish, beans, dairy products, and nuts. To boost the protein in your meals:

- Spread nut butter on toast, crackers, fruit, or vegetables.
- Add cottage cheese to fruit and tomatoes.
- Add canned tuna to casseroles and salads.
- Add shredded cheese to sauces, soups, omelets, baked potatoes, and steamed vegetables.
- Eat yogurt on your cereal or fruit.
- Eat hard-boiled (hard-cooked) eggs. Use them in egg-salad sandwiches or slice and dice them for tossed salads.

- Add diced or chopped meats to soups, salads, and sauces.
- Add dried milk powder or egg white powder to foods (like scrambled eggs, casseroles, and milkshakes).

To add calories to your diet

The best way to increase calories is to add carbohydrates and some extra fat to your meals.

Carbohydrates include both starches and simple sugars. Starches are in:

- breads, muffins, biscuits, crackers
- oatmeal and cold cereals
- pasta
- potatoes
- rice
- Simple sugars are in:
- fresh or dried fruit (raisins, dates, apricots, etc)
- jelly, honey, and maple syrup added to cereal, pancakes, and waffles

Fats are more concentrated sources of calories. Add moderate amounts of the following to your meals:

- butter, margarine, sour cream, cream cheese, peanut butter
- gravy, sour cream, cream cheese, grated cheese
- avocados, olives, salad dressing

How can I maintain my appetite?

When you become ill, you often lose your appetite. This can lead to weight loss, which can make it harder for your body to fight infection. Here are some tips for increasing your appetite:

- Try a little exercise, like walking or doing yoga. This can often stimulate your appetite and make you feel like eating more.
- Eat smaller meals more often. For instance, try to snack between meals.
- Eat whenever your appetite is good.

- Avoid drinking too much right before or during meals. This can make you feel full.

- Avoid carbonated (fizzy) drinks and foods such as cabbage, broccoli, and beans. These foods and drinks can create gas in your stomach and make you feel full and bloated.

- Eat with your family or friends.

- Choose your favorite foods, and make meals as attractive to you as possible. Try to eat in a pleasant location.

How much water do I need?

Drinking enough liquids is very important when you have HIV. Fluids transport the nutrients you need through your body.

Extra water can:

- reduce the side effects of medications

- help flush out the medicines that have already been used by your body

- help you avoid dehydration (fluid loss), dry mouth, and constipation

- make you feel less tired

Many of us don't drink enough water every day. You should be getting at least 8-10 glasses of water (or other fluids, such as juices or soups) a day.

Here are some tips on getting the extra fluids you need:

- Drink more water than usual. Try other fluids, too, like Gatorade or Sprite.

- Avoid colas, coffee, tea, and cocoa. These may contain caffeine and can actually dehydrate you. Read the labels on drinks to see if they have caffeine in them.

- Avoid alcohol.

- Begin and end each day by drinking a glass of water.

- Suck on ice cubes and popsicles.

Note: If you have diarrhea or are vomiting, you will lose a lot of fluids and will need to drink more than usual.

Do I need supplements?

Our bodies need vitamins and minerals, in small amounts, to keep our cells working properly. They are essential to our staying healthy. People with HIV need extra vitamins and minerals to help repair and heal cells that have been damaged.

Even though vitamins and minerals are present in many foods, your health care provider may recommend a vitamin and mineral supplement (a pill or other form of concentrated vitamins and minerals). While vitamin and mineral supplements can be useful, they can't replace eating a healthy diet.

If you are taking a supplement, here are some things to remember:

- Always take vitamin pills on a full stomach. Take them regularly.

- Some vitamins and minerals, if taken in high doses, can be harmful. Talk with your health care provider before taking high doses of any supplement.

- Some minerals (like calcium, magnesium, and iron) may interfere with certain HIV medicines—talk with your health care provider about whether or when to take these minerals.

What should I know about food safety?

Paying attention to food and water safety is important when you have HIV, because your immune system is already weakened and working hard to fight off infections.

If food is not handled or prepared in a safe way, germs from the food can be passed on to you. These germs can make you sick.

You need to handle and cook food properly to keep those germs from getting to you.

Here are some food safety guidelines:

- Keep everything clean! Clean your counters and utensils often.

- Wash your hands with soap and warm water before and after preparing and eating food.

- Check expiration dates on food packaging. Do not eat foods that have a past expiration date.

- Rinse all fresh fruits and vegetables with clean water.

- Thaw frozen meats and other frozen foods in the refrigerator or in a microwave. Never thaw foods at room temperature. Germs that grow at room temperature can make you very sick.

Table 37.1. Vitamins and minerals that affect the immune system

Name	What It Does	Where to Get It	About Supplements
Vitamin A and beta-carotene	Keeps skin, lungs, and stomach healthy.	liver, whole eggs, milk, dark green, yellow, orange, and red vegetables and fruit (like spinach, pumpkin, green peppers, squash, carrots, papaya, and mangoes). Also found in orange and yellow sweet potatoes	It's best to get vitamin A from food. Vitamin A supplements are toxic in high doses. Supplements of beta-carotene (the form of vitamin A in fruits and vegetables) have been shown to increase cancer risk in smokers.
Vitamin B-group (B-1, B-2, B-6, B-12, Folate)	Keeps the immune and nervous system healthy.	white beans, potatoes, meat, fish, chicken, watermelon, grains, nuts, avocados, broccoli, and green leafy vegetables	
Vitamin C	Helps protect the body from infection and aids in recovery.	citrus fruits (like oranges, grapefruit, and lemons), tomatoes, and potatoes	
Vitamin E	Protects cells and helps fight off infection.	green leafy vegetables, vegetable oils, and peanuts	Limit to 400 IU per day.
Iron	Not having enough iron can cause anemia.	green leafy vegetables, whole grain breads and pastas, dried fruit, beans, red meat, chicken, liver, fish, and eggs	Limit to 45 mg per day unless otherwise instructed by your doctor. Iron may be a problem for people with HIV because it can increase the activity of some bacteria. Supplements that do not contain iron may be better. Ask your doctor.
Selenium	Important for the immune system.	whole grains, meat, fish, poultry, eggs, peanut butter, and nuts	Limit to 400 mcg per day.
Zinc	Important for the immune system.	meat, fish, poultry, beans, peanuts, and milk and dairy products	Limit to 40 mg per day.

- Clean all cutting boards and knives (especially those that touch chicken and meat) with soap and hot water before using them again.

- Make sure you cook all meat, fish, and poultry "well-done." You might want to buy a meat thermometer to help you know for sure that it is done. Put the thermometer in the thickest part of the meat and not touching a bone. Cook the meat until it reaches 165 to 212 degrees Fahrenheit on your thermometer.

- Do not eat raw, soft-boiled, or "over easy" eggs, or Caesar salads with raw egg in the dressing.

- Do not eat sushi, raw seafood, or raw meats, or unpasteurized milk or dairy products.

- Keep your refrigerator cold, set no higher than 40 degrees. Your freezer should be at 0 degrees.

- Refrigerate leftovers at temperatures below 40 degrees F. Do not eat leftovers that have been sitting in the refrigerator for more than 3 days.

- Keep hot items heated to over 140 degrees F, and completely reheat leftovers before eating.

- Throw away any foods (like fruit, vegetables, and cheese) that you think might be old. If food has a moldy or rotten spot, throw it out. When in doubt, throw it out.

- Some germs are spread through tap water. If your public water supply isn't totally pure, drink bottled water.

Can diet help ease side effects and symptoms?

Many symptoms of HIV, as well as the side effects caused by HIV medicines, can be helped by using (or avoiding) certain types of foods and drinks.

Below are some tips for dealing with common problems people with HIV face.

Nausea

- Try the BRATT Diet (Bananas, Rice, Applesauce, Tea, and Toast).

- Try some ginger—in tea, ginger ale, or ginger snaps.

- Don't drink liquids at the same time you eat your meals.

- Eat something small, like crackers, before getting out of bed.

- Keep something in your stomach; eat a small snack every 1-2 hours.

- Avoid foods like:

  - Fatty, greasy, or fried foods

  - Very sweet foods (candy, cookies, or cake)

  - Spicy foods

  - Foods with strong odors

Mouth and swallowing problems

- Avoid hard or crunchy foods such as raw vegetables.

- Try eating cooked vegetables and soft fruits (like bananas and pears).

- Avoid very hot foods and beverages. Cold and room temperature foods will be more comfortable to your mouth.

- Do not eat spicy foods. They can sting your mouth.

- Try soft foods like mashed potatoes, yogurt, and oatmeal.

- Also try scrambled eggs, cottage cheese, macaroni and cheese, and canned fruits.

- Rinse your mouth with water. This can moisten your mouth, remove bits of food, and make food taste better to you.

- Stay away from oranges, grapefruit, and tomatoes. They have a lot of acid and can sting your mouth.

Diarrhea

- Try the BRATT Diet (Bananas, Rice, Applesauce, Tea, and Toast).

- Keep your body's fluids up (hydrated) with water, Gatorade, or other fluids (those that don't have caffeine).

- Limit sodas and other sugary drinks.

- Avoid greasy and spicy foods.

- Avoid milk and other dairy products.

- Eat small meals and snacks every hour or 2.

- Try taking Glutamine protein powder to help repair the intestinal lining.

Points to remember

You may feel that many things are out of your control if you have HIV. But you can control what you eat and drink, and how much. Good nutrition is an important part of your plan to stay well.

- Eating right can make your body and your immune system stronger.

- When you are HIV-positive, you may need to eat more. Be sure to eat a diet that is high in proteins and calories.

- Exercise can stimulate your appetite and make you feel like eating more.

- Drink plenty of liquids to help your body deal with any medications you are taking. If you are vomiting or have diarrhea, you will need to drink more than usual.

- Practice food safety. Keep your kitchen clean, wash foods, and be careful about food preparation and storage. If your tap water isn't pure, drink bottled water.

- You can use certain foods and beverages to help you deal with symptoms and side effects.

- Before taking vitamin and mineral supplements, check with your health care provider.

Remember, there is no one "right" way to eat. Eating well means getting the right amount of nutrients for your particular needs. Your health care provider can refer you to a dietitian or nutritionist who can help design a good diet for you.

Section 37.2

HIV and Exercise

This section includes excerpts from "Exercise," AIDS.gov,
June 1, 2012; and text from "Exercise and HIV: Entire Lesson," U.S.
Department of Veterans Affairs (VA), September 27, 2015.

Get Up And Get Moving

Regular physical activity has lots of benefits. It increases your
physical strength and endurance, and it can help prevent problems
with your *metabolism* (like high cholesterol, obesity, and diabetes)
that often affect people who don't exercise or maintain a healthy
weight.

Exercise is good for everyone—and the guidelines for physical activity apply, regardless of your HIV status. The U.S. Surgeon General's
report on exercise suggests 30–45 minutes a day of brisk walking,
bicycling, or working around the house. This amount of exercise can
reduce your risks of developing coronary heart disease, high blood
pressure, colon cancer, and diabetes.

If you are living with HIV/AIDS, however, consult your healthcare
provider before you begin an exercise routine. You'll want to develop
a exercise regimen that is appropriate for you and reflects your HIV
care plan. You will also want to maintain a healthy weight and healthy
eating habits.

You also need to talk to your provider before you start an exercise
program if you have any other health problems, especially cardiovascular (heart disease), pulmonary (asthma), or joint problems (arthritis
or joint replacement).

Overview

Being HIV positive is no different from being HIV negative
when it comes to exercise. Regular exercise is part of a healthy
lifestyle.

Early in the AIDS epidemic, HIV-positive persons had many health problems. They often had trouble keeping their normal weight and muscle mass. People wasted away and died.

Now that anti-HIV drugs have become available, many long-term survivors have stronger immune systems. Newly infected persons have hope for a normal lifespan, if they take care of their bodies. And that includes getting regular exercise.

Benefits of exercise

Following are some of the benefits of exercise:

- Maintains or builds muscle mass
- Reduces cholesterol and triglyceride levels (less risk of heart disease)
- Increases energy
- Regulates bowel function
- Strengthens bones (less risk of osteoporosis)
- Improves blood circulation
- Increases lung capacity
- Helps with sound, restful sleep
- Lowers stress
- Improves appetite

Before starting

Before starting an exercise program, talk to your doctor about what you have done in the past for exercise; mention any problems that you had. Consider your current health status and other medical conditions that may affect the type of exercise you can do.

Make sure you can set aside time for your exercise program. Experts recommend about 150 minutes (2-1/2 hours) of moderately vigorous exercise per week. That means about 30 minutes of brisk walking, bicycling, or working around the house, 5 days a week. This amount of exercise can reduce risks of developing coronary heart disease, high blood pressure, colon cancer, and diabetes.

If this amount of time seems too much, consider starting with 3 times a week. The important thing is consistency. This is an ongoing program and you will not benefit without consistency.

Types of exercise

Two types of exercise are resistance training and aerobic exercise. Resistance training—sometimes called strength training—helps to build muscle mass. Aerobic exercise is important because it strengthens your lungs and your heart.

Resistance training

Resistance or strength training is important for people with HIV because it can help offset the loss of muscle sometimes caused by the disease. This form of exercise involves exertion of force by moving (pushing or pulling) objects of weight. They can be barbells, dumbbells, or machines in gyms. You can also use safe, common household objects such as plastic milk containers filled with water or sand, or you can use your own body weight in exercises such as push-ups or pull-ups. The purpose of resistance training is to build muscle mass.

Use the correct amount of weight for the exercise you are performing. You should not feel pain during the exercise. When starting a resistance training program, you should feel a little sore for a day or two, but not enough to limit your regular activities. If you do feel very sore, you have used too much weight or have done too many repetitions. Rest an extra day and start again using less weight.

Aerobic exercise

Aerobic exercise strengthens your lungs and heart. Walking, jogging, running, swimming, hiking, and cycling are forms of this exercise.

This movement increases the rate and depth of your breathing, which in turn increases how much blood and oxygen your heart pumps to your muscles. To achieve the maximum benefit of this kind of exercise, your heart rate should reach the target rate for at least 20 minutes. It may take you weeks to reach this level if you haven't been exercising much.

Designing a program

When beginning an exercise program, start slow and build. Start any exercise session with a warmup. This can be as short as a few stretches, if you are working out later in the day when your muscles and joints are already loose, or a short 10-minute stretch session if you are working out first thing in the morning, when your muscles and joints are still tight. Your warmup should not tire you out but invigorate you and decrease the risk of joint or muscle injury.

If you join a gym, ask about what comes with the membership. Many gyms offer a free evaluation, weighing and measuring you and asking what your goals are. Some gym memberships come with a free workout with a personal trainer and program to help you achieve your goals.

Finding a workout partner can be helpful for support and encouragement, and your workout partner can help with the last repetition of an exercise, which can help improve your strength.

A balanced exercise program is best. Starting with an aerobic exercise is a good warmup to a resistance training session. Remember that learning the correct form in a weight training program will lessen the chance of injury. Go at your own pace. You are not competing with anyone. Listen to your body. If it hurts, stop.

Exercise cautions

After an exercise session, you should feel a little tired. A little while later, however, you should have some energy.

Water – Drink it before, during, and after you exercise. When you feel thirsty you have already lost important fluids and electrolytes and may be dehydrated.

Eat well – Exercising tears down muscle in order to build it up stronger. You need nutrition to provide the raw materials to rebuild your muscles.

Sleep – While you sleep, your body is rebuilding.

Listen to your body – It will tell you to slow down or speed up.

If you are sick or have a cold, take a break. Your body will thank you.

Section 37.3

Mental Health

Text in this section is excerpted from "Mental Health," AIDS.gov,
March 7, 2014.

PEOPLE LIVING WITH HIV ARE AT INCREASED RISK
FOR DEVELOPING MENTAL HEALTH CONDITIONS.
THESE CONDITIONS ARE TREATABLE AND, WITH
HELP, YOU CAN RECOVER.

POSITIVE MENTAL HEALTH
IS AN IMPORTANT PART OF STAYING
HEALTHY WHEN LIVING WITH HIV.

DISCUSS YOUR MENTAL HEALTH WITH YOUR
HEALTHCARE TEAM THROUGHOUT YOUR HIV
TREATMENT. BE OPEN AND HONEST ABOUT
ANY CHANGES IN THE WAY YOU ARE
THINKING OR FEELING.

Figure 37.1. *Mental Health and HIV*

What Is Mental Health?

"Mental health" refers to your emotional, psychological, and social
well-being. It is an important part of staying healthy when living with
HIV. Your mental health affects how you think, feel, and act. It also
helps determine how you handle stress, relate to others, and make
choices.

Positive mental health allows you to:

- realize your full potential

- cope with the stresses of life

- work productively

- make meaningful contributions to your community

Positive mental health is important for all individuals at every
stage of life, and there are some particular considerations for people
living with HIV.

Why Is Positive Mental Health Important for People Living With HIV?

Your mental health is just as important as your physical health. When you have positive mental health, you generally are able to:

- function better at work, at school, and in relationships.

- cope more effectively with life's difficulties, such as the death of a loved one, ending a relationship, job stress, health issues, and family or financial problems.

- take better care of yourself physically.

- provide better care for your children or other family members.

But mental health problems can affect the way you think, feel, and behave, and can change how well you function at work and at home. If you are living with HIV, mental health problems can affect your physical health by:

- making it harder for you to take all your HIV medicines on time.

- making it harder for you to keep your health appointments or take advantage of your support network.

- interfering with your healthy behaviors, such as getting enough sleep and exercise and avoiding risk behaviors such as having unprotected sex.

- impairing your ability to cope with the stresses of daily life.

Mental health problems are very common among all Americans, not just those living with HIV. In fact, in 2012, about:

- One in five American adults experienced a diagnosable mental illness.

- Nearly one in 10 young people experienced a period of major depression.

- Four percent of American adults lived with a serious mental illness, such as schizophrenia, bipolar disorder, or major depression.

As a person living with HIV, it is important for you to be aware that you have an increased risk for developing mood, anxiety, and cognitive disorders. **These conditions are treatable. People who experience mental health problems can get better and**

many recover completely. You can better manage your overall health and well-being if you know how having HIV can affect your mental health and what resources are available to help you if you need it.

What Causes Mental Health Problems?

Mental health problems are not caused by "personal weakness." Most are caused by a combination of family history and environmental, biological, and *psychosocial* factors.

Common factors include:

- a family history of mental health problems and other genetic factors.

- stressful life events or psychosocial reasons, including trauma, sexual and physical abuse, neglect, and illness.

- psychological factors such as unhealthy thinking patterns and trouble managing feelings.

In addition, some forms of stress can contribute to mental health problems for people living with HIV, including:

- having trouble getting the services you need.

- experiencing a loss of social support, resulting in isolation.

- experiencing a loss of employment or worries about whether you will be able to perform your work as you did before.

- having to tell others you are HIV-positive.

- managing your HIV medicines.

- going through changes in your physical appearance or abilities due to HIV/AIDS.

- dealing with loss, including the loss of relationships or even death.

- facing the stigma and discrimination associated with HIV/AIDS.

Starting *antiretroviral therapy* also can affect your mental health in different ways. Sometimes, it can relieve your anxiety because knowing that you are taking care of yourself can give you a sense of security. However, it can also increase your emotions because coping with the reality of living with HIV can be complicated. In addition, antiretroviral medications may cause a variety of symptoms, including depression, anxiety, and sleep disturbance, and may make some mental health issues worse.

The HIV virus itself also can contribute to mental health problems. Some *opportunistic infections* (which occur when your immune system is damaged by HIV) can affect your nervous system and lead to changes in your behavior and functioning. Other disorders, such as mild cognitive changes or more severe cognitive conditions, such as dementia, are associated with advanced HIV disease.

For these reasons, it is important to talk to your healthcare provider about your mental health. A conversation about mental health should be part of your complete medical evaluation before starting antiretroviral medications. And you should continue to discuss your mental health with your healthcare team throughout treatment. Be open and honest with your provider about any changes in the way you are thinking, or how you are feeling about yourself and life in general. Also discuss any alcohol or substance use with your provider so that he or she can help connect you to treatment if necessary.

In addition, tell your healthcare provider about any over-the-counter or prescribed medications you may be taking, including any psychiatric medications, because some of these drugs may interact with antiretroviral medications.

How Do I Know If Something Is Wrong and How Can I Find Help?

Almost everyone faces mental health challenges at some point. This is true for all individuals, not just those living with HIV. It's normal to experience some degree of worrying or fear, particularly after you have been diagnosed with HIV, or when you are experiencing changes in your health, or adjusting to antiretroviral medications. A support network can help you cope during these tough times. But when your mental health symptoms begin to affect your ability to cope and carry out typical functions in your life, it's important to get help.

So how do you know when it's time to get help? Sometimes, you can notice a change in yourself—and, sometimes, the people around you are the ones who notice. Some changes that might be significant include:

- No longer finding enjoyment in activities which usually make you happy

- Withdrawing from social interaction

- Change in memory functioning

- Sleeping too much—or being unable to sleep
- Feeling "sad" or "empty" much of the time
- Feeling guilty
- Feeling tired all the time
- Experiencing sudden and repeated attacks of fear known as "panic attacks"
- Having racing thoughts
- Loss of sexual interest
- Worrying what others are thinking about you
- Hearing voices in your head
- Feelings of wanting to hurt yourself or others
- Intense anger or rage toward others

Depression

Depression is a serious medical illness. It's more than just a feeling of being "down in the dumps" or "blue" for a few days. Depression is a disorder of the brain. There are a variety of causes, including genetic, environmental, psychological, and biochemical factors. Depression can range from mild to severe, and symptoms can include many of feelings or behaviors listed above.

HIV does not directly cause depression. But depression is one of the most common mental health conditions experienced by people living with HIV, just as it is by the general population. Only a mental health provider can accurately diagnose and treat depression. Recovery from depression takes time but treatments are effective.

Other Mental Health Conditions

Other mental health conditions include anxiety disorders, mood disorders, and personality disorders.

Remember: a mental health disorder may be a pre-existing condition that already was a problem for a person before they had HIV; it may be first seen after an HIV diagnosis; or it may be directly or indirectly caused by the progression of the disease.

Get Help

If you feel that something might be different or "wrong," it's important to tell your doctor or other healthcare provider—including your nurse, case manager, or social worker—so that he or she can help you. Don't be embarrassed to talk about your feelings. Your feelings are important and valid and the members of your healthcare team should be concerned about you and respect you.

If what you are describing is pattern of behavior and feelings you have experienced over time, your healthcare provider may offer treatment or a referral to a mental health services provider. Mental health providers (psychologists, therapists, psychiatrists, social workers, or nurses) can use many forms of treatment, including medications and/ or "talk therapy."

Finding Treatment

One of the hardest parts of having mental health condition is that you may not feel like seeking treatment or going to your appointments once you schedule them. If you are feeling this way, consider asking a friend or family member to help you make and keep your appointments, and share these feelings with your mental health provider. When you follow through, your medical and mental health providers can help you feel better, and can improve your chances of successful HIV treatment. Also you can call 1-800-273-TALK (8255) if you need help in a crisis or are experiencing emotional distress.

Living with HIV can sometimes be overwhelming to deal with, but do not neglect your mental health. The most important thing to remember is that **you are not alone**; there are support systems in place to help you, including doctors, psychiatrists, family members, friends, support groups, and other services.

Section 37.4

Sex and Sexuality and HIV

Text in this section is excerpted from "Sex and Sexuality and HIV: Entire Lesson," U.S. Department of Veterans Affairs (VA), September 17, 2015.

Overview

If you just tested positive for HIV, you may not want to think about having sex. Some people who get HIV feel guilty or embarrassed. These are common reactions, especially if you got HIV through sex. Chances are, however, that you will want to have sex again. The good news is that there is no reason why you can't. People with HIV enjoy sex and fall in love, just like other people.

> You can have a good sex life, even if you have HIV.

If you are having a hard time dealing with negative feelings like anger or fear, you can get help. Talk to your doctor about support groups or counseling. Sex is a very tough topic for many people with HIV—you are not alone.

By reading this information, you are already taking a good first step toward a healthy sex life. Having good information will help you make good decisions.

Talking to your doctor

Your doctor or other members of your health care team may ask you about your sexual practices each time you go in for a checkup. It may feel embarrassing at first to be honest and open with your doctor. But he or she is trying to help you stay healthy.

Your doctor and staff will still give you care if you have had sex with someone of the same sex or someone other than your spouse. The is not there to judge you. It's OK to tell your doctor the truth. It will not affect your medical benefits. It will help your health care team take better care of you.

Make sure you set aside time to ask your doctor questions about safer sex, sexually transmitted diseases (STDs), re-infection, or any other questions you might have. If you feel that you need help dealing with your feelings, ask about support groups or counseling.

Many people with HIV ask their doctor or nurse to talk with them and their partners about HIV and how it is transmitted. They can answer technical questions and address the specifics of your situation. If you live with someone, he or she may have questions about everyday contact as well as sexual contact.

Telling your sexual partners

This may be one of the hardest things you have to do. But you need to tell your sexual partner that you are HIV positive, whether you have a primary partner such as a spouse or girlfriend or boyfriend, have more than one partner, or are single or casually dating.

What follows are tips for talking to your main partner, other partners, and former partners.

Talking to your main partner

If you are in a relationship, one of the first things you will probably think about after learning that you have HIV is telling your partner or partners. For some couples, a positive HIV test may have been expected. For others, the news will be a surprise that can bring up difficult issues.

Your partner may not be prepared to offer you support during a time when you need it. Your partner may be worrying about his or her own HIV status. On the other hand, if you think you may have contracted HIV from your partner, you are probably dealing with your own feelings.

If your partner is not already HIV positive, he or she should get an HIV test right away. Don't assume that the results will come back positive, even if you have been having unsafe sex or sharing needles. Until he or she has been tested, your partner may assume the worst and may blame you for possibly spreading the disease. It is important that you discuss these feelings with each other in an open and honest way, perhaps with a licensed counselor.

Talking to new partners

Talking about HIV with someone you are dating casually or some-one you met recently may be difficult. You might not know this person very well or know what kind of reaction to expect. When telling a casual partner or someone you are dating, each situation is different and you might use a different approach each time. Sometimes you may feel comfortable being direct and saying, "Before we have sex, I want you to know that I have HIV."

Other times, you may want to bring it up by saying something like, "Let's talk about safer sex." Whichever approach you choose, you probably want to tell the person that you have HIV before you have sex the first time. Otherwise, there may be hurt feelings or mistrust later. Also be sure to practice safer sex.

Talking to former partners

With people you have had sex with in the past or people you have shared needles with, it can be very difficult to explain that you have HIV. However, it is important that they know so that they can decide whether to get tested.

If you need help telling people that you may have been exposed to HIV, most city or county health departments will tell them for you, without using your name. Ask your doctor about this service.

Remember

Before telling your partner that you have HIV, take some time alone to think about how you want to bring it up.

- Decide when and where would be the best time and place to have a conversation. Choose a time when you expect that you will both be comfortable, rested, and as relaxed as possible.

- Think about how your partner may react to stressful situations. If there is a history of violence in your relationship, consider your safety first and plan the situation with a case manager or counselor.

- Imagine several ways in which your partner might react to the news that you are HIV positive. Write down what she or he might say, and then think about what you might say in response.

What is "safer sex"?

We know a lot about how HIV is transmitted from person to person. Having safer sex means you take this into account and avoid risky practices.

There are two reasons to practice safer sex: to protect yourself and to protect others.

Protecting yourself

If you have HIV, you need to protect your health. When it comes to sex, this means practicing safer sex to avoid sexually transmitted diseases like herpes, hepatitis, and even HIV. HIV makes it harder for your body to fight off diseases. What might be a small health problem for someone without HIV could be big health problem for you.

Practicing safer sex can protect you from getting re-infected or "super-infected" with a different strain of HIV. Some strains are resistant to certain drugs, so getting a new strain of HIV could make the disease harder to treat. Experts believe that re-infection is possible although not very likely.

Protecting your partner

Taking care of others means making sure that you do not pass along HIV to them. If your sex partners already have HIV, you should still avoid infecting them with another sexually transmitted disease you may be carrying.

Most people would agree that you owe it to your sexual partners to tell them that you have HIV. This is being honest with them. Even though it can be very hard to do, in the long run you will probably feel much better about yourself.

Some people with HIV have found that people who love them think that unsafe sex is a sign of greater love or trust. If someone offers to have unsafe sex with you, it is still up to you to protect them by being safe.

"Being safe" usually means protecting yourself and others by using condoms for the highest-risk sex activities, specifically for anal and vaginal sex. When done correctly, condom use is very effective at preventing HIV transmission. In recent years, "being safe" has come to include two other strategies for reducing HIV infections; these are HIV treatment for HIV-positive people and PrEP for HIV negatives. HIV experts are still figuring out the best roles for each of these prevention tools, and the best combinations. One or more of them is likely to be appropriate for you—be sure to ask your health care provider about them.

What about pre-exposure prophylaxis (PrEP)?

Some HIV-negative individuals may, under the supervision of their health care providers, take anti-HIV medications every day to prevent themselves from becoming infected. We call this pre-exposure prophylaxis, or PrEP. Usually these are persons who are at relatively high risk of becoming infected with HIV (for example, because they have an HIV-infected partner, they have risky sexual exposures, or they share injection drug equipment). The medication used for PrEP is Truvada, a combination tablet containing Emtriva and Viread. PrEP appears to be quite effective if it is taken every day, and is not effective if it is taken irregularly. Your health care provider can tell you more about the potential benefits and shortcomings of PrEP for HIV-negative persons.

What is risky sex?

HIV is passed through body fluids such as semen, vaginal fluid, or blood. The less contact you have with these, the lower the risk. The most sensitive areas where these fluids are risky are in the vagina or anus (ass). The skin there is thin, and is easily torn, which makes it easier for the virus to enter your body.

In general, vaginal or anal sex without a condom is the most risky. Kissing, touching, hugging, and mutual masturbation are very low risk. Saliva (spit) and tears aren't risky.

Here is a list of sexual activities organized by level of risk to help you and your partner make decisions:

High risk

- Anal sex *without a condom* (penis in the anus)
- Vaginal sex *without a condom* (penis in the vagina)

Low risk

- Sex with a condom *when you use it right*
- Oral sex, but don't swallow semen (cum)
- Deep kissing (French kissing or tongue kissing)
- Sharing sex toys that have been cleaned or covered with a new condom between uses

491

No risk

- Hugging, massage
- Masturbation
- Fantasizing
- Dry kissing
- Phone sex
- Cyber sex
- Sex toys you don't share

Talking about safer sex

You and your partners will have to decide what you are comfortable doing sexually. If you aren't used to talking openly about sex, this could be hard to get used to.

Here are some tips:

- Find a time and place outside the bedroom to talk.
- Decide what are your boundaries, concerns and desires before you start to talk.
- Make sure you clearly state what you want. Use only "I" statements, for example: "I want to use a condom when we have sex."
- Make sure you don't do, or agree to do, anything that you're not 100% comfortable with.
- Listen to what your partner is saying. Acknowledge your partner's feelings and opinions. You will need to come up with solutions that work for both of you.
- Be positive. Use reasons for safer sex that are about you, not your partner.

Of course, only you and your partner can decide what level of risk you are willing to take.

Birth control and HIV

The only forms of birth control that will protect against HIV are abstinence and using condoms while having sex. Other methods of birth control offer protection against unplanned pregnancy, but do not protect against HIV or other sexually transmitted diseases.

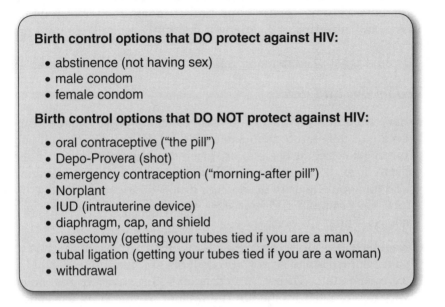

Birth control options that DO protect against HIV:

- abstinence (not having sex)
- male condom
- female condom

Birth control options that DO NOT protect against HIV:

- oral contraceptive ("the pill")
- Depo-Provera (shot)
- emergency contraception ("morning-after pill")
- Norplant
- IUD (intrauterine device)
- diaphragm, cap, and shield
- vasectomy (getting your tubes tied if you are a man)
- tubal ligation (getting your tubes tied if you are a woman)
- withdrawal

Considerations for HIV-positive women

If you are in a monogamous relationship and **your partner also is HIV positive**, you may decide to use a birth control method other than condoms. (These methods won't protect against other STDs or re-infection.)

Safe methods of birth control for HIV-positive women with an HIV-positive partner include:

- using a diaphragm
- tubal ligation (getting your tubes tied)
- IUD (intrauterine device)

Use only after checking with your provider (these may interact with your anti-HIV medications):

- birth control pills
- Depo-Provera
- Norplant

Tips for using condoms and dental dams

Some people think that using a condom makes sex less fun. Other people have become creative and find condoms sexy. Not having to worry about infecting someone will definitely make sex much more enjoyable!

If you are not used to using condoms: practice, practice, practice.

Condom dos and don'ts

- Shop around: Use lubricated latex condoms. Always use latex, because lambskin condoms don't block HIV and STDs, and polyurethane condoms break more often than latex (if you are allergic to latex, polyurethane condoms are an option). Shop around and find your favorite brand. Try different sizes and shapes (yes, they come in different sizes and shapes!). There are a lot of choices—one will work for you.

- Keep it fresh: Store condoms loosely in a cool, dry place (not your wallet). Make sure your condoms are fresh—check the expiration date. Throw away condoms that have expired, been very hot, or been washed in the washer. If you think the condom might not be good, get a new one. You and your partner are worth it.

- Take it easy: Open the package carefully, so that you don't rip the condom. Be careful if you use your teeth. Make sure that the condom package has not been punctured (there should be a pocket of air). Check the condom for damaged packaging and signs of aging such as brittleness, stickiness, and discoloration.

- Keep it hard: Put on the condom after the penis is erect and before it touches any part of a partner's body. If a penis is uncircumcised (uncut), the foreskin must be pulled back before putting on the condom.

- Heads up! Make sure the condom is right-side out. It's like a sock—there's a right side and a wrong side. Before you put it on the penis, unroll the condom about half an inch to see which direction it is unrolling. Then put it on the head of the penis and hold the tip of the condom between your fingers as you roll it all the way down the shaft of the penis from head to base. This keeps out air bubbles that can cause the condom to break. It also leaves a space for semen to collect after ejaculation.

494

- Slippery when wet: If you use a lubricant (lube), it should be a water-soluble lubricant (for example, ID Glide, K-Y Jelly, Slippery Stuff, Foreplay, Wet, Astroglide) in order to prevent breakdown of the condom. Products such as petroleum jelly, massage oils, butter, Crisco, Vaseline, and hand creams are not considered water-soluble lubricants and should not be used.

- Slippery when wet—part 2: Put lubricant on after you put on the condom, not before—it could slip off. Add more lube often. Dry condoms break more easily.

- Come and go...: Withdraw the penis immediately after ejaculation, while the penis is still erect; grasp the rim of the condom between your fingers and slowly withdraw the penis (with the condom still on) so that no semen is spilled.

- Clean up: Throw out the used condom right away. Tie it off to prevent spillage or wrap it in bathroom tissue and put it in the garbage. Condoms can clog toilets. Use a condom only once. Never use the same condom for vaginal and anal intercourse. Never use a condom that has been used by someone else.

Do you have to use a condom for oral sex?

It is possible for oral sex to transmit HIV, whether the infected partner is performing or receiving oral sex. But the risk is low compared with unprotected vaginal or anal sex.

If you choose to perform oral sex, and your partner is male, you may:

- use a latex condom on the penis; or

- if you or your partner is allergic to latex, plastic (polyurethane) condoms can be used.

If you choose to have oral sex, and your partner is female, you may:

- use a latex barrier (such as a natural rubber latex sheet, a dental dam, or a cut-open condom that makes a square) between your mouth and the vagina. A latex barrier such as a dental dam reduces the risk of blood or vaginal fluids entering your mouth. Plastic food wrap also can be used as a barrier.

If you choose to perform oral sex with either a male or female partner and this sex includes oral contact with your partner's anus (anilingus or rimming),

- use a latex barrier (such as a natural rubber latex sheet, a dental dam, or a cut-open condom that makes a square) between your mouth and the anus. Plastic food wrap also can be used as a barrier. This barrier is to prevent getting another sexually transmitted disease or parasites, not HIV.

If you choose to share sex toys, such as dildos or vibrators, with your partner,

- each partner should use a new condom on the sex toy; and be sure to clean sex toys between each use.

Female condom

Most people have never heard of these, but they may be helpful for you. The female condom is a large condom fitted with larger and smaller rings at each end that help keep it inside the vagina. They may seem a little awkward at first, but can be an alternative to the male condom. They are made of nitrile, so any lubricant can be used without damaging them. Female condoms generally cost more than male condoms, and if you aren't used to them, you'll definitely need to practice.

- Store the condom in a cool dry place, not in direct heat or sunlight.

- Throw away any condoms that have expired—the date is printed on individual condom wrappers.

- Check the package for damage and check the condom for signs of aging such as brittleness, stickiness, and discoloration. The female condom is lubricated, so it will be somewhat wet.

- Before inserting the condom, you can squeeze lubricant into the condom pouch and rub the sides together to spread it around.

- Put the condom in before sex play because pre-ejaculatory fluid, which comes from the penis, may contain HIV. The condom can be inserted up to 8 hours before sex.

- The female condom has a firm ring at each end of it. To insert the condom, squeeze the ring at the closed end between the fingers (like a diaphragm), and push it up into the back of the vagina. The open ring must stay outside the vagina at all times, and it will partly cover the lip area.

- Do not use a male condom with the female condom.

- Do not use a female condom with a diaphragm.

- If the penis is inserted outside the condom pouch or if the outer ring (open ring) slips into the vagina, stop and take the condom out. Use a new condom before you start sex again.

- Don't tear the condom with fingernails or jewelry.

- Use a female condom only once and properly dispose of it in the trash (not the toilet).

Dental dams and plastic wrap

Even though oral sex is a low-risk sexual practice, you may want to use protection when performing oral sex on someone who has HIV.

Dental dams are small squares of latex that were made originally for use in dental procedures. They are now commonly used as barriers when performing oral sex on women, to keep in vaginal fluids or menstrual blood that could transmit HIV or other STDs.

Some people use plastic wrap instead of a dental dam. It's thinner. Here are some things to remember:

- Before using a dental dam, first check it visually for any holes.

- If the dental dam has cornstarch on it, rinse that off with water (starch in the vagina can lead to an infection).

- Cover the woman's genital area with the dental dam.

- For oral-anal sex, cover the opening of the anus with a new dental dam.

- A new dental dam should be used for each act of oral sex; it should never be reused.

Chapter 38

Avoiding Infections When You Have HIV/AIDS

Chapter Contents

Section 38.1

Preventing Exposure

Text in this section is excerpted from "Recommendations to Help
HIV-infected Patients Avoid Exposure to, or Infection from,
Opportunistic Pathogens," AIDS*info*, May 7, 2013.

Male latex condoms, when used consistently and correctly during
every act of sexual intercourse, are highly effective in preventing the
sexual transmission of HIV and can reduce the risk for acquiring other
sexually transmitted diseases (STDs), including chlamydia, gonorrhea,
and trichomoniasis. Correct and consistent use of male latex condoms
not only reduces the risk of HIV transmission but might reduce the risk
for transmission of herpes simplex virus, syphilis, and chancroid when
the infected area or potential site of exposure is covered, although data
for this effect are more limited.

Male condoms also appear to reduce the risk for human papillomavirus associated diseases (i.e., genital warts, cervical cancer) and
thereby mitigate the adverse consequences of infection with HPV.
Although data for female condoms are limited, women should consider
using them to prevent the acquisition of STDs and reduce their risk of
transmitting HIV. Spermicides containing nonoxynol-9 are not effective for HIV/STD prevention and may increase risk of transmission to
uninfected partners; nonoxynol-9 **should not be used** as a microbicide
or lubricant during vaginal or anal intercourse.

As with many non-sexually transmitted opportunistic infections,
intercurrent infections with sexually transmitted pathogens (especially
pathogens that cause genital ulcers such as herpes simplex, syphilis,
and chancroid) can, if untreated, stimulate increases in HIV viral load
and consequent declines in CD4 T lymphocyte (CD4) count. Furthermore, acquisition of STDs by HIV-infected patients indicates participation in high-risk sexual behavior that is capable of transmitting HIV
to others, the risk for which is substantially increased in the presence
of genital tract inflammation (e.g., from gonorrhea or chlamydia) and
genital ulcer disease (e.g., herpes simplex virus-2 infection, syphilis).

All HIV-infected persons, including those who are asymptomatic, should be tested at initial evaluation for trichomoniasis in

women; syphilis, urogenital gonorrhea, and chlamydia in men and women; and oral gonorrhea, rectal gonorrhea, and rectal chlamydia for male patients reporting receptive sex at these anatomic sites. Nucleic acid amplification testing methods are the most sensitive and specific method for the diagnosis of anogenital, oral, and rectal chlamydia and gonorrhea infection. For all sexually active patients, screening should be repeated at least annually and more frequently depending on individual risk or symptoms. In addition to identifying and treating STDs, providers should communicate prevention messages, discuss sexual and drug-use behaviors, positively reinforce safer behaviors, refer patients for services such as substance abuse treatment, and facilitate partner notification, counseling, and testing.

Specific sex practices should be avoided that might result in oral exposure to feces (e.g., oral-anal contact) to reduce the risk for intestinal infections (e.g., cryptosporidiosis, shigellosis, campylobacteriosis, amebiasis, giardiasis, lymphogranuloma venereum [LGV] serovars of *C. trachomatis,* hepatitis A [HAV]). Persons who wish to reduce their risk for exposure might consider using dental dams or similar barrier methods for oral-anal and oral-genital contact, changing condoms after anal intercourse, and wearing latex gloves during digital-anal contact. Frequent washing of hands and genitals with warm soapy water during and after activities that might bring these body parts in contact with feces might further reduce risk for illness.

Sexual transmission of hepatitis C virus (HCV) and infection can occur, especially among HIV-infected men who have sex with men (MSM). HIV-infected MSM not known to be infected with HCV, and who present with new and unexplained increases in alanine aminotransferase, should be tested for HCV virus infection. Routine (e.g., annual) HCV testing should be considered for MSM with high risk sexual behaviors or with a diagnosis of an ulcerative STD.

HAV can be transmitted sexually, therefore vaccination is recommended for all susceptible MSM, as well as others with indications for HAV vaccination (e.g., injection-drug users, persons with chronic liver disease or who are infected with hepatitis B [HBV]). HAV vaccination is also recommended for other HIV-infected persons (e.g., injection-drug users, persons with chronic liver disease or who are infected with HBV or HCV). HBV vaccination is recommended for all susceptible HIV-infected patients. HBV infection can occur when mucous membranes are exposed to blood or body fluids that contain blood, which might occur during some types of sexual contact. HIV-infected patients coinfected with HBV or HCV should be reminded that use of latex condoms not only reduces their risk of transmitting HIV to sexual partners but reduces their risk of transmitting these viral hepatitis infections as well.

Injection-Drug-Use Exposures

Injection-drug use is a complex behavior that puts HIV-infected persons at risk for HBV and HCV infection, additional possibly drug-resistant strains of HIV, and other bloodborne pathogens. Providers should assess a person's readiness to change this practice and encourage activities to provide education and support directed at recovery. Patients should be counseled to stop using injection drugs and to enter and complete substance abuse treatment, including relapse prevention programs.

For patients who continue to inject drugs, health-care providers should advise them to adhere to the following practices:

- Never reuse or share syringes, needles, water, or drug-preparation equipment; if injection equipment that has been used by other persons is shared, the implements should first be cleaned with bleach and water before use.

- Use only sterile syringes and needles obtained from a reliable source (e.g., pharmacies or syringe-exchange programs).

- Use sterile (e.g., boiled) water to prepare drugs, and if this is not feasible, use clean water from a reliable source (e.g., fresh tap water); use a new or disinfected container (i.e., cooker) and a new filter (i.e., cotton) to prepare drugs.

- Clean the injection site with a new alcohol swab before injection.

- Safely dispose of syringes and needles after one use.

All susceptible injection-drug–users should be vaccinated against HBV and HAV infection. HIV-infected injection drug users not known to be HCV infected who present with new and unexplained increases in alanine aminotransferase should be tested for HCV infection. Routine (e.g., annual) HCV testing should be considered for injection drug users who continue to inject drugs.

Environmental and Occupational Exposures

Certain activities or types of employment might increase the risk for exposure to tuberculosis (TB). These include residency or occupation in correctional institutions and shelters for the homeless, other settings identified as high risk by local health authorities, as well as volunteer work or employment in health-care facilities where patients with TB are treated. Decisions regarding the risk of occupational exposure to TB should be made in conjunction with a health-care provider and should be based on such factors as the patient's specific duties in the workplace, the prevalence of TB in the community, and the degree to which precautions designed to prevent the transmission of TB are taken in the workplace. These decisions will affect the frequency with which the patient should be screened for TB.

Day care providers and parents of children in child care are at increased risk for acquiring cytomegalovirus infection, cryptosporidiosis, and other infections (e.g., HAV, giardiasis) from children. The risk for acquiring infection can be diminished by practicing optimal hygienic practices (e.g., washing hands with soap and water, or alcohol-based hand sanitizers if soap and water are unavailable) after fecal contact (e.g., during diaper changing) and after contact with urine or saliva.

Occupations involving contact with animals (e.g., veterinary work and employment in pet stores, farms, or slaughterhouses) might pose a risk for toxoplasmosis, cryptosporidiosis, salmonellosis, campylobacteriosis, Bartonella infection, *E. coli* infection, and other infections of concern to any immunocompromised host (e.g., leptospirosis, brucellosis, *Capnocytophaga spp.*). However, available data are insufficient to justify a recommendation against HIV-infected persons working in such settings. Wearing gloves and good hand hygiene can reduce the risk of infection.

Contact with young farm animals, specifically animals with diarrhea, should be avoided to reduce the risk for cryptosporidiosis. Since soils and sands can be contaminated with *Toxoplasma gondii* and *Cryptosporidium parvum,* persons who have extended contact with these materials (e.g., gardening; playing in or cleaning sandboxes) should wash their hands thoroughly with soap and water following exposure.

In areas where histoplasmosis is endemic, patients should avoid activities known to be associated with increased risk (e.g., creating dust when working with surface soil; cleaning chicken coops that are heavily contaminated with compost droppings; disturbing soil beneath bird-roosting sites; cleaning, remodeling or demolishing old buildings; and cave exploring). In areas where coccidioidomycosis is endemic, when possible, patients should avoid activities associated with increased risk, including extensive exposure to disturbed native soil (e.g., building excavation sites, during dust storms).

Pet-Related Exposures

Health-care providers should advise HIV-infected persons of the potential risk posed by pet ownership. However, they should be sensitive to the psychological benefits of pet ownership and should **not** routinely advise HIV-infected persons to part with their pets. Specifically, providers should advise HIV-infected patients of the following precautions.

General

HIV-infected persons should avoid direct contact with stool from pets or stray animals. Veterinary care should be sought when a pet develops diarrheal illness. If possible, HIV-infected persons should avoid contact with animals that have diarrhea.

When obtaining a new pet, HIV-infected patients should avoid animals aged <6 months (or <1 year for cats) and specifically animals with diarrhea. Because the hygienic and sanitary conditions in pet-breeding facilities, pet stores, and animal shelters vary, patients should be cautious when obtaining pets from these sources. Stray animals should also be avoided, and specifically those with diarrhea.

Gloves should always be worn when handling feces or cleaning areas that might have been contaminated by feces from pets. Patients should wash their hands after handling pets and also before eating. Patients, especially those with CD4 cell counts < 200 cells/μL should avoid direct contact with all animal feces to reduce the risk for toxoplasmosis, cryptosporidiosis, salmonellosis, campylobacteriosis, *E. coli* infection, and other infectious illnesses.

HIV-infected persons should limit or avoid direct exposure to calves and lambs (e.g., farms, petting zoos). Paying attention to hand hygiene (i.e., washing hands with soap and water, or alcohol-based hand sanitizers if soap and water are unavailable) and avoiding direct contact with stool are important when visiting premises where these animals are housed or exhibited.

Patients should not allow pets, particularly cats, to lick patients' open cuts or wounds and should take care to avoid any animal bites. Patients should wash all animal bites, animal scratches, or wounds licked by animals promptly with soap and water and seek medical attention. A course of antimicrobial therapy might be recommended if the wounds are moderate or severe, demonstrate crush injury and edema, involve the bones of a joint, involve a puncture of the skin near a joint, or involve a puncture of a joint directly.

Cats

Patients should be aware that cat ownership may under some circumstances increase their risk for toxoplasmosis and *Bartonella* infection, and enteric infections. Patients who elect to obtain a cat should adopt or purchase an animal aged >1 year and in good health to reduce the risk for cryptosporidiosis, *Bartonella* infection, salmonellosis, campylobacteriosis, and *E. coli* infection.

Litter boxes should be cleaned daily, preferably by an HIV-negative, non-pregnant person; if HIV-infected patients perform this task, they should wear gloves and wash their hands thoroughly afterward to reduce the risk for toxoplasmosis. To further reduce the risk for toxoplasmosis, HIV-infected patients should keep cats indoors, not allow them to hunt, and not feed them raw or undercooked meat. Although declawing is not usually advised, patients should avoid activities that might result in cat scratches or bites to reduce the risk for *Bartonella* infection.

Patients should also wash sites of cat scratches or bites promptly and should not allow cats to lick patients' open cuts or wounds. Care of cats should include flea control to reduce the risk for *Bartonella* infection. Testing cats for toxoplasmosis or *Bartonella* infection **is not recommended**, as such tests cannot accurately identify animals that pose a current risk for human infection.

Birds

Screening healthy birds for *Cryptococcus neoformans, Mycobacterium avium,* or *Histoplasma capsulatum* **is not recommended**.

Other

HIV-infected persons should avoid or limit contact with reptiles (e.g., snakes, lizards, iguanas, and turtles) and chicks and ducklings because of the high risk for exposure to *Salmonella spp*. Gloves should be used during aquarium cleaning to reduce the risk for infection with *Mycobacterium marinum*. Contact with exotic pets (e.g., nonhuman primates) should be avoided.

Food- and Water-Related Exposures

Food

Contaminated food is a common source of enteric infections. Transmission most often occurs by ingestion of undercooked foods or by cross-contamination of foods in the kitchen.

Health-care providers should advise HIV-infected persons, particularly those with a CD4 count <200 cells/μL, not to eat raw or undercooked eggs, including specific foods that might contain raw eggs (e.g., certain preparation of Hollandaise sauce, Caesar salad dressings, homemade mayonnaises, uncooked cookie and cake batter, eggnog); raw or undercooked poultry, meat, and seafood (raw shellfish in particular); unpasteurized dairy products (including milk and cheese); unpasteurized fruit juices; and raw seed sprouts (e.g., alfalfa sprouts or mung bean sprouts).

Meat and poultry are safest when adequate cooking is confirmed by thermometer. Current U.S. Department of Agriculture (USDA) guidance is that the internal temperature be at least 145°F (63°C) for whole cuts of meat, 160°F (71°C) for ground meat excluding poultry, and 165°F (74°C) for poultry; whole cuts of meat and poultry should rest at least three minutes before carving and consuming. Immunocompromised persons who wish to maximally ensure their cooked meats are safe to eat may choose to use the following recommendations: the internal temperature should be at least 165°F (74°C) for all types of red meats and 180°F (82°C) for poultry. If a thermometer is not used when cooking meats, the risk for illness is decreased by eating poultry and meat that have no trace of pink color. However, color change of the meat (e.g., absence of pink) does not always correlate with internal temperature.

Irradiated meats, if available, are predicted to eliminate the risk of foodborne enteric infection. Use of microwaves as a primary means of cooking of potentially contaminated foods (e.g., meats, hot dogs) should be avoided because microwave cooking is not uniform.

Produce items should be washed thoroughly; providers may wish to advise patients that produce is safest when cooked.

Health-care providers should advise HIV-infected persons to avoid cross-contamination of foods. Salad preparation prior to handling of raw meats or other uncooked, potentially contaminated foods decreases risk. Uncooked meats, including hot dogs, and their juices should not come into contact with other foods. Hands, cutting boards, counters, knives, and other utensils should be washed thoroughly (preferably in a dish washer on hot cycle) after contact with uncooked foods.

Soft cheeses (e.g., feta, Brie, Camembert, blue-veined, and Mexican-style cheese such as queso fresco) and prepared deli foods (including coldcuts, salads, hummus, hot dogs, pâtés) are potential sources of *Listeria monocytogenes* infection, which can lead to serious, even fatal, systemic infection in HIV-infected patients with low CD4 cell counts; consumption of these foods should be avoided.

Hard cheeses, processed cheeses, cream cheese, including slices and spreads; cottage cheese or yogurt; and canned or shelf-stable pâté and meat spreads need not be avoided. Avoid raw or unpasteurized milk, including goat's milk, or foods that contain unpasteurized milk or milk products.

Water

Patients should **not** drink water directly from lakes or rivers because of the risk for cryptosporidiosis, giardiasis, and toxoplasmosis. Waterborne infection can also result from swallowing water during recreational activities. All HIV-infected patients should avoid swimming in water that is probably contaminated with human or animal waste and should avoid swallowing water during swimming. Patients, especially those with CD4 cell counts <200 cells/μL, should also be made aware that swimming or playing in lakes, rivers, and oceans as well as some swimming pools, recreational water parks, and ornamental water fountains can expose them to enteric pathogens (e.g., *Cryptosporidium, Giardia,* norovirus, Shiga toxin-producing *E. coli*) that cause diarrheal illness and to which their HIV infection makes them more susceptible.

Outbreaks of diarrheal illness have been linked to drinking water from municipal water supplies. During outbreaks or in other situations in which a community boil-water advisory is issued, boiling water for >1 minute will eliminate the risk for most viral, bacterial, and parasitic causes of diarrhea, including cryptosporidiosis. Using submicron, personal-use water filters (home/office types) or drinking bottled water might also reduce the risk from municipal and from well water.

Available data are inadequate to support a recommendation that all HIV-infected persons boil or otherwise avoid drinking tap water in non-outbreak settings. However, persons who wish to take independent action to reduce their risk for waterborne cryptosporidiosis might take precautions similar to those recommended during outbreaks. Such decisions are best made in conjunction with a health-care provider. Persons who choose to use a personal-use filter or bottled water should be aware of the complexities involved in selecting the appropriate products, the lack of enforceable standards for destruction or removal of oocysts, product cost, and the difficulty of using these products consistently.

Patients taking precautions to avoid acquiring pathogens from drinking water should be advised that ice made from contaminated tap water also can be a source of infection. Patients should also be made aware that fountain beverages served in restaurants, bars, theaters, and other public places also might pose a risk, because these beverages, and the ice they might contain, are usually made from tap water.

Nationally distributed brands of bottled or canned water and carbonated soft drinks are safe to drink. Commercially packaged (i.e., sealed at the factory and unopened), non-carbonated soft drinks and fruit juices that do not require refrigeration until after they are opened (i.e., those that can be stored unrefrigerated on grocery shelves) also are safe. Nationally distributed brands of frozen fruit juice concentrate are safe if they are reconstituted by users with water from a safe source.

Fruit juices that must be kept refrigerated from the time they are processed to the time they are consumed might be either fresh (i.e., unpasteurized) or heat treated (i.e., pasteurized); only juices labeled as pasteurized should be considered safe to consume. Other pasteurized beverages and beers also are considered safe.

Travel-Related Exposures

HIV-infected travelers to developing countries, especially travelers who are severely immunosuppressed, risk exposure to both opportunistic and non-opportunistic pathogens not prevalent in the United States. Health-care providers or specialists in travel medicine should be consulted 4 to 6 weeks in advance of travel to fully review and implement all measures necessary to prevent illness abroad.

The Centers for Disease Control and Prevention (CDC) maintain a website (www.cdc.gov/travel) accessible to travelers and their care providers and regularly publishes recommendations for prevention of disease while traveling in the CDC's Yellow Book (Health Information for International Travel). The CDC's travel website allows users to locate prevention recommendations according to geographic destination and to find updates on international disease outbreaks that might pose a health threat to travelers.

The following summary advice should be considered for all HIV-infected travelers but does substitute for destination-specific consultation with a travel medicine specialist.

The risk for foodborne and waterborne infections among HIV-infected persons is magnified during travel to economically developing countries. Travelers to such countries may wish to additionally consult the section *Food- and Water-Related Exposures*, as well as recommendations for food and water precautions and water disinfection in the CDC Yellow Book (Health Information for Travelers).

Specifically, persons who travel to economically developing areas should avoid foods and beverages that might be contaminated, as well as tap water, ice made with tap water, and items sold by street vendors. Raw fruits or vegetables that might have been washed in tap water should be avoided. Foods and beverages that are usually safe include steaming hot foods, fruits that are peeled by the traveler, unopened and properly bottled (including carbonated) beverages, hot coffee and tea, beer, wine, and water that is brought to a rolling boil for 1 minute. Treating water with iodine or chlorine can be as effective as boiling for preventing infections with most pathogens. Iodine and chlorine treatments may not prevent infection with *Cryptosporidium;* however these treatments can be used when boiling is not practical.

Waterborne infections might result from swallowing water during recreational activities. To reduce the risk for parasitic (e.g., cryptosporidiosis, giardiasis, toxoplasmosis) and bacterial infections, patients should avoid swallowing water during swimming and should not swim in water that might be contaminated (e.g., with sewage or animal waste). HIV-infected persons traveling to developing countries should also be advised to **not** use tap water to brush their teeth.

Scrupulous attention to safe food and water consumption and good hygiene (i.e., regularly washing hands with soap and water, or alcohol-based hand sanitizers if soap and water are unavailable) are the most effective methods for reducing risk of travelers' diarrhea. Antimicrobial prophylaxis for travelers' diarrhea **is not recommended** routinely for HIV-infected persons traveling to developing countries. Such preventive therapy can have adverse effects, can promote the emergence of drug-resistant organisms, and can increase the risk of *C. difficile*-associated diarrhea.

Nonetheless, studies (none involving an HIV-infected population) have reported that prophylaxis can reduce the risk for diarrhea among travelers. Under selected circumstances (e.g., those in which the risk for infection is high and the period of travel brief), the health-care provider and patient might weigh the potential risks and benefits and decide that antibiotic prophylaxis is warranted.

HIV-infected travelers to developing countries should consider carrying a sufficient supply of an antimicrobial agent to be taken empirically if diarrhea occurs. Antimicrobial resistance among enteric bacterial pathogens outside the United States is a growing public health problem; therefore, the choice of antibiotic should be made in consultation with a clinician based on the traveler's destination. Travelers should consult a physician if they develop severe diarrhea that does not respond to empirical therapy, if their stools contain blood, they develop fever with shaking chills, or dehydration occurs. Antiperistaltic agents (e.g., diphenoxylate and loperamide) are used for treating diarrhea; however, they should not be used by patients with high fever or with blood in the stool, and their use should be discontinued if symptoms persist for more than 48 hours.

Live-virus vaccines should, in general, **not** be used. An exception is measles vaccine, which is recommended for non-immune persons. However, measles vaccine **is not recommended** for persons who are severely immunosuppressed. Severely immunosuppressed persons who must travel to measles-endemic countries should consult a travel medicine specialist regarding possible utility of prophylaxis with immune globulin.

Another exception is varicella vaccine, which can be administered to asymptomatic susceptible persons with a CD4 cell count ≥200 cells/μL. For adults and adolescents with CD4 cell counts <200 cells/μL, varicella-zoster immune globulin (VariZIG™) is indicated after close contact with a person who has active varicella or zoster and anti-herpetic antiviral therapy (e.g., acyclovir, famciclovir, valacyclovir) is recommended in the event vaccination or exposure results in clinical disease. Persons at risk for and non-immune to polio and typhoid fever or who require influenza vaccination should be administered only inactivated formulations of these vaccines **not** live-attenuated preparations.

Yellow fever vaccine is a live-virus vaccine with uncertain safety and efficacy among HIV-infected persons. Travelers with asymptomatic HIV infection who cannot avoid potential exposure to yellow fever should be offered vaccination. If travel to a zone with yellow fever is necessary and vaccination is not administered, patients should be advised of the risk, instructed in methods for avoiding the bites of vector mosquitoes, and provided a vaccination waiver letter. Preparation for travel should include a review and updating of routine vaccinations, including diphtheria, tetanus, acellular pertussis, and influenza.

Killed and recombinant vaccines (e.g., influenza, diphtheria, tetanus, rabies, HAV, HBV, Japanese encephalitis, meningococcal vaccines) should usually be used for HIV-infected persons just as they would be used for non-HIV–infected persons anticipating travel.

Section 38.2

Safe Food and Water

Text in this section is excerpted from "Food Safety for People
with HIV/AIDS," U.S. Food and Drug Administration (FDA),
January 29, 2015.

Foodborne Illness in the United States

When certain disease-causing bacteria, viruses or parasites contaminate food, they can cause foodborne illness. Another word for
such a bacteria, virus, or parasite is "pathogen." Foodborne illness,
often called *food poisoning*, is an illness that comes from a food you
eat.

- The food supply in the United States is among the safest
  in the world—but it can still be a source of infection for all
  persons.

- According to the Centers for Disease Control and Prevention, 48
  million persons get sick, 128,000 are hospitalized, and 3,000 die
  from foodborne infection and illness in the United States each
  year. Many of these people are children, older adults, or have
  weakened immune systems and may not be able to fight infection normally.

Since foodborne illness can be serious—or even fatal—it is important for you to know and practice safe food-handling behaviors to help
reduce your risk of getting sick from contaminated food.

Food Safety: It's Especially Important for You

As a person with the Human Immunodeficiency Virus/Acquired
Immunodeficiency Syndrome (HIV/AIDS), you are susceptible to many
types of infection, like those that can be brought on by disease-causing
bacteria and other pathogens that cause foodborne illness.

- A properly functioning immune system works to clear infection
  and other foreign agents from your body. When the HIV virus

511

that causes AIDS damages or destroys the body's immune system, you become more vulnerable to developing and opportunistic infection, such as Pneumocystis carinii pneumonia, or contracting an infection, such as foodborne illness.

- As with many types of infection, because you have HIV/AIDS, you are more likely to have a lengthier illness, undergo hospitalization, or even die, should you contract a foodborne illness.

- Because your immune system is weakened, you must be especially vigilant when handling, preparing, and consuming foods.

- To avoid contracting a foodborne illness, you must be vigilant when handling, preparing, and consuming foods.

Make safe handling a lifelong commitment to minimize your risk of foodborne illness. Be aware that as you age, your immunity to infection naturally is weakened.

Table 38.1. Major Pathogens That Cause Foodborne Illness

Campylobacter	
Associated Foods	**Symptoms and Potential Impact**
• Untreated or contaminated water • Unpasteurized ("raw") milk • Raw or undercooked meat, poultry, or shellfish	• Fever, headache, and muscle pain followed by diarrhea (sometimes bloody), abdominal pain, and nausea. Symptoms appear 2 to 5 days after eating and may last 2 to 10 days. May spread to bloodstream and cause life-threatening infection.
Cryptosporidium	
Associated Foods/Sources	**Symptoms and Potential Impact**
• Swallowing contaminated water, including that from recreational sources (e.g., swimming pool or lake) • Eating uncooked or contaminated food • Placing a contaminated object in the mouth • Soil, food, water, contaminated surfaces	• Watery diarrhea, dehydration, weight loss, stomach cramps or pain, fever, nausea, and vomiting; respiratory symptoms may also be present. • Symptoms begin 7 to 10 days after becoming infected and may last 2 to 14 days. In those with a weakened immune system, including people with HIV/AIDS, symptoms may subside and return over weeks to months.

Table 38.1. Continued

Clostridium perfringens	
Associated Foods/ Sources	**Symptoms and Potential Impact**
• Many outbreaks result from food left for long periods in steam tables or at room temperature and time and/or temperature abused foods. • Meats, meat products, poultry, poultry products , and gravy	• Onset of watery diarrhea and abdominal cramps within about 16 hours. The illness usually begins suddenly and lasts for 12 to 24 hours. In elderly, symptoms may last 1 to 2 weeks. • Complications and/or death occur only very rarely.

Listeria monocytogenes **Can grow slowly at refrigerator temperatures**	
Associated Foods	**Symptoms and Potential Impact**
• Improperly reheated hot dogs, luncheon meats, cold cuts, fermented or dry sausage, and other deli-style meat and poultry • Unpasteurized (raw) milk and soft cheeses made with unpasteurized (raw) milk • Smoked seafood and salads made in the store such as ham salad, chicken salad, or seafood salads • Raw vegetables	• Fever, chills, headache, backache, sometimes upset stomach, abdominal pain, and diarrhea. May take up to 2 months to become ill. • Gastrointestinal symptoms may appear within a few hours to 2 to 3 days, and disease may appear 2 to 6 weeks after ingestion. The duration is variable. • Those at-risk (including people with HIV/AIDS and others with weakened immune systems) may later develop more serious illness; death can result from this bacteria. • Can cause problems with pregnancy, including miscarriage, fetal death, or severe illness or death in newborns.

Escherichia coli O157:H7 **One of several strains of *E. coli* that can cause human illness**	
Associated Foods	**Symptoms and Potential Impact**
• Undercooked beef, especially ground beef • Unpasteurized milk and juices, like "fresh" apple cider • Contaminated raw fruits and vegetables, and water • Person-to-person contact	• Severe diarrhea that is often bloody, abdominal cramps, and vomiting. Usually little or no fever. • Can begin 1 to 9 days after contaminated food is eaten and lasts about 2 to 9 days. • Some, especially the very young, may develop hemolytic-uremic syndrome (HUS), which cause acute kidney failure, and can lead to permanent kidney damage or even death.

Table 38.1. Continued

Noroviruses (and other caliciviruses)	
Associated Foods	**Symptoms and Potential Impact**
• Shellfish and fecally-contaminated foods or water • Ready-to-eat foods touched by infected food workers; for example, salads, sandwiches, ice, cookies, fruit	• Nausea, vomiting, stomach pain usually start between 24 and 48 hours, but cases can occur within 12 hours of exposure. Symptoms usually last 12 to 60 hours. • Diarrhea is more prevalent in adults and vomiting is more prevalent in children.
Salmonella (over 2,300 types)	
Associated Foods	**Symptoms and Potential Impact**
• Raw or undercooked eggs, poultry, and meat • Unpasteurized (raw) milk or juice • Cheese and seafood • Fresh fruits and vegetables	• Stomach pain, diarrhea (can be bloody), nausea, chills, fever, and/or headache usually appear 6 to 72 hours after eating; may last 4 to 7 days. • In people with a weakened immune system, such as people with HIV/AIDS, the infection may be more severe and lead to serious complications including death.
Toxoplasma gondii	
Associated Foods/Sources	**Symptoms and Potential Impact**
• Accidental contact of cat feces through touching hands to mouth after gardening, handling cats, cleaning cat's litter box, or touching anything that has come in contact with cat feces. • Raw or undercooked meat.	• Flu-like illness that usually appears 10 to 13 days after eating, may last months. Those with a weakened immune system, including people with HIV/AIDS, may develop more serious illness. • Can cause problems with pregnancy, including miscarriage and birth defects.
Vibrio vulnificus	
Associated Foods	**Symptoms and Potential Impact**
• Undercooked or raw seafood (fish or shellfish)	• Diarrhea, stomach pain, and vomiting may appear within 4 hours to several days and last 2 to 8 days. May result in a blood infection. May result in death for those with a weakened immune system, including people with HIV/AIDS, cancer or liver disease.

Eating at Home: Making Wise Food Choices

Some foods are more risky for you than others. In general, the foods that are most likely to contain harmful bacteria or viruses fall in two categories:

- **Uncooked** fresh fruits and vegetables

- **Some animal products**, such as unpasteurized (raw) milk; soft cheeses made with raw milk; and raw or undercooked eggs, raw meat, raw poultry, raw fish, raw shellfish and their juices; luncheon meats and deli-type salads (without added preservatives) prepared on site in a deli-type establishment.

Interestingly, the risk these foods may actually pose depends on the *origin or source of the food* and *how the food is processed, stored, and prepared*. Follow these guidelines (see table 38.2.) for safe selection and preparation of your favorite foods.

If You Have Questions
.... about Wise Food Choices:
Be sure to consult with your doctor or healthcare provider. He or she can answer any specific questions or help you in your choices.

...about Particular Foods:
If you are not sure about the safety of a food in your refrigerator, don't take the risk.

When in doubt, throw it out!
Wise choices in your food selections are important.
All consumers need to follow the Four Basic Steps to Food Safety: *Clean, Separate, Cook* and *Chill*.

Taking Care: Handling and Preparing Food Safely

Foodborne pathogens are sneaky. Food that appears completely fine can contain pathogens—disease-causing bacteria, viruses, or parasites—that can make you sick. You should never taste a food to determine if it is safe to eat.

As a person with HIV/AIDS, it is especially important that you – or those preparing your food – are always careful with food handling and preparation. The easiest way to do this is to Check Your Steps—*clean, separate, cook,* and *chill* – from the *Food Safe Families Campaign*.

515

Table 38.2. Common Foods: Select the Lower Risk Options

Type of Food	Higher Risk	Lower Risk
Meat and Poultry	• Raw or undercooked meat or poultry	• Meat or poultry cooked to a safe minimum internal temperature
Tip: Use a food thermometer to check the internal temperature on the "Is It Done Yet?" chart for specific safe minimum internal temperature.		
Seafood	• Any raw or undercooked fish, or shellfish, or food containing raw or undercooked seafood e.g., sushi, sashimi, found in some sushi or ceviche. Refrigerated smoked fish • Partially cooked seafood, such as shrimp and crab	• Previously cooked seafood heated to 165 °F • Canned fish and seafood • Seafood cooked to 145 °F
Milk	• Unpasteurized (raw) milk	• Pasteurized milk
Eggs	Foods that contain raw/undercooked eggs, such as: • Homemade Caesar salad dressings* • Homemade raw cookie dough* • Homemade eggnog*	*At home:* • Use pasteurized eggs/egg products when preparing recipes that call for raw or undercooked eggs *When eating out:* • Ask if pasteurized eggs were used
Tip: Most pre-made foods from grocery stores, such as Caesar dressing, pre-made cookie dough, or packaged eggnog are made with pasteurized eggs.		
Sprouts	• Raw sprouts (alfalfa, bean, or any other sprout)	• Cooked sprouts
Vegetables	• Unwashed fresh vegetables, including lettuce/salads	• Washed fresh vegetables, including salads • Cooked vegetables

Table 38.2. Continued

Type of Food	Higher Risk	Lower Risk
Cheese	• Soft cheeses made from unpasteurized (raw) milk, such as: – Feta – Brie – Camembert – Blue-veined – Queso fresco	• Hard cheeses • Processed cheeses • Cream cheese • Mozzarella • Soft cheeses that are clearly labeled "made from pasteurized milk"
Hot Dogs and Deli Meats	• Hot dogs, deli and luncheon meats that have not been reheated	• Hot dogs, luncheon meats, and deli meats reheated to steaming hot or 165 ºF
	Tip: You need to reheat hot dogs, deli meats and luncheon meats before eating them because the bacteria, Listeria monocytogenes grows at refrigerated temperatures (40 ºF or below). This bacteria may cause severe illness, hospitalization, or even death. Reheating these foods until they are steaming hot destroys these dangerous bacteria and makes these foods safe for you to eat.	
Pâtés	• Unpasteurized, refrigerated pâtés or meat spreads	• Canned or shelf-stable pâtés or meat spreads

517

Four Basic Steps to Food Safety

1. Clean: **Wash Hands and Surfaces Often**

Bacteria can spread throughout the kitchen and get onto cutting boards, utensils, counter tops, and food.

To ensure that your hands and surfaces are clean, be sure to:

- Wash hands in warm soapy water for at least 20 seconds before and after handling food and using the bathroom, changing diapers, or handling pets.

- Wash cutting boards, dishes, utensils, and counter tops with hot soapy water between the preparation of raw meat, poultry, and seafood products and preparation of any other food that will not be cooked. As an added precaution, sanitize cutting boards and counter tops by rinsing them in a solution made of one tablespoon of unscented liquid chlorine bleach per gallon of water, or, as an alternative, you may run the plastic board through the wash cycle in your automatic dishwasher.

- Use paper towels to clean up kitchen surfaces. If using cloth towels, you should wash them often in the hot cycle of the washing machine.

- Wash produce. Rinse fruits and vegetables, and rub firm-skin fruits and vegetables under running tap water, including those with skins and rinds that are not eaten.

- With canned goods: remember to clean lids before opening.

2. Separate: **Don't Cross-Contaminate**

Cross-contamination occurs when bacteria are spread from one food product to another. This is especially common when handling raw meat, poultry, seafood, and eggs. The key is to keep these foods—and their juices—away from ready-to-eat foods.

To prevent cross-contamination, remember to:

- Separate raw meat, poultry, seafood, and eggs from other foods in your grocery shopping cart, grocery bags, and in your refrigerator.

- Never place cooked food on a plate that previously held raw meat, poultry, seafood, or eggs without first washing the plate with hot soapy water.

- Don't reuse marinades used on raw foods unless you bring them to a boil first.

- Consider using one cutting board only for raw foods and another only for ready-to-eat foods, such as bread, fresh fruits and vegetables, and cooked meat.

3. Cook: ***Cook to Safe Temperatures***

Foods are safely cooked when they are heated to the USDA-FDA recommended safe minimum internal temperatures, as shown on the "Is it Done Yet" chart.

To ensure that your foods are cooked safely, always:

- Use a **food thermometer** to measure the internal temperature of cooked foods. Check the internal temperature in several places to make sure that the meat, poultry, seafood, or egg product is cooked to safe minimum internal temperatures.

- Cook **ground beef** to at least 160 °F and **ground poultry** to a safe minimum internal temperature of 165 °F. Color of food is not a reliable indicator of safety or doneness.

- Reheat **fully cooked hams** packaged at a USDA-inspected plant to 140 °F. For fully cooked ham that has been repackaged in any other location or for leftover fully cooked ham, heat to 165 °F.

- Cook **seafood** to 145 F. Cook **shrimp, lobster, and crab** until they turn red and the flesh is pearly opaque. Cook **clams, mussels, and oysters** until the shells open. If the shells do not open, do not eat the seafood inside.

- Cook **eggs** until the yolks and whites are firm. Use only recipes in which the eggs are cooked or heated to 160 °F.

- Cook all raw **beef, lamb, pork, and veal steaks, roasts, and chops** to 145 °F with a 3-minute rest time after removal from the heat source.

- Bring **sauces, soups, and gravy** to a boil when reheating. Heat other leftovers to 165 °F.

- Reheat **hot dogs, luncheon meats, bologna, and other deli meats** until steaming hot or 165 °F.

- When cooking in a microwave oven, cover food, stir, and rotate for even cooking. If there is no turntable, rotate the dish by hand once or twice during cooking. Always allow standing time, which completes the cooking, before checking the internal temperature with a food thermometer. Food is done when it reaches the USDA- FDA recommended safe minimum internal temperature.

Is It Done Yet?

Use a food thermometer to be most accurate. You can't always tell by looking.

USDA-FDA Recommended Safe Minimum Internal Temperatures

- Beef, Pork, Veal, Lamb, Steaks, Roasts and Chops

  145 °F with 3-minute rest time

- Fish

  145 °F

- Beef, Pork, Veal, Lamb Ground

  160 °F

- Egg Dishes

  160 °F

- Turkey, Chicken and Duck Whole, Pieces and Ground

  165 °F

4. Chill: ***Refrigerate Promptly***

Cold temperatures slow the growth of harmful bacteria. Keep-ing a constant refrigerator temperature of **40 °F or below** is one of the most effective ways to reduce risk of foodborne illness. Use an appliance thermometer to be sure the refrigera-tor temperature is consistently 40 °F or below and the freezertemperature is 0 °F or below.

To chill foods properly:

- Refrigerate or freeze meat, poultry, eggs, seafood, and other perishables within 2 hours of cooking or purchasing. Refrigerate within 1 hour if the temperature outside is above 90 °F.

- Never thaw food at room temperature, such as on the counter top. It is safe to thaw food in the refrigerator, in cold water, or in the microwave. If you thaw food in cold water or in the micro-wave, you should cook it immediately.

Divide large amounts of food into shallow containers for quicker cooling in the refrigerator.

- Follow the recommendations in the abridged USDA-FDA Cold Storage Chart (Table 38.3.).

USDA-FDA Cold Storage Chart

These time limit guidelines will help keep refrigerated food safe to eat. Because freezing keeps food safe indefinitely, recommended storage times for frozen foods are for quality only.

Table 38.3. Cold Storage Chart

Product	Refrigerator (40 ºF)	Freezer (0 ºF)
Eggs		
Fresh, in shell	3 to 5 weeks	Don't freeze
Hard cooked	1 week	Don't freeze well
Liquid Pasteurized Eggs, Egg Substitutes		
Opened	3 days	Don't freeze well
Unopened	10 days	1 year
Deli and Vacuum-Packed Products		
Egg, chicken, ham, tuna, and macaroni salads	3 to 5 days	Don't freeze well
Hot Dogs		
Opened package	1 week	1 to 2 months
Unopened package	2 weeks	1 to 2 months
Luncheon Meat		
Opened package	3 to 5 days	1 to 2 months
Unopened package	2 weeks	1 to 2 months
Bacon and Sausage		
Bacon	7 days	1 month
Sausage, raw – from chicken, turkey, pork, beef	1 to 2 days	1 to 2 months
Hamburger and Other Ground Meats		
Hamburger, ground beef, turkey, veal, pork, lamb, and mixtures of them	1 to 2 days	3 to 4 months

Table 38.3. Continued

Product	Refrigerator (40 ºF)	Freezer (0 ºF)
Fresh Beef, Veal, Lamb, Pork		
Steaks	3 to 5 days	6 to 12 months
Chops	3 to 5 days	4 to 6 months
Roast	3 to 5 days	4 to 12 months
Fresh Poultry		
Chicken or turkey, whole	1 to 2 days	1 year
Chicken or turkey, pieces	1 to 2 days	9 months
Seafood		
Lean fish (flounder, haddock, halibut, etc.)	1 to 2 days	6 to 8 months
Fatty fish (salmon, tuna, etc.)	1 to 2 days	2 to 3 months
Leftovers		
Cooked meat or poultry	3 to 4 days	2 to 6 months
Chicken nuggets, patties	3 to 4 days	1 to 3 months
Pizza	3 to 4 days	1 to 2 months

In the Know: Becoming a Better Shopper

Follow these safe food-handling practices while you shop:

- Carefully read food labels while in the store to make sure food is not past its "sell by" date.

- Put raw packaged meat, poultry, or seafood into a plastic bag before placing it in the shopping cart so that its juices will not drip on – and contaminate – other foods. If the meat counter does not offer plastic bags, pick some up from the produce section before you select your meat, poultry, and seafood.

- Buy only pasteurized milk, cheese, and other dairy products from the refrigerated section. When buying fruit juice from the refrigerated section of the store, be sure that the juice label says it is **pasteurized**.

- Purchase eggs in the shell from the refrigerated section of the store. (Note: store the eggs in their original carton in the main part of your refrigerator once you are home.) For recipes that call for eggs that are raw or undercooked when the dish is served – homemade Caesar salad dressing and homemade ice cream are two examples – use either shell eggs that have been treated to destroy *Salmonella* by pasteurization or pasteurized egg products. When consuming raw eggs, using pasteurized eggs is the safer choice.

- **Never** buy food that is displayed in unsafe or unclean conditions.

- When purchasing canned goods, make sure that they are free of dents, cracks, or bulging lids. (Once you are home, remember to clean each lid before opening the can.)

- Purchase produce that is not bruised or damaged.

- Check Your Steps:

  - Check "Sell-By" date.

  - Put raw meat, poultry, or seafood in plastic bags.

  - Buy only pasteurized milk, soft cheeses made with pasteurized milk, and pasteurized or juices that have been otherwise treated to control harmful bacteria.

  - When buying eggs, purchase refrigerated shell eggs. If your recipe calls for raw eggs, purchase pasteurized, refrigerated liquid eggs.

  - Don't buy food displayed in unsafe or unclean conditions.

Food Product Dating

Types of Open Dates:

Open dating is found primarily on perishable foods such as meat, poultry, eggs, and dairy products.

- A"**Sell-By**" date tells the store how long to display the product for sale. You should buy the product before the date expires.

- A "**Best if Used By (or Before)**" date is recommended for best flavor or quality. It is not a purchase or safety date.

- A "**Use-By**" date is the last date recommended for the use of the product while at peak quality. The date has been determined by the manufacturer of the product.

- **"Closed or coded dates"** are packing numbers for use by the manufacturer. "Closed" or "coded" dating might appear on shelf-stable products such as cans and boxes of food.

Transporting Your Groceries

Follow these tips for safe transporting of your groceries:

- Pick up perishable foods last, and plan to go directly home from the grocery store.

- Always refrigerate perishable foods within 2 hours of cooking or purchasing.

- Refrigerate within 1 hour if the temperature outside is above 90 °F.

- In hot weather, take a cooler with ice or another cold source to transport foods safely.

Being Smart When Eating Out

Eating out can be lots of fun – so make it an enjoyable experience by following some simple guidelines to avoid foodborne illness. Remember to observe your food when it is served, and don't ever hesitate to ask questions before you order. Waiters and waitresses can be quite helpful if you ask how a food is prepared. Also, let them know you don't want any food item containing raw meat, poultry, seafood, sprouts, or eggs.

Basic Rules for Ordering

- Ask whether the food contains uncooked ingredients such as eggs, sprouts, meat, poultry, or seafood. If so, choose something else.

- Ask how these foods have been cooked. If the server does not know the answer, ask to speak to the chef to be sure your food has been cooked to a safe minimum internal temperature.

- If you plan to get a "doggy bag" or save leftovers to eat at a later time, refrigerate perishable foods as soon as possible – and always within 2 hours after purchase or delivery. If the leftover is in air temperatures above 90 °F, refrigerate within 1 hour.

If in doubt, make another selection!

Table 38.4. Smart Menu Choices

Higher Risk:	Lower Risk:
• Soft cheese made from unpasteurized (raw) milk.	• **Hard or processed cheeses. Soft cheeses** only if they are made from **pasteurized milk**.
• Refrigerated smoked seafood and raw or undercooked seafood.	• **Fully cooked fish or seafood.**
• Cold or improperly heated hot dogs.	• **Hot dogs reheated to steaming hot.** If the hot dogs are served cold or lukewarm, ask to have them reheated until steaming, or choose something else.
• Sandwiches with cold deli or luncheon meat.	• **Grilled sandwiches** in which the meat or poultry is heated until steaming.
• Raw or undercooked fish, such as sashimi, non-vegetarian sushi or cerviche.	• **Fully cooked fish** that is firm and flaky.
• Soft-boiled or "over-easy" eggs, as the yolks are not fully cooked.	• **Fully cooked eggs** with firm yolk and whites.
• Salads, wraps, or sandwiches containing raw (uncooked) or lightly cooked sprouts.	• Salads, wraps, or sandwiches containing **cooked sprouts.**

Tips for Transporting Food

- Keep cold food cold, at 40 °F or below. To be safest, place cold food in cooler with ice or frozen gel packs. Use plenty of ice or frozen gel packs. Cold food should be at 40 °F or below the entire time you are transporting it.

- Hot food should be kept at 140 °F or above. Wrap the food well and place in an insulated container.

Stay "Food Safe" When Traveling Internationally

Discuss your travel plans with your physician before traveling to other countries. Your physician may have specific recommendations for the places you are visiting, and may suggest extra precautions or medications to take on your travels.

Foodborne Illness: Know the Symptoms

Despite your best efforts, you may find yourself in a situation where you suspect you have a foodborne illness. Foodborne illness often presents itself with flu-like symptoms.

These symptoms include:

- Nausea
- Vomiting
- Diarrhea
- Fever

If you suspect that you could have a foodborne illness, there are four key steps that you should take. Follow the guidelines in the Foodborne Illness Action Plan (below), which begins with contacting your physician or healthcare provider right away.

When in doubt, contact your physician or healthcare provider!

Foodborne Illness Action Plan

If you suspect you have a foodborne illness, follow these general guidelines:

1. Consult your physician or healthcare provider, or seek medical treatment as appropriate.

   As a person with HIV/AIDS, you are at increased risk for severe infection.

   - Contact your physician immediately if you develop symptoms or think you may be at risk.

   - If you develop signs of infection as discussed with your physician, seek out medical advice and/or treatment immediately.

2. Preserve the food.

   - If a portion of the suspect food is available, wrap it securely, label it to say "DANGER," and freeze it.

   - The remaining food may be used in diagnosing your illness and in preventing others from becoming ill.

3. Save all the packaging materials, such as cans or cartons.

   - Write down the food type, the date and time consumed, and when the onset of symptoms occurred. Write down as many foods and beverages you can recall consuming in the past week (or longer), since the onset time for various foodborne illnesses differ.

- Save any identical unopened products.

- If the suspect food is a USDA-inspected meat, poultry, or egg product, call the USDA Meat and Poultry Hotline, **1-888-MPHotline (188-674-6854)**. For all other foods, call the FDA office of Emergency Operations at 1-866-300-4374 or 301-796-8240.

4. Call your local health department if you believe you became ill from food you ate in a restaurant or other food establishment.

- The health department staff will be able to assist you in determining whether any further investigation is warranted.

- To locate your local health department, visit Health Guide USA.

Section 38.3

Staying Healthy while Traveling

Text in this section is excerpted from "Travel Abroad," Centers for Disease Control and Prevention (CDC), January 16, 2015.

- Before you go on a trip outside the United States, talk to your doctor about your destinations and planned activities.
- Take special care with food and water.
- Protect your health (and the health of others) just as you do at home.

Each year, millions of Americans travel abroad. Even though travel outside the United States can be risky for anyone, it may require special precautions for individuals living with HIV infection. For example, travel to some developing countries can increase the risk of getting an **opportunistic infection**. For some destinations, certain vaccines that contain live viruses may be required, and your health care provider needs to review your medical record to ensure they are safe for you.

The most important things you can do is **see your health care provider before you travel**, know the medical risks you might face, and learn how to protect yourself.

Before You Travel

- Talk to your health care provider or an expert in travel medicine about health risks in the places you plan to visit. Ideally, this conversation should take place at least 4–6 weeks before your scheduled departure. Your health care provider can advise you on preventive medicines you may need, specific measures you need to take to stay healthy, and what to watch out for. He or she may also be able to provide you with the name(s) of health care providers or clinics that treat people with HIV infection in the region you plan to visit. Your health care provider may also:

  - recommend you pack a supply of medicine, such as antibiotics to treat travelers' diarrhea;

  - recommend certain vaccinations.

- Consult CDC Health Information for International Travel (commonly called the Yellow Book). The section on Immunocompromised Travelers has an extensive amount of information that may be useful for you. Make sure your health care provider knows about this source of information.

- If you are traveling to an area where insect-borne diseases (such as dengue fever, yellow fever, or malaria) are common, minimize the risk of getting bitten by mosquitoes or ticks. Remember to:

  - Pack a good supply of insect repellant that contains at least 30 percent DEET;

  - Wear lightweight long pants and shirts with long sleeves;

  - Wear a hat and inspect your scalp and body daily for ticks.

- You doctor may also recommend:

  - Sleeping under a mosquito net to prevent mosquito bites;

  - Taking medicine to prevent getting malaria.

- Educate and prepare yourself.

- **About your destination**: Make sure you know if the countries you plan to visit have special health rules for visitors, especially visitors with HIV infection.

- **About your insurance policies**:

  - Review your medical insurance to see what coverage it provides when you are away from home. You may purchase supplemental traveler's insurance to cover the cost of emergency medical evacuation by air and the cost of in-country care, if these costs may are not covered by your regular insurance.

  - Take proof of insurance, such as a photocopy or scan your policy and send the image to an e-mail address you can access both in the United States and abroad. Leave a copy at home and tell your friends or family where it is located.

When You Travel Abroad

- **Food and water** in developing countries may contain germs that could make you sick.

  - **Do not**
    - eat raw fruit or vegetables that you do not peel yourself;
    - eat raw or undercooked seafood or meat;
    - eat unpasteurized dairy products;
    - eat anything from a street vendor;
    - drink tap water (in developing countries some hotels may purify their own water but it is safer to avoid it), drinks made with tap water, or ice made from tap water.

  - **Do** eat and drink:
    - hot foods;
    - hot coffee or tea;
    - bottled water and drinks (make sure the seals are original and have not been tampered with);
    - water that you bring to a rolling boil for one full minute then cool in a covered and clean vessel;
    - fruits that you peel;
    - wine, beer and other alcoholic beverages are also safe.

- **Tuberculosis** is very common worldwide, and can be severe in people with HIV. Avoid hospitals and clinics where coughing TB patients are treated. See your doctor upon your return to discuss whether you should be tested for TB.

- **Animal wastes**, such as fecal droppings in soil or on sidewalks, can pose hazards to individuals with weakened immune systems. Physical barriers, such as shoes, can protect you from direct contact. Likewise, towels can protect you from direct contact when lying on a beach or in parks. If you are in physical contact with animals, wash your hands thoroughly afterwards with soap and water.

- **Take all your medications** on schedule, as usual.

- **Stick to your special diet**, if you are on one.

- **Take the same precautions** that you take at home to prevent transmitting HIV to others.

Section 38.4

Vaccinations

This section includes excerpts from "Vaccines," AIDS.gov, May 12, 2014; and text from "Recommended Vaccines for Adults," Centers for Disease Control and Prevention (CDC), January 25, 2013.

What are vaccines and what do they do?

A vaccine—also called a "shot" or "immunization"—is a substance that teaches your body's immune system to recognize and defend against harmful viruses or bacteria **before** you get infected. These are called "preventive vaccines" or "prophylactic vaccines," and you get them while you are healthy. This allows your body to set up defenses against those dangers ahead of time. That way, you won't get sick if you're exposed to them later. Preventive vaccines are widely used to prevent diseases like polio, chicken pox, measles, mumps, rubella, influenza (flu), and hepatitis A and B.

In addition to preventive vaccines, there are also therapeutic vaccines. These are vaccines that are designed to treat people who already have a disease. Some scientists prefer to refer to therapeutic vaccines as "therapeutic immunogens." Currently, there is only one FDA-approved therapeutic vaccine for advanced prostate cancer in men.

HIV Infection and Adult Vaccination

Vaccines are especially critical for people with chronic health conditions such as HIV infection.

If you have HIV infection and your CD4 count is 200 or greater, talk with your doctor about:

- Influenza vaccine each year to protect against seasonal flu

- Tdap vaccine to protect against whooping cough and tetanus

- Pneumococcal vaccine to protect against pneumonia and other pneumococcal diseases

- Hepatitis B vaccine series to protect against hepatitis B

- HPV vaccine series to protect against human papillomavirus if you are a man or woman up to age 26 years

- MMR vaccine to protect against measles, mumps, and rubella if you were born in 1957 or after and have not gotten this vaccine or have immunity to these diseases

- Varicella vaccine to protect against chickenpox if you were born in 1980 or after and have not gotten two doses of this vaccine or have immunity to this disease

If you have HIV infection and your CD4 count is less than 200, talk with your doctor about:

- Influenza vaccine each year to protect against seasonal flu

- Tdap vaccine to protect against whooping cough and tetanus

- Pneumococcal vaccine to protect against pneumonia and other pneumococcal diseases

- Hepatitis B vaccine series to protect against hepatitis B

- HPV vaccine series to protect against human papillomavirus if you are a man or woman up to age 26 years

Chapter 39

Life Issues When You Have HIV/AIDS

Chapter Contents

533

Section 39.1

Dating, Marriage, and HIV

Text in this section is excerpted from "Dating and Marriage," AIDS.
gov, August 13, 2014.

If you are living with HIV, you may be wondering whether you can
ever date or get married. The answer is: "Yes!"

It's true that the issue of having a sexual relationship with a
partner can cause anxiety when you are living with HIV. But you
have to remember—"living with HIV" means just that: Living! Having HIV does not prevent you from dating or marrying—it just may
require a little more responsibility and trust from you and your
partner.

PEOPLE LIVING WITH HIV LIVE FULL & HEALTHY LIVES, INCLUDING HAVING INTIMATE RELATIONSHIPS

HAVING HIV DOESN'T PREVENT YOU FROM DATING & MARRYING—IT JUST MAY REQUIRE A LITTLE MORE RESPONSIBILITY & TRUST FROM BOTH PARTNERS.

IF YOU ARE HIV+ & YOUR PARTNER IS HIV−, THERE ARE STEPS YOU CAN TAKE TO REDUCE THE RISK OF TRANSMITTING HIV FROM YOU TO HIM OR HER.

Figure 39.1. *Dating and HIV*

When Should You Tell Someone You Have HIV?

Disclosing your HIV-positive status to a potential intimate partner
may be one of the most personal and stressful situations you will face.
But when that information is shared, you and your partner can both
make informed choices about safer sex, including using condoms and
medicines that prevent and treat HIV.

There is no "right" way to disclose, but here are some tips that can
help you:

- **Don't wait until the heat of the moment to start talking
  about HIV.** It's better to talk about it earlier than later—certainly before you have sex.

- **Some people living with HIV have suggested that it helps to talk about your status earlier in the relationship than later.** Disclosing you are HIV-positive after you've become close to someone can cause your partner to feel as though you have kept something important from him or her.

- **Don't force it.** Find the right time and place to have a conversation. You can schedule a time to talk or have spontaneous conversations in a setting where you are comfortable.

- **Try scheduling regular check-ins or "talkiversaries."** The key to having a healthy relationship is having an open dialogue throughout the relationship. It can be hard to find the right time to bring these things up. If you agree to schedule them in advance, no one has to wonder about the timing of the conversations.

- **A conversation does not have to be face-to-face.** Whether you talk, type, or text, what is important is that you start the conversation about HIV.

Also, it's important to keep in mind that many states have laws that require you to tell your sexual partners if you are HIV-positive before you have sex (anal, vaginal, or oral). In some states, you can be charged with a crime if you don't tell your partner your HIV status, even if your partner doesn't become infected.

In addition, to promote safe and voluntary HIV disclosure and address the barriers that may prevent some people living with HIV from disclosing their status, the President's Advisory Council on HIV/AIDS (PACHA) and the CDC/HRSA Advisory Committee on HIV, Viral Hepatitis and STD Prevention and Care (CHAC) have issued Joint Recommendations on Safe and Voluntary Disclosure of HIV in the United States.

Serosorting

Some people living with HIV choose to practice "serosorting"—having sex only with partners of the same HIV status, often to engage in unprotected sex, in order to reduce the risk of transmitting the virus to an HIV-negative person. However, the CDC does not recommend serosorting as a safer sex practice. Among the reasons it is not recommended is that serosorting does not protect against other sexually transmitted infections (STIs), such as hepatitis B virus (HBV), hepatitis C virus (HCV), syphilis, and herpes. There is also the risk of HIV re-infection (infection with another strain of HIV), which can result in harder-to-treat HIV superinfection.

Keep Yourself and Your Partner Healthy

If you are living with HIV and your partner is HIV-negative, here are steps you can take to reduce the risk of transmitting HIV from you to him or her:

- **Use antiretroviral therapy (ART).** ART reduces the amount of virus in your blood and body fluids. ART can keep you healthy for many years, and greatly reduce your chance of transmitting HIV to your sexual partner(s) if you take it consistently and correctly.

- **If you are taking ART, follow your healthcare provider's advice.** Visit your provider regularly and always take your medicine as directed.

- **Use condoms consistently and correctly.** When used correctly and consistently, condoms are highly effective in preventing HIV infection, as well as other sexually transmitted diseases (STDs). Both male and female condoms are available.

- **Choose less risky sexual behaviors.** Oral sex is much less risky than anal or vaginal sex. Anal sex is the highest-risk sexual activity for HIV transmission. During anal sex, it is less risky for you as the HIV-positive partner to be the receptive partner (bottom) than the insertive partner (top). Sexual activities that do not involve the potential exchange of bodily fluids carry no risk for getting HIV (e.g., touching).

- **Talk to your partner about pre-exposure prophylaxis (PrEP).** PrEP is a way for people who don't have HIV to prevent HIV infection by taking a pill every day. The pill contains two medicines that are also used to treat HIV. Along with other prevention methods like condoms, PrEP can offer good protection against HIV if taken every day. CDC recommends PrEP be considered for people who are HIV-negative and at substantial risk for HIV infection. This includes HIV-negative individuals who are in an ongoing relationship with an HIV-infected partner.

- **Talk to your partner about post-exposure prophylaxis (PEP) if you think they have had a possible exposure to HIV.** An example of a possible exposure is if you have anal or vaginal sex without a condom or the condom breaks and your partner is not on PrEP. Your partner's chance of exposure to HIV is lower if you are taking ART consistently and correctly, especially if your viral load is undetectable. Your partner should talk to his/her doctor right away (within 3 days) if they think they have had a possible exposure to HIV. Starting medicine immediately (known as post-exposure prophylaxis, or PEP) and taking it daily for 4 weeks reduces your partner's chance of getting HIV.

- **Get tested and treated for STDs and encourage your partner to do the same.** If you are sexually active, get tested at least once a year. STDs can have long-term health consequences. If you are living with HIV, STDs can also increase your risk of transmitting it to others. You should also encourage your partner to get tested for HIV at least once a year so they are sure about their HIV status and can take action to keep them healthy. They may benefit from more frequent testing (e.g., every 3-6 months).

Frequently Asked Questions

Can a heterosexual mixed-status couple conceive a baby without passing the virus to the uninfected partner or the baby?

Mixed-status couples can have healthy children, but it's important to talk to a healthcare provider about what you can do to lower the risk of passing HIV to the uninfected partner or the baby. PrEP is one of several options to protect the uninfected partner during conception and pregnancy, and there are also ways to get pregnant without having unprotected sex. The risks of transmitting HIV are different for men and women, and your provider can give you information to help you conceive safely.

If I have an undetectable viral load, can I still transmit HIV to my partner?

Yes. Having an undetectable viral load greatly lowers your chance of transmitting the virus to your sexual partners who are HIV-negative. However, even if you have an undetectable viral load, you still have HIV in your body, which means there is still a chance that you could potentially infect a partner. Taking other actions, like using a condom consistently and correctly, can lower your chances of transmitting HIV even more.

Section 39.2

Having Children

Text in this section is excerpted from "Family Planning," AIDS.gov,
October 2, 2015.

Can I Have Children If I Have HIV?

Yes, someone living with HIV can become a parent. But, since there
is a potential to transmit HIV to an uninfected partner during conception or to the baby during pregnancy and childbirth, it is important to
learn about the multiple ways to reduce these risks.

Discuss your hopes and plans for having children during your regular medical visits with your health care provider. These discussions
(called "preconception care") can help you, your partner, and your
health care provider plan for a healthy pregnancy and delivery.

Here are some questions to ask your health care provider if you
are considering starting a family. (The specific questions and answers
will vary depending on whether you are a man or a woman living with
HIV):

1. When do I wish to conceive a baby?

2. Is my viral load undetectable?

3. What's the safest way for my partner and I to conceive?

4. How do I avoid transmitting HIV to my partner, surrogate, or
    baby during conception, pregnancy, and delivery?

5. If my partner is on pre-exposure prophylaxis (PrEP), will we
    have a lower chance of transmitting HIV to our baby?

6. If I become pregnant, will HIV cause problems for me during
    pregnancy or delivery?

7. Will my baby have HIV?

8. Will my HIV treatment cause problems for my baby?

9. If I become pregnant, what medical and community programs
    and support groups can help me and my baby?

Answers to these questions can help you make the best-informed family planning decisions possible.

Contraception and HIV

If you don't want to become pregnant, talk to your healthcare provider about the best birth control methods for you. Be sure to discuss methods for both protecting against unintended pregnancy and HIV transmission or getting or transmitting sexually transmitted infections (STIs).

How Can I Reduce the Chance of Transmitting HIV to My Baby?

If you are a woman living with HIV, you can greatly lower your risk of passing HIV to your baby by taking a combination of HIV medicines (called antiretroviral therapy or ART), during pregnancy, labor, and delivery. Newborn babies born to HIV-infected mothers are also given HIV medicines to protect them.

Talk to your healthcare provider about HIV medicines for you and your baby before, during, and after your delivery.

And if you are already on ART, don't stop taking your medicine. It is important to stay on treatment to protect your health and prevent passing HIV to your baby. But your HIV regimen may change during pregnancy. Work closely with your healthcare provider to find an HIV regimen that is right for you and always talk to your provider before making any changes.

Also talk to your health care provider about delivery options. For example, for women with a high or unknown HIV viral load near the time of delivery, a scheduled cesarean delivery (sometimes called a C-section) at 38 weeks of pregnancy is recommended to reduce the risk of mother-to-child transmission of HIV.

And because HIV can spread in breast milk, women with HIV in the United States should not breastfeed their babies. In the United States, infant formula is a safe and healthy alternative to breast milk.

If you are HIV-negative woman but your partner has HIV, ask your health care provider about PrEP, a daily pill that can prevent HIV during conception and pregnancy. Encourage your partner to get and stay on ART, which greatly reduces the chance that your partner will pass HIV to you.

Get tested for HIV when you are planning a pregnancy or as soon as possible after you find out you are pregnant.

You should be tested again in your third trimester if you engage in behaviors that put you at risk for HIV.

Is Adoption an Option?

Adopting a baby can be an option for people with HIV who want to begin or expand their families.

The American with Disabilities Act does not allow adoption agencies to discriminate against individuals or couples with HIV. If you are interested in adoption, contact a local HIV service provider for help in getting referred to organizations or agencies.

Section 39.3

Aging with HIV/AIDS

Text in this section is excerpted from "Aging with HIV/AIDS,"
AIDS.gov, July 10, 2015.

Growing Older with HIV

At the start of the epidemic more than 30 years ago, people who were diagnosed with HIV/AIDS could expect to live only 1-2 years after that diagnosis. This meant that the issues of aging were not a major focus for people with HIV disease.

But in recent days, thanks to improvements in the effectiveness antiretroviral therapy (ART), people with HIV who are diagnosed early in their infection, and who get and stay on ART can keep the virus suppressed and live as long as their HIV-negative peers. For this reason, a growing number of people living with HIV in the United States are aged 55 and older. Many of them have been living with HIV for years; others are recently infected or diagnosed. According to CDC, people aged 55 and older accounted for more than one-quarter (26% or 313,2000) of the estimated 1.2 million people living with HIV in the U.S. in 2011.

Complications Associated with Aging

So the good news is that people with HIV are living longer, healthier lives if they are on treatment and achieve and maintain a suppressed viral load. However, with this longer life expectancy Individuals living with long-term HIV infection exhibit many clinical characteristics commonly observed in aging: multiple chronic diseases or conditions, the use of multiple medications, changes in physical and cognitive abilities, and increased vulnerability to stressors.

Complications Associated with Long-Term HIV Infection

While effective HIV treatments have decreased the likelihood of AIDS-defining illnesses among people aging with HIV, HIV-associated non-AIDS conditions are more common in individuals with long-standing HIV infection. These conditions include cardiovascular disease, lung disease, certain cancers, HIV-Associated Neurocognitive Disorders (HAND), and liver disease (including hepatitis B and hepatitis C), among others.

In addition, HIV appears to increase the risk for several age-associated diseases as well as to cause chronic inflammation throughout the body. Chronic inflammation is associated with a number of health conditions, including cardiovascular disease, lymphoma, and type 2 diabetes. Researchers are working to better understand what causes chronic inflammation, even when people are being treated with ART for their HIV disease.

HIV and its treatment can also have profound effects on the brain. Although AIDS-related dementia, once relatively common among people with HIV, is now rare, researchers estimate that more than 50 percent of people with HIV have an HIV-Associated Neurocognitive Disorder (HAND). HAND may include deficits in attention, language, motor skills, memory, and other aspects of cognitive function that may significantly affect a person's quality of life. People who have HAND may also experience depression or psychological distress. Researchers are studying how HIV and its treatment affect the brain, including the affects on older people living with HIV.

Late HIV Diagnosis

Older Americans are more likely than younger Americans to be diagnosed with HIV infection late in the course of their disease, meaning they get a late start to treatment and possibly more damage to their immune system. This can lead to poorer prognoses and shorter survival after an HIV diagnosis. Late diagnoses can occur because health care providers may not always test older people for HIV infection, and older people may mistake HIV symptoms for those of normal aging and don't consider HIV as a cause.

The Importance of Support Services

Living with HIV presents certain challenges, no matter what your age. But older people with HIV may face different issues than their younger counterparts, including greater social isolation and loneliness. Stigma is also a particular concern among older people with HIV. Stigma negatively affects people's quality of life, self-image, and behaviors, and may prevent them disclosing their HIV status or seeking HIV care.

Therefore, it is important for older people with HIV to get linked to HIV care and have access to mental health and other support services to help them stay healthy and remain engaged in HIV care. You can find support services through your healthcare provider, your local community center, or HIV/AIDS service organization. Or use the AIDS.gov HIV Testing and Care Services Locator to find services near you.

Section 39.4

Employment

Text in this section is excerpted from "Employment," AIDS.gov, October 10, 2014.

Working with HIV/AIDS

With proper care and treatment, many people living with HIV/AIDS lead normal, healthy lives, including having a job. Most people with HIV/AIDS can continue working at their current jobs or look for a new job in their chosen field. Your overall well-being and financial health can be more stable when you are gainfully employed.

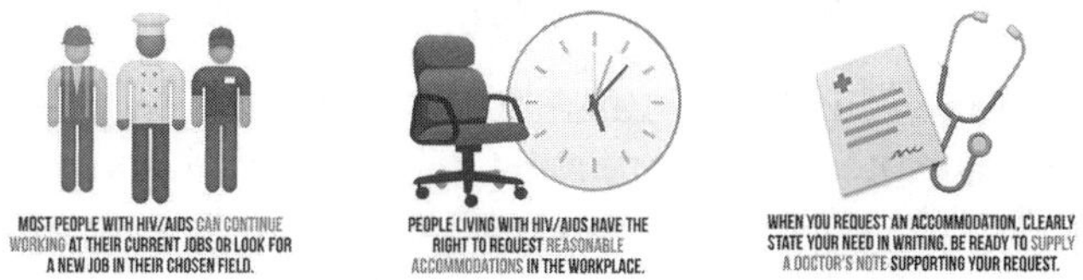

MOST PEOPLE WITH HIV/AIDS CAN CONTINUE WORKING AT THEIR CURRENT JOBS OR LOOK FOR A NEW JOB IN THEIR CHOSEN FIELD.

PEOPLE LIVING WITH HIV/AIDS HAVE THE RIGHT TO REQUEST REASONABLE ACCOMMODATIONS IN THE WORKPLACE.

WHEN YOU REQUEST AN ACCOMMODATION, CLEARLY STATE YOUR NEED IN WRITING. BE READY TO SUPPLY A DOCTOR'S NOTE SUPPORTING YOUR REQUEST.

Figure 39.2. *Working with HIV/AIDS*

Getting a New Job or Returning to Work

Working will affect a lot of your life: your medical status, your finances, your social life, the way you spend your time, and perhaps even your housing or transportation needs. Before taking action on getting a new job or returning to work, you may want to get information and perspectives from:

- Your HIV/AIDS case manager or counselor, if you have one

- Benefits counselors at an AIDS service organization or other community organization

- The Social Security Administration's Work Incentives Planning and Assistance Program (WIPA)

- Other people living with HIV who are working, or have returned to work

- Providers of any of your housing, medical, or financial benefits

- Public and non-profit employment and training service providers

Here are some questions to discuss with them:

- What are my goals for employment?

- What kind of work do I want to do?

- What are the resources that can help me set and achieve a new career goal?

- Are there state or local laws that further strengthen anti-discrimination protections in the ADA?

- How do I access training or education that will help me achieve my goals?

- How can I plan to take care of my health if I go to work?

- How will my going to work impact the benefits I am receiving?

543

Requesting Reasonable Accommodations

Qualified individuals with disabilities, including people living with HIV/AIDS, have the right to request reasonable accommodations in the workplace. A reasonable accommodation is any modification or adjustment to a job or work environment that enables a qualified person with a disability to apply for or perform a job. An accommodation may be tangible (for example, a certain type of chair) or non-tangible (for example, a modified work schedule for someone with a medical condition requiring regular appointments with a health care provider). You are "qualified" if you are able to perform the essential functions of the job, with or without reasonable accommodation.

Your supervisor may not be trained in reasonable accommodations or know how to negotiate them. For that reason, often it's best to go directly to the person responsible for human resources at your employer, even if that person works in a different location. In a small business, that person may well be the owner.

When you request an accommodation, state clearly what you need (for example, time off for a clinic visit every third Tuesday of the month, a certain type of chair, or a change in your work hours) and be ready to supply a doctor's note supporting your request. The initial note need not contain your diagnosis, but it should verify that you are under that doctor's care and that he/she believes you need the accommodation to maintain your health or to be able to fulfill essential functions of your job.

Many people living with HIV/AIDS do not want to give a lot of details about their health. If you prefer not to provide a lot of information, you may want to limit the medical information you initially give to your employer. However, if your need for accommodation is not obvious, your employer may require that you provide medical documentation to establish that you have a disability as defined by the ADA, to show that the employee needs the requested accommodation, and to help determine effective accommodation options. This can, but often does not, include disclosing your specific medical condition.

Be aware that not all people with HIV/AIDS will need accommodations to perform their jobs and many others may only need a few or simple accommodations. The U.S. Department of Labor's (DOL) Job Accommodation Network (JAN) provides free, expert, and confidential technical assistance to both employees and employers on workplace accommodations and disability employment issues, which includes resources for employees living with HIV/AIDS (see AskJAN.org or call 800-526-7234 Voice or 877-781-9403 TTY for one-on-one guidance).

Chapter 40

HIV/AIDS Patients and Legal Rights

Chapter Contents

545

Section 40.1

Legal Disclosure Requirements and Other Considerations

Text in this section is excerpted from "Legal Disclosure," AIDS.gov,
June 01, 2012.

HIV Disclosure Policies and Procedures

If your HIV test is positive, the clinic or other testing site will report the results to your state health department. They do this so that public health officials can monitor what's happening with the HIV epidemic in your city and state. (It's important for them to know this, because Federal and state funding for HIV/AIDS services is often targeted to areas where the epidemic is strongest.)

Your state health department will then remove all of your personal information (name, address, etc.) from your test results and send the information to the U.S. Centers for Disease Control and Prevention (CDC). CDC is the Federal agency responsible for tracking national public health trends. CDC does not share this information with anyone else, including insurance companies.

Many states and some cities have *partner-notification laws*—meaning that, if you test positive for HIV, you (or your healthcare provider) may be legally obligated to tell your sex or needle-sharing partner(s). In some states, if you are HIV-positive and don't tell your partner(s), you can be charged with a crime. Some health departments require healthcare providers to report the name of your sex and needle-sharing partner(s) if they know that information—even if you refuse to report that information yourself.

Some states also have laws that require clinic staff to notify a "third party" if they know that person has a significant risk for exposure to HIV from a patient the staff member knows is infected with HIV. This is called *duty to warn*. The *Ryan White HIV/AIDS Program* requires that health departments receiving money from the Ryan White program show "good faith" efforts to notify the marriage partners of a patient with HIV/AIDS.

Disclosure Policies In Correctional Facilities

If you are serving time in a jail or prison, your HIV status may be disclosed legally under the Occupational Safety and Health Administration's (OSHA) Standard for Occupational Exposure to *Bloodborne Pathogens*. State or local laws may also require that your HIV status be reported to public health authorities, parole officers spouses, or sexual partners.

Section 40.2

Your Rights in the Workplace

Text in this section is excerpted from "Workplace," AIDS.gov, October 10, 2014.

HIV At Work

The impact of the HIV/AIDS epidemic on the workplace gets bigger each year. That's because people between the ages of 20-44 are most affected by HIV/AIDS—and they also make up over 50% of our nation's 143 million workers.

Thanks to advances in antiretroviral therapy (ART), with the proper care and treatment, people living with HIV can live healthy lives and continue to contribute their skills and talents to America's labor force.

If you are living with HIV, it's important that you know how HIV/AIDS laws affect you at work. Here are some of the most important ones:

- The **Americans with Disabilities Act of 1990 (ADA)** prohibits employment discrimination on the basis of disability. The ADA covers businesses that employ 15 or more people and applies to employment decisions at all stages. U.S. courts have ruled that, even if you have *asymptomatic HIV*, you are protected under this law.

- The mission of the **Occupational Safety and Health Administration (OSHA)** is to save lives, prevent injuries, and protect the health of America's workers. To accomplish this, Federal and state governments work in partnership with the more than 100 million working men and women and their 6.5 million employers who are covered by the Occupational Safety and Health Act of 1970.

- The **Family Medical Leave Act of 1993 (FMLA)** applies to private-sector employers with 50 or more employees within 75 miles of the work site. If you are eligible, you can take leave for serious medical conditions or to provide care for an immediate family member with a serious medical condition, including HIV/AIDS. You are entitled to a total of 12 weeks of job-protected, unpaid leave during any 12-month period.

- The **Health Insurance Portability and Accountability Act of 1996 (HIPAA)** addresses some of the barriers to healthcare you may face if you are living with HIV. If you have group health coverage, HIPAA protects you from discriminatory treatment by your insurance provider. HIPAA also makes it easier for small groups (such as businesses with a small number of employees) to get and keep health insurance coverage, and gives people who lose (or leave) their group health coverage new options for buying individual coverage.

- The **Consolidated Omnibus Budget Reconciliation Act of 1986 (COBRA)**allows employees to continue their health insurance coverage at their own expense for a period of time after their employment ends. For most employees, ceasing work for health reasons, the period of time to which benefits may be extended ranges from 18 to 36 months.

Frequently Asked Questions

I am an HIV/AIDS Service Provider. What resources are available to help me support people living with HIV in securing employment or returning to the labor force?

Getting to Work is an online, multi-media training curriculum developed collaboratively by the U.S. Department of Labor and the U.S. Department of Housing and Urban Development to assist HIV service providers and housing providers to better understand how employment can add value for individuals, families and communities, and to provide strategies they can implement to incorporate employment into their approach.

Section 40.3

Affordable Care Act

Text in this section is excerpted from "The Affordable Care Act Helps People Living with HIV/AIDS," Centers for Disease Control and Prevention (CDC), June 2, 2014.

On March 23, 2010, President Obama signed the Affordable Care Act and set into place an effort that will help ensure Americans have secure, stable, affordable health insurance. Historically, people living with HIV and AIDS have had a difficult time obtaining private health insurance and have been particularly vulnerable to insurance industry abuses. Consistent with the goals of the President's National HIV/ AIDS Strategy, the Affordable Care Act makes considerable strides in addressing these concerns and advancing equality for people living with HIV and AIDS.

Improving Access to Coverage

Currently, fewer than one in five (17%) people living with HIV has private insurance and nearly 30% do not have any coverage. Medicaid, the Federal-state program that provides health care benefits to people with low incomes and those living with disabilities, is a major source of coverage for people living with HIV/AIDS, as is Medicare, the Federal program for seniors and people with disabilities. The Ryan White HIV/ AIDS Program is another key source of funding for health and social services for this population.

The Affordable Care Act is one of the most important pieces of legislation in the fight against HIV/AIDS in our history. As of September 23, 2010, insurers are no longer able to deny coverage to children living with HIV or AIDS. The parents of as many as 17.6 million children with pre-existing conditions no longer have to worry that their children will be denied coverage because of a pre-existing condition. Insurers also are prohibited from cancelling or rescinding coverage to adults or children because of a mistake on an application. And insurers can no longer impose lifetime caps on insurance benefits. Because of the law, 105 million Americans no longer have a lifetime dollar limit on essential health benefits. These changes will begin to improve access to insurance for people living with HIV/AIDS and other disabling conditions and help people with these conditions retain the coverage they have.

For people who have been locked out of the insurance market because of their health status, including those living with HIV/AIDS, the law created the Pre-existing Condition Insurance Plan. More than 90,000 people—some of whom are living with HIV or AIDS—have enrolled in this program, which has helped change lives and, in many cases, save them.

These changes will provide an important bridge to the significant changes in 2014 as the Affordable Care Act is fully implemented. Beginning in 2014, insurers will not be allowed to deny coverage to anyone or impose annual limits on coverage. People with low and middle incomes will be eligible for tax subsidies that will help them buy coverage from new state health insurance Exchanges. The Affordable Care Act also broadens Medicaid eligibility to generally include individuals with income below 133% of the Federal poverty line ($14,400 for an individual and $29,300 for a family of 4), including single adults without children who were previously not generally eligible for Medicaid. As a result, in many states, a person living with HIV who meets this income threshold will no longer have to wait for an AIDS diagnosis in order to become eligible for Medicaid.

The Affordable Care Act also closes, over time, the Medicare Part D prescription drug benefit "donut hole," giving Medicare enrollees living with HIV and AIDS the peace of mind that they will be better able to afford their medications. Beneficiaries receive a 50% discount on covered brand-name drugs while they are in the "donut hole," a considerable savings for people taking costly HIV/AIDS drugs. And in the years to come, they can expect additional savings on their prescription drugs while they are in the coverage gap until it is closed in 2020.

In addition, as a result of the health care law, AIDS Drug Assistance Program (ADAP) benefits are now considered as contributions toward Medicare Part D's True Out of Pocket Spending Limit ("TrOOP"). This is a huge relief for ADAP clients who are Medicare Part D enrollees, since they will now be able to move through the donut hole more quickly, which was difficult, if not impossible, for ADAP clients to do before this change.

Ensuring Quality Coverage

The Affordable Care Act also helps people with public or private coverage have access to the information they need to get the best quality care. This includes:

- Better information. Because of the Affordable Care Act, people living with HIV and AIDS will also be offered more information and services. Plans are required to provide information in a user-friendly manner that clearly explains what is and isn't covered.

- Quality, comprehensive care. The law ensures health plans in the individual and small-group markets beginning in 2014 offer benefits similar to that of a typical employer plan, including prescription drugs, preventive services and chronic disease management, and mental health and substance use disorder services.

- Preventive care. Many private health insurance plans must now cover recommended preventive services, like certain cancer screenings, at no additional cost. HIV screening for adults and adolescents at higher risk and HIV screening and counseling for women are also covered without cost-sharing in most private plans. Medicare also covers certain recommended preventive services, including HIV screening for individuals at increased risk, without cost-sharing or deductibles. These services will help people living with HIV and AIDS stay healthy and prevent the spread of HIV as well.

- Coordinated care. The law also recognizes the value of patient-centered medical homes (coordinated, integrated, and comprehensive care) as an effective way to strengthen the quality of care, especially for people with complex chronic conditions. The Ryan White HIV/AIDS Program is the pioneer in the development of this model in the HIV health care system.

Increasing Opportunities for Health and Well-Being

Despite significant advances in HIV treatment and education, there are an estimated 50,000 new HIV infections annually, and there are significant racial and gender disparities with the majority of new infections among gay men, African Americans, and Latinos. The health of people living with HIV and AIDS is influenced not only by their ability to get coverage but also economic, social, and physical factors.

- Prevention and wellness. The law makes critical investments in prevention, wellness, and public health activities to improve public health surveillance, community-based programs, and outreach efforts. This includes increasing coverage for HIV testing.

- Diversity and cultural competency. The Affordable Care Act expands initiatives to strengthen cultural competency training for all health care providers and ensure all populations are treated equitably. It also bolsters the Federal commitment to reducing health disparities.

- Health care providers for underserved communities. The Affordable Care Act expands the health care workforce and increases funding for community health centers, an important safety-net for low-income individuals and families. A key recommendation of the National HIV/AIDS Strategy is to increase the number and diversity of available providers of clinical care and related services for people living with HIV. Thanks to the Affordable Care Act, the National Health Service Corps is providing loans and scholarships to more doctors, nurses, and other health care providers that in recent days serve approximately 10.4 million patients across the country. The National Health Service Corps has nearly tripled since 2008, a critical healthcare workforce expansion to better serve vulnerable populations.

Section 40.4

How the Laws Apply to Persons with HIV

This section includes excerpts from "HIV and the Law," Centers for Disease Control and Prevention (CDC), August 13, 2015; and text from "Legal Issues," AIDS.gov, February 9, 2012.

Fast Facts

Laws and policies are structural interventions that can be facilitators or barriers to effective HIV prevention and care activities. Examples of these laws and policies include:

- 49 states plus D.C. now have HIV testing laws that are consistent with CDC's 2006 recommendations, nearly twice as many as when the recommendations were released.
- 32 state Medicaid programs reimburse for routine HIV screening of adults aged 15-65 years, regardless of risk.
- 42 states plus D.C. require reporting of all CD4 and viral load laboratory data to HIV surveillance programs.

What's Law Got to Do with It?

Law impacts nearly every aspect of our lives. Laws and explicit policies can be viewed as structural interventions for achieving HIV prevention goals.

What CDC is Doing

Given the importance of law in HIV prevention work, the Division of HIV/AIDS Prevention (DHAP) has implemented public health law research methods to systematically collect and assess statutory and regulatory frameworks across a range of legal domains to help determine whether these legal frameworks act as barriers or facilitators to effective HIV prevention environments. DHAP has focused on the public health implications of state statutes and regulations across key HIV prevention topic areas, such as HIV testing, Medicaid reimbursement for routine HIV screening, laboratory reporting of CD4 and viral load data for HIV surveillance purposes, and criminalization of potential HIV exposure.

Legal Issues

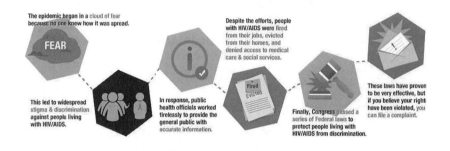

Figure 40.1. *AIDS and Legal Issues*

History

HIV/AIDS has been unlike any other public health issue of our time. The epidemic began in a cloud a fear because, at first, no one knew how it was spread. When it became clear that HIV was infectious, and that it was potentially fatal, there was no treatment. This led to widespread stigma and discrimination against people living with HIV/AIDS.

In response, public health officials worked tirelessly to provide the general public with accurate information about how HIV was, and was not, transmitted, and how people could protect themselves. Public health officials realized that the stigma attached to HIV/AIDS was getting in the way of testing and prevention efforts and keeping people from getting healthcare.

Despite the best efforts of public health officials, medical professionals, HIV/AIDS advocates, and people living with HIV/AIDS, HIV-related discrimination continued. People living with HIV/AIDS—and even some people who were merely rumored to have HIV—were fired from their jobs, evicted from their homes, and denied access to medical care and social services based on their HIV status.

After years of widespread discrimination, Congress passed a series of Federal laws to protect people living with HIV/AIDS from discrimination based on their HIV status and to give them the same legal protections as any other person with a medical disability.

One of the first legal protections was the **1990** *Americans with Disabilities Act (ADA)*. It expanded the reach of the *Rehabilitation Act of 1973* and made discrimination on the basis of disability unlawful. In the first Supreme Court case involving HIV/AIDS discrimination, the Court ruled that Congress intended HIV infection to be included as a disability under the ADA. HIV infection has been found to meet the definition of disability under Federal and state laws protecting the disabled from all forms of discrimination.

A few years later, Congress enacted another important legal protection, the *Health Insurance Portability and Accountability Act of 1996 (HIPAA)*. HIPAA is designed to protect the privacy of patients' medical records and other health information. It also provides patients with access to their medical records and with significant control over how their personal health information is used and disclosed. HIPAA has proven to be very effective in preventing discrimination against people living with HIV/AIDS by preventing others from knowing their HIV status.

People with HIV/AIDS who believe that their health information privacy rights have been violated may be eligible to file a complaint.

Frequently Asked Questions

Does the Americans with Disabilities Act (ADA) prohibit housing discrimination?

Housing discrimination is not covered by the ADA. However, the Fair Housing Amendments Act of 1988, which is primarily enforced by the U.S. Department of Housing and Urban Development (HUD), prohibits housing discrimination against people with disabilities, including those living with HIV/AIDS.

Can my insurance company drop me now that I have been diagnosed with HIV?

There are no simple answers to that question. You do have some protections. The Health Insurance Portability and Accountability Act of 1996 (HIPAA) helps people with HIV/AIDS get and keep their health insurance. HIPAA provides several protections important to people with HIV/AIDS:

- It limits (but doesn't eliminate) the ability of insurance companies to exclude you from coverage if you have a pre-existing condition.

Chapter 41

Insurance and Housing Options for People with HIV

Chapter Contents

Section 41.1

Insurance Options for People with HIV

Text in this section is excerpted from "Insurance," AIDS.gov,
June 1, 2012.

Because it can be very expensive to treat HIV, it's important to
know what your health insurance options are if you are living with
HIV disease. Some of the options include:

Group Health Insurance Plans

Group health insurance is private insurance often comes with
employment. Many of these programs cover comprehensive medical
care, including hospital visits, outpatient care (clinic settings) prescription coverage and specialist visits. In some cases, however, you
may still have to pay for some of your healthcare costs, even if you
have private insurance. Some of these costs might include co-pays or
premiums.

Individual Health Insurance Policies

You may be able to buy an individual health insurance policy, but
they tend to be more expensive and require a pre-screening application that may exclude coverage for pre-existing conditions, like HIV
disease.

Public Healthcare Programs

If you don't have health insurance—or you need help because your
insurance doesn't pay for the care you need—the programs listed
below can help by paying for care that is delivered by local and state
agencies.

- *Ryan White HIV/AIDS Program* – Funds outpatient primary
  care, HIV/AIDS drugs, and supportive services only when other
  public or private sources are not available.

- **Medicaid** – Supports healthcare for low-income individuals
  who meet eligibility requirements. Medicaid is administered by
  states, and each state sets its own guidelines for eligibility and
  services.

- **Medicare** – Federal health insurance program that supports medical care for those who qualify based on work history, age, and disability status.

- **Other programs that pay for HIV/AIDS medications** – These include: the Ryan White AIDS Drug Assistance Program (ADAP); Medicare Part D; patient assistance programs; and clinical trials.

HIPAA

The **Health Insurance Portability and Accountability Act of 1996 (HIPAA)** is not a type of insurance—but it was designed to make it easier for people to get and keep health insurance.

HIPAA has three main functions:

- It protects people with group insurance coverage from discriminatory treatment.

- It enables small groups (such as businesses with a small number of employees) to get, and keep, health insurance coverage more easily.

- It gives people new options for getting individual coverage when they lose or leave their group insurance (because of a job change or being fired/laid off, etc.)

This law provides several protections important to people with HIV/AIDS:

- It limits (but doesn't eliminate) the ability of insurance companies to exclude you from coverage if you have a pre-existing condition.

- If you have a family member who has had health problems in the past, or is having them now, HIPAA keeps group health plans from denying you coverage or charging additional fees for coverage because of your family member's health.

- It guarantees certain small business employers (and certain individuals who lose job-related coverage) the right to purchase individual health insurance.

- HIPAA guarantees, in most cases, that employers or individuals who purchase health insurance can renew the coverage, regardless of any health conditions of individuals covered under the insurance policy.

Frequently Asked Questions

Will my HIV test results be given to my insurance company?

In general, testing laboratories are not required to share your test results with insurance companies and can only share them with the "authorized person," which usually means you (the patient) and/or your healthcare provider who ordered the test and is responsible for using the results. This may vary from state to state and between insurance plans, however. If you file insurance claims for treatment for HIV or AIDS, then your insurance company will know you have HIV disease.

Will my insurance company drop me if I've been tested for HIV?

Your insurance company should not drop you for being tested for HIV—or for being HIV-positive. Certain insurance plans have restrictions on what they will pay for, including pre-existing conditions, but they should not drop you for taking an HIV test.

Section 41.2

Housing Options for People with HIV

Text in this section is excerpted from "Housing," AIDS.gov, June 1, 2012.

To help take care of the housing needs of low-income people who are living with HIV/AIDS and their families, the U.S. Department of Housing and Urban Development (HUD) manages the Housing Opportunities for Persons with AIDS (HOPWA) program.

Many different HOPWA programs and projects provide short-term and long-term rental assistance, operate community residences, or provide other supportive housing facilities that have been created to address the needs of people who are living with HIV/AIDS and the challenges that come with the disease.

- **Statewide HOPWA Information**

Find current contacts listed by state, maps, Executive Summaries, histories, and accomplishments for HOPWA grantees.

- **Technical Support of HOPWA Providers**

HOPWA Technical Assistance is available to all HOPWA grantees and project sponsors through the HOPWA National Technical Assistance program. Grantees interested in accessing HOPWA Technical Assistance may contact their local HUD Field Office or any HOPWA Technical Assistance provider directly for more information.

Other HUD Programs for Persons with HIV/AIDS

In addition to the HOPWA program, people living with HIV/AIDS are eligible for any HUD program for which they might otherwise qualify (such as being low-income or homeless). Programs include public housing, Section 8 housing assistance, Community Development Block Grants, and the Continuum of Care Homeless Assistance programs.

Chapter 42

National HIV Testing Day

National HIV Testing Day is a reminder to get the facts, get tested, and get involved to take care of yourself and your partners.

An estimated 1.2 million people in the United States are living with HIV, and that number grows by almost 50,000 every year. One in eight people who have HIV don't know it. That means they aren't getting the medical care they need to stay healthy and avoid passing HIV to others.

CDC has found that more than 90 percent of new HIV infections in the United States could be prevented by testing and diagnosing people who have HIV and ensuring they receive prompt, ongoing care and treatment. Early linkage to and retention in HIV care is central to managing HIV and promoting health among all people living with HIV. HIV medicines can keep people with HIV healthy for many years, and greatly reduce the chance of transmitting HIV to their sex partners.

Get the Facts

Protecting yourself and others against HIV starts with knowledge. Knowing the facts about HIV will help you make informed decisions about sex, drug use, and other activities that may put you and your partners at risk for HIV.

Text in this chapter is excerpted from "June 27 is National HIV Testing Day," Centers for Disease Control and Prevention (CDC), June 25, 2015.

- Learn the basics about HIV, how to prevent HIV transmission, and the steps you can take to protect yourself and others.

- Talk about what you learn with your friends and other people who are important to you.

- Empower even more people via social media. Share your new knowledge with your friends online.

Get Tested

The only way to know if you are infected with HIV is to get tested. CDC recommends that everyone between the ages of 13 and 64 get tested for HIV at least once as part of routine health care, and that people with certain risk factors get tested more often. People with more than one sex partner, people with sexually transmitted diseases (STDs), and people who inject drugs are likely to be at high risk and should get tested at least once a year. Sexually active gay and bisexual men may benefit from even more frequent testing, depending on their risk. To protect your own health, you should also get tested if you have been sexually assaulted.

If you are pregnant or planning to become pregnant, CDC recommends HIV testing with each pregnancy, both for your own benefit and to reduce the risk of transmitting HIV to your baby.

Knowing your HIV status gives you the power to control your health and your future. And getting tested has never been easier. You can ask your health care provider to test you for HIV. Many medical clinics, substance abuse programs, community health centers, and hospitals offer HIV testing. Testing is often free of charge. You can also

- Visit GetTested (gettested.cdc.gov) and enter your ZIP code.

- Text your ZIP code to KNOWIT (566948), and you will receive a text back with a testing site near you.

- Call 800-CDC-INFO (800-232-4636) to ask for free testing sites in your area.

- Contact your local health department.

- Get a home testing kit (the Home Access HIV-1 Test System or the OraQuick In-Home HIV Test) from a drugstore.

Get Involved

HIV testing is only one step. We can all do something to help stop HIV. Here are some ideas about how you and your friends can get involved.

- **Share** your knowledge of HIV or your personal HIV story with others. One of the best ways to increase awareness is through a personal connection with others. Participants featured in CDC's HIV awareness campaign Let's Stop HIV Together, shared their voices and personal stories to raise HIV awareness, reduce stigma, and champion the power of relationships in the personal and public fight to stop HIV.

- **Use social media to increase HIV awareness.** Follow @ TalkHIV and tweet about National HIV Testing Day using #NHTD. You can also like *Act Against AIDS* on Facebook and create your own Let's Stop HIV Together meme. Share your ad and encourage others to do the same.

- **Support people living with HIV.** Have an open, honest conversation about staying safe and healthy. Listen to the challenges that people living with HIV face and provide support for their special needs.

- **Volunteer in your community.** The first step to getting involved in HIV prevention is to contact your local AIDS service organizations and/or community health departments. These groups can help identify opportunities or other organizations that may need the support of volunteers.

In addition, CDC's Act Against AIDS campaign materials promote HIV awareness and testing in high-risk populations.

- *Let's Stop HIV Together* (www.cdc.gov/actagainstaids/campaigns/lsht/index.html) is a general-awareness campaign to reduce stigma by urging everyone to "Get the facts. Get tested. Get involved."

- *Start Talking. Stop HIV.* (www.cdc.gov/actagainstaids/campaigns/starttalking/index.html) encourages gay and bisexual men to communicate about testing and other HIV prevention issues.

- *Reasons* (www.cdc.gov/actagainstaids/campaigns/reasons/index.html) promotes HIV testing among gay and bisexual Hispanic/Latino men.

- *Testing Makes Us Stronger* (gettested.cdc.gov/Stronger/index.html) encourages African American gay and bisexual men to get tested for HIV.

- *Take Charge. Take the Test.* (gettested.cdc.gov/takecharge/index. aspx) encourages African American women to get tested for HIV.

- *One Test. Two Lives.* (www.cdc.gov/actagainstaids/campaigns/ ottl/index.html) focuses on ensuring that all women are tested for HIV early in their pregnancy.

Part Seven

Clinical Trials and Ongoing Research

Chapter 43

HIV/AIDS Clinical Trials –
Basic Information

Clinical Trials

- HIV/AIDS clinical trials are research studies done to look at new ways to prevent, detect, or treat HIV/AIDS. Clinical trials are the fastest way to determine if new medical approaches to HIV/AIDS are safe and effective in people.

- Examples of HIV/AIDS clinical trials under way include studies of new HIV medicines, studies of vaccines to prevent or treat HIV, and studies of medicines to treat infections related to HIV.

- The benefits and possible risks of participating in an HIV/AIDS clinical trial are explained to study volunteers before they decide whether to participate in a study.

- Use the AIDS*info* clinical trial search to find HIV/AIDS studies looking for volunteer participants. Some HIV/AIDS clinical trials enroll only people infected with HIV. Other studies enroll people who aren't infected with HIV.

Text in this chapter is excerpted from "HIV/AIDS Clinical Trials," AIDS*info*, September 15, 2015.

What is a clinical trial?

A clinical trial is a research study done to evaluate new medical approaches in people. New approaches can include:

- new medicines or new combinations of medicines

- new surgical procedures or devices

- new ways to use an existing medicine or device

Clinical trials are the fastest way to determine whether new medical approaches are safe and effective in people.

What is an HIV/AIDS clinical trial?

HIV/AIDS clinical trials help researchers find better ways to prevent, detect, or treat HIV/AIDS. All the medicines used to treat HIV/AIDS in the United States were first studied in clinical trials.

Examples of HIV/AIDS clinical trials under way include:

- studies of new medicines to treat HIV

- studies of vaccines to prevent or treat HIV

- studies of medicines to treat infections related to HIV

Can anyone participate in an HIV/AIDS clinical trial?

It depends on the study. Some HIV/AIDS clinical trials enroll only people infected with HIV. Other studies include people who aren't infected with HIV.

Other factors such as age, gender, HIV treatment history, or other medical conditions may also restrict who can participate in an HIV/AIDS clinical trial.

What are the benefits of participating in an HIV/AIDS clinical trial?

Participating in an HIV/AIDS clinical trial can provide benefits. For example, many people participate in HIV/AIDS clinical trials because they want to contribute to HIV/AIDS research. They may have HIV or know somebody who is infected with HIV.

People with HIV who participate in an HIV/AIDS clinical trial may benefit from new HIV medicines before they are widely available. They can also receive regular and careful medical care from a research team that includes doctors and other health professionals. Often the medicines and medical care are free of charge.

Sometimes people get paid for participating in a clinical trial. For example, they may receive money or a gift card. They may be reimbursed for the cost of meals or transportation.

Are HIV/AIDS clinical trials safe?

Researchers try to make HIV/AIDS clinical trials as safe as possible. However, volunteering to participate in a study that is testing an experimental treatment for HIV can involve risks of varying degrees. Risks can include unpleasant, serious, or even life-threatening side effects from the treatment being studied.

In a process called informed consent, study volunteers are informed of the possible risks and benefits of a clinical trial. Understanding the risks and benefits helps volunteers decide whether to participate in the study.

If I decide to participate in a clinical trial, will my personal information be shared?

The privacy of study volunteers is important to everyone involved in an HIV/AIDS clinical trial. The informed consent process includes an explanation of how a study volunteer's personal information is protected.

How can I find an HIV/AIDS trial in which to participate?

To find an HIV/AIDS clinical trial looking for volunteers, use the AIDS*info* clinical trial search. For help with your search, call an AIDS*info* health information specialist at 1-800-448-0440 (free) or e-mail contactus@aidsinfo.nih.gov.

Chapter 44

Ongoing Research

Chapter Contents

Section 44.1

Behavioral and Clinical Surveillance

This section includes excerpts from "Behavioral and Clinical
Surveillance," Centers for Disease Control and Prevention
(CDC), September 17, 2015; and text from "Youth Risk Behavior
Surveillance System (YRBSS)," Centers for Disease Control and
Prevention (CDC), May 15, 2015.

HIV behavioral and clinical surveillance and research help local,
state, and national organizations to better understand who is at risk
for HIV infection, who is recently diagnosed with HIV, and who has
illness related to HIV.

CDC HIV-Related Programs

MMP

The Medical Monitoring Project (MMP) is a surveillance project
designed to learn more about the experiences and needs of people
who are receiving care for HIV. It is supported by several government
agencies and conducted by state and local health departments along
with the CDC.

Youth

The Youth Risk Behavior Surveillance System (YRBSS) includes
a national school-based survey conducted by CDC and state, territorial, tribal, and local surveys conducted by state, territorial, and local
education and health agencies and tribal governments.

NHBS

National HIV Behavioral Surveillance (NHBS) data are used to
provide a behavioral context for trends seen in HIV surveillance data.
They also describe populations at increased risk for HIV infection and
thus provide an indication of the leading edge of the epidemic.

Cost-Effectiveness

The CDC Division of HIV/AIDS Prevention is pleased to provide a basic guide to the cost-effectiveness analysis of prevention interventions for HIV infection and AIDS. The purpose of this guide is to help prevention program staff and planners become more familiar with potential uses of economic evaluation.

Youth Risk Behavior Surveillance System (YRBSS)

The Youth Risk Behavior Surveillance System (YRBSS) monitors six types of health-risk behaviors that contribute to the leading causes of death and disability among youth and adults, including—

- Behaviors that contribute to unintentional injuries and violence

- Sexual behaviors that contribute to unintended pregnancy and sexually transmitted diseases, including HIV infection

- Alcohol and other drug use

- Tobacco use

- Unhealthy dietary behaviors

- Inadequate physical activity

YRBSS also measures the prevalence of obesity and asthma among youth and young adults.

YRBSS includes a national school-based survey conducted by CDC and state, territorial, tribal, and local surveys conducted by state, territorial, and local education and health agencies and tribal governments.

575

Section 44.2

Medical Monitoring Project

This section includes excerpts from "Medical Monitoring Project
(MMP)," Centers for Disease Control and Prevention (CDC),
February 23, 2015; and text from "Information for Potential
Participants," Centers for Disease Control and Prevention (CDC),
February 23, 2015.

About Medical Monitoring Project (MMP)

The Medical Monitoring Project (MMP) is a surveillance system
designed to learn more about the experiences and needs of people who
are living with HIV. It is supported by several government agencies
and conducted by state and local health departments along with the
Centers for Disease Control and Prevention (CDC).

By collecting locally and nationally representative behavioral
and medical record data from people living with HIV, MMP will help
answer the following questions:

- How many people living with HIV are receiving medical care for
  HIV?

- How easy is it to access medical care, prevention, and support
  services?

- What are the met and unmet needs of people living with HIV?

- How is treatment affecting people living with HIV?

To improve the usefulness of MMP data, in 2015 MMP was expanded
to include people living with HIV who are not receiving medical care.
This information can be used to guide policy and funding decisions
aimed at increasing engagement in care and improving quality of care
for people living with HIV throughout the United States.

Importance/Significance

MMP is important because it provides information about the behaviors, medical care, and health status of people living with HIV.

MMP is unique in that it describes comprehensive clinical and behavioral information from persons carefully sampled to represent everyone diagnosed with HIV in the United States. Because MMP's estimates are designed to be representative, information gathered from MMP may be used by prevention planning groups, policy leaders, health care providers, and people living with HIV to highlight disparities in care and services and advocate for needed resources.

Sampling Overview

From 2005–2014, MMP sampled persons from HIV care facilities, so only people receiving HIV medical care were included in the project. Starting in 2015, MMP introduced a new sampling method to include all adults diagnosed with HIV in the United States. This is accomplished using a two stage sampling strategy.

First Stage: State Level

All 50 states, the District of Columbia and Puerto Rico were eligible for inclusion in MMP.

A sample of states was based on the number of AIDS cases within each area. A total of 16 states and 1 U.S. territory were selected.

Second Stage: Person Level

A sample of about 400 HIV infected individuals from each area is selected each year from the National HIV Surveillance System. These individuals must be at least 18 years old and diagnosed with HIV. People who are selected are asked to participate in an interview during which they answer questions about their behavior and HIV medical care. They also give the MMP project staff permission to review their medical chart.

Sampled people's participation is very important – those who participate represent HIV-positive individuals like them who were not selected to participate.

Confidentiality

MMP project staff follow strict protocols to ensure participants' confidentiality. All information collected is kept confidential including patient and healthcare facility names. Names of selected people and facilities are NOT sent to CDC and will NOT be used in any reports.

Information for Potential Participants

How are people chosen to participate in MMP?

All HIV diagnoses are reported to public health departments. From this list, the Medical Monitoring Project (MMP) randomly chooses people living with HIV who are 18 years of age or older to participate in MMP. People are selected once a year so if you were not selected this year you may be selected next year.

If I am chosen for MMP, what will I be asked to do?

You will be asked to answer some questions related to your HIV and the care you receive. We will also ask permission to review your medical records.

Why should I participate?

This is your chance to share your experiences. This is important because your experience matters! Everyone with HIV is not selected to participate. You will represent other people living with HIV, so your participation is important. Your responses will help us collect information that truly represents the experiences of all people living with HIV.

Do I have to participate in MMP if I'm selected?

No, you do not have to participate and you can change your mind about participating at any time.

Will I be compensated for my time?

People who participate will receive a token of appreciation for their participation.

Is the information collected kept confidential?

Yes, all information collected will be kept confidential including your name, your contact information, and, if you have a health care provider, your provider's name or the facility where he or she practices. Participants' names, facility names and provider names are NOT sent to the CDC and will NOT be used in any reports.

Which areas are participating in MMP?

The following areas are participating: California; Chicago, IL; Delaware; Florida; Georgia; Houston, TX; Illinois; Indiana; Los Angeles,

CA; Michigan; Mississippi; New Jersey; New York City, NY; New York State; North Carolina; Oregon; Pennsylvania; Philadelphia, PA; Puerto Rico; San Francisco, CA; Texas; Virginia; and Washington State.

If I am selected to participate, who will be contacting me?

In most states, health department staff will contact you either by phone or by mail about being a part of MMP. In a few states, your healthcare provider my contact you first.

Where can I learn more about MMP?

You can contact your state or local health department or call the MMP Information Line for more information about MMP.

Community Advisory Board (CAB)

MMP works with a National Community Advisory Board (CAB) made up of local people from each MMP area who care about people living with HIV and the services they receive. They act as a link between MMP staff and people who participate in MMP. CAB members make sure the voice of people living with HIV is heard at the city, state, and national levels. They work with their local health department to make sure MMP respects participants' rights and protects their privacy. CAB members also make sure the information collected by MMP answers important public health questions. In addition, in some areas CAB members can answer questions about MMP and let you know how MMP helps the local community.

Part Eight

Additional Help and Information

Chapter 45

Glossary of HIV/AIDS-Related Terms

acquired immunodeficiency syndrome (AIDS): A disease of the immune system due to infection with HIV. HIV destroys the CD4 T lymphocytes (CD4 cells) of the immune system, leaving the body vulnerable to life-threatening infections and cancers. Acquired immunodeficiency syndrome (AIDS) is the most advanced stage of HIV infection. To be diagnosed with AIDS, a person with HIV must have an AIDS-defining condition or have a CD4 count less than 200 cells/mm^3 (regardless of whether the person has an AIDS-defining condition).

acute HIV infection: Early stage of HIV infection that extends approximately 1 to 4 weeks from initial infection until the body produces enough HIV antibodies to be detected by an HIV antibody test. During acute HIV infection, HIV is highly infectious because the virus is multiplying rapidly. The rapid increase in HIV viral load can be detected before HIV antibodies are present.

adherence: Taking medications (or other treatment) exactly as instructed by a health care provider. The benefits of strict adherence to an HIV regimen include sustained viral suppression, reduced risk of drug resistance, improved overall health and quality of life, and decreased risk of HIV transmission.

This glossary contains terms excerpted from documents produced by several sources deemed reliable.

AIDS-defining condition: Any HIV-related illness included in the Centers for Disease Control and Prevention's (CDC) list of diagnostic criteria for AIDS. AIDS-defining conditions include opportunistic infections and cancers that are life-threatening in a person with HIV.

alanine aminotransferase: A liver enzyme that plays a role in protein metabolism. Abnormally high blood levels of ALT are a sign of liver inflammation or damage from infection or drugs. A normal level is below approximately 50 IU/L.

amebiasis: An inflammation of the intestines caused by infection with Entamoeba histolytica (a type of ameba) and characterized by frequent, loose stools flecked with blood and mucus.

antiretroviral therapy (ART) : The daily use of a combination of HIV medicines (called an HIV regimen) to treat HIV infection. A person's initial HIV regimen generally includes three antiretroviral (ARV) drugs from at least two different HIV drug classes.

assay: A qualitative or quantitative analysis of a substance; a test.

asymptomatic: Without symptoms or not sick. Usually used in HIV/ AIDS literature to describe a person who has a positive reaction to one of several tests for HIV antibodies but who shows no clinical symptoms of the disease and who is not sick. Even though a person is asymptomatic, he or she may still infect another person with HIV.

baseline: An initial measurement used as the basis for future comparison. For people infected with HIV, baseline testing includes CD4 count, viral load (HIV RNA), and resistance testing. Baseline test results are used to guide HIV treatment choices and monitor effectiveness of antiretroviral therapy (ART).

CD4 cell: A type of lymphocyte. CD4 T lymphocytes (CD4 cells) help coordinate the immune response by stimulating other immune cells, such as macrophages, B lymphocytes (B cells), and CD8 T lymphocytes (CD8 cells), to fight infection. HIV weakens the immune system by destroying CD4 cells.

CD4 cell count: A laboratory test that measures the number of CD4 T lymphocytes (CD4 cells) in a sample of blood. In people with HIV, the CD4 count is the most important laboratory indicator of immune function and the strongest predictor of HIV progression. The CD4 count is one of the factors used to determine when to start antiretroviral therapy (ART). The CD4 count is also used to monitor response to ART.

cervical cancer: Cancer that forms in tissues of the cervix (the organ connecting the uterus and vagina). It is usually a slow-growing cancer that may not have symptoms but can be found with regular Pap tests (a procedure in which cells are scraped from the cervix and looked at under a microscope). Cervical cancer is almost always caused by human papillomavirus (HPV) infection.

chemotherapy: In general, it is the use of medicines to treat any disease. It is more commonly used to describe medicines to treat cancer.

chlamydia: A sexually transmitted disease (STD) caused by Chlamydia trachomatis that infects the genital tract. The infection is frequently asymptomatic (i.e. shows no symptoms), but if left untreated, it can cause sterility in women.

chronic HIV infection: Also known as asymptomatic HIV infection or clinical latency. The stage of HIV infection between acute HIV infection and the onset of AIDS. During chronic HIV infection, HIV levels gradually increase and the number of CD4 cells decrease. Declining CD4 cell levels indicate increasing damage to the immune system. Antiretroviral therapy (ART) can prevent HIV from destroying the immune system and advancing to AIDS.

clinical progression: Advance of disease that can be measured by observable and diagnosable signs or symptoms. For example, HIV progression can be measured by change in CD4 count.

coccidioidomycosis: An infectious fungal disease caused by the breathing in of Coccidioides immitis, which are carried on windblown dust particles.

coinfection: When a person has two or more infections at the same time. For example, a person infected with HIV may be coinfected with hepatitis C (HCV) or tuberculosis (TB) or both.

combination therapy: Two or more drugs or treatments used together to obtain the best results against HIV infection and/or AIDS. Combination drug therapy (treatment) has proven more effective than monotherapy (single-drug therapy) in controlling the growth of the virus. An example of combination therapy would be the use of two drugs such as zidovudine and lamivudine together.

core biopsy: The removal of a tissue sample with a wide needle for examination under a microscope. Also called core needle biopsy.

CT scan: A procedure that uses a computer linked to an x-ray machine to make a series of detailed pictures of areas inside the body. The pictures are taken from different angles and are used to create 3-dimensional (3-D) views of tissues and organs. A dye may be injected into a vein or swallowed to help the tissues and organs show up more clearly. A CT scan may be used to help diagnose disease, plan treatment, or find out how well treatment is working. Also called CAT scan, computed tomography scan, computerized axial tomography scan, and computerized tomography.

drug resistance: When a bacteria, virus, or other microorganism mutates (changes form) and becomes insensitive to (resistant to) a drug that was previously effective. Drug resistance can be a cause of HIV treatment failure.

dysplasia: Cells that look abnormal under a microscope but are not cancer.

endocervical curettage: A procedure in which a sample of abnormal tissue is removed from the cervix using a small, spoon-shaped instrument called a curette. The tissue is then checked under a microscope for signs of cervical cancer. This procedure may be done if abnormal cells are found during a Pap test.

enzyme-linked immunosorbent assay (elisa): A laboratory test to detect the presence of HIV antibodies in the blood, oral fluid, or urine. The immune system responds to HIV infection by producing HIV antibodies. A positive result on an enzyme-linked immunosorbent assay (ELISA) must be confirmed by a second, different antibody test (a positive Western blot) for a person to be definitively diagnosed with HIV infection.

excisional biopsy: A surgical procedure in which an entire lump or suspicious area is removed for diagnosis. The tissue is then examined under a microscope.

false negative: A negative test result that incorrectly indicates that the condition being tested for is not present when, in fact, the condition is actually present. For example, a false negative HIV test indicates a person does not have HIV when, in fact, the person is infected with HIV.

false positive: A positive test result that incorrectly indicates that the condition being tested for is present when, in fact, the condition is actually not present. For example, a false positive HIV test indicates a person has HIV when, in fact, the person is not infected with HIV.

highly active antiretroviral therapy (HAART): The name given to treatment regimens recommended by HIV experts to aggressively decrease viral multiplication and progress of HIV disease. The usual HAART treatment combines three or more different drugs, such as two nucleoside reverse transcriptase inhibitors (NRTIs) and a protease inhibitor, two NRTIs and a non-nucleoside reverse transcriptase inhibitor (NNRTI), or other combinations. These treatment regimens have been shown to reduce the amount of virus so that it becomes undetectable in a patient's blood.

Hodgkin lymphoma: A cancer of the immune system that is marked by the presence of a type of cell called the Reed-Sternberg cell. The two major types of Hodgkin lymphoma are classical Hodgkin lymphoma and nodular lymphocyte-predominant Hodgkin lymphoma. Symptoms include the painless enlargement of lymph nodes, spleen, or other immune tissue. Other symptoms include fever, weight loss, fatigue, or night sweats. Also called Hodgkin disease.

human herpesvirus 8: A type of virus that causes Kaposi sarcoma (a rare cancer in which lesions grow in the skin, lymph nodes, lining of the mouth, nose, and throat, and other tissues of the body). Human herpesvirus 8 also causes certain types of lymphoma (cancer that begins in cells of the immune system). Also called HHV8, Kaposi sarcoma-associated herpesvirus, and KSHV.

human immunodeficiency virus (HIV): The virus that causes AIDS, which is the most advanced stage of HIV infection. HIV is a retrovirus that occurs as two types.

human papillomavirus: A type of virus that can cause abnormal tissue growth (for example, warts) and other changes to cells. Infection for a long time with certain types of human papillomavirus can cause cervical cancer. Human papillomavirus may also play a role in some other types of cancer, such as anal, vaginal, vulvar, penile, oropharyngeal, and squamous cell skin cancers. Also called HPV.

immune system: A complex network of cells, tissues, organs, and the substances they make that helps the body fight infections and other diseases. The immune system includes white blood cells and organs and tissues of the lymph system, such as the thymus, spleen, tonsils, lymph nodes, lymph vessels, and bone marrow.

immunocompromised : When the body is unable to produce an adequate immune response. A person may be immunocompromised because of a disease or an infection, such as HIV, or as the result of treatment with drugs or radiation.

immunodeficiency : Inability to produce an adequate immune response because of an insufficiency or absence of antibodies, immune cells, or both. Immunodeficiency disorders can be inherited, such as severe combined immunodeficiency; they can be acquired through infection, such as with HIV; or they can result from chemotherapy.

immunosuppression: A state of the body in which the immune system is damaged and does not perform its normal functions. Immunosuppression may be induced by drugs (e.g. in chemotherapy) or result from certain disease processes, such as HIV infection.

incisional biopsy: A surgical procedure in which a portion of a lump or suspicious area is removed for diagnosis. The tissue is then examined under a microscope to check for signs of disease.

incubation period: The time between infection with a pathogen and the onset of disease symptoms.

Kaposi sarcoma: A type of cancer in which lesions (abnormal areas) grow in the skin, lymph nodes, lining of the mouth, nose, and throat, and other tissues of the body. The lesions are usually purple and are made of cancer cells, new blood vessels, and blood cells. They may begin in more than one place in the body at the same time. Kaposi sarcoma is caused by Kaposi sarcoma-associated herpesvirus (KSHV). In the United States, it usually occurs in people who have a weak immune system caused by AIDS or by drugs used in organ transplants. It is also seen in older men of Jewish or Mediterranean descent, or in young men in Africa.

latency: The period when an infecting organism is in the body but is not producing any clinically noticeable ill effects or symptoms. In HIV disease, clinical latency is an asymptomatic period in the early years of HIV infection. The period of latency is characterized by near-normal CD4+ T-cell counts. Recent research indicates that HIV remains quite active in the lymph nodes during this period.

lymphocyte: A type of immune cell that is made in the bone marrow and is found in the blood and in lymph tissue. The two main types of lymphocytes are B lymphocytes and T lymphocytes. B lymphocytes make antibodies, and T lymphocytes help kill tumor cells and help control immune responses. A lymphocyte is a type of white blood cell.

lymphoma: Cancer of the lymphoid tissues. Lymphomas are often described as being large-cell or small-cell types, cleaved or noncleaved, or diffuse or nodular. The different types often have different prognoses (i.e. prospect of survival or recovery). Lymphomas can also be referred to by the organs where they are active, such as CNS lymphomas, which are in the central nervous system, and GI lymphomas, which are in the gastrointestinal tract. The types of lymphomas most commonly associated with HIV infection are called non-Hodgkin lymphomas or B-cell lymphomas. In these types of cancers, certain cells of the lymphatic system grow abnormally. They divide rapidly, growing into tumors.

monotherapy: Using only one drug to treat an infection or disease. Monotherapy for the treatment of HIV is not recommended outside of a clinical trial. The optimal regimen for initial treatment of HIV includes three antiretroviral (ARV) drugs from at least two different HIV drug classes.

non-Hodgkin lymphoma: Any of a large group of cancers of lymphocytes (white blood cells). Non-Hodgkin lymphomas can occur at any age and are often marked by lymph nodes that are larger than normal, fever, and weight loss. There are many different types of non-Hodgkin lymphoma. These types can be divided into aggressive (fast-growing) and indolent (slow-growing) types, and they can be formed from either B-cells or T-cells. B-cell non-Hodgkin lymphomas include Burkitt lymphoma, chronic lymphocytic leukemia/small lymphocytic lymphoma (CLL/SLL), diffuse large B-cell lymphoma, follicular lymphoma, immunoblastic large cell lymphoma, precursor B-lymphoblastic lymphoma, and mantle cell lymphoma. T-cell non-Hodgkin lymphomas include mycosis fungoides, anaplastic large cell lymphoma, and precursor T-lymphoblastic lymphoma. Lymphomas that occur after bone marrow or stem cell transplantation are usually B-cell non-Hodgkin lymphomas. Prognosis and treatment depend on the stage and type of disease. Also called NHL.

non-nucleoside reverse transcriptase inhibitor (NNRTI): Antiretroviral (ARV) HIV drug class. Non-nucleoside reverse transcriptase inhibitors (NNRTIs) bind to and block HIV reverse transcriptase (an HIV enzyme). HIV uses reverse transcriptase to convert its RNA into DNA (reverse transcription). Blocking reverse transcriptase and reverse transcription prevents HIV from replicating.

nucleoside reverse transcriptase inhibitor (NRTI): Antiretroviral (ARV) HIV drug class. Nucleoside reverse transcriptase inhibitors (NRTIs) block reverse transcriptase (an HIV enzyme). HIV uses reverse transcriptase to convert its RNA into DNA (reverse transcription). Blocking reverse transcriptase and reverse transcription prevents HIV from replicating.

opportunistic infection (OI): An infection that occurs more frequently or is more severe in people with weakened immune systems, such as people with HIV or people receiving chemotherapy, than in people with healthy immune systems.

PET scan: A procedure in which a small amount of radioactive glucose (sugar) is injected into a vein, and a scanner is used to make detailed, computerized pictures of areas inside the body where the glucose is taken up. Because cancer cells often take up more glucose than normal cells, the pictures can be used to find cancer cells in the body. Also called positron emission tomography scan.

post-exposure prophylaxis (PEP): Short-term treatment started as soon as possible after high-risk exposure to an infectious agent, such as HIV, hepatitis B virus (HBV), or hepatitis C virus (HCV). The purpose of post-exposure prophylaxis (PEP) is to reduce the risk of infection. An example of a high-risk exposure is exposure to an infectious agent as the result of unprotected sex.

protease inhibitor: Antiretroviral (ARV) HIV drug class. Protease inhibitors (PIs) block protease (an HIV enzyme). By blocking protease, PIs prevent new (immature) HIV from becoming a mature virus that can infect other CD4 cells.

rapid HIV test: A screening test for detecting antibody to HIV that produces very quick results, usually in 5 to 30 minutes. For diagnosis of HIV infection, a positive rapid test is confirmed with a second rapid test made by a different manufacturer.

rapid test: A type of HIV antibody test used to screen for HIV infection. A rapid HIV antibody test can detect HIV antibodies in blood or oral fluid in less than 30 minutes. A positive rapid HIV antibody test must be confirmed by a second, different antibody test (a positive Western blot) for a person to be definitively diagnosed with HIV infection.

reverse transcription: The third of seven steps in the HIV life cycle. Once inside a CD4 cell, HIV releases and uses reverse transcriptase (an HIV enzyme) to convert its genetic material—HIV RNA—into HIV DNA. The conversion of HIV RNA to HIV DNA allows HIV to enter the CD4 cell nucleus and combine with the cell's genetic material—cell DNA.

seroconversion: The transition from infection with HIV to the detectable presence of HIV antibodies in the blood. When seroconversion occurs (usually within a few weeks of infection), the result of an HIV antibody test changes from HIV negative to HIV positive.

serologic test: Any number of tests that are performed on the clear fluid portion of blood. Often refers to a test that determines the presence of antibodies to antigens such as viruses.

superinfection: When a person who is already infected with HIV becomes infected with a second, different strain of HIV. Superinfection may cause HIV to advance more rapidly. Superinfection can also complicate treatment if the newly acquired strain of HIV is resistant to antiretroviral (ARV) drugs in the person's current HIV treatment regimen.

syphilis: A primarily sexually transmitted disease resulting from infection with the spirochete (a bacterium) Treponema pallidum. Syphilis can also be acquired in the uterus during pregnancy.

T cell: A type of lymphocyte. There are two major types of T lymphocytes

treatment failure: When an antiretroviral (ARV) regimen is unable to control HIV infection. Treatment failure can be clinical failure, immunologic failure, virologic failure, or any combination of the three. Factors that can contribute to treatment failure include drug resistance, drug toxicity, or poor treatment adherence.

tuberculosis (TB): Infection with the bacteria Mycobacterium tuberculosis, as evidenced by a positive tuberculin skin test (TST) that screens for infection with this organism. Sometimes, TST is called a purified protein derivative (PPD) or Mantoux test. A positive skin test might or might not indicate active TB disease. Thus, any person with a positive TST should be screened for active TB and, once active TB is excluded, evaluated for treatment to prevent the development of TB disease. TB infection alone is not considered an opportunistic infection indicating possible immune deficiency.

undetectable viral load: When the amount of HIV in the blood is too low to be detected with a viral load (HIV RNA) test. Antiretroviral (ARV) drugs may reduce a person's viral load to an undetectable level; however, that does not mean the person is cured. Some HIV, in the form of latent HIV reservoirs, remain inside cells and in body tissues.

viral load (VL): The amount of HIV in a sample of blood. Viral load (VL) is reported as the number of HIV RNA copies per milliliter of blood. An important goal of antiretroviral therapy (ART) is to suppress a person's VL to an undetectable level—a level too low for the virus to be detected by a VL test.

viral set point: The viral load (HIV RNA) that the body settles at within a few weeks to months after infection with HIV. Immediately after infection, HIV multiplies rapidly and a person's viral load is typically very high. After a few weeks to months, this rapid replication of HIV declines and the person's viral load drops to its set point.

western blot: A type of antibody test used to confirm a positive result on an HIV screening test. (The initial screening test is usually a different type of antibody test or, less often, a viral load test). The immune system responds to HIV infection by producing HIV antibodies. A Western blot for confirmatory HIV testing is done using a blood sample.

window period: The time period from infection with HIV until the body produces enough HIV antibodies to be detected by standard HIV antibody tests. The length of the window period varies depending on the antibody test used. During the window period, a person can have a negative result on an HIV antibody test despite being infected with HIV.

Chapter 46

Directory of Organizations for People with HIV/AIDS and Their Families and Friends

Government Agencies That Provide Information about HIV/AIDS

AIDSInfo (AIDS Information Service)
P.O. Box 6303
Rockville, MD 20849-6303
Toll-Free: 800-HIV-0440 (448-0440)
Phone: 301-315-2816
Fax: 301-315-2818
Website: www.aidsinfo.nih.gov
E-mail: ContactUs@aidsinfo.gov

CDC National Prevention Information Network
P.O. Box 6003
Rockville, MD 20849-6003
Toll-Free: 800-458-5231
Website: npin.cdc.gov

Centers for Disease Control and Prevention
1600 Clifton Rd.
Atlanta, GA
Toll-Free: 800-232-4636
Website: www.cdc.gov

Resources in this chapter were compiled from several sources deemed reliable; all contact information was verified and updated in September 2015.

Effective Interventions
Toll-Free: 866-532-9565
Website: effectiveinterventions.
cdc.gov
E-mail: interventions@danya.
com

**HIV Testing and Care
Services Locator**
Website: locator.aids.gov

National Cancer Institute
NCI Office of Communications
and Education, Public Inquiries
Office
6116 Executive Blvd.
Ste. 300
Bethesda, MD 20892-8322
Toll-Free: 800-4-CANCER
(800-422-6237)
Website: www.cancer.gov

**National Institute of Allergy
and Infectious Diseases**
6610 Rockledge Dr.
MSC 6612
Bethesda, MD 20892-6612
Toll-Free: 866-284-4107
Phone: 301-496-5717
Website: www.niaid.nih.gov

National Institute on Aging
Information Center
P.O. Box 8057
Gaithersburg, MD 20898-8057
Toll-Free: 800-222-2225
Website: www.nia.nih.gov

**National Prevention
Information Network**
Website: npin.cdc.gov
E-mail: NPIN-info@cdc.gov

Office of AIDS Research
National Institutes of Health
5635 Fishers Ln.
MSC 9310
Bethesda, MD 20892-9310
Phone: 301-496-0357
Fax: 301-496-2119
Website: www.oar.nih.gov
E-mail: oartemp1@od31em1.
od.nih.gov

Positive Spin
 U.S. Department of Health &
Human Services
Website: positivespin.hiv.gov
E-mail: contact@aids.gov

**U.S. Department of Health &
Human Services**
200 Independence Ave., S.W.
Washington, DC
Toll-Free: 877-696-6775
Website: www.hhs.gov

**U.S. Department of Veterans
Affairs**
Clinical Public Health Programs:
HIV/AIDS
810 Vermont Ave., N.W.
Washington, DC
Toll-Free: 800-273-8255
Website: www.hiv.va.gov
E-mail: publichealth@va.gov

**U.S. Food and Drug
Administration**
10903 New Hampshire Ave.
Silver Spring, MD
Toll-Free: 888-463-6332
Website: www.fda.gov

Private Agencies That Provide Information about HIV/AIDS

AIDS InfoNet
P.O. Box 810
Arroyo Seco, NM
Website: www.aidsinfonet.org

AIDS Vaccine Advocacy Coalition (AVAC)
101 W. 23rd St., #2227
New York, NY
Phone: 212-367-1279
Fax: 646-365-3452
Website: www.avac.org
E-mail: avac@avac.org

AIDSmeds.com
462 Seventh Ave., 19th Fl.
New York, NY 10018-7424
Website: www.aidsmeds.com

AIDSVu
Website: www.aidsvu.org
E-mail: info@aidsvu.org

American Academy of Family Physicians
P.O. Box 11210
Shawnee Mission, KS
66207-1210
Toll-Free: 800-274-2237
Phone: 913-906-6000
Fax: 913-906-6075
Website: www.aafp.org

American Academy of HIV Medicine
1705 DeSales St., N.W., Ste. 700
Washington, DC
Phone: 202-659-0699
Fax: 202-659-0976
Website: www.aahivm.org

American Sexual Health Association
P.O. Box 13827
Research Triangle Park, NC
Phone: 919-361-8400
Website: www.ashasexualhealth.org
E-mail: info@ashasexualhealth.org

Antiretroviral Pregnancy Registry
Research Park
1011 Ashes Dr.
Wilmington, NC
Toll-Free: 800-258-4263
Fax: 800-800-1052
Website: www.apregistry.com

AVERT
4 Brighton Rd., Horsham
West Sussex,
RH13 5BA
United Kingdom
Website: www.avert.org

The Body.com
250 West 57th St.
Ste. 1614
New York, NY
Phone: 212-541-8500
Website: www.thebody.com

Center for AIDS Information and Advocacy
P.O. Box 66306
Houston, TX 77266-6306
Toll-Free: 800-341-1788
Phone: 713-527-8219
Fax: 713-521-3679
Website: www.centerforaids.org
E-mail: info@centerforaids.org

595

Center for AIDS Prevention Studies—University of California at San Francisco
AIDS Research Institute, University of California at San Francisco
50 Beale St.
Ste. 1300
San Francisco, CA
Phone: 415-597-9100
Fax: 415-597-9213
Website: www.caps.ucsf.edu
E-mail: CAPS.Web@ucsf.edu

Clinician Consultation Center
 UCSF at San Francisco General Hospital
1001 Potrero Ave.
Bldg. 20, Ward 2203
San Francisco, CA 94110-3518
Toll-Free: 800-933-3413
Fax:415-476-3454
Website: nccc.ucsf.edu

Elizabeth Glaser Pediatric AIDS Foundation
1140 Connecticut Ave., N.W.
Ste. 200
Washington, DC
Toll-Free: 888-499-HOPE (-4673)
Phone: 202-296-9165
Fax: 202-296-9185
Website: www.pedaids.org
E-mail: info@pedaids.org

Elton John AIDS Foundation
584 Broadway
Ste. 906
New York, NY
Website: www.ejaf.org

Foundation for AIDS Research (amfAR)
120 Wall St., 13th Floor
New York, NY 10005-3908
Phone: 212-806-1600
Fax: 212-806-1601
Website: www.amfar.org
E-mail: information@amfar.org

HIV InfoSource
NYU School of Medicine
550 First Ave., Old Bellevue
C&D Bldg.
Rm. 558
New York, NY
Website: www.med.nyu.edu

HIV Medicine Association
1300 Wilson Blvd.
Ste. 300
Arlington, VA
Phone: 703-299-1215
Fax: 703-299-8766
Website: www.hivma.org
E-mail: info@hivma.org

HIV Vaccine Trials Network
1100 Eastlake Ave. E.
Seattle,
Washington
Phone: 206-667-6300
Fax: 206-667-6366
Website: www.hvtn.org
E-mail: info@hvtn.org

International AIDS Vaccine Initiative (IAVI)
110 William St.
Fl. 27
New York, NY 10038-3901
Phone: 212-847-1111
Website: www.iavi.org

Microbicide Trials Network
204 Craft Ave.
Pittsburgh, PA
Phone: 412-641-8999
Fax: 412-641-6170
Website: www.mtnstopshiv.org

National Association of People with AIDS (NAPWA)
8401 Colesville Rd.
Ste. 505
Silver Spring, MD
Toll-Free: 866-846-9366
Phone: 240-247-0880
Fax: 240-247-0574
Website: www.napwa.org

National Minority AIDS Council
1931 13th St., N.W.
Washington, DC
Phone: 202-483-6622
Website: www.nmac.org
E-mail: info@nmac.org

National NeuroAIDS Tissue Consortium
401 N. Washington St., Ste. 700
Rockville, MD
Phone: 866-668-2272 or 301-251-1161
Fax: 301-576-4597
Website: nntc.org/
E-mail: nntc@emmes.com

North American Syringe Exchange Network
Ste. 113
Tacoma, WA
Phone: 253-272-4857
Fax: 253-272-8415
Website: www.nasen.org

One Test Two Lives
Toll-Free: 866-588-4948
Website: www.1test2lives.org
E-mail: info@1test2lives.org

Pacific AIDS Education and Training Program
University of California, San Francisco
550 16th St., 3rd Floor
San Francisco, CA 94158-2549
Phone: 415-476-6153
Website: www.paetc.org
E-mail: paetcmail@ucsf.edu

Project Inform
1375 Mission St.
San Francisco, CA 94103–2621
Phone: 415-558-8669
Fax: 415-558-0684
Website: www.projectinform.org

Services & Advocacy for Gay, Lesbian, Bisexual & Transgender Elders (SAGE)
305 7th Ave., 6th Floor
New York, NY
Phone: 212-741-2247
Website: www.sageusa.org

U.S. Military HIV Research Program
6720A Rockledge Dr., Ste. 400
Bethesda, MD
Phone: 301-500-3600
Fax: 301-500-3666
Website: www.hivresearch.org
E-mail: info@hivresearch.org

Well Project
Toll-Free: 888-616-WELL (9355)
Website: www.thewellproject.org
E-mail: info@thewellproject.org

Patient Assistance Programs for HIV Drugs

Delavirdine (Rescriptor®)
ViiV Healthcare Patient
Assistance Program
P.O. Box 52037
Phoenix, AZ
Toll-Free: 877-784-4842
Fax: 877-784-4004
Website: www.
viivhealthcareforyou.com

Epivir/Ziagen (Epzicom®)
ViiV Healthcare Patient
Assistance Program
P.O. Box 52037
Phoenix, AZ
Toll-Free: 877-784-4842
Fax: 877-784-4004
Website: www.
viivhealthcareforyou.com

Etravirine (Intelence®)
Johnson & Johnson Patient
Assistance Foundation, Inc.
P.O. Box 221857
Charlotte, NC 28222-1857
Toll-Free: 800-652-6227
Website: www.intelence.com
Website: www.jjpaf.org

Lamivudine (Epivir®)
ViiV Healthcare Patient
Assistance Program
P.O. Box 52037
Phoenix, AZ
Toll-Free: 877-784-4842
Fax: 877-784-4004
Website: www.
viivhealthcareforyou.com

Recombinant (Cervarix®)
GSK For You
Toll-Free: 888-825-5249
Website: www.gskforyou.com

Recombinant (Gardasil®)
Merck Patient Assistance
Program
Toll-Free: 800-727-5400
Website: www.gardasil.com
Website: www.merckhelps.com

Retrovir/Epivir (Combivir®)
ViiV Healthcare Patient
Assistance Program
P.O. Box 52037
Phoenix, AZ
Toll-Free: 877-784-4842
Fax: 877-784-4004
Website: www.
viivhealthcareforyou.com

Rilpivirine (Edurant®)
Johnson & Johnson Patient
Assistance Foundation, Inc.
P.O. Box 221857
Charlotte, NC 28222-1857
Toll-Free: 800-652-6227
Website: www.edurant.com
Website: www.jjpaf.org

Truvada® for PrEP Medication Assistance Program
Toll-Free: 855-330-5479
Website: www.truvada.com
Website: www.gilead.com/
responsibility/us-patient-access

Viread / Emtriva (Truvada®)
U.S. Advancing Access®
program
Toll-Free: 800-226-2056
Website: www.viread.com
Website: www.gilead.com/
responsibility/us-patient-access

Zidovudine (Retrovir®)
ViiV Healthcare Patient
Assistance Program
P.O. Box 52037
Phoenix, AZ
Toll-Free: 877-784-4842
Fax: 877-784-4004
Website: www.
viivhealthcareforyou.com

Index

Index

Page numbers followed by 'n' indicate a footnote. Page numbers in italics indicate a table or illustration.